PH17

FLEET HISTORY

OF

DEVON GENERAL

OMNIBUS AND TOURING COMPANY LIMITED

PUBLISHED BY

THE PSV CIRCLE

MAY 2015

FOREWORD

The draft for this publication is a substantially revised and updated version of an earlier Fleet History 2PH1, published in 1966, initially complied by Ron Maybray. This has been further improved with the assistance of Peter Bates, David Corke, Les Folkard, Richard Gadsby, Dave Godley, Roger Grimley, Tony Holdsworth, Colin Martin, Hugh Pincott, Philip Platt, Peter Tulloch, Fred Ward and the Devon General Society. Acknowledgement is also made to the publications "Devon General - A Fascinating Story" by Leslie Folkard (published by the Devon General Society 2007) and "Glory Days - Devon General" (published by Ian Allan 2006).

This publication contains all material available in April 2015.

Photographs have been supplied by Alan Cross, Arthur Ingram, CF Klapper, Geoffrey Morant (courtesy Richard Morant), GHF Atkins (courtesy SJ Butler), The Omnibus Society, Peter Yeomans, RF Mack, Roy Marshall, Surfleet Photographs, The Omnibus Society XLM Collection. Thanks also to Mike Eyre for preparing the photographs for publication.

Notes:

This is one of a range of publications produced by The PSV Circle primarily as a service to its members. The information contained herein has been taken from the range of sources indicated above; either from observation or other research, as well as the content of PSV Circle monthly news sheets and also includes information provided from other reputable sources. Considerable time and effort has been taken to ensure that the content of this publication is as complete and accurate as possible but no responsibility can be accepted for any errors or omissions.

Contents:

Any general comments on this publication may be sent to the Publications Manager, Unit GK, 436 Essex Road, London, N1 3QP or via email to publications.manager@psv-circle.org.uk.

Details of how to join The PSV Circle and a list of all our publications can be obtained from The PSV Circle website - www.psv-circle.org.uk.

ISBN: 978-1-908953-58-2

Published by the PSV Circle
© The PSV Circle May 2015

INTRODUCTION

The Devon General Omnibus & Touring Co Ltd was incorporated on 22nd May 1919, with its registered office at the home of the Mill family, two of whom were principal proprietors. The administrative headquarters were established at Blackboy Road, Exeter on completion of the building in 7/21, remaining there until a move to Torquay in October 1933.

The original fleet consisted of three reconditioned AEC YC chassis fitted with modified London General B type bodies retaining their original London General livery, which operated on two services connecting Exeter with Torquay via different routes. Like many other operators at the time, in 1920 and 1921 further reconditioned AEC and Daimler chassis were acquired and fitted with a variety of bodies.

Devon General and Torquay Tramways were originally two separate entities, the latter having been operating tramcars on five routes in the Torquay area going back to 1907. Torquay Tramways, which was a subsidiary of the London based National Electric Construction Co Ltd, began operating buses in addition to its trams, in response to competition from Devon General in 1920 and quickly built up a bus fleet outnumbering that of its rival. In 1922 Torquay Tramways Co Ltd, acquired a controlling interest in Devon General, as a result of which the buses of the Tramways Company were then transferred to Devon General with effect from 1st June 1922 (see page 13), although the tram services continued to run as before.

The services of the newly combined operation formed the nucleus of Devon General's bus operations. Between 1924 and 1952 expansion throughout the South Devon area, was facilitated by the introduction of new services and acquiring those of several stage service operators, with in some cases, these operators continuing their coaching operations. A number of competitors operating from Torquay into the Paignton and Brixham area were financially induced to cease operations at the same time in 1931, giving the company a near monopoly in this area.

The vehicles transferred from Torquay Tramways consisted of similar AEC and Daimler chassis, some of which had been purchased new and others being based on reconditioned ex military chassis. Further similar vehicles were acquired in the following two years, but 1925 saw the introduction of ten new Dennis chassis, of two types, with bodywork by Hall Lewis. This coachbuilder and its successor, Park Royal would supply many more bodies to the company over the next few years. 1928 saw the first new Leylands entering service, again with Hall Lewis bodies, which included six Lioness coaches intended for limited stop express services which became a feature of Devon General operations for many years. From this time until the outbreak of World War Two almost all new single-deck deliveries consisted of either Leyland or AEC chassis of various types.

Just over two years later, in November 1924, Devon General bought the Fleet Cars coaching business (for further details see page 123). This continued to operate as a subsidiary for a further nine years, until November 1933.

In a further expansion of coaching activities, Devon General acquired control of Grey Cars Ltd from its, then owner, L Timpson & Sons of London, on 1st March 1932. Both Grey Cars and existing subsidiary Fleet Cars, continued to operate independently as subsidiaries until the following year. On 1st November 1933, the three operations were integrated when the vehicles and assets of both Grey Cars and Fleet Cars were transferred to Devon General, with both subsidiary companies being wound up on 1st January 1934. Devon General continued to operate its tours using the name and livery of 'Grey Cars' until 1938. Use of the Grey Cars name and livery was reintroduced in 1945.

The last Torquay trams ran on the 31st January 1934 and despite an abortive scheme to introduce trolleybuses, a fleet of AEC Regents with Short bodies were purchased instead as replacements. These were the first of many AEC Regents of various models to serve the company, right through to the end of operations in 1971. With the exception of these tram replacement Regents, very few double-deckers operated for the company until the war years.

On 1st July 1934 the National Electric Construction Co was absorbed by the British Electric Traction Co Ltd, with Devon General therefore becoming a subsidiary of that organisation.

The last AEC Regal single-deckers to pre-war specification, entered service at the beginning of 1940, from around which time all normal vehicle production ceased. Throughout the war the Ministry of War Transport allocated the limited numbers of new buses to operators according to need and availability. The first such vehicle was a Leyland TD7, believed to have been intended for Newport Corporation, which appeared at the end of 1942. The following year saw the short-lived return of Daimler chassis and the first of a number of Guy Arabs, a new make as far as Devon General were concerned. Although the wartime utility bodies fitted to the Guys were not up to the usual standards, the chassis proved robust and reliable, with the result that a number of these were rebuilt and rebodied for further service in the 1950s. In company with many other operators throughout the country during World War Two, Devon General purchased a number of producer gas trailer units. These were used with a number of pre-war buses, but proved rather less than successful in the hilly territory served. To the relief of many, this scheme for buses was abandoned in November 1944.

With the return of peace towards the end of 1945, supplies slowly returned to a more normal footing, although it was the latter end of 1946 before any new buses built to full peacetime standards were delivered. These consisted of AEC Regent double-deckers and Regal single-deckers all with bodies by Weymann. This combination was to supply most of the company's service bus requirements for a number of years.

The demand for coach travel soon manifested itself, so as a stop-gap measure several pre-war 'express service' saloons with higher specification seating were hurriedly refurbished and painted in Grey Cars livery for use on local tours. The first new coaches to appear were a batch of Bedford OB/Duple Vista delivered in the early part of 1948. Once coach deliveries got back into full swing, these were downgraded for bus use on lightly trafficked routes. Delivered after the end of the 1948 holiday season, but not actually entering service until the following year were the first batch of AEC Regal III/Duple coaches, to be followed by similar examples which went in service in 1950. These proved to be the last new front-engined coaches to be purchased, apart from a single Bedford SB, which had been ordered by an operator whose business had been taken over.

The first underfloor engined single-deckers appeared in 1951, which despite the recent increase in permitted vehicle dimensions, were only 7ft 6in wide, though of 30ft length. These also marked a temporary return to Leyland with the then new Royal Tiger chassis, with bodies supplied by Willowbrook, who later went on to supply several further batches of both buses and coaches through into the 1960s. Also entering service in 1951 were six Leyland PD2s with Leyland's own lowbridge bodies, intended for a specific route which required such vehicles. These were the last Leylands to be purchased until the advent of the rear engined Atlantean models in 1959. Batches of AEC Regent III/Weymann double-deckers continued to be delivered through to 1954.

By 1952 there was a surplus of single-deck vehicles, largely because of the conversion of a number of routes to double-deck operation, made possible largely by the influx of AEC Regent III since the end of the War. Some thirty two pre-war AEC Regals were sold to three fellow BET Group companies, Mexborough & Swinton, Rhondda Transport and Thomas Bros of Port Talbot. Six Regals dating from 1946 were exchanged with Leicester Corporation for six Regent II double-deckers of similar vintage, which ran for several months in Leicester livery.

Underfloor engined coaches made their first appearance in 1953, being again based on AEC chassis, the Regal IV, with Willowbrook bodies. More Regal IVs coaches followed the following year, but this time with Park Royal bodies.

A total of twenty 'new' double-deckers were constructed using the running units from pre-war AEC Regent and Regals, with reconditioned chassis frames fitted with new bodies by Weymann and Saunders-Roe. For further details see 1953 and 1954.

By 1955, although the company still favoured AEC as their chassis supplier, the Regent had been updated to the Mk V version and the Regal IV had been superseded by the lighter Reliance. Many examples of both these chassis types were to follow over the next few years, mainly with Marshall, Weymann and Willowbrook bodywork.

The following year saw the first Beadle-Commer chassisless coaches and less common buses, enter service, with Devon General being one of several BET Group operators to use this model.

During the 1950s the services and coach operations of a number of businesses were taken over, in some cases introducing a handful of non-standard vehicles into the fleet.

To replace the Bedford OBs used on stage services, following demonstrations, a batch of thirty-one seat Albion Nimbuses entered service in 1958, again with Willowbrook bodies. These were followed by a further three with Harrington bodies in 1962, this body manufacturer also finding favour with its coach bodies on Reliance chassis.

The rear-engined Leyland Atlantean was introduced into the fleet in 1959, with MCCW bodywork, which proved to be the first of many of this type to enter service right through to 1969. Later deliveries on this chassis included examples with Roe and Willowbrook bodies. However the AEC Regent V continued to be favoured for routes more suited to its configuration and because of dissatisfaction with the reliability of the early Atlanteans.

The AEC Reliance continued to be purchased to meet both bus and coach requirements during the 1960s, with bodywork supplied by several builders.

With effect from 1st March 1968 the BET Group, of which Devon General was a subsidiary, was acquired by the Transport Holding Co. Under the terms of the 1968 Transport Act the interests of the Transport Holding Co were then absorbed by the National Bus Co (NBC) of which Devon General therefore became a subsidiary on 1st January 1969. From this time coaches in Grey Cars livery began to be repainted into an all white, with grey band 'corporate' livery, having the Grey Cars fleetname in large letters. This continued until after the takeover by Western National in 1971, at which point, under the auspices of the NBC, the Devon General coaching operations were taken over by Greenslades Tours of Exeter.

On 1ST April 1970 the vehicles and operations of the Exeter Corporation transport undertaking passed to Devon General, following their acquisition by the NBC.

The end of Devon General in this form came with a rationalisation of NBC operations, as part of which the vehicles and operations were taken over by the neighbouring Western National Omnibus Co Ltd, who were also by now, part of the NBC 'family'. This takeover was effective from 1st January 1971, subsequent events being outside the scope of this publication.

LIVERY:

From the earliest days Devon General buses were painted in various combinations of red and white, with the white supplanted later by ivory, for bands and roof. Wings were painted black until superseded by maroon from 1952.

With the takeover of the Grey Cars fleet, the grey & maroon livery in use on these coaches was retained until 1938, when the first of the new AEC Ranger coaches was delivered in grey but the rest were painted in a new saxe blue livery. When coach tours recommenced in 1945 two further coaches were repainted in saxe blue on rebuilding, but a modified version of the earlier Grey Cars livery was then reintroduced, which included cream window surrounds and this continued in use until after the formation of the NBC (see above).

The six AEC Regents that were converted to open-top in 1955 introduced a new livery of ivory with red bands and maroon wings. For the 1960 season they were repainted with red wings and fleetnames. The replacement Leyland Atlantean convertible-top double-deckers delivered in 1961 carried a similar livery.

DEPOTS:
Ashburton (West Street)
Purchased with the Babington business 5/27; closed 1928.
Brixham (Bell's Garage, New Road)
Rented from 1935; closed 1939.
Churston (Prout's Garage)
Premised rented from c1925 until 1930.
Crediton (Mill Street)
Rented premises, in use from around 1928 until 7/54.
Crockernwell
One bus stabled overnight, at first in rented premises, later on open land, from 1942 until 1957.
Exmouth (Imperial Road)
Opened in 9/31 to replace earlier premises in use since 1921. Passed to Western National 1/71.
Exeter (Blackboy Road)
Opened 7/21. These premises were also the administrative headquarters until 10/33. Closed shortly after Western National takeover 3/71.
Exeter (Heavitree Road)
Acquired with the Exeter Corporation undertaking in 4/70. Passed to Western National 1/71.
Kingsteignton (Newton Road)
Rented from around 1921, purchased 4/23; closed and sold 1960.
Moretonhampstead (Court Street)
Premises acquired to replace earlier rented/leased accommodation in 5/31. Passed to Western National 1/71.
Paignton (Orient Road, Preston)
Purchased in 5/25 to accommodate the Fleet Cars vehicles; sold 7/34.
Sidmouth (Woolbrook)
Opened 1930. Passed to Western National 1/71.
Teignmouth
Various premises used to house a handful of vehicles from 1936, continuing through to the Western National takeover in 1/71.
Tiverton (Chapel Street)
Rented from 3/24 until 1938.
Tiverton (Lodge Road, later known as Old Road)
Opened 9/37. Passed to Western National 1/71.
Torquay (Court Garages, Belgrave Road)
Rented temporarily during the War, acquired with Court business 9/66.

Torquay (Newton Road)
> Depot, workshops and offices opened 1931, became administrative headquarters 10/33. Passed to Western National 1/71.

Torquay (Torwood Street)
> Acquired from Grey Cars Ltd, having been built during Timpson ownership in 1930. Passed to Western National 1/71, then to Greenslades Tours, with the coaching interests 5/71.

Torquay (Westhill Avenue/St Marychurch)
> Originally Torquay Tramways tram depot, extended to accommodate buses as well. Closed and sold to Torquay Corporation, following cessation of tram services 1934.

DEVON COUNTY COUNCIL REGISTRATION NUMBERS:

It should be noted that after October 1926 Devon County Council issued registration numbers in a different sequence to the majority of other licensing authorities. From ATA to JOD the prime marks (TA, TT, UO, DV, OD) were taken in chronological order and issued in as many combinations as had been allotted by the latest statutory instrument, before proceeding to the next prime mark. From KTA to YOD and for all reverse issues simple alphabetical order was followed. It should also be noted that for a time in the early T xxxx series, cars and heavy motor cars were allocated even serial numbers only, with odd numbers being reserved for motorcycles.

ATA	6/34	CTA	9/36	DDV	12/38	GTT	11/44	JDV	10/47
BTA	10/34	DTA	11/36	EDV	2/39	HTT	11/45	FOD	12/47
ATT	12/34	CTT	4/37	COD	5/39	JTT	3/46	(GOD	not issued)
BTT	3/35	DTT	6/37	DOD	8/39	FUO	6/46	HOD	3/48
AUO	5/35	ETT	9/37	EOD	12/39	GUO	9/46	JOD	5/48
BUO	8/35	CUO	12/37	FTA	7/40	HUO	11/46	KTA	7/48
ADV	11/35	DUO	3/38	GTA	7/41	JUO	1/47	KTT	9/48
BDV	1/36	EUO	5/38	HTA	4/42	FDV	3/47	KUO	12/48
AOD	3/36	CDV	938	JTA	1/48	GDV	5/47	KDV	2/49
BOD	6/36			FTT	10/43	HDV	7/47	KOD	5/49

Acknowledgement is made for this information contained in "A History of Motor Vehicle Registration in the United Kingdom" by LH Newall.

THE TORQUAY TRAMWAYS COMPANY LIMITED

Tramways in Torquay were operated by the Torquay Tramway Co Ltd, which was a subsidiary of the National Electric Construction Co Ltd with registered office at 88 Kingsway, London WC2. The first routes were opened in April 1907 using the Dolter stud-contact current collection system, this being replaced by conventional trolley and overhead wires in 1911, with a new line to Paignton added in July of the same year. The gauge was 3ft 6ins and the livery was maroon and cream.

The routes were:-

Torre Station	-	Beacon Quay
Torre Station	-	St Marychurch
Torquay (Strand)	-	St Marychurch via Wellswood (circular)
Torquay (Strand)	-	St Marychurch via Ellacombe (circular)
Torquay (Strand)	-	Paignton

The main depot was at Westhill Avenue, Torquay, and there was also a smaller depot at Preston. This depot housed the cars on the Paignton route, to which the bogie cars were always confined.

In 1920 a fleet of buses was purchased, which were also housed at Westhill Avenue and operated over a wide area of South Devon. The Tramways Company acquired a controlling interest in the Devon General Omnibus & Touring Co Ltd in 1922 and the Tramways Company buses were transferred to the reconstituted Devon General company with effect from 1st June 1922.

Torquay Corporation built a cliff railway in 1926 to serve Oddicombe Beach, which was then leased to the Tramways Company.

The trams continued to operate until 31st January 1934, when they were replaced by Devon General buses. Westhill Avenue depot was then transferred to Torquay Corporation and Preston depot sold to a firm of motor engineers. The company was finally wound up on 19th April 1934.

Torquay Corporation (now Torbay Council) took over operation of the cliff railway, which is still providing a useful service to this day.

ELECTRIC TRAMS

1907

New Cars:

1	Brush	M & G Radial	2 x 35 hp GE58-4T	27/22	-/07	-/34?
2	Brush	M & G Radial	2 x 35 hp GE58-4T	27/22	-/07	-/34?
3	Brush	M & G Radial	2 x 35 hp GE58-4T	27/22	-/07	-/34?
4	Brush	M & G Radial	2 x 35 hp GE58-4T	27/22	-/07	-/34?
5	Brush	M & G Radial	2 x 35 hp GE58-4T	27/22	-/07	-/34?
6	Brush	M & G Radial	2 x 35 hp GE58-4T	27/22	-/07	-/34?
7	Brush	M & G Radial	2 x 35 hp GE58-4T	27/22	-/07	-/34?
8	Brush	M & G Radial	2 x 35 hp GE58-4T	27/22	-/07	-/34?
9	Brush	M & G Radial	2 x 35 hp GE58-4T	27/22	-/07	-/34?
10	Brush	M & G Radial	2 x 35 hp GE58-4T	27/22	-/07	-/34?
11	Brush	M & G Radial	2 x 35 hp GE58-4T	27/22	-/07	-/34?
12	Brush	M & G Radial	2 x 35 hp GE58-4T	27/22	-/07	-/34?
13	Brush	M & G Radial	2 x 35 hp GE58-4T	27/22	-/07	-/34?
14	Brush	M & G Radial	2 x 35 hp GE58-4T	27/22	-/07	-/34?
15	Brush	M & G Radial	2 x 35 hp GE58-4T	27/22	-/07	-/34?
16	Brush	M & G Radial	2 x 35 hp GE58-4T	27/22	-/07	-/34?
17	Brush	M & G Radial	2 x 35 hp GE58-4T	27/22	-/07	-/34?
18	Brush	M & G Radial	2 x 35 hp GE58-4T	27/22	-/07	-/34?

Notes:

1-18: Open top double-deck, unvestibuled, three bay, four wheel cars.

1: Remounted on a Brill 21E truck during 1920s.
7: Remounted on a Brill 21E truck during 1920s.
9-10: Remounted on Brill 21E trucks during 1920s.
16-18: Remounted on Brill 21E trucks during 1920s.

Disposals:
>1-6: Scrapped at Torquay.
>7: Plymouth Corporation Tramways 16 1934.
>9-10: Plymouth Corporation Tramways 17-18 1934.
>11-15: Scrapped at Torquay.
>16-18: Plymouth Corporation Tramways 19-21 1934.

1910

New Cars:

19	Brush	Brill 21E	2 x 35 hp GE58-4T	27/22?	-/10	-/34?
20	Brush	Brill 21E	2 x 35 hp GE58-4T	27/22?	-/10	-/34?
21	Brush	Brill 21E	2 x 35 hp GE58-4T	27/22?	-/10	-/34?
22	Brush	Brill 21E	2 x 35 hp GE58-4T	27/22?	-/10	-/34?
23	Brush	Brill 21E	2 x 35 hp GE58-4T	27/22?	-/10	-/34?
24	Brush	Brill 21E	2 x 35 hp GE58-4T	27/22?	-/10	-/34?
25	Brush	Brill 21E	2 x 35 hp GE58-4T	27/22?	-/10	-/34?
26	Brush	Brill 21E	2 x 35 hp GE58-4T	27/22?	-/10	-/34?
27	Brush	Brill 21E	2 x 35 hp GE58-4T	27/22?	-/10	-/34?
28	Brush	Brill 21E	2 x 35 hp GE58-4T	27/22?	-/10	-/34?
29	Brush	Brill 21E	2 x 35 hp GE58-4T	27/22?	-/10	-/34?
30	Brush	Brill 21E	2 x 35 hp GE58-4T	27/22?	-/10	-/34?
31	Brush	Brill 21E	2 x 35 hp GE58-4T	27/22?	-/10	-/34?
32	Brush	Brill 21E	2 x 35 hp GE58-4T	27/22?	-/10	-/34?
33	Brush	Brill 21E	2 x 35 hp GE58-4T	27/22?	-/10	-/34?

Notes:
>19-33: Open top double-deck, three bay, unvestibuled, four wheel cars.

Disposals:
>19-33: Scrapped at Torquay.

1921

Cars acquired from Taunton Electric Traction Co Ltd:

34	Brush	Brush	2 x 25 hp Brush 1002D	24	-/05	-/34?
35	Brush	Brush	2 x 25 hp Brush 1002D	24	-/05	-/34?
36	Brush	Brush	2 x 25 hp Brush 1002D	24	-/05	-/34?

Previous history:
>These cars were new to Taunton Electric Traction Co and were from the series numbered 1-6.

Notes:
>34-36: Single-deck, four bay, unvestibuled four wheel cars.

Disposals:
>34-36: Scrapped at Torquay.

1923

New Cars:

37	Brush	Brush	2 x 37 hp BTH 249RA	76	-/23	-/34
38	Brush	Brush	2 x 37 hp BTH 249RA	76	-/23	-/34

Notes:
>37-38: Open top double-deck, five bay, vestibuled, bogie cars.

Disposals:
>37-38: Plymouth Corporation Tramways 12-13 1934.

1925

New Cars:

39	Brush	Brush	2 x 37 hp BTH 249RA	76	-/25	-/34
40	Brush	Brush	2 x 37 hp BTH 249RA	76	-/25	-/34

Notes:
      39-40: Open top double-deck, five bay, vestibuled, bogie cars.

Disposals:
      39-40: Plymouth Corporation Tramways 14-15 1934.

1928

New Cars:

41	Brush	Brush		2 x 37 hp BTH 249RA	72	-/28	-/34
42	Brush	Brush		2 x 37 hp BTH 249RA	72	-/28	-/34

Notes:
      41-42: Open top double-deck, five bay, vestibuled, bogie cars.

Disposals:
      41-42: Plymouth Corporation Tramways 10-11 1934.

MOTOR BUSES

1920

New Vehicles:

1	T 8188	AEC YC	14896	Brush	B32F	5/20	6/22
2	T 8190	AEC YC	14894	Brush	B32F	5/20	6/22
3	T 8192	AEC YC	14895	Brush	B32F	5/20	6/22
9	T 8194	AEC YC	14899	Brush	B32F	5/20	6/22
4?	T 8196	AEC YC	14893	Brush	B32F	5/20	6/22
5?	T 8198	AEC YC	14892	Brush	B32F	5/20	6/22
6?	T 8200	AEC YC	14897	Brush	B32F	5/20	6/22
7?	T 8202	AEC YC	14898	Brush	B32F	5/20	6/22
8	T 8204	AEC YC	14901	Brush	B32F	5/20	6/22

Notes:
      The registration T 8206 was allocated to a further AEC YC on order, which was subsequently cancelled. These vehicles were re-seated to B26F at an unknown date.

      T 8192 (3): Body destroyed in a depot explosion 6/21; rebodied Strachan & Brown B32F and re-registered TA 3094 3/22. The registration T 8192 was reissued to Daimler Y ch.6613 (see below).

Disposals:
      All these vehicles were transferred to Devon General 1/6/22.

1921

New Vehicles:

	TA 1004	AEC K	20505	LGOC	O24/22RO	4/21	6/22
	TA 1005	AEC K	20506	LGOC	O24/22RO	4/21	6/22
14	TA 1006	AEC K	20507	LGOC	O24/22RO	4/21	6/22
	TA 1168	AEC K	20508	LGOC	O24/22RO	4/21	6/22
	TA 1169	AEC K	20509	LGOC	O24/22RO	4/21	6/22
	TA 1170	AEC K	20510	LGOC	O24/22RO	4/21	6/22

Disposals:
      All these vehicles were transferred to Devon General 1/6/22 (qv).

Vehicles acquired from War Department (GOV):

23	T 8192	Daimler Y	6613	?	Ch30	6/21	6/22
	TA 1008	Daimler Y	6008	Roberts?	Ch30	4/21	6/22
	TA 1009	Daimler Y	6580	Roberts?	Ch30	4/21	6/22
	TA 1010	Daimler Y	6631	Roberts?	Ch30	4/21	6/22
	TA 1676	Daimler Y	6329	Roberts?	Ch30	7/21	6/22

2	TA 1677	Daimler Y	5601	Roberts?	Ch30	7/21	6/22
	TA 1678	Daimler Y	7002	Roberts?	Ch30	7/21	6/22
5	TA 1679	Daimler Y	6516	Roberts?	Ch30	7/21	6/22
84	TA 1934	Daimler Y	6166	Roberts?	Ch30	7/21	6/22

Previous history:

The chassis of these vehicles are believed to have all originated with the War Department (GOV), being rebuilt, rebodied and re-registered prior to entering service on the dates listed above. The vehicles listed with Roberts bodies were supplied by JM Roberts (dealer), London W12 but the bodies are likely to have actually been built by a sub-contractor.

T 8192 (23): Chassis new 1916.
TA 1934 (84): Chassis new 1916.

Disposals:

All these vehicles were transferred to Devon General 1/6/22 (qv).

1922

Vehicles acquired from War Department (GOV):

	TA 3794	Daimler Y	5881	Strachan & Brown	B32F	5/22	6/22
	TA 3795	Daimler Y	5891	Strachan & Brown	B32F	5/22	6/22
29	TA 3796	Daimler Y	6500	Strachan & Brown	B32F	5/22	6/22
28	TA 3797	Daimler Y	6300	?	Ch28	5/22	6/22
6	TA 3798	Daimler Y	4382	Strachan & Brown	B32F	5/22	6/22
33	TA 3799	Daimler Y	4327	Strachan & Brown	B32F	5/22	6/22
36	TA 3800	Daimler Y	6561	Strachan & Brown	B32F	5/22	6/22
	TA 3801	Daimler Y	6529	Strachan & Brown	B32F	5/22	6/22
25	TA 3802	Daimler Y	5999	?	Ch28	5/22	6/22
26	TA 3803	Daimler Y	6984	?	Ch28	5/22	6/22
27	TA 3848	Daimler Y	6324	?	Ch28	5/22	6/22
	TA 3849	Daimler Y	6541	Strachan & Brown	B32F	5/22	6/22

Previous history:

The chassis of these vehicles are believed to have all originated with the War Department (GOV), being rebuilt, rebodied and re-registered prior to entering service on the dates listed above.

Disposals:

All these vehicles were transferred to Devon General 1/6/22 (qv).

ANCILLARY FLEET

T 7518	Wolseley	5455	Lorry	-/14	11/19	-/21
TA 1803	AEC B	B204	Tower wagon	-/10	7/21	6/33

Previous history:

T 7518: Acquired from War Department (GOV).
TA 1803: Chassis new to London General Omnibus Co Ltd, London SW1 (LN) B204 as a bus registered LC 3841; probably acquired via War Department (GOV); re-registered and fitted with tower wagon body on acquisition.

Disposals:

T 7518: Moor & Son, South Molton (DN) 1921; WJ Cole, South Molton (GDN) 10/21; last licensed 12/24; scrapped 7/29.
TA 1803: Transferred to Devon General 6/33 (qv).

DEVON GENERAL OMNIBUS & TOURING COMPANY LIMITED

MOTOR BUSES

1919

Vehicles acquired from the War Department (GOV):

1	T 6942	AEC YC	11423	Hora	O18/22RO	6/19	-/30
2	T 6944	AEC YC	10459	Hora	O18/22RO	6/19	12/27
3	T 6946	AEC YC	11311	Hora	O18/22RO	6/19	6/32

Previous history:

The chassis of these vehicles were rebuilt and fitted with surplus London General Omnibus Co Ltd B type bodies by AEC and re-registered prior to entering service on the dates listed above.

T 6942 (1): Chassis new 1918.
T 6944 (2): Chassis new 1918.

Notes:

T 6942 (1): Named "Sir Francis Drake"; later events relating to this vehicle are contradictory. It has been reported as being fitted with a Hora B35R of the same type, or possibly transferred from, either T 7750 or 7752 (see 1920); alternatively it is recorded as fitted with an East Kent Road Car Co Ltd, Canterbury (KT) single-deck body in 10/21; the original Hora body is quoted as transferred to LF 8399 (11) (in 10/21?); finally a photo dating from the latter part of the 1920s shows a charabanc carrying the registration T 6942 with a Daimler radiator. This latter report is contradicted by the disposal (from Motor Tax records) shown below.

T 6944 (2): Named "Sir Walter Raleigh"; rebuilt as single deck configuration unknown by 1921; rebodied by an unidentified manufacturer as Ch32 and renumbered by 1927 (new fleet number not known).

T 6946 (3): Named "Sir John Hawkins"; rebuilt as single deck configuration unknown by 1921; rebuilt and rebodied by an unidentified manufacturer as O26/24RO and renumbered 72 1926.

Disposals:

T 6942 (1): Smith & Blackwell, London N1 as Ch32 9/24.
T 6944 (2): No further user; original body used as a caravan at Stepps Bridge; scrapped during World War Two.
T 6946 (72): No further user.

1920

New Vehicles:

4	T 7750	AEC YC	15087	Hora	B35R	1/20	-/22
5	T 7752	AEC YC	15086	Hora	B35R	1/20	-/30
6	T 8328	AEC YC	15296	Dowell	Ch28	4/20	12/28
7	T 8330	AEC YC	15297	Dowell	Ch28	4/20	12/30
10	T 9234	Federal 25 hp	216	?	Lorry/Ch--	7/20	-/22

Notes:

T 7752 (5): Reputedly re-licensed as a Daimler Y with an unidentified Ch30 body and renumbered 4 by 1928; which may mean it was fitted with a Daimler radiator and a different body, from an unknown source.

T 8328 (6): Rebodied by an unknown manufacturer as O26/24RO and renumbered 71 1926.

T 8330 (7): Rebodied Hall Lewis B32F and renumbered 87 1927. This body was one of six Hall Lewis convertible bodies, described as a 'charabuses', which were a centre-gangway bus body from which the roof, windows and upper rear panel could be removed as one unit, to create an open tourer.

T 9234 (10): Had a lorry body which was converted to a charabanc for weekend use.

Disposals:

T 7750 (4): Rhondda Transport Company Ltd, Porth (GG) 13 (or 16) 1922; to service 1923; Hendy Quarry Company Ltd, Pontyclun (GGG) as a tipper at an unknown date; last licensed 12/38.
T 7752 (4): R Charlton, London SE5 (GLN) as lorry 1930; last licensed 12/31.
T 8328 (71): No further user.

T 8330 (87): W Mack, London WC2 (GLN) as lorry at an unknown date.
T 9234 (10): Cooper (showman), Exeter at an unknown date; withdrawn 12/29.

Vehicle acquired from London General Omnibus Co Ltd, London SW1 (LN) 3/20:

8	T 8232	AEC YC		10179	?		B27R	3/20	-/22
9	T 8234	AEC YC		12817	?		B27R	3/20	12/30

Previous history:

T 8232: New to War Department (GOV); London General with lorry body fitted with bench seats for 27, registered LU 8066 1918; from whom it was acquired via AEC Ltd.
T 8234: New to War Department (GOV); London General with lorry body fitted bench seats for 27, registered LU 8153 1918; from whom it was acquired via AEC Ltd.

Notes:

T 8232 (8): Also used for carriage of goods; fitted with a (second-hand?) Hora B32R body (1920?).
T 8234 (9): Also used for carriage of goods; fitted with a second-hand B--F body acquired from East Kent Road Car Co Ltd, Canterbury (KT) by 1926; rebodied Hall Lewis B32F ('charabus' body see note for T 8330 above) and renumbered 89 1927.

Disposals:

T 8232 (8): Rhondda Transport Company Ltd, Porth (GG) 16; to service 1923; fitted with 1920 B26- body by an unidentified builder transferred from AEC YC L 6479 (2) with the Hora body being transferred to L 6479 in exchange in 1924, both vehicles retaining the identity of the donor vehicle; withdrawn by 1932; not traced further.
T 8234 (89): W Mack, London WC2 (GLN) as lorry at an unknown date; last licensed 12/30.

Vehicle acquired from London General Omnibus Co Ltd, London SW1 (LN) 12/20:

11	LF 8399	AEC B		B1629	LGOC		O18/16RO	6/12	-/22

Previous history:

This vehicle was new to London General as B1629.

Notes:

LF 8399 (11): Re-registered TA 820 and possibly fitted with the Hora double-deck body, cut-down as B20R from AEC YC T 6942 (1) in 10/21.

Disposal:

TA 820 (ex LF 8399) (11): JA Torbat, Stanley (PH) 10/22, last licensed 12/24; scrapped 11/25.

1921

Vehicles acquired from the War Department (GOV):

12	FJ 1696	AEC YC	7198	Dodson	B32R	5/21	12/30
14	FJ 1697	AEC YC	8872	Dodson	B32R	5/21	12/27
15	FJ 1698	AEC YC	11588	Dodson	B32R	5/21	12/27
	FJ 1780	Daimler Y	4122	?	B32-	7/21	12/27
	FJ 1781	Daimler Y	6428	?	B32-	7/21	-/30
17	FJ 1782	Daimler Y	7312	?	B32F	7/21	-/29
	FJ 1794	Daimler Y	4241	?	Ch32	7/21	9/31
	FJ 1795	Daimler Y	4185	?	Ch32	7/21	9/31
	FJ 1796	Daimler Y	3377	?	Ch32	7/21	9/26

Previous history:

The chassis of these vehicles were acquired via Slough Trading Co Ltd and were rebuilt, rebodied and re-registered prior to entering service on the dates listed above.

FJ 1696-1698: The Dodson bodies were new.
FJ 1780-1782: Had second-hand bodies, two of which were acquired from East Kent Road Car Co Ltd, Canterbury (KT), the origin of the third is unknown.
FJ 1794-1796: The bodies were probably second-hand and were also acquired from Slough Trading.

Notes:

Details of the AEC YCs are confused. The registration/chassis number combinations quoted above are listed as they appear in Devon Motor Tax records, but ch.7198 is also quoted as one of these vehicles. The batch is also quoted as being FJ 1697-1699 (14-16), omitting FJ 1696, which perhaps suggests there was a fourth similar vehicle. They are also quoted as B34R.

FJ 1696 (12): Rebodied Hall Lewis B32F ('charabus' body see note for T 8330 p12) and renumbered 86
 1927, although the same vehicle was reputedly licensed as a charabanc by 1926 and
 relicensed as a Daimler Y by 1927.
FJ 1698 (15): Licensed as a charabanc by 1926, having presumably been rebodied.

Disposals:

FJ 1696 (86): W Mack, London WC2 (GLN) as lorry 12/30; becoming Macks Haulier Ltd at an unknown
 date; scrapped 1937.
FJ 1697 (14): ADC Sales Ltd (dealer), Walthamstow 12/27; AJ Smith, London SW4 use and date
 unknown.
FJ 1698 (15): ADC Sales Ltd (dealer), Walthamstow 10/27; AJ Smith, London SW4 use and date
 unknown.
FJ 1752 (17): WJ Lavinder Ltd (dealer), Worcester Park at an unknown date.
FJ 1780: ADC Sales Ltd (dealer), Walthamstow Ltd, Southall 10/27; AJ Smith, London SW4 use and date
 unknown.
FJ 1781 (40?): EG Vitoria {GV Transport Ltd}, London N22 (GLN) as lorry at an unknown date; last
 licensed 6/32.
FJ 1782 (17): Transferred to Ancillary Fleet 1929.
FJ 1794-1795: WJ Lavinder Ltd (dealer), Worcester Park 9/31.
FJ 1796: Scrapped

1922

Vehicles transferred from Torquay Tramways Co Ltd, Torquay (DN) 1/6/22:

60	T 8188	AEC YC	14896	Brush	B26F	3/20	9/29
61	T 8190	AEC YC	14894	Brush	B26F	3/20	9/29
85	T 8192	Daimler Y	6613	?	Ch30	4/21	-/30
63	T 8194	AEC YC	14899	Brush	B26F	3/20	3/29
64	T 8196	AEC YC	14893	Brush	B26F	3/20	9/29
65	T 8198	AEC YC	14892	Brush	B26F	3/20	9/31
66	T 8200	AEC YC	14897	Brush	B26F	3/20	9/29
67	T 8202	AEC YC	14898	Brush	B26F	3/20	9/31
68	T 8204	AEC YC	14901	Brush	B26F	3/20	3/29
	TA 1004	AEC K	20505	LGOC	O24/22RO	4/21	-/26
	TA 1005	AEC K	20506	LGOC	O24/22RO	4/21	8/26
	TA 1006	AEC K	20507	LGOC	O24/22RO	4/21	-/26
	TA 1008	Daimler Y	6008	Roberts?	Ch30	4/21	9/27
	TA 1009	Daimler Y	6580	Roberts?	Ch30	4/21	-/30
	TA 1010	Daimler Y	6631	Roberts?	Ch30	4/21	-/30
	TA 1168	AEC K	20508	LGOC	O24/22RO	4/21	-/26
	TA 1169	AEC K	20509	LGOC	O24/22RO	4/21	-/26
	TA 1170	AEC K	20510	LGOC	O24/22RO	4/21	8/26
	TA 1676	Daimler Y	6329	Roberts?	Ch30	7/21	10/29
	TA 1677	Daimler Y	5601	Roberts?	Ch30	7/21	-/30
	TA 1678	Daimler Y	7002	Roberts?	Ch30	7/21	-/29
	TA 1679	Daimler Y	6516	Roberts?	Ch30	7/21	9/31
	TA 1934	Daimler Y	6166	Roberts?	Ch30	7/21	-/31
62	TA 3094	AEC YC	14895	Strachan & Brown	B32F	5/20	-/30
19	TA 3794	Daimler Y	5881	Strachan & Brown	B32F	5/22	3/30
20	TA 3795	Daimler Y	5891	Strachan & Brown	B32F	5/22	10/29
21	TA 3796	Daimler Y	6500	Strachan & Brown	B32F	5/22	-/30
6	TA 3797	Daimler Y	6300	?	Ch28	5/22	-/30
	TA 3798	Daimler Y	4382	Strachan & Brown	B32F	5/22	3/30
	TA 3799	Daimler Y	4327	Strachan & Brown	B32F	5/22	3/30
36	TA 3800	Daimler Y	6561	Strachan & Brown	B32F	5/22	-/30
	TA 3801	Daimler Y	6529	Strachan & Brown	B32F	5/22	10/29
	TA 3802	Daimler Y	5999	?	Ch28	5/22	9/31

3	TA 3803	Daimler Y	6984 ?		Ch28	5/22	-/30
	TA 3848	Daimler Y	6324 ?		Ch28	5/22	9/31
	TA 3849	Daimler Y	6541	Strachan & Brown	B32F	5/22	3/30

Previous history:

These vehicles were transferred from Torquay Tramways Co Ltd, who had acquired a controlling interest in Devon General in 1922. The buses of the Tramways Company then being transferred to Devon General. See p10-11 for details of previous history.

Notes:

The fleet numbers shown are the first known Devon General numbers, with subsequent changes shown below, however records are incomplete, therefore some of these numbers may not have been the first numbers allocated. Numbers 19-24 are believed to have been allocated to 1921 charabancs (including TA 1676-1679 & 1934) in unknown order and 29-36 were allocated to Daimler Y TA 3794-3796, 3798-3801 & 3849 also in unknown order.

The Daimler Y chassis listed with Roberts bodies above, were supplied by JM Roberts (dealer), London W12, but the bodies are likely to have been actually built by a sub-contractor.

One of the AEC K type was latterly numbered 49.

T 8192 (23): Had a reissued registration (originally carried by an AEC YC); rebodied Hall Lewis B32F ('charabus' body see note for T 8330 p12) and renumbered 85 1927.
T 8198: Fitted with a Ch-- body and renumbered 18 at an unknown date.
T 8202: Fitted with a Ch-- body and renumbered 12 at an unknown date.
TA 1008-1009 (10-11): Re-seated to Ch29 at an unknown date.
TA 1010 (12): Also recorded as 29 and 32 seat.
TA 1676: Also recorded as 26 and 29 seat.
TA 1677 (2): Also recorded as 29 and 32 seat.
TA 1678: Also recorded as 29 and 32 seat.
TA 1679 (5): Re-seated to Ch29 at an unknown date.
TA 1934: Rebodied Hall Lewis B32F ('charabus' body see note for T 8330 p12) and renumbered 84 1927.
TA 3094 (ex T 8192) (3): New with a Brush B32F body, which was destroyed in a depot explosion 6/21; rebodied Strachan & Brown B32F and re-registered TA 3094 3/22; re-seated to B32F at an unknown date.
TA 3848: Also recorded as 29 seat.

Disposals:

T 8188 (1): No further user.
T 8190: No further user.
T 8192 (85): W Mack, London WC2 (GLN) as lorry at an unknown date; last licensed 12/30; scrapped.
T 8194: No further user.
T 8196: No further user.
T 8198: Sold to unknown owner; last licensed 9/30.
T 8200: No further user.
T 8202: Sold to unknown owner; last licensed 9/31.
T 8204: Sold to unknown owner; last licensed 4/29.
TA 1004: ADC Sales Ltd (dealer), Walthamstow in part exchange 1926; London General Omnibus Co, London SW1 (LN) K1127 11/26; withdrawn 10/30.
TA 1005: ADC Sales Ltd (dealer), Walthamstow in part exchange 1926; London General Omnibus Co, London SW1 (LN) K1128 11/26; withdrawn 3/31.
TA 1006: ADC Sales Ltd (dealer), Walthamstow in part exchange 1926; London General Omnibus Co, London SW1 (LN) K1129 11/26; withdrawn 5/31.
TA 1008: No further user.
TA 1009: G Bailey & Sons Ltd, London SW1 (GLN) as a van at an unknown date; last licensed 1/39.
TA 1010: JT & T Latham, Beauchamp Roding (GEX) as lorry at an unknown date; last licensed 12/35.
TA 1168: ADC Sales Ltd (dealer), Walthamstow in part exchange 1926; London General Omnibus Co, London SW1 (LN) K1130 11/26; withdrawn 4/31.
TA 1169: ADC Sales Ltd (dealer), Walthamstow in part exchange 1926; London General Omnibus Co, London SW1 (LN) K1131 11/26; withdrawn 6/31.
TA 1170: ADC Sales Ltd (dealer), Walthamstow in part exchange 1926; London General Omnibus Co, London SW1 (LN) K1132 11/26; withdrawn 5/31.
TA 1676: No further user.
TA 1677: Pullinger, London SW9 (GLN) as lorry at an unknown date; withdrawn 6/33.

TA 1678: Davis, London E6 (GLN) as lorry at an unknown date; last licensed 6/31.
TA 1679: No further user.
TA 1934 (84): W Mack, London WC2 (GLN) as lorry at an unknown date.
TA 3094 (62): Gliddon, Upminster (GEX) as lorry at an unknown date; last licensed 12/37; scrapped 8/41.
TA 3794: No further user.
TA 3795: No further user.
TA 3796 (21): Barnard, Stowmarket (GEK) as lorry at an unknown date; last licensed 11/34.
TA 3797 (6): Bailey, London WC1 (GLN) as lorry at an unknown date; last licensed 1/39.
TA 3798: No further user.
TA 3799: Sold to unidentified owner date and use unknown; scrapped 2/40.
TA 3800 (36): Excervis Transport Company, Tooting (GSR) as lorry at an unknown date; withdrawn 12/36.
TA 3801-3802: No further user.
TA 3803 (3): C Froud, London SE10 (GLN) at an unknown date; last licensed 8/33.
TA 3848-3849: No further user.

Vehicles acquired from the War Department (GOV):

	MX 9272	Daimler Y	3353	?	B26-	-/16	c-/28
27	TA 4625	Daimler Y	4357	Strachan & Brown	B40F	10/22	-/30
	TA 4645	Daimler CB	?	Strachan & Brown	B20F	10/22	-/27
28	TA 4701	Daimler Y	?	Strachan & Brown	B40F	10/22	-/30
	TA 4754	Daimler CB	?	Strachan & Brown	B20F	11/22	-/27

Previous history:
The chassis of these vehicles were acquired via JM Roberts (dealer), London W12 and were rebuilt, rebodied and re-registered prior to entering service on the dates listed above.

Notes:
TA 4625 & TA 4701 (27-28): Originally licensed to seat 40 including tip-up seats across the gangway, but this practice ceased after 1926 and the seating was reduced to B32F.

Disposals:
MX 9272: No disposal known.
TA 4625 (27): Bailey, London WC1 (GLN) as a van at an unknown date; last licensed 9/37.
TA 4645: Glasgow General Omnibus & Motor Services Ltd, Glasgow (LK) 6/27; last licensed 6/27 (not operated?).
TA 4701 (28): Mack, London WC2 (GLN) as a van at an unknown date; last licensed 7/42.
TA 4754: Glasgow General Omnibus & Motor Services Ltd, Glasgow (LK) 6A 1927; last licensed 5/29.

1923

Vehicles acquired from the War Department (GOV):

29	TA 5222	Daimler Y	8580	Strachan & Brown	B32F	1/23	10/30
30?	TA 5223	Daimler Y	?	Strachan & Brown	B32F	1/23	12/29
31	TA 5440	Daimler Y	6580	Strachan & Brown	B32F	2/23	10/30
58	TA 5441	Daimler Y	6516	Strachan & Brown	B32F	2/23	10/29
16?	TA 6339	Daimler Y	4262	?	Ch28	5/23	9/30
	TA 7157	Daimler Y	3987	?	B32-	7/23	3/28
	TA 7256	Daimler Y	2105	?	Ch--	7/23	-/31

Previous history:
These chassis of these vehicles were acquired via JM Roberts (dealer), London W12 and were rebuilt, rebodied and re-registered prior to entering service on the dates listed above.

In addition an AEC chassis was acquired for spares (no further details known).

Notes:
TA 5440 (31): Originally licensed to seat 40 using tip-up seats across the gangway, but this practice ceased after 1926 and the seating reduced to 32.
TA 5441 (58): Originally licensed to seat 40 using tip-up seats across the gangway, but this practice ceased after 1926 and the seating reduced to 32; renumbered 32 at an unknown date.
TA 6339 (16?): Body acquired from MB Down & C Boucher, Kingsteignton (DN).

TA 7256 (88): Had a canvas roof with sidescreens; rebodied Hall Lewis B32F ('charabus' body see note for T 8330 p12) and renumbered 88 1927.

Disposals:
TA 5222 (29): No further users.
TA 5223 (30?): No further users.
TA 5440 (31): No further users.
TA 5441 (32): No further users.
TA 6339 (16?): No further users.
TA 7157: ADC Sales Ltd (dealer), Walthamstow at an unknown date.
TA 7256 (88): W Mack, London WC2 (GLN) as lorry at an unknown date; last licensed 12/37.

1924

Vehicles acquired from Croscols Ltd, Tiverton (DN) 3/24:

T 9364	Napier 25/30 hp	3213N	?	Ch19	7/20	n/a
FM 1941	Daimler CK	?	Eaton	B26R	c1/21	-/27
FM 1942	Daimler CK	?	Eaton	B26R	c1/21	-/27
TA 1870	FIAT F2	?	?	Ch14	7/21	-/27
TA 4851	Daimler CB	1918	Roberts?	B20F	12/22	-/27
TA 5391	Daimler CB	2469	Roberts?	B20F	2/23	-/27

Previous history:
These vehicles were acquired with the Croscols business; their previous histories are detailed in the Vehicles of Acquired Operators section.

Notes:
T 9364: Not operated by Devon General.
TA 1870: Quoted with engine number 16044, chassis number unknown.

Disposals:
T 9364: Chassis sold 1924.
FM 1941: H Russett {Royal Blue}, Bristol (GL) by 1930.
FM 1942: No disposal known.
TA 1870: Transferred to Ancillary Fleet (qv).
TA 4851: H & E Ashley, Catford (GKT) at an unknown date; last licensed 6/35.
TA 5391: H & E Ashley, Catford (GKT) as lorry at an unknown date; last licensed 12/33.

Vehicles acquired from the War Department (GOV):

33	TA 9408	Daimler Y	6208	Strachan & Brown	B40F	4/24	-/30
34	TA 9409	Daimler Y	4202	Strachan & Brown	B40F	4/24	3/30
	TA 9540	Daimler Y	7198?	Thompson	B32F	4/24	12/28
35	TT 193	Daimler Y	7031	Strachan & Brown	B40F	6/24	10/30
36	TT 194	Daimler Y	6137	Strachan & Brown	B40F	6/24	-/30
	TT 485	Daimler Y	4070	?	Ch28	7/24	10/29
	TT 486	Daimler Y	?	?	Ch28	7/24	-/30

Previous history:
The chassis of these vehicles were acquired via Slough Trading Co Ltd and were rebuilt, rebodied and re-registered prior to entering service on the dates listed above. It is believed that a further similar chassis was acquired from the same source, which may have been fitted with a 'charabus' body similar to TA 9540. An AEC chassis is also believed to have been acquired for spares.

Notes:
TA 9408-9409 (33-34): Originally licensed to seat 40 using tip-up seats across the gangway, but this practice ceased after 1926 and the seating reduced to 32. Original fleet numbers not known, those quoted were applied at an unknown date.
TA 9540: This vehicle had a convertible body, described as a 'charabus', which was a centre-gangway bus body from which the roof, windows and upper rear panel could be removed as one unit, to create an open tourer.
TT 193-194 (35-36): Originally licensed to seat 40 using tip-up seats across the gangway, but this practice ceased after 1926 and the seating reduced to 32. Original fleet numbers not known, those quoted were applied at an unknown date.

Disposals:

TA 9408 (33): Bailey, London WC1 (GLN) as lorry at an unknown date; Wargent, Ashperton (GHR) at an unknown date; last licensed 11/35.

TA 9409 (34?): No further user.

TA 9540: No disposal known.

TT 193 (35): No further user.

TT 194 (36): Rockman, London E15 (GLN) as lorry 1930; last licensed 9/34.

TT 485: No further user.

TT 486: Bailey, London WC1 (GLN) as lorry 1930.

1925

New Vehicles:

50	TT 4077	Dennis 4 ton	40340	Hall Lewis	B26F	5/25	-/31
51	TT 4078	Dennis 4 ton	40342	Hall Lewis	B26F	5/25	-/31
52	TT 4079	Dennis 4 ton	40352	Hall Lewis	B26F	5/25	-/31
53	TT 4080	Dennis 4 ton	40354	Hall Lewis	B26F	5/25	-/31
54	TT 4563	Dennis 2½ ton	45093	Hall Lewis	B28F	7/25	-/31
55	TT 4564	Dennis 2½ ton	45095	Hall Lewis	B28F	7/25	-/30
56	TT 4565	Dennis 2½ ton	45061	Hall Lewis	B28F	7/25	-/31
57	TT 4566	Dennis 2½ ton	45060	Hall Lewis	B28F	7/25	-/30
58	TT 4567	Dennis 2½ ton	45050	Hall Lewis	B28F	7/25	-/31
59	TT 4568	Dennis 2½ ton	45052	Hall Lewis	B28F	7/25	-/31

Notes:

TT 4563-4568 (54-59): Re-seated to B32F at an unknown date.

Disposals:

TT 4077 (50): Unidentified dealer, London 1931; Essex & Kent Farmers, Southend-on-Sea (GEX) as lorry at an unknown date.

TT 4078 (51): Unidentified dealer, London 1931; Gibson, London E8 (GLN) as lorry at an unknown date.

TT 4079 (52): Unidentified dealer, London 1931; Beadle, London SE5 (GLN) as lorry at an unknown date.

TT 4080 (53): Unidentified dealer, London 1931; Bennett, Croydon (SR) as lorry at an unknown date.

TT 4563 (54): Unidentified dealer, London 1931; Bennett, Croydon (SR) as lorry at an unknown date.

TT 4564 (55): Body sold, chassis dismantled.

TT 4565 (56): Unidentified dealer, London 1931; Lobjoit, Langley (GBK) as lorry at an unknown date.

TT 4566 (57): Body sold, chassis dismantled.

TT 4567 (58): Unidentified dealer, London 1931; Val de Travers (contractor), London EC2 (GLN) as lorry at an unknown date.

TT 4568 (59): Unidentified dealer, London 1931; Hibberd, Bramford (GEK) as lorry at an unknown date.

Vehicles acquired from the War Department (GOV):

	TT 2236	Daimler Y	5740	Thompson	B32F	1/25	-/28

Previous history:

TT 2236: Chassis acquired via Lowe (dealer), location unknown; rebuilt, rebodied and re-registered prior to entering service 1/25.

Notes:

TT 2236: This vehicle had a convertible body, described as a 'charabus', which was a centre-gangway bus body from which the roof, windows and upper rear panel could be removed as one unit, to create an open tourer.

Disposals:

TT 2236: No further user.

Vehicles transferred from Fleet Cars Ltd, Paignton (DN):

	DB 1567	Dennis 35 hp	?	?	Ch28	7/19	-/27
	DB 1569	Dennis 35 hp	?	?	Ch28	7/19	-/27
	DB 1723	Dennis 35 hp	?	?	Ch28	1/20	-/27
	DB 1724	Dennis 35 hp	?	?	Ch28	1/20	-/27
80	TA 6347	Lancia Tetraiota	189	?	Ch18	5/23	-/31

Previous history:

These vehicles were all new to Fleet Cars.

Notes:

The four Dennis vehicles were numbered 76-79 in unknown order.

TA 6347 (80): Believed to have been renumbered 101 at an unknown date.

Disposals:

DB 1567: Unidentified owner Devon 1927; scrapped by 9/34.
DB 1569: Unidentified owner Devon 1927; scrapped by 10/29.
DB 1723: Unidentified owner Devon 1927; scrapped by 1/28.
DB 1724: Unidentified owner Devon 1927; scrapped by 9/38.
TA 6347 (80/101): WV Glanville, Taunton (GSO) as lorry 1931; last licensed 9/33.

1926

New Vehicles:

73	TT 9268	AEC 506	506033?	Hall Lewis	B32F	7/26	-/33
74	TT 9269	AEC 506	506028	Hall Lewis	B32F	7/26	-/33
75	TT 9270	AEC 506	506035?	Hall Lewis	B32F	7/26	-/33
76	TT 9271	AEC 506	506029?	Hall Lewis	B32F	7/26	-/33
77	TT 9480	AEC 506	506027	Hall Lewis	B32F	8/26	-/32
78	TT 9494	AEC 506	506034	Hall Lewis	B32F	8/26	-/32

Notes:

These vehicles were received in part-exchange for six AEC K types (TA 1004-1006 & TA 1168-1170).

TT 9268 & 9270 (73 & 75): The chassis numbers of TT 9268 & 9270 both appear as ch.506033 in Devon Motor Tax records, but one is thought to have been ch.506035. This chassis number is later attributed to UO 928 (see 1927), suggesting an identity exchange between UO 928 and either TT 9268 or 9270 when with WJ Lavinder Ltd (dealer) (see below).
TT 9271 (76): Chassis number is quoted as both ch.506029 and 506039.

Disposals:

TT 9268 (73): WJ Lavinder Ltd (dealer), Worcester Park at an unknown date; H Yager (London) Ltd {Charlotte Cabinet Company}, Ponders End (GMX) as lorry at an unknown date; last licensed 3/35.
TT 9269 (74): WJ Lavinder Ltd (dealer), Worcester Park at an unknown date; Aberford Motor Co Ltd, Aberford (GWR) as lorry at an unknown date; last licensed 3/44.
TT 9270 (75): WJ Lavinder Ltd (dealer), Worcester Park at an unknown date; Aberford Motor Co Ltd, Aberford (GWR) at an unknown date; Road Haulage Executive, Aberford (GWR) at an unknown date; last licensed, as a tractor unit, 12/49.
TT 9271 (76): WJ Lavinder Ltd (dealer), Worcester Park at an unknown date; London Plywood & Timber Co Ltd, London EC1 (GLN) as lorry at an unknown date; last licensed 3/38.
TT 9480 (77): WJ Lavinder Ltd (dealer), Worcester Park at an unknown date. Perry & Priest, London SE5 (GLN) as lorry at an unknown date; last licensed 12/44.
TT 9494 (78): WJ Lavinder Ltd (dealer), Worcester Park at an unknown date; last licensed 12/37.

Vehicle transferred from Fleet Cars Ltd, Paignton (DN):

100?	TA 6433	Lancia Tetraiota	137	?	Ch20	5/23	9/31

Previous history:

TA 6433 (100?): New to W Langbridge & WP Tucker {Comfy Cars}, Paignton (DN); to Fleet Cars 1/26.

Disposals:

TA 6433 (100?): No further operator.

Vehicle acquired from Whitton, Cullompton (GDN):

41?	TA 5708	AEC YC	8303	Thompson?	B28F	3/23	-/30

Previous history:

TA 5708: New to Whitton, Cullompton (GDN) as lorry; acquired as a chassis only and fitted with the body listed prior to entering service.

Notes:

TA 5708: This vehicle had a convertible body, described as a 'charabus', which was a centre-gangway bus body from which the roof, windows and upper rear panel could be removed as one unit, to create an open tourer. It is not confirmed that this was one of the Thompson bodies.

Disposals:

TA 5708: J Small, London NW9 (GLN) as lorry at an unknown date; last licensed 12/41.

1927

New Vehicles:

79	UO 845	ADC 506	506121	Hall Lewis	B28F	1/27	-/33
80	UO 846	ADC 506	506122	Hall Lewis	B28F	1/27	-/33
81	UO 927	ADC 506	506123	Hall Lewis	B28F	1/27	-/33
82	UO 928	ADC 506	506124	Hall Lewis	B28F	1/27	-/33
83	UO 980	ADC 506	506143	Hall Lewis	B28F	1/27	-/32
90	UO 4164	ADC 506	506275	Hall Lewis	B32F	10/27	-/33
91	UO 4165	ADC 506	506274	Hall Lewis	B32F	10/27	-/33
92	UO 4189	ADC 506	506273	Hall Lewis	B32F	10/27	-/33
93	UO 4227	ADC 506	506276	Hall Lewis	B32F	10/27	-/33
94.	UO 4675	ADC 506	506284	Hall Lewis	B32F	12/27	-/33
95	UO 4676	ADC 506	506283	Hall Lewis	B32F	12/27	-/33

Notes:

UO 845-846 (79-80): Reseated to B32F at unknown dates.
UO 927-928 (81-82): Reseated to B32F at unknown dates.
UO 980 (83): Reseated to B32F at an unknown date.

Disposals:

UO 845 (79): WJ Lavinder Ltd (dealer), Worcester Park at an unknown date.
UO 846 (80): WJ Lavinder Ltd (dealer), Worcester Park at an unknown date; Hepplewhite, Hillingdon (GMX) at an unknown date.
UO 927 (81): WJ Lavinder Ltd (dealer), Worcester Park at an unknown date; Aberford Motor Co Ltd, Aberford (GWR) as lorry at an unknown date; scrapped 10/43.
UO 928 (82): WJ Lavinder Ltd (dealer), Worcester Park at an unknown date; last licensed 12/37. See note for TT 9268 & 9270 (1926).
UO 980 (83): H Yager (London) Ltd {Charlotte Cabinet Company}, Ponders End (GMX) as lorry at an unknown date; last licensed 6/36.
UO 4164 (90): WJ Lavinder Ltd (dealer), Worcester Park at an unknown date; Aberford Motor Co Ltd, Aberford (GWR) at an unknown date; Road Haulage Executive, Aberford (GWR) (1948?); last licensed 12/48.
UO 4165 (91): WJ Lavinder Ltd (dealer), Worcester Park at an unknown date; Fox's Motors Ltd, Manchester (GLA) as a tipper at an unknown date; last licensed 9/38.
UO 4189 (92): WJ Lavinder Ltd (dealer), Worcester Park at an unknown date; Aberford Motor Co Ltd, Aberford (GWR) at an unknown date; Road Haulage Executive, Aberford (GWR) (1948?); last licensed 12/51.
UO 4227 (93): WJ Lavinder Ltd (dealer), Worcester Park at an unknown date; Aberford Motor Co Ltd, Aberford (GWR) at an unknown date; Road Haulage Executive, Aberford (GWR) (1948?); last licensed 8/50.
UO 4675 (94): WJ Lavinder Ltd (dealer), Worcester Park at an unknown date; Aberford Motor Co Ltd, Aberford (GWR) as lorry at an unknown date; last licensed 4/48.
UO 4676 (95): WJ Lavinder Ltd (dealer), Worcester Park at an unknown date; Aberford Motor Co Ltd, Aberford (GWR) as lorry at an unknown date; fitted with an oil engine type and date unknown; last licensed 3/42.

Vehicle acquired from Torquay-Chelston Car Co Ltd (DN) 1/27:

98	TA 3098	Leyland G7	12371	Leyland	B31D	3/22	-/27
99	TT 8164	Leyland LSC1	45154	Leyland	B31F	5/26	-/33

Previous history:

These vehicles were acquired with the Torquay-Chelston Car Co business; their previous histories are detailed in the Vehicles of Acquired Operators section.

Disposal:

TA 3098 (98): Transferred to Ancillary Fleet 1929 (qv).
TT 8164 (99): Lamb, Middleton St George (GDM) as lorry at an unknown date; withdrawn 12/47.

Vehicle transferred from Fleet Cars Ltd, Paignton (DN):

102?	TA 6434	Lancia Z1	4097	?	Ch14	5/23	-/27
103	TA 9441	Lancia Tetraiota	163	?	Ch18	4/24	-/31
104	TT 3356	Lancia Pentaiota	625	?	Ch20	4/25	9/34

Previous history:

These vehicles had all been new to the Comfy Cars business which was originally a partnership between W Langridge & WP Tucker, becoming WP Tucker alone, probably in 1924; to Fleet Cars 1/26.

Notes:

TA 9441 (103): Also quoted as Ch20.
TT 3356 (104): Re-seated to Ch18 at an unknown date.

Disposals:

TA 6434 (102?): Transferred to Ancilliary fleet (qv).
TA 9441 (103): HM Wargent, Ashperton (GHR) as lorry at an unknown date; last licensed 11/35.
TT 3356 (104): Scrapped.

Vehicles acquired from EO Babington {Blue Cars}, Ashburton (DN) 20/5/27:

	EB 2187	FIAT 15/20hp	?	Dowell	Ch14	4/20	c-/27
	EB 2188	FIAT 15/20hp	?	Dowell	Ch14	4/20	c-/27
	TA 5449	Maxwell 30 cwt	E21890	?	Ch14-	2/23	n/a
	TA 7282	Berliet 35 cwt	10583	?	B20F	7/23	n/a
105	TA 7490	Lancia Tetraiota	203	?	B20F	8/23	-/31
106	TT 1761	Lancia Pentaiota	539	?	B20F	11/24	12/29
69	TT 6254	Albion PJ24	4129G	?	B24F	12/25	-/33
70	TT 6255	Albion PJ24	4129K	?	B24F	12/25	-/33
	TT 8954	Berliet	30754	?	B20F	7/26	c-/30
107	UO 97	Berliet CBOH	30762	?	B20F	11/26	c-/28
	?	Maxwell 30 cwt	?	?	Ch14-	-/--	c-/27

Previous history:

These vehicles were acquired with the Babington business; their previous histories are detailed in the Vehicles of Acquired Operators section.

Only one of either EB 2187 or 2188 was acquired.

Notes:

TA 5449: Had been withdrawn 9/26; not operated by Devon General.
TA 7282: Probably not operated.
TT 8954: Also quoted as B22F.

Disposals:

EB 2187-2188: No disposals known.
TA 5449: Last licensed (9/23?); scrapped 11/28.
TA 7282: Last licensed 3/27; scrapped 11/28.
TA 7490 (105): EJ Dunn, Taunton (SO) at an unknown date; last licensed 9/32.
TT 1761: Scrapped.
TT 6254-6255 (69-70): Taylor, Ipswich (GEK) as lorries at an unknown date.
TT 8954: Heath Bros, Bovey Tracey (GDN) as lorry at an unknown date; last licensed 6/32.
UO 97 (107): Guest, Loddiswell (GDN) as lorry at an unknown date; last licensed 10/33.

1928

New vehicles:

96	UO 4960	ADC 506	506281	Hall Lewis	B32F	1/28	-/33
97	UO 4961	ADC 506	506282	Hall Lewis	B32F	1/28	-/33
110	UO 6853	Leyland LSC3	46673	Hall Lewis	B32D	6/28	-/34
111	UO 6854	Leyland LSC3	46670	Hall Lewis	B32D	6/28	-/34
112	UO 6855	Leyland LSC3	46671	Hall Lewis	B32D	6/28	-/34

113	UO 7303	Leyland LSC3	46747	Hall Lewis	B32D	7/28	-/34
114	UO 7304	Leyland LSC3	45745	Hall Lewis	B32D	7/28	-/34
116	UO 7469	Leyland LSC3	46746	Hall Lewis	B32D	7/28	-/34
115	UO 7470	Leyland LSC3	46748	Hall Lewis	B32D	7/28	-/34
117	UO 7471	Leyland LSC3	46749	Hall Lewis	B32D	7/28	-/34
118	UO 7851	Leyland LC1	47423	Hall Lewis	C26D	8/28	-/34
119	UO 7852	Leyland LC1	47424	Hall Lewis	C26D	8/28	-/34
120	UO 7910	Leyland LC1	47425	Hall Lewis	C26D	8/28	-/34
121	UO 7911	Leyland LC1	47426	Hall Lewis	C26D	8/28	-/34
122	UO 7950	Leyland LC1	47427	Hall Lewis	C26D	8/28	-/34
123	UO 7951	Leyland LC1	47428	Hall Lewis	C26D	8/28	-/34

Notes:
The six Leyland LC1 coaches were for use on "Limited Stop" services.

Disposals:
UO 4960 (96): WJ Lavinder Ltd (dealer), Worcester Park at an unknown date; Fox Motors Ltd, Manchester (GLA) as a tipper 9/38; unidentified owner, Sheffield (GWR) at an unknown date.

UO 4961 (97): WJ Lavinder Ltd (dealer), Worcester Park at an unknown date; Aberford Motor Company, Aberford (GWR) as a tanker at an unknown date; last licensed 12/41.

UO 6853 (110): Mann, Crossman & Paulin, London (GLN) as lorry at an unknown date; last licensed 12/48; scrapped at an unknown date.

UO 6854 (111): Mann, Crossman & Paulin, London (GLN) as lorry at an unknown date; to an unidentified showman at an unknown date; last licensed 11/47; scrapped at an unknown date.

UO 6855 (112): Mann, Crossman & Paulin, London (GLN) as lorry at an unknown date, to an unidentified showman at an unknown date; last licensed 4/48; scrapped at an unknown date.

UO 7303 (113): H Roberts, Connah's Quay (FT) at an unknown date; Crosville Motor Services Ltd, Chester (CH) B101 7/36; unidentified owner, Wolverhampton (GST) as lorry by 6/46; Road Haulage Executive, Dudley (GWO) (1948?); last licensed 12/49.

UO 7304 (114): AT Crabtree, Grantham (LI) as B31D 1934; last licensed 3/35.

UO 7469 (116): AE Doulin {Thorpe Coaches}, London E17 (LN) by 9/38; J Abbot, Ipswich as a caravan 9/46.

UO 7470 (115): A Mellors (showman), Nottingham at an unknown date; last licensed 6/52; scrapped.

UO 7471 (117): C Hunt {Kineton Green Bus Service}, Kineton (WK) 9/34; becoming Kineton Green Bus Services Ltd, Kineton (WK) 11/34; El Peake, Pontnewynydd (MH) 1/37; SJ Davies, Penygraig (GG) at an unknown date; J Jones, Ynysybwl (GG) (1947?).

UO 7851 (118): C Hunt {Kineton Green Bus Service}, Kineton (WK) 9/34; becoming Kineton Green Bus Services Ltd, Kineton (WK) 11/34; last licensed 12/36; no further operator.

UO 7852 (119): C Hunt {Kineton Green Bus Service}, Kineton (WK) 9/34; becoming Kineton Green Bus Services Ltd, Kineton (WK) 11/34; last licensed 11/36; no further operator.

UO 7910 (120): OW Owen, Rhostryfan (CN) by 8/36; last licensed 12/38; scrapped 8/43.

UO 7911 (121): W Jarvill & A Vessey {Lily}, Scunthorpe (LI) at an unknown date; last licensed 3/36.

UO 7950 (122): DM Pritchard, Llanrug (CN) 1934; Crosville Motor Services Ltd, Chester (CH) K111 3/36; withdrawn 1936; AE Banwell, Biddisham (SO) 1936; not operated.

UO 7951 (123): H Semmence & Co, Wymondham (GNK) as C25F 6/37; withdrawn 6/40; believed converted to goods vehicle with same operator; last licensed 3/51.

Vehicles transferred from Fleet Cars Ltd, Paignton (DN):

109	ML 4014	Lancia	342	?	Ch18	4/27	-/34
108	UO 2811	Lancia 30 hp	3813	?	Ch18	6/27	9/34

Previous history:
ML 4014 (109): New to GG Gullick {Heather Tours}, Paignton (DN), supplied through and registered by Curtis Automobile Co Ltd (Lancia dealer), London NW10; acquired by Fleet Cars from Gullick 5/28.

UO 2811 (108): New to GG Gullick {Heather Tours}, Paignton (DN); to Fleet Cars 5/28.

Disposals:
ML 4014: Sold 1934; Park Street Garage, London N16 (GLN?) probably as lorry, at an unknown date; last licensed 9/44.

UO 2811: Sold 1934; no further user.

1929

New Vehicles:

135	DV 116	Leyland TS2	60464	Hall Lewis	C26D	5/29	-/39
136	DV 160	Leyland TS2	60465	Hall Lewis	C26D	4/29	-/39
137	DV 226	Leyland TS2	60466	Hall Lewis	C26D	5/29	-/39
138	DV 225	Leyland TD1	70538	Hall Lewis	L24/24RO	5/29	-/36
128	DV 925	Leyland LT1	50130	Hall Lewis	B31D	6/29	12/37
129	DV 926	Leyland LT1	50129	Hall Lewis	B31D	6/29	-/36
130	DV 1044	Leyland LT1	50131	Hall Lewis	B31D	6/29	11/36
131	DV 1616	Leyland LT1	50132	Hall Lewis	B31D	7/29	2/37
139	DV 2149	Leyland TD1	70537	Hall Lewis	L24/24RO	8/29	-/36
140	DV 2304	Leyland TD1	70536	Hall Lewis	L24/24RO	8/29	-/36
144	DV 2326	Leyland TS2	60347	Hall Lewis	C30D	8/29	-/36
145	DV 2355	Leyland TS2	60346	Hall Lewis	C30D	8/29	12/35
141	DV 2356	Leyland TD1	70539	Hall Lewis	L24/24RO	8/29	-/36
124	UO 9690	Leyland LSC3	47514	Hall Lewis	B32D	3/29	-/34
125	UO 9691	Leyland LSC3	47513	Hall Lewis	B32D	3/29	-/34
126	UO 9692	Leyland LSC3	47512	Hall Lewis	B32D	3/29	-/34
132	UO 9759	Leyland TS2	60463	Hall Lewis	C26D	3/29	-/39
133	UO 9779	Leyland TS2	60461	Hall Lewis	C26D	3/29	-/47
134	UO 9780	Leyland TS2	60462	Hall Lewis	C26D	3/29	-/39
127	UO 9813	Leyland LSC3	47511	Hall Lewis	B32D	3/29	-/34

Notes:

The Leyland TS2 coaches were for use on "Limited Stop" services.

DV 116 (135): Re-seated to C30D 1935.

DV 160 (136): Re-seated to C30D 1935.

DV 225 (138): Returned to Hall Lewis and fitted with replacement L24/24RO body, original body remounted on Thornycroft LC chassis (UH 8231-8234 series) for sale to Cardiff Corporation (GG).

DV 226 (137): Re-seated to C30D 1935.

DV 2149 (139): Returned to Hall Lewis and fitted with replacement L24/24RO body, original body remounted on Thornycroft LC chassis (UH 8231-8234 series) for sale to Cardiff Corporation (GG).

DV 2304 (140): Returned to Hall Lewis and fitted with replacement L24/24RO body, original body remounted on Thornycroft LC chassis (UH 8231-8234 series) for sale to Cardiff Corporation (GG).

DV 2356 (141): Exhibited at the 1929 Commercial Motor Show; returned to Hall Lewis and fitted with replacement L24/24RO body, original body remounted on Thornycroft LC chassis (UH 8231-8234 series) for sale to Cardiff Corporation (GG).

UO 9759 (132) Re-seated to C30D 1935.

UO 9779 (133): Re-seated to C30D 1935; allocated number XL133 1939, but not carried; earmarked for conversion to a service vehicle but used instead for experiments with producer gas in 1940, when it was repainted grey and renumbered SL133. It was then stored until 1946 when it was converted back to petrol and returned to service still in grey livery.

UO 9780 (134): Re-seated to C30D 1935.

Disposals:

DV 116 (135): Auctioned via London Horse & Motor Depository, London SE1 4/39; HN Trewren {Marigold Service}, Lanner (CO) 1939; scrapped 1946; registration void 1948.

DV 160 (136): Auctioned via London Horse & Motor Depository, London SE1 4/39; TJ & MA King {Monarch Coaches}, Bristol (GL) 1939; GW Bailey, Mexborough (WR) by 1945; A & C Wigmore, Dinnington (WR) at an unknown date; withdrawn 5/48; scrapped.

DV 225 (138): E & N Sanderson {Millburn Garage} (dealer), (dealer) Glasgow at an unknown date; W Alexander & Sons Ltd, Falkirk (SN) R186 6/37; fitted with the 1933 Pickering H24/24R body transferred from Crossley Condor GS 3920 and Leyland 8.6 litre oil engine; to service 9/37, reseated to H30/26R 1/41; James Sutherland (Peterhead) Ltd (AD) 91 1/45; returned to W Alexander & Sons Ltd, Falkirk (SN) R665 3/50; withdrawn 1950; MacLean, Peterhead use unknown 8/50.

DV 226 (137): Auctioned via London Horse & Motor Depository, London SE1 4/39; T Allsopp (dealer), Sheffield at an unknown date; Berresford Motors Ltd, Cheddleton (ST) 12/42; scrapped 3/50.

DV 925 (138): GJ Dawson (Clapham) Ltd (dealer), London SW9 at an unknown date; no further owner.

DV   926 (129): GJ Dawson (Clapham) Ltd (dealer), London SW9 at an unknown date; B Mitchell, Glyncorrwg (GG) c1937; last licensed 3/39; GH Morgan (South Wales) Motor Traders Ltd (dealer), Newport at an unknown date.
DV 1044 (130): GJ Dawson (Clapham) Ltd (dealer), London SW9 at an unknown date.
DV 1616 (131): GJ Dawson (Clapham) Ltd (dealer), London SW9 at an unknown date.
DV 2149 (139): J Laurie & Son {Chieftain}, Hamilton (LK) 1936; withdrawn 6/38.
DV 2304 (140): No further user.
DV 2326 (144): Bedlington and District Luxury Coaches Ltd, Ashington (ND) as C32F at an unknown date.
DV 2355 (145): No further user.
DV 2356 (141): E & N Sanderson {Millburn Garage} (dealer), (dealer), Glasgow at an unknown date; W Alexander & Sons Ltd, Falkirk (SN) R191, fitted with the 1933 Pickering H24/24R body transferred from Crossley Condor GS 3919 and Leyland 8.6 litre oil engine 9/37, reseated to H30/26R in 10/41; James Sutherland (Peterhead) Ltd (AD) 92 1/45; returned to W Alexander & Sons Ltd, Falkirk (SN) R666 3/50; withdrawn 1950; Davidson, Nigg as a hut 6/50.
UO 9690 (124): C Hunt {Kineton Green Bus Service}, Kineton (WK) 15 9/34; becoming Kineton Green Bus Services Ltd, Kineton (WK) 15 11/34; G Osborne (showman), Wellingborough 4/47; last licensed 9/53; scrapped.
UO 9691 (125): FT Tagg (dealer?), Sutton-in-Ashfield 9/37; G Bell, Sutton-in-Ashfield as a caravan 1937; scrapped 2/38.
UO 9692 (126): Simmons-Hodge Transport Ltd, Truro (GCO) as a van at an unknown date; last licensed 12/39; scrapped 9/43.
UO 9759 (132): Auctioned via London Horse & Motor Depository, London SE1 4/39; T Allsopp (dealer) Sheffield 1939; George Wimpey & Co Ltd (contractor) London W6 (XLN) by 5/42; Baldwin & Barlow Ltd, Tow Law (DM) by 1946; rebuilt by Raine as B33R; last licensed 7/52.
UO 9779 (SL 133): AE Banwell, Biddisham (SO) at an unknown date; Gratton Bros Ltd, Burnham-on-Sea (SO) at an unknown date; Monarch Coaches Ltd, Bristol (GL) rebodied Heaver C33F 1950; to service 5/51; last licensed 9/55; sold for scrap 6/56.
UO 9780 (134): Auctioned via London Horse & Motor Depository, London SE1 4/39; T Allsopp (dealer) Sheffield at an unknown date; Stone's Brewery, Sheffield (GWR) as lorry at an unknown date; last licensed 2/49.
UO 9813 (127): Mann, Crossman & Paulin Ltd, London E1 (GLN) as lorry at an unknown date; last licensed 9/46.

Vehicle on loan from Associated Equipment Co Ltd, Southall:

MT 1257	AEC 426	426106 Bell	B32D	12/28

Notes:

MT 1257: On demonstration for an unknown period early 1929.

Vehicles acquired from Great Western Railway, London W2 (LN) 7/29:

142	UO 5995	Leyland LSC1	46333 Leyland	B31R	4/28	-/33
143	UO 7430	Leyland LSC3	47132 Metcalfe	B32-	7/28	-/33

Notes:

UO 5995 (142): New to Ashcroft's Motors Ltd {Devonian Cars}, Paignton (DN); to GWR as 1046 1/29.
UO 7430 (143): New to Ashcroft's Motors Ltd {Devonian Cars}, Paignton (DN); to GWR as 1048 1/29.

Disposals:

UO 5995 (142): Guymer, Barking (GEX) as lorry at an unknown date; withdrawn 12/42.
UO 7430 (143): Heanor & District Omnibus Co Ltd, Heanor (DE) 1 1934; Midland General Omnibus Co Ltd, Langley Mill (DE) 4/38; not operated; no further operator.

1930

New Vehicles:

146	DV 3898	Leyland LT1	50722 Hall Lewis	B32D	3/30	-/36
147	DV 3899	Leyland LT1	50723 Hall Lewis	B32D	3/30	-/36
148	DV 3900	Leyland LT1	50717 Hall Lewis	B32D	3/30	-/36
149	DV 3901	Leyland LT1	50727 Hall Lewis	B32D	3/30	-/36
150	DV 3902	Leyland LT1	50725 Hall Lewis	B32D	4/30	-/36
151	DV 3903	Leyland LT1	50718 Hall Lewis	B32D	3/30	-/36
152	DV 4114	Leyland LT1	50716 Hall Lewis	B31D	4/30	-/37
153	DV 4115	Leyland LT1	50721 Hall Lewis	B31D	4/30	-/36

154	DV 4116	Leyland LT1	50720	Hall Lewis	B31D	4/30	-/36
155	DV 4117	Leyland LT1	50728	Hall Lewis	B31D	4/30	-/36
156	DV 4118	Leyland LT1	50724	Hall Lewis	B31D	4/30	-/36
157	DV 4119	Leyland LT1	50729	Hall Lewis	B31D	4/30	-/36
158	DV 4120	Leyland LT1	50719	Hall Lewis	B31D	4/30	10/36
159	DV 4121	Leyland LT1	50726	Hall Lewis	B31D	4/30	-/36
162	DV 4889	Leyland TS2	60819	Hall Lewis	C31D	4/30	10/35
160	DV 4890	Leyland TS2	60821	Hall Lewis	C31D	4/30	10/35
161	DV 4891	Leyland TS2	60820	Hall Lewis	C31D	4/30	10/35
163	DV 4925	Leyland TS2	60823	Hall Lewis	C30D	4/30	10/35
164	DV 5475	Leyland TS2	60822	Hall Lewis	C30D	5/30	10/35
165	DV 5476	Leyland TS2	60818	Hall Lewis	C30D	5/30	10/35
166	DV 5477	Leyland TS3	61220	Hall Lewis	C30D	5/30	10/35
167	DV 5478	Leyland TS3	61223	Hall Lewis	C30D	5/30	10/35
168	DV 5479	Leyland TS3	61221	Hall Lewis	C30D	5/30	10/35
169	DV 5480	Leyland TS3	61222	Hall Lewis	C30D	5/30	10/35
170	DV 5481	Leyland LT2	51092	Hall Lewis	B31D	5/30	-/36
171	DV 5482	Leyland LT2	51088	Hall Lewis	B31D	5/30	-/36
172	DV 5483	Leyland LT2	51093	Hall Lewis	B31D	5/30	-/36
173	DV 5484	Leyland LT2	51089	Hall Lewis	B31D	5/30	-/36
175	DV 5765	Leyland LT2	51091	Hall Lewis	B31D	6/30	-/36
174	DV 5766	Leyland LT2	51090	Hall Lewis	B31D	6/30	-/36
176	DV 5767	Leyland LT2	50916	Hall Lewis	C32D	6/30	-/35
178	DV 5834	Morris (R?)	6620(R?)	Hall Lewis	B12F	7/30	-/38
177	DV 5835	Leyland LT2	50917	Hall Lewis	C30D	7/30	-/35
179	DV 6853	Morris (R?)	7914(R?)	Hall Lewis	B12F	9/30	-/38
1	DV 7307	Leyland LT2	51260	Park Royal	B31D	11/30	-/37
2	DV 7308	Leyland LT2		Park Royal	B31D	11/30	-/37
3	DV 7424	Leyland LT2	51262	Park Royal	B31D	12/30	-/37
4	DV 7425	Leyland LT2		Park Royal	B31D	12/30	-/37
5	DV 7426	Leyland LT2	51265	Park Royal	B31D	12/30	-/37
6	DV 7428	Leyland LT2	51268	Park Royal	B31D	12/30	-/37
7	DV 7429	Leyland LT2	51263	Park Royal	B31D	12/30	-/37
8	DV 7430	Leyland LT2	51267	Park Royal	B31D	12/30	-/37
14	DV 7709	Leyland LT2	51272	Park Royal	B31D	12/30	-/37
9	DV 7710	Leyland LT2	51266	Park Royal	B31D	12/30	-/37
10	DV 7712	Leyland LT2	51269	Park Royal	B31D	12/30	-/37
11	DV 7713	Leyland LT2	51270	Park Royal	B31D	12/30	-/37
12	DV 7714	Leyland LT2	51271	Park Royal	B31D	12/30	-/37
13	DV 7715	Leyland LT2	51274	Park Royal	B31D	12/30	-/37

Notes:

The Leyland TS2 and TS3 coaches were for use on "Limited Stop" services.

DV 7308 & 7425 (2 & 4): The chassis numbers for these two vehicles were 51261 & 51264 in unknown order.

Disposals:

DV 3898 (146): GJ Dawson (Clapham) Ltd (dealer), London SW9 by 3/37; last licensed 12/37.

DV 3899 (147): GJ Dawson (Clapham) Ltd (dealer), London SW9 by 3/37; JH Hill & Sons, Barry (GG) as B32F 4/37; Western Welsh Omnibus Co Ltd, Cardiff (GG) 3 11/38; delicensed 11/39; fitted with Weymann B32F body transferred from an unidentified Leyland TS7 chassis and reinstated 1/46; withdrawn7/50; J Thompson (dealer), Cardiff for scrap 2/51.

DV 3900 (148): GJ Dawson (Clapham) Ltd (dealer), London SW9 by 3/37.

DV 3901 (149): GJ Dawson (Clapham) Ltd (dealer), London SW9 by 3/37; C Randall, Caerau (GG) 1937; last licensed 12/37.

DV 3902 (150): GJ Dawson (Clapham) Ltd (dealer), London SW9 by 3/37; DT Davies & Son {Cream Line Services}, Tonmawr (GG) c4/37; last licensed 9/38.

DV 3903 (151): GJ Dawson (Clapham) Ltd (dealer), London SW9 by 3/37; Whiting, Sheffield (GWR) as lorry at an unknown date; last licensed 6/47.

DV 4114 (152): GJ Dawson (Clapham) Ltd (dealer), London SW9 by 3/37; Pencoed Motor Co Ltd, Bridgend (GG) 1937; Western Welsh Omnibus Co Ltd, Cardiff (GG) 496 7/37; renumbered 7 1/46; withdrawn 11/50.

DV 4115 (153): GJ Dawson (Clapham) Ltd (dealer), London SW9 by 3/37; last licensed 12/37.

DV 4116 (154): GJ Dawson (Clapham) Ltd (dealer), London SW9 by 3/37; JH Hill & Son, Barry (GG) 4/37; Western Welsh Omnibus Co Ltd, Cardiff (GG) 5 11/38; delicensed 11/39; fitted with an unidentified body transferred from a Leyland TS7 chassis and relicensed 1/46; withdrawn 3/50; sold 4/50.

DV 4117 (155): GJ Dawson (Clapham) Ltd (dealer), London SW9 by 3/37; W Williamson, Bridlington (ER) 24 by 1947; GB Hirst, Holmfirth (WR) 5/47; not traced further.

DV 4118 (156): GJ Dawson (Clapham) Ltd (dealer), London SW9 by 3/37; Davies, Kenfig Hill (GG) at an unknown date; unidentified showman by 8/39; last licensed 12/39.

DV 4119 (157): GJ Dawson (Clapham) Ltd (dealer), London SW9 by 3/37; Seldon, Maesteg (GG) at an unknown date; last licensed 12/38.

DV 4120 (158): GJ Dawson (Clapham) Ltd (dealer), London SW9 by 3/37; last licensed 10/36.

DV 4121 (159): GJ Dawson (Clapham) Ltd (dealer), London SW9 by 3/37; RH Tye, Mendlesham (EK) 4/37; withdrawn 4/41; Tyler (showman) Sandringham at an unknown date; last licensed 3/48.

DV 4889 (162): Southern National Omnibus Co Ltd, Exeter (DN) 3570 10/35; Western National Omnibus Co Ltd, Exeter (DN) 3570 rebodied Beadle C32R (485) 3/36; withdrawn 1/53.

DV 4890 (160): Western National Omnibus Co Ltd, Exeter (DN) 3568 10/35; rebodied Beadle C32R (482) 3/36; withdrawn 10/53.

DV 4891 (161): Western National Omnibus Co Ltd, Exeter (DN) 3569 10/35; rebodied Beadle C32R (484) 3/36; withdrawn 1/53.

DV 4925 (163): Southern National Omnibus Co Ltd, Exeter (DN) 3571 10/35; Western National Omnibus Co Ltd, Exeter (DN) 3571 rebodied Beadle C32R (483) 3/36; rebuilt by Beadle 1941; withdrawn 10/53.

DV 5475 (164): Southern National Omnibus Co Ltd, Exeter (DN) 3572 10/35; Western National Omnibus Co, Exeter (DN) 10/35; Western National Omnibus Co Ltd, Exeter (DN) rebodied Beadle C32R (481) 3/36; rebuilt by Beadle 1941; withdrawn 12/52; sold 1/53.

DV 5476 (165): Southern National Omnibus Co Ltd, Exeter (DN) 3573 10/35; Western National Omnibus Co Ltd, Exeter (DN) 3573 rebodied Beadle C32R (486) 3/36; rebuilt by Beadle 1940; last licensed 12/51; sold 10/53.

DV 5477 (166): Southern National Omnibus Co Ltd, Exeter (DN) 3574 10/35; rebodied Beadle C28R (477) 3/36; withdrawn 1950; sold 6/50.

DV 5478 (167): Southern National Omnibus Co Ltd, Exeter (DN) 3575 10/35; rebodied Beadle C28R (480) 3/36; last licensed 12/50; sold for scrap 9/52.

DV 5479 (168): Southern National Omnibus Co Ltd, Exeter (DN) 3576 10/35; rebodied Beadle C28R (478) 3/36; withdrawn 1952; Airship Club, Moordown, Bournemouth (XHA) 6/52; last licensed 9/52.

DV 5480 (169): Southern National Omnibus Co Ltd, Exeter (DN) 3577 10/35; rebodied Beadle C28R (479) 3/36; last licensed 12/50; sold for scrap 9/52.

DV 5481 (170): GJ Dawson (Clapham) Ltd (dealer), London SW9 by 3/37; F Stephens, Tredegar (MH) 1937; last licensed 12/40.

DV 5482 (171): GJ Dawson (Clapham) Ltd (dealer), London SW9 by 3/37; C Randall, Caerau (GG) at an unknown date; last licensed 9/38; South Wales Motor Traders (dealer), Newport for scrap at an unknown date.

DV 5483 (172): GJ Dawson (Clapham) Ltd (dealer), London SW9 by 3/37; JH Hill & Sons, Barry (GG) at 1937; Western Welsh Omnibus Co Ltd, Cardiff (GG) 4 11/38; delicensed 11/39; fitted with an unidentified body transferred from a Leyland TS7 chassis and relicensed 1/46; withdrawn 2/50; sold 7/50.

DV 5484 (173): GJ Dawson (Clapham) Ltd (dealer), London SW9 by 3/37; JH Hill & Sons, Barry (GG) 1937, Western Welsh Omnibus Co Ltd, Cardiff (GG) 6 11/38; delicensed 11/39; relicensed 1/46; withdrawn and sold 5/49.

DV 5765 (175): GJ Dawson (Clapham) Ltd (dealer), London SW9 by 3/37; C Randall, Caerau (GG) 1937; last licensed 11/37.

DV 5766 (174): GJ Dawson (Clapham) Ltd (dealer), London SW9 by 3/37; RJ Guppy, Barry Dock (GG) by 10/37; sold 1944; EJ Parfitt, Rhymney Bridge (GG) at an unknown date; also recorded with T Vowles, Merthyr Vale (GG) at an unknown date (operator sequence uncertain).

DV 5767 (176): W Hunter, Loanhead (MN) by 1936; G Dickson, Dundee (AS) at an unknown date; A & C McLennan, Spittalfield (PH) c1947; last licensed 12/50.

DV 5834 (178): FT Marshall, Torrington (DN) 11/38; Brock, Torquay (GDN) as lorry c12/38; Peck (dealer?), Tavistock at an unknown date.

DV 5835 (177): Gorman Bros, Coatbridge (LK) by 1938; GH Austin, Woodseaves (ST) 31 c1941 as 31 seat; last licensed 9/49; Martin (dealer), Penkridge for scrap 1950.

DV 6853 (179): FT Marshall, Torrington (DN) 11/38; Braunton, Torrington (as goods?) 7/46; Peck, Tavistock (GDN) as a van at an unknown date; last licensed 9/50.

DV 7307 (1): Unidentified dealer 1937; Griffin Motor Co Ltd, Brynmawr (BC) 72 as B30F by 8/39; Gibbs Bros, Pontllanfraith (MH) 24 by 7/44; R Thomas {Morning Star}, Nelson (GG) at an unknown date; Praill (dealer), Hereford at an unknown date; scrapped 6/49.

DV 7308 (2): Unidentified dealer 1937; HM Admiralty {Royal Navy} (GOV) at an unknown date; noted at Skegness 8/44.

DV 7424 (3): Unidentified dealer 1937; S Harfoot, Barry Dock (GG) as B31F 1937; Western Welsh Omnibus Co Ltd, Cardiff (GG) 495 7/38; not licensed; relicensed and renumbered 2 1/46; withdrawn 5/49; last licensed 1/49; sold 7/50.

DV 7425 (4): Unidentified dealer 1937; AT Hardwick {Glider Coaches}, Bilston (ST) by 8/49; withdrawn 12/50; Hales Bros (hauliers), Farcet (GPR) at an unknown date; not licensed.

DV 7426 (5): Unidentified dealer 1937; GE Martindale, Ferryhill (DM) 1937; withdrawn 12/40.

DV 7428 (6): Unidentified dealer 1937; Griffin Motor Co Ltd, Brynmawr (BC) 71 as B30F by 8/39; withdrawn by 1/46; AT Chivers, Clydach (MH) at an unknown date, with unidentified B35R body; last licensed 12/47.

DV 7429 (7): Unidentified dealer 1937; LG Potter, Skewen (GG) 6/42; not traced further.

DV 7430 (8): Unidentified dealer 1937; T Evans, New Tedegar (MH) at an unknown date; last licensed 9/39; scrapped.

DV 7709 (14): Unidentified dealer 1937; WH John {Coity Motors}, Coity (GG) 1937; LG Potter, Skewen (GG) at an unknown date; not traced further.

DV 7710 (9): Unidentified dealer 1937; Stanhope Motor Services Ltd, Stanhope (DM) 1937; withdrawn 12/49.

DV 7712 (10): Unidentified dealer 1937; FG Carter, Northwold (NK) rebodied Eaton C32F 2/37; withdrawn 12/51.

DV 7713 (11): Unidentified dealer 1937; EI Peake, Pontnewydd (MH) as B31F c1937; SJ Davies, Penygraig (GG) at an unknown date; J Jones, Ynysybwl (GG) at an unknown date.

DV 7714 (12): Unidentified dealer 1937; Griffin Motor Co Ltd, Brynmawr (BC) 67 as B30F by 8/39; AT Chivers, Clydach (MH) as B32F at an unknown date; withdrawn 12/49.

DV 7715 (13): Unidentified dealer 1937; War Department (GOV) at an unknown date; Western National Omnibus Co Ltd, Exeter (DN) for spares 9/47.

Vehicle on loan from Willowbrook Ltd, Loughborough:

DV 5055	Daimler CF6		7340S	Willowbrook	2331	B32-	11/29

Notes:

This vehicle was first registered for use on demonstration by Devon General during 4/30.

1931

New vehicles:

15	DV 7890	Leyland LT2		51273	Park Royal	B31D	1/31	-/37
16	DV 8082	Leyland LT2		51275	Park Royal	B31D	1/31	-/37
17	DV 8083	Leyland LT2		51277	Park Royal	B31D	2/31	-/37
18	DV 8084	Leyland LT2		51276	Park Royal	B31D	1/31	-/37
19	DV 8504	Leyland LT2		51278	Park Royal	B31D	3/31	-/37
20	DV 8505	Leyland LT2		51279	Park Royal	B31D	3/31	-/37
21	DV 8506	Leyland LT2		51435	Park Royal	C31F	3/31	-/37
22	DV 8507	Leyland LT2		51436	Park Royal	C31F	3/31	-/37
23	DV 8508	Leyland LT2		51437	Park Royal	C31F	3/31	-/37
24	DV 8509	Leyland LT2		51438	Park Royal	C31F	3/31	-/37
180	DV 9216	AEC Regal		662681	Park Royal	C26F	5/31	-/38
181	DV 9217	AEC Regal		662679	Park Royal	C26F	5/31	-/37
182	DV 9218	AEC Regal		662680	Park Royal	C26F	5/31	-/38
183	DV 9219	AEC Regal		662678	Park Royal	C26F	5/31	-/37
184	DV 9220	AEC Regal		662676	Park Royal	C26F	5/31	-/38
185	DV 9333	AEC Regal		662804	Park Royal	C26F	6/31	-/37
186	DV 9334	AEC Regal		662807	Park Royal	C26F	6/31	-/37
187	DV 9335	AEC Regal		662806	Park Royal	C26F	6/31	-/38
188	DV 9336	AEC Regal		662805	Park Royal	C26F	6/31	-/38
189	DV 9337	AEC Regal		662677	Park Royal	C26F	6/31	-/38
25	DV 9338	Leyland LT3		51608	Park Royal	B31F	6/31	-/38
26	DV 9339	Leyland LT3		51609	Park Royal	B31F	6/31	-/38
27	DV 9572	Leyland LT3		51607	Park Royal	B31F	6/31	9/39
28	DV 9655	Leyland LT3		51610	Park Royal	B31F	7/31	-/38
29	DV 9721	Leyland LT3		51612	Park Royal	B31F	7/31	-/38

| 30 | DV 9722 | Leyland LT3 | 51611 | Park Royal | | B31F | 7/31 | -/38 |
| 31 | OD 832 | Leyland LT5 | 101 | Park Royal | B3184 | B31F | 12/31 | -/38 |

Notes:

DV 8506-8509 (21-24): Had Park Royal body numbers B3010-3013 in unknown order.

DV 9216-9220 (180-184) & DV 9333-9337 (185-189): Had Park Royal body numbers B3090-3099 in unknown order and were for use on "Limited Stop" services; re-seated to C32F at an unknown date.

DV 9338-9339, 9572, 9655 & 9721-9722 (25-30): Had Park Royal body numbers B3106-3011 in unknown order.

OD 832 (31): Was the prototype Leyland LT5 and had been exhibited at the 1931 Commercial Motor Show on the Park Royal stand.

Disposals:

DV 7890 (15): Unidentified dealer 1937; Pridham Bros, Lamerton (DN) by 8/37; rebodied by an unknown builder as C31F 1949; withdrawn 8/63; CT Shears, Exeter (DN) for preservation 10/64; A Dodsley, Ripley for preservation 6/81; P Holmes, Morton for preservation by 6/83; Kirkby's, Anston for preservation 1983; East Yorkshire Motor Services Ltd, Kingston upon Hull (HE) 99 for preservation 12/89; North East Bus Breakers (dealer) Annfield Plain 3/02; HJ Snaith, Otterburn (ND) for preservation 3/03; current 8/11.

DV 8082 (16): Unidentified dealer 1937; Pencoed Motor Co Ltd, Pencoed (GG) 1937; Western Welsh Omnibus Co Ltd, Cardiff (GG) 497 7/37; renumbered 9 1/46; last licensed 12/49; withdrawn 3/50; scrapped.

DV 8083 (17) Unidentified dealer 1937; Griffin Motor Co Ltd, Brynmawr (BC) (73?) as B30F; re-seated to B31F at an unknown date; Gibbs Bros, Pontllanfraith (MH) 25 as B32F by 7/44; R Thomas {Morning Star}, Nelson (GG) 5 at an unknown date; JH Kinder (showman), Porthcawl at an unknown date; last licensed 5/57; W Lewis (dealer), Aberdare for scrap 5/60.

DV 8084 (18): Unidentified dealer 1937; Pridham Bros, Lamerton (DN) by 8/37; withdrawn 12/49; derelict in a field at Lamerton 1962; scrapped 8/63.

DV 8504 (19): Unidentified dealer 1937; OE James, Port Talbot (GG) 1937; Thomas Bros Ltd, Port Talbot (GG) by 5/44; last licensed 12/50; Bird's Commercial Motors Ltd (dealer), Stratford-upon-Avon for scrap at an unknown date.

DV 8505 (20): Unidentified dealer 1937; Griffin Motor Co Ltd, Brynmawr (BC) 66 as B30F by 8/39; C Davies, Pontllotyn (GG) at an unknown date; withdrawn 12/49.

DV 8506 (21): Unidentified dealer 1937; Griffin Motor Co Ltd, Brynmawr (BC) 70 as B30F by 8/39; C Davies, Pontllotyn (GG) at an unknown date; withdrawn 9/51.

DV 8507 (22): Unidentified dealer 1937; A Habberfield, Neath (GG) as B31F at an unknown date; WJ Hall, Pengam (MH) 7/48; withdrawn 6/51; scrapped 1952.

DV 8508 (23): Unidentified dealer 1937; Pencoed Motor Co Ltd, Pencoed (GG) 1937; Western Welsh Omnibus Co Ltd, Cardiff (GG) 498 7/37; renumbered 10 1/46; withdrawn 3/50.

DV 8509 (24): Unidentified dealer 1937; Jones, Abertillery (MH) at an unknown date; W Carpenter & Sons, Blaengarw (GG) as B31F at an unknown date; withdrawn 6/40.

DV 9216 (180): Greenslades Tours Ltd, Exeter (DN) 10/38; withdrawn 1939; Gough's Garages Ltd {Queen of the Road}, Bristol (GL) 1939; War Department (GOV) 6/40; James Motor Garage, Liverpool (LA) 6/46; re-registered GKF 20 7/46; fitted with oil engine (type unknown), 10/48; not traced further.

DV 9217 (181): GJ Dawson (Clapham) Ltd (dealer), London SW9 1937; War Department (GOV) c1940; WL Williams {Rhymney Transport Services}, Rhymney (MH) at an unknown date; W & R Dunlop Ltd, Greenock (RW) 1/43; withdrawn by 1947; J Knapp, RAF Acklington use and date unknown; last licensed 3/50. NB. The disposal records for this vehicle and DV 9219 (below) are confused, what appears here is believed to be the correct version.

DV 9218 (182): Greenslades Tours Ltd, Exeter (DN) 10/38; withdrawn 1940; War Department (GOV) M1260485 7/40; GJ Miller {GJ Miller & Son}, Cirencester (GL) 1943; AH Kearsey Ltd, Cheltenham (GL) 41 5/46; rebodied Burlingham C33F (2971) 8/47; withdrawn 1/55; GB Green & TH Griffin {G & G Coaches}, Leamington Spa (WK) 3/54; FS Dunn, Bestwood Village (NG) by 9/57; withdrawn 6/58; Reliance Garage (Norwich) Ltd (dealer) for scrap (1958?).

DV 9219 (183): GJ Dawson (Clapham) Ltd (dealer), London SW9 1937; Mrs NR Howe Beeston (NG) 1937; JW Smalley, Martin (KN) c1938; AE Olive, Billinghay (KN) c1/47; MA & WR Towler, Liverpool (LA) 8/48; rebodied Withnell C33F, rebuilt as FC33F at an unknown date; MA Towler & Sons Ltd, Liverpool (LA) 6/50; withdrawn 3/54; Godfrey Abbott & Co, Sale (CH) at an unknown date; not licensed. See note above relating to this vehicle and DV 9217.

DV 9220 (184): Greenslades Tours Ltd, Exeter (DN) 10/38; withdrawn 1940; War Department (GOV) M1260486 7/40; GJ Miller {GJ Miller & Son}, Cirencester (GL) 1945; AH Kearsey Ltd, Cheltenham (GL) 39 5/46; withdrawn 10/51; scrapped at an unknown date.

DV 9333 (185): GJ Dawson (Clapham) Ltd (dealer) London SW9 1937; RG Smith {White Line Coaches}, London N1 (LN) 5/38; HH Mills, Sherston (WI) at an unknown date; Wemyss Bros, Ardersier (IV) at an unknown date; W Alexander & Sons Ltd, Falkirk (SN) A98 6/50; withdrawn 1951; Christison, Troon (XAR) 1/51; E Hepworth (showman), Doncaster at an unknown date; last licensed 9/54.

DV 9334 (186): GJ Dawson (Clapham) Ltd (dealer), London SW9 1937; L Coleman, Tydd St Giles (CM) 12/37; withdrawn 5/53.

DV 9335 (187): Greenslades Tours, Exeter (DN) 10/38; War Department (GOV) 1939; Gough's Garages Ltd {Queen of the Road}, Bristol (GL) 1944; Bristol Co-operative Society Ltd {Queen of the Road}, Bristol (GL) 21 11/47; withdrawn 1/51; scrapped.

DV 9336 (188): Greenslades Tours, Exeter (DN) 10/38; War Department (GOV) 1939; Gough's Garages Ltd {Queen of the Road}, Bristol (GL) 1944; Bristol Co-operative Society Ltd {Queen of the Road}, Bristol (GL) 11/47; possibly not operated.

DV 9337 (189): Greenslades Tours, Exeter (DN) 10/38; War Department (GOV) 1939; Gough's Garages Ltd (Queen of the Road), Bristol (GL) 1944; Bristol Co-operative Society Ltd {Queen of the Road}, Bristol (GL) 22 11/47; rebuilt by Longwell Green as C33F between 1947 and 1950; withdrawn 9/52; scrapped.

DV 9338 (25): Auctioned via London Horse & Motor Depository (dealer), London SE1 4/39; Gratton Bros, Burnham-on-Sea (SO) (as 25 seat?) by 1943; PW Cole, (showman), Martock by 6/46, last licensed 6/51.

DV 9339 (26): Auctioned via London Horse & Motor Depository (dealer), London SE1 4/39; WW Petherick & Sons Ltd, Bude (GCO) as lorry at an unknown date; last licensed 7/53.

DV 9572 (27): Sold 1941; not traced further.

DV 9655 (28): Auctioned via London Horse & Motor Depository (dealer) London SE1 4/39; Somerset County Council as an ambulance at an unknown date; last licensed 12/41; R Street (dealer), Yeovil for scrap at an unknown date.

DV 9721 (29): Auctioned via London Horse & Motor Depository (dealer) London SE1 4/39; WW Petherick & Sons Ltd, Bude (GCO) as lorry at an unknown date; last licensed 2/52.

DV 9722 (30): Auctioned via London Horse & Motor Depository (dealer) London SE1 4/39; Somerset County Council as an ambulance at an unknown date; last licensed 12/41; scrapped.

OD 832 (31): Auctioned via London Horse & Motor Depository (dealer) London SE1 4/39; Somerset County Council as a mobile first aid post at an unknown date; last licensed 12/40.

1932

New vehicles:

32	OD 1827	Leyland LT5	371	Weymann	C313	B31F	3/32	-/38
33	OD 1828	Leyland LT5	374	Weymann	C316	B31F	3/32	-/38
34	OD 1829	Leyland LT5	372	Weymann	C314	B31F	3/32	-/38
35	OD 1830	Leyland LT5	377	Weymann	C319	B31F	3/32	-/38
36	OD 1831	Leyland LT5	373	Weymann	C315	B31F	3/32	-/38
38	OD 1832	Leyland LT5	379	Weymann	C321	B31F	3/32	-/38
39	OD 1833	Leyland LT5	380	Weymann	C322	B31F	3/32	-/38
40	OD 1834	Leyland LT5	572	Weymann	C324	B31F	3/32	-/38
41	OD 1835	Leyland LT5	574	Weymann	C326	B31F	3/32	-/38
42	OD 1836	Leyland LT5	376	Weymann	C318	B31F	3/32	-/38
191	OD 2259	AEC Regent	6611806	Brush		L26/26R	4/32	-/37
190	OD 2260	AEC Regent	6611808	Brush		L26/26R	4/32	-/37
192	OD 2261	AEC Regent	6611807	Brush		L26/26R	4/32	-/37
46	OD 2290	Leyland LT5	552	Weymann	C362	DP31F	5/32	-/41
45	OD 2291	Leyland LT5	551	Weymann	C361	DP31F	5/32	-/39
44	OD 2292	Leyland LT5	375	Weymann	C320	B31F	5/32	-/38
43	OD 2293	Leyland LT5	378	Weymann	C325	B31F	5/32	-/38
37	OD 2294	Leyland LT5	573	Weymann	C362	B31F	5/32	-/40
47	OD 2540	Leyland LT5	546	Weymann	C364	DP31F	5/32	12/39
48	OD 2541	Leyland LT5	548	Weymann	C358	DP31F	5/32	9/39
49	OD 2542	Leyland LT5	549	Weymann	C359	DP31F	5/32	9/39
50	OD 2543	Leyland LT5	550	Weymann	C360	DP31F	5/32	9/39
51	OD 2544	Leyland LT5	545	Weymann	C363	DP31F	5/32	-/40
52	OD 2545	Leyland LT5	547	Weymann	C357	DP31F	5/32	-/40
100	OD 2836	Leyland KP3	620	Weymann	C432	C20F	6/32	-/39

| 101 | OD 2837 | Leyland KP3 | 622 | Weymann | C434 | C20F | 6/32 | -/39 |
| 102 | OD 2838 | Leyland KP3 | 621 | Weymann | C433 | C20F | 6/32 | -/39 |

Notes:

OD 2290 (46): Was a Sun Saloon with opening roof; re-seated to DP30F 1938; allocated number SK46 1939, but probably never carried.

OD 2291 (45): Was a Sun Saloon with opening roof; re-seated to DP30F 1938; allocated number SK45 1939, but probably never carried.

OD 2540-2545 (47-52): Were Sun Saloons with opening roofs; re-seated to DP30F 1938; allocated numbers SK47-52 1939, but probably never carried.

OD 2836-2838 (100-102): Were "all-weather" coaches with canvas roof sections between the front and rear domes.

Disposals:

OD 1827 (32): Auctioned via London Horse & Motor Depository, London SE1 4/39; R Barr (Leeds) Ltd, Leeds (GWR) as lorry 1939; PM Morrell Ltd (dealer), Leeds at an unknown date; last licensed 12/47.

OD 1828 (33): Auctioned via London Horse & Motor Depository, London SE1 4/39; GE Martindale, Ferryhill (DM) 1938; withdrawn 12/50.

OD 1829 (34): Auctioned via London Horse & Motor Depository, London SE1 4/39; J Booth, Killamarsh (DE) at an unknown date; withdrawn 12/45.

OD 1830 (35): Auctioned via London Horse & Motor Depository, London SE1 4/39; GE Martindale, Ferryhill (DM) 1938; burnt out 12/47.

OD 1831 (36): Auctioned via London Horse & Motor Depository, London SE1 4/39; WA Richardson, Walworth (GSR) as lorry; withdrawn 12/42; scrapped at an unknown date.

OD 1832 (38): Auctioned via London Horse & Motor Depository, London SE1 4/39; probably to War Department (GOV) (1939?); Williams, Treorchy (GG) c1950; AE Marsh Ltd {Black & White Coaches}, Harvington (WO) c1950; fitted with a second-hand ECOC (C32F?) body, probably from an ex Ribble Leyland LZ2; Scaffolding (Great Britain) Ltd Sports Club, Birmingham (XWK) 4/57; last licensed 3/61.

OD 1833 (39): Auctioned via London Horse & Motor Depository, London SE1 4/39; A Waters, Barry (GG) by 7/43; Western Welsh Omnibus Co Ltd, Cardiff (GG) 8 1/44; withdrawn and sold 2/49

OD 1834 (40): Auctioned via London Horse & Motor Depository, London SE1 4/39; J & EH Jones, Pantdu (GG) at an unknown date; Thomas Bros Ltd, Port Talbot (GG) at an unknown date; not operated; last licensed 12/45; scrapped at an unknown date.

OD 1835 (41): Auctioned via London Horse & Motor Depository, London SE1 4/39; DJ Morrison, Tenby (PE) 5 c1938; Rhymney Transport Services Ltd, Rhymney (MH) c1951; withdrawn 9/51; GH Morgan (South Wales) Motor Traders Ltd (dealer), Newport by 6/54.

OD 1836 (42): Auctioned via London Horse & Motor Depository, London SE1 4/39; ATC Chivers, Brynmawr (BC) at an unknown date; withdrawn 9/49; remains still there 1/73.

OD 2259 (191): GJ Dawson (Clapham) Ltd (dealer), London SW9 9/37; Valliant Direct Coaches Ltd, London W5 (LN) 1/38; rebodied by the operator as C32F and re-registered HMX 552 4/38; HM Admiralty {Royal Navy} (GOV) by 4/43; Superior Coaches Ltd, London N17 (LN) 8/46; SV Twigg {County Coaches}, Rayleigh (EX) as C31F 11/48; withdrawn 9/51.

OD 2260 (190): GJ Dawson (Clapham) Ltd (dealer), London SW9 9/37; Valliant Direct Coaches Ltd, London W5 (LN) 1/38; rebodied by the operator as C32F and re-registered HMX 553 4/38; HM Admiralty {Royal Navy} (GOV) by 4/43; Dunstable Coaches Ltd, Dunstable (BD) 9/47; withdrawn 10/47; J Hannington, Kettering (NO) at an unknown date; unidentified showman 8/50.

OD 2261 (192): GJ Dawson (Clapham) Ltd (dealer), London SW9 9/37; Valliant Direct Coaches Ltd, London W5 (LN) 1/38; rebodied by the operator as C32F and re-registered HMX 554 4/38.

OD 2290 (46): Valliant Direct Coaches Ltd, London W5 (LN) 1940; A Rowe & Sons, Cudworth (WR) 8/49; rebuilt (by Brighouse Motors?); last licensed 10/52.

OD 2291 (45): Torquay Corporation Waterworks (XDN) 1939; reacquired 1941 (qv).

OD 2292 (44): Auctioned via London Horse & Motor Depository, London SE1 4/39; J Parsons, Holsworthy (DN) as B26F (1939?); AE Thomas, Chagford (DN) at an unknown date; J Green, Brierley Hill (ST) by 10/40; WA Noakes {Dothwill Coaches}, Pensnett (ST) by 6/48; H & H Motorways Ltd {Bunty}, Kenilworth (WK) 6/49; last licensed 9/54.

OD 2293 (43): Auctioned via London Horse & Motor Depository, London SE1 4/39; AE Thomas, Chagford (DN) 1938; C Simmonds (showman), South Wigston at an unknown date; last licensed 3/48.

OD 2294 (37): Auctioned via London Horse & Motor Depository, London SE1 4/39; J Jewitt, Spennymoor (DM) by 5/41; rebodied Raine B32F 1946; JJ Baker Ltd (G & B Motor Services), Quarrington Hill (DM) at an unknown date; withdrawn 4/54; body rebuilt and lengthened as B39F and transferred to 1946 AEC Regal chassis GPT 678 1954.

OD 2540 (47): HM Admiralty {Royal Navy} (GOV) 12/39.

OD 2541-2542 (48-49): Air Ministry {Royal Air Force} (GOV) 9/39.

OD 2543 (50): Valliant Direct Coaches Ltd, London W5 (LN) 9/39; probably to HM Government 4/40; WA Noakes {Dothwill Coaches}, Pensnett (ST) re-registered ORE 177 9/47, rebodied Auto-Cellulose C33F 2/48; H & H Motorways Ltd {Bunty}, Kenilworth (WK) 6/49.

OD 2544 (51): HM Admiralty {Royal Navy} (GOV) 8057 RN 12/39; noted derelict at the premises of Hall & Co, Fratton, Portsmouth 9/59.

OD 2545 (52): Probably to HM Government 1940; A Rowe & Sons, Cudworth (WR) at an unknown date; last licensed 12/52.

OD 2836 (100): Auctioned via London Horse & Motor Depository, London SE1 4/39; probably to HM Government (1940?); B Smith (showman), Stopsley, Bedfordshire by 1946; last licensed 6/51.

OD 2837 (101): Auctioned via London Horse & Motor Depository, London SE1 4/39; AJ James {Mendip Queen Coaches}, High Littleton (SO) 1939; Burnell Bros {Lorna Doone}, Weston-super-Mare (SO) at an unknown date; withdrawn 3/48; scrapped;.

OD 2838 (102): Auctioned via London Horse & Motor Depository, London SE1 4/39; Hereford Motor Co Ltd, Hereford (HR) at an unknown date; last licensed 10/43; withdrawn 12/43.

1933

New Vehicles:

53	OD 5854	Leyland LT5	2589	Weymann	W938	B31F	5/33	12/39
54	OD 5855	Leyland LT5	2590	Weymann	W937	B31F	5/33	12/39
55	OD 5856	Leyland LT5	2591	Weymann	W939	B31F	5/33	12/39
56	OD 5857	Leyland LT5	2592	Weymann	W940	B31F	5/33	12/39
57	OD 5858	Leyland LT5	2593	Weymann	W941	B31F	5/33	12/39
58	OD 5859	Leyland LT5	2595	Weymann	W943	B31F	6/33	-/40
59	OD 5860	Leyland LT5	2594	Weymann	W942	B31F	5/33	-/40
60	OD 5861	Leyland LT5	2596	Weymann	W944	B31F	6/33	12/39
61	OD 5862	Leyland LT5	2602	Weymann	W950	B31F	5/33	12/39
63	OD 5863	Leyland LT5	2597	Weymann	W945	DP31F	5/33	12/39
64	OD 5864	Leyland LT5	2598	Weymann	W946	DP31F	5/33	-/40
65	OD 5865	Leyland LT5	2599	Weymann	W947	DP31F	5/33	12/39
66	OD 5866	Leyland LT5	2600	Weymann	W948	DP31F	5/33	12/39
67	OD 5867	Leyland LT5	2601	Weymann	W949	DP31F	5/33	12/39
68	OD 5868	Leyland LT5	2605	Weymann	W953	DP31F	5/33	12/39
69	OD 5869	Leyland LT5	2606	Weymann	W954	DP31F	5/33	12/39
62	OD 6148	Leyland LT5	2604	Weymann	W952	B31F	6/33	12/39
70	OD 6149	Leyland LT5	2603	Weymann	W951	DP31F	6/33	12/39

Notes:

OD 5454-5862 (53-61): Allocated numbers SK53-61 1939, but probably never carried.

OD 5863-5869 (63-69): Were Sun Saloons with opening roofs and may have been originally ordered for City of Oxford Motor Services Ltd, in whose name the bodies appear in Weymann's records; allocated numbers SK63-69 1939, but probably never carried.

OD 6148 (62): Allocated number SK62 1939, but probably never carried.

OD 6149 (70): Was a Sun Saloon with opening roof and may have been originally ordered for City of Oxford Motor Services Ltd, in whose name the body appears in Weymann's records; allocated number SK70 1939, but probably never carried.

Disposals:

OD 5854-5857 (53-56): Auctioned via London Horse & Motor Depository (dealer), London SE1 12/39; Air Ministry {Royal Air Force} (GOV) 12/39.

OD 5858 (57): Auctioned via London Horse & Motor Depository (dealer), London SE1 12/39.

OD 5859 (58): Auctioned via London Horse & Motor Depository (dealer), London SE1 12/39; War Department (GOV) (1940?); WA Noakes {Dothwill Coaches}, Pensnett (ST) by 1948; rebodied Willenhall C33F 1948; B Davenport {Bestway Coaches}, Netherton (WO) by 8/49; Ward's Tours Ltd {Bantam Coaches}, Glasgow (LK) at an unknown date; G Pennington {Cosy Coaches}, Meadowfield (DM) by 7/56; H Allison (showman), Houghton le Spring by 6/59; last licensed 9/60.

OD 5860 (59): Auctioned via London Horse & Motor Depository (dealer), London SE1 12/39; Valliant Direct Coaches Ltd, London W5 (LN) 4/40; R Dixon Snr, Annfield Plain (DM) at an unknown date; recorded as B32R (original body rebuilt?); withdrawn and scrapped 9/53.

OD 5861 (60): Auctioned via London Horse & Motor Depository (dealer), London SE1 12/39; probably to HM Government 4/40; WA Noakes {Dothwill Coaches}, Pensnett (ST) by 2/49; rebodied Burlingham B35F c1948; last licensed 12/55; scrapped at an unknown date.

OD 5862 (61): Auctioned via London Horse & Motor Depository (dealer), London SE1 12/39; Air Ministry {Royal Air Force} (GOV) 12/39.

OD 5863 (63): Auctioned via London Horse & Motor Depository (dealer), London SE1 12/39; HM Admiralty {Royal Navy} (GOV) 12/39.

OD 5864 (64): Auctioned via London Horse & Motor Depository (dealer), London SE1 12/39; Valliant Direct Coaches Ltd, London W5 (LN) 4/40; J Booth, Killamarsh (DE) as B32F by 5/46; withdrawn 12/50.

OD 5865-5866 (65-66): Auctioned via London Horse & Motor Depository (dealer), London SE1 12/39; Air Ministry {Royal Air Force} (GOV) 12/39.

OD 5867 (67): Auctioned via London Horse & Motor Depository (dealer), London SE1 12/39; Air Ministry {Royal Air Force} (GOV) 12/39; AE Marsh Ltd {Black & White Coaches}, Harvington (WO) re-registered GUY 434 2601 as B34F 4/48; WA Blencowe, Shipston-on-Stour (WO) 5/52; not operated; last licensed 5/52.

OD 5868 (68): Auctioned via London Horse & Motor Depository (dealer), London SE1 12/39; Air Ministry {Royal Air Force} (GOV) 12/39; recorded as written off 1948 but believed to have passed to CW Banfield, London SE17 (LN) having assumed the identity of OD 6149 (see below) and was re-registered HUC 273 7/46, withdrawn 10/50; sold for use as a store/caravan, Little Common, Bexhill by 9/54; C Durham, Meopham for preservation 9/79; CT Shears, Winkleigh (DN) for preservation c8/80; still owned 1/15.

OD 5869 (69): Auctioned via London Horse & Motor Depository (dealer), London SE1 12/39; Valliant Direct Coaches Ltd, London W5 (LN) 4/40; War Department (GOV) (1940?); H & W Davies, Summerhill (DH) withdrawn 7/52; Sykes Motors Tours Ltd, Sale (CH) at an unknown date; AC Goulding & CT Smyth {G & S Motors}, Hooton (CH) 5/54; withdrawn 2/56; Peters Bros, Llanarmon-yn-Ial (FT) at an unknown date; T Jones, Mold (GFT) as lorry at an unknown date; last licensed 12/57; HG Billington (dealer), Birkenhead for scrap (1958?).

OD 6148 (62): Auctioned via London Horse & Motor Depository (dealer), London SE1 12/39; Air Ministry {Royal Air Force} (GOV) 12/39; written off 1948.

OD 6149 (70): HM Admiralty {Royal Navy} (GOV) 12/39. A vehicle with the registration OD 6149 passed to CW Banfield, London SE17 (LN) and was re-registered HUC 273 7/46, but it is believed that OD 5868 had acquired the identity of OD 6149 and that OD 5868 probably did not return to civilian use (see also OD 5868 above).

Vehicles acquired from Grey Cars Ltd, Torquay (DN) 1/11/33:

	DV 1521	Lancia Tetraiota	131	?	Ch20	7/23	n/a
	DV 2242	Lancia Tetraiota	214	?	Ch20	7/23	n/a
	DY 4573	Lancia Pentaiota	?	?	C26D	5/27	n/a
	DY 4574	Lancia Pentaiota	?	?	C26D	5/27	n/a
	DY 4575	Lancia Pentaiota	?	?	C26D	5/27	n/a
301	GC 4841	AEC Mercury	640009	Harrington	C23D	6/30	9/37
302	GC 4842	AEC Mercury	640004	Harrington	C23D	6/30	9/37
303	GC 4843	AEC Mercury	640013	Harrington	C23D	6/30	9/37
304	GC 4844	AEC Mercury	640008	Harrington	C23D	6/30	9/37
305	GC 4845	AEC Mercury	640006	Harrington	C23D	7/30	9/37
306	GC 4846	AEC Mercury	640011	Harrington	C23D	7/30	9/35
307	GC 4847	AEC Mercury	640012	Harrington	C23D	6/30	9/35
308	GC 4848	AEC Mercury	640007	Harrington	C23D	6/30	9/35
309	GC 4849	AEC Mercury	640005	Harrington	C23D	6/30	9/37
310	GC 4850	AEC Mercury	640010	Harrington	C23D	6/30	9/35
319	GN 7302	AEC Ranger	665014	Harrington	C26D	5/31	10/39
320	GN 7303	AEC Ranger	665017	Harrington	C26D	5/31	10/39
321	GN 7304	AEC Ranger	665018	Harrington	C26D	5/31	10/39
322	GN 7305	AEC Ranger	665013	Harrington	C26D	5/31	10/39
323	GN 7306	AEC Ranger	665016	Harrington	C26D	5/31	10/39
324	GN 7307	AEC Ranger	665015	Harrington	C26D	5/31	10/39
325	GN 7308	AEC Ranger	665019	Harrington	C26D	5/31	10/39
326	GN 7309	AEC Ranger	665020	Harrington	C26D	5/31	10/39
327	GN 7310	AEC Ranger	665021	Harrington	C26D	5/31	10/39
328	GN 7311	AEC Ranger	665022	Harrington	C26D	5/31	10/39
311	GN 7316	AEC Mercury	640063	Harrington	C22D	3/31	9/37
312	GN 7317	AEC Mercury	640069	Harrington	C22D	3/31	9/37
313	GN 7318	AEC Mercury	640071	Harrington	C22D	3/31	9/35

314	GN 7319	AEC Mercury	640070	Harrington	C22D	3/31	9/35
315	GN 7320	AEC Mercury	640068	Harrington	C22D	3/31	9/35
316	GN 7321	AEC Mercury	640072	Harrington	C22D	3/31	9/35
317	GN 7322	AEC Mercury	640073	Harrington	C22D	5/31	9/35
318	GN 7323	AEC Mercury	640128	Harrington	C22D	3/31	9/35
	PP 816	Lancia	?	?	?	-/26	n/a
	TT 4046	Lancia Pentaiota	836	Bartle?	Ch20	5/25	n/a
	TT 4047	Lancia Pentaiota	837	Bartle?	Ch20	5/25	n/a
	TT 4048	Lancia Pentaiota	838	Bartle?	Ch20	5/25	n/a
	TT 4049	Lancia Pentaiota	840	Bartle?	Ch20	5/25	n/a
	TT 4545	Lancia Pentaiota	887	Bartle?	Ch20	6/25	n/a
	TT 4546	Lancia Pentaiota	897	Bartle?	Ch20	6/25	n/a
	TT 8217	Lancia Pentaiota	1223	?	Ch20	6/26	n/a
	TT 8218	Lancia Pentaiota	1229	?	Ch20	6/26	n/a
	TT 8816	Lancia Pentaiota	1230	?	Ch20	7/26	n/a
	UO 2694	Lancia Pentaiota	1472	?	Ch20	5/27	-/34
	UO 6715	Lancia Pentaiota	2446	?	C25F	5/28	-/34
329	UO 7253	Lancia Pentaiota	2437	?	C26F	6/28	9/34
330	UO 7254	Lancia Pentaiota	2447	?	C26F	6/28	9/34
331	UO 7255	Lancia Pentaiota	2448	?	C26F	6/28	9/34
332	UO 7256	Lancia Pentaiota	2449	?	C26F	6/28	9/34
333	UO 7257	Lancia Pentaiota	2450	?	C26F	6/28	9/34

Previous history:
These vehicles were all new to Greys Cars except for:-

DV 1521: New to Hampton Motor Co Ltd, Torquay (DN) with unidentified Ch20 body registered TA 6901; rebodied and re-registered DV 1521 6/29; Grey Cars 9/29 (qv); last licensed 9/33; acquired as a withdrawn vehicle.

DV 2242: New to Hampton Motor Co Ltd, Torquay (DN) with unidentified Ch20 body registered TA 7231; rebodied and re-registered DV 2242 8/29; Grey Cars 9/29 (qv); not operated by Devon General.

DY 4573: New to A Timpson & Sons Ltd, London SE6 (LN); operated at Hastings before transfer to Grey Cars as 53 4/29.

DY 4574: New to A Timpson & Sons Ltd, London SE6 (LN); operated at Hastings before transfer to Grey Cars as 55 6/29.

DY 4575: New to A Timpson & Sons Ltd, London SE6 (LN); operated at Hastings before transfer to Grey Cars as 54 4/29.

GC 4841-4845 (301-305): New to A Timpson & Sons Ltd, London SE6 (LN) 221-225 as C22D; transferred to Grey Cars as 1-5 7/32.

GC 4846-4850 (306-310): New to A Timpson & Sons Ltd, London SE6 (LN) 226-230 as C22D; transferred to Grey Cars as 6-10 7/31.

GN 7302-7304 (319-321): New to A Timpson & Sons Ltd, London SE6 (LN) 302-304; transferred to Grey Cars as 19-21 7/32.

GN 7316-7317 (311-312): New to A Timpson & Sons Ltd, London SE6 (LN) 316-317; transferred to Grey Cars as 11-12 7/32.`

GN 7318-7323 (313-318): New to A Timpson & Sons Ltd, London SE6 (LN) 328-323; transferred to Grey Cars as 13-18 7/31.

PP 816: New to an unidentified operator; GG Gullick {White Heather}, Torquay (DN) at an unknown date; Grey Cars 4/25 (qv).

TT 4046: Acquired as a withdrawn vehicle, having been withdrawn by Grey Cars 9/32.

TT 4047-4049: Acquired as withdrawn vehicles, having been withdrawn by Grey Cars 9/31.

TT 4545: Acquired as a withdrawn vehicle, having been withdrawn by Grey Cars 6/29.

TT 4546: Acquired as a withdrawn vehicle, having been withdrawn by Grey Cars 9/33.

TT 8816: Acquired as a withdrawn vehicle, having been withdrawn by Grey Cars 9/33.

UO 2694: New to Hampton Motor Co Ltd, Torquay (DN); from whom it was acquired 9/29.

Notes:
DV 1521, DV 2242, DY 4573-4575, TT 4046-4049, 8217-8218, 8816, UO 2694 & UO 6715 were not operated by Devon General.

GN 7302-7311 (319-328): It had been intended to rebody these vehicles in 1939, but this was not proceeded with because of the War.

Disposals:

DV 1521 (ex TA 6901): Goodman Price Ltd, London E8 (GLN) as lorry 1934.

DV 2242 (ex TA 7231): Goodman Price Ltd, London E8 (GLN) as lorry 1934; last licensed 6/37.

DY 4573-4575: Goodman Price Ltd, London E8 (GLN) as lorries 1934.

GC 4841 (301): GJ Dawson (Clapham) Ltd (dealer), London SW9 1937; Fitzpatrick (contractor), Clough, Co Down as goods 3/39; last licensed 1/45.

GC 4842 (302): GJ Dawson (Clapham) Ltd (dealer), London SW9 1937.

GC 4843 (303): GJ Dawson (Clapham) Ltd (dealer), London SW9 1937; unidentified owner at an unknown date; last licensed 3/48.

GC 4844 (304): GJ Dawson (Clapham) Ltd (dealer), London SW9 1937; Fitzpatrick (contractor), Clough, Co Down as goods 3/39; last licensed 1/43.

GC 4845 (305): GJ Dawson (Clapham) Ltd (dealer), London SW9 1937; Fitzpatrick (contractor), Clough, Co Down as goods 3/39; last licensed 1/47.

GC 4846 (306): GJ Dawson (Clapham) Ltd (dealer), London SW9 9/35; RC Vanscolina {Court Coaches}, Torquay (DN) 5/36 as C25R; Sunbeam Coaches (Torquay) Ltd, Torquay (DN) 3/46; withdrawn 5/49; scrapped 12/49.

GC 4847 (307): GJ Dawson (Clapham) Ltd (dealer), London SW9 9/35; RC Vanscolina {Court Coaches}, Torquay (DN) 5/36 as C25R; Cream Cars (Torquay) Ltd, Torquay (DN) 11/49; withdrawn at an unknown date; derelict on premises; then scrapped 1956.

GC 4848 (308): GJ Dawson (Clapham) Ltd (dealer), London SW9 9/35; LH Prescott {City Coach Co} Bath (SO) 3/36 as C22R; Evenny, location unknown (private owner) 11/40; last licensed 4/42.

GC 4849 (309): GJ Dawson (Clapham) Ltd (dealer), London SW9 1937; no further operator.

GC 4850 (310): GJ Dawson (Clapham) Ltd (dealer), London SW9 9/35; AE Townsend, Torquay (DN) 9/35; SH Blake, Delabole (CO) 11/41; SK Hill, Stibb Cross (DN) 1942; Dunn's Motors Ltd, Taunton (SO) at an unknown date; withdrawn 5/50.

GN 7302-7305 (319-322): War Department (GOV) 10/39.

GN 7306 (323): War Department (GOV) M1261505 10/39.

GN 7307 (324): War Department (GOV) 10/39; Ribblesdale Coachways Ltd, Blackburn (LA) 4/43; Miltons Motors Ltd, Colne (LA) 11/47; L Shann, Leeds (WR) 2/48; withdrawn 3/49; H Pemberton, Upton (WR) 1949; Maltby Miners Home Coal & Transport Service Ltd, Maltby (WR) 3/50; not operated; scrapped 6/51.

GN 7308-7311 (325-328): War Department (GOV) 10/39.

GN 7316 (311): GJ Dawson (Clapham) Ltd (dealer), London SW9 1937.

GN 7317 (312): GJ Dawson (Clapham) Ltd (dealer), London SW9 1937; unidentified owner as a tanker at an unknown date; Wessex Machinery Museum, Andover for preservation by 5/76; A Pring, location unknown, for preservation by 1981; advertised for sale by unidentified owner Leamington Spa by 3/83; possibly to unidentified owner, Hampshire c1983.

GN 7318 (313): GJ Dawson (Clapham) Ltd (dealer), London SW9 9/35; Newquay Motor Co Ltd {Red & White Coaches}, Newquay as C20R 5/36.

GN 7319 (314): GJ Dawson (Clapham) Ltd (dealer), London SW9 9/35; Newquay Motor Co Ltd {Red and White Coaches}, Newquay as C20R 5/36; Richards & Osborn, Fraddon (CO) at an unknown date; Dunn's Motors Ltd, Taunton (SO) by 1946; Fox Bros & Co Ltd, Wellington (SO) 3/50; withdrawn 11/54.

GN 7320 (315): GJ Dawson (Clapham) Ltd (dealer), London SW9 9/35; SH Dingle & NTD Weston, Looe (CO) as C20R 5/36; NTD Weston, Looe (CO) 3/38; WH Hawkey, Newquay (CO) 4/38; MG Rowe, Dobwalls (CO) 1/46; withdrawn 2/49 and scrapped.

GN 7321 (316): GJ Dawson (Clapham) Ltd (dealer), London SW9 9/35; C Hopkins & Sons {Blue Moorland Coaches}, Dawlish (DN) 3/36; withdrawn 12/49; EE Down, Newton Abbot (GDN) as lorry.

GN 7322 (317): GJ Dawson (Clapham) Ltd (dealer), London SW9 9/35; Newquay Motor Co Ltd {Red & White Coaches}, Newquay (CO) as C20R 5/36; WH Hawkey, Newquay (CO) 11/40; MG Rowe, Dobwalls (CO) 4/45; withdrawn 4/50.

GN 7323 (318): GJ Dawson (Clapham) Ltd (dealer), London SW9 9/35; C Hopkins & Sons {Blue Moorland Coaches}, Dawlish (DN) 3/36; United Steel Co Ltd, Colsterworth (XKN) 5/49; scrapped 1/55.

TT 4046: Goodman Price Ltd, London E8 (GLN) as lorry 1934; not operated; last licensed 9/32.

TT 4047-4049: Goodman Price Ltd, London E8 (GLN) as lorries 1934; not operated; last licensed 9/31.

TT 4545-4546: Sold 1934; no disposals known.

TT 8217: Goodman Price Ltd, London E8 (GLN) as lorry1934; last licensed 12/34.

TT 8218: Goodman Price Ltd, London E8 (GLN) as lorry 1934; last licensed 1/37.

TT 8816: Sold 1934; No disposal known.

UO 2694: Goodman Price Ltd, London E8 (GLN) as lorry 1934; not operated; last licensed 9/33.

UO 6715: Goodman Price Ltd, London E8 (GLN) as lorry 1934; last licensed 6/37.

UO 7253 (329): GJ Dawson (Clapham) Ltd (dealer), London SW9 9/34; Penn, London SE3 (GLN) as lorry at an unknown date.

UO 7254 (330): GJ Dawson (Clapham) Ltd (dealer), London SW9 9/34; no further user.

UO 7255 (331): GJ Dawson (Clapham) Ltd (dealer), London SW9 9/34; Penn, London SE3 (GLN) as lorry at an unknown date; Royal Arsenal Co-operative Society Ltd, London SE18 (GLN) as lorry at an unknown date; scrapped at an unknown date.

UO 7256-7257 (332-333): GJ Dawson (Clapham) Ltd (dealer), London SW9 9/34; no further user.

Vehicles acquired from Fleet Cars Ltd, Paignton (DN) 1/11/33:

	TA 3753	Lancia Tetraiota	64	Weymann	C337	C20F	5/22	n/a
	TT 3162	Lancia Pentaiota	711	?		C20F	3/25	n/a
	TT 3163	Lancia Pentaiota	725	?		C20F	3/25	n/a
	TT 3164	Lancia Pentaiota	726	?		C18F	3/25	n/a
	TT 3165	Lancia Pentaiota	727	?		C18F	3/25	n/a
	TT 3328	Lancia Pentaiota	754	?		C18F	4/25	n/a
	TT 3620	Lancia Pentaiota	755	?		C18F	5/25	n/a
	TT 3621	Lancia Pentaiota	756	?		C18F	5/25	n/a
	TT 3840	Lancia Pentaiota	786	?		C18F	5/25	n/a
	TT 3841	Lancia Pentaiota	782	?		C18F	5/25	n/a
	TT 4105	Lancia Pentaiota	784	?		C18F	5/25	n/a
	TT 4667	Lancia Pentaiota	865	?		C18F	7/25	n/a
	TT 4668	Lancia Pentaiota	863	?		C18F	7/25	n/a
	TT 4893	Lancia Pentaiota	877	?		C20F	7/25	n/a
	TT 4894	Lancia Pentaiota	?	?		C20F	7/25	n/a
	TT 4895	Lancia Pentaiota	878	?		C20F	7/25	n/a
	TT 8647	Lancia Pentaiota	1046	?		C20F	6/26	n/a
336	UO 2720	Lancia Pentaiota	1483	?		C20D	6/27	9/34
337	UO 2721	Lancia Pentaiota	1484	?		C20D	6/27	9/34
335	UO 2722	Lancia Pentaiota	1485	?		C20D	6/27	9/34
338	UO 2723	Lancia Pentaiota	1486	?		C20D	6/27	9/34
334	UO 2724	Lancia Pentaiota	1487	?		C20D	6/27	9/34

Previous history:

These vehicles were all-weather coaches with detachable canvas roofs and celluloid side screens. Only UO 2720-2724 operated for Devon General. Fleet numbers quoted in brackets are their Fleet Cars numbers.

TA 3753: New to W Langbridge & WP Tucker {Comfy Coaches}, Paignton (DN) with an unidentified Ch-- body; becoming WP Tucker alone probably in 1924; to Fleet Cars 1/26; rebodied as listed above 1932.

TT 3162-3163: Originally C18F; had been re-seated to C20F at an unknown date.

TT 8647: Originally C18F; had been re-seated to C20F at an unknown date.

Notes:

Of the above vehicles, only UO 2720-2724 were operated by Devon General (still in Fleet Cars livery).

Disposals:

TA 3753: Goodman Price Ltd, London E8 (GLN) as lorry 1934; last licensed 6/36.

TT 3162: Sold 1934; no further operator.

TT 3163: Goodman Price Ltd, London E8 (GLN) as lorry 1934; last licensed 7/35.

TT 3164: Goodman Price Ltd, London E8 (GLN) as lorry 1934; last licensed 2/37.

TT 3165: Sold 1934; no further operator.

TT 3328: Goodman Price Ltd, London E8 (GLN) as lorry 1934; last licensed 12/36.

TT 3620: Sold 1934; no further operator.

TT 3621: Goodman Price Ltd, London E8 (GLN) as lorry 1934; last licensed 3/37.

TT 3840: Sold 1934; no further operator.

TT 3841: Goodman Price Ltd, London E8 (GLN) as lorry 1934; last licensed 5/37.

TT 4105: Sold 1934; no further operator.

TT 4667: Sold 1934; no further operator.

TT 4668: Goodman Price Ltd, London E8 (GLN) as lorry 1934; last licensed 3/37.

TT 4893: Bowler, Bishops Frome (GHR) as lorry 1934; last licensed 12/36.

TT 4894: Sold 1934; no further operator.

TT 4895: Goodman Price Ltd, London E8 (GLN) as lorry 1934; last licensed 3/35.

TT 8647: Goodman Price Ltd, London E8 (GLN) as lorry 1934; last licensed 5/37.

UO 2720 (336): Barber, Mitcham (GSR) as lorry 1934; last licensed 9/38.
UO 2721 (337): Nunn (showman), March 1934; last licensed 9/38.
UO 2722 (335): B Berkin, London E7 (GLN) as lorry at an unknown date; last licensed 2/35.
UO 2723 (338): Sold 1934; no further operator.
UO 2724 (334): RR Allen (Broadland Coaches Ltd), Norwich (NK) at an unknown date; last licensed 8/36; withdrawn 1937.

1934

New Vehicles:

200	OD 7487	AEC Regent	O6612437	Short	H28/24R	1/34	-/57
201	OD 7488	AEC Regent	O6612440	Short	H28/24R	1/34	-/56
202	OD 7489	AEC Regent	O6612435	Short	H28/24R	1/34	-/57
203	OD 7490	AEC Regent	O6612439	Short	H28/24R	1/34	6/61
204	OD 7491	AEC Regent	O6612438	Short	H28/24R	1/34	5/57
205	OD 7492	AEC Regent	O6612436	Short	H28/24R	1/34	-4/61
206	OD 7493	AEC Regent	O6612441	Short	H28/24R	1/34	-/57
207	OD 7494	AEC Regent	O6612442	Short	H28/24R	1/34	-/57
208	OD 7495	AEC Regent	O6612444	Short	H28/24R	1/34	12/55
209	OD 7496	AEC Regent	O6612443	Short	H28/24R	1/34	-/56
210	OD 7497	AEC Regent	O6612445	Short	H28/24R	1/34	-/61
211	OD 7498	AEC Regent	O6612446	Short	H28/24R	1/34	-/56
212	OD 7499	AEC Regent	O6612447	Short	H28/24R	2/34	-/57
213	OD 7500	AEC Regent	O6612448	Short	H28/24R	2/34	-/57
214	OD 7501	AEC Regent	O6612449	Short	H28/24R	1/34	-/57
215	OD 7502	AEC Regent	O6612450	Short	H28/24R	3/34	-/53
216	OD 7503	AEC Regent	O6612451	Short	H28/24R	3/34	-/57
217	OD 7504	AEC Regent	O6612452	Short	H28/24R	5/34	12/56
218	OD 7505	AEC Regent	O6612453	Short	H28/24R	5/34	6/61
219	OD 7506	AEC Regent	O6612454	Short	H28/24R	5/34	8/61
220	OD 7507	AEC Regent	O6612455	Short	H28/24R	5/34	-/57
221	OD 7508	AEC Regent	O6612456	Short	H28/24R	5/34	12/56
222	OD 7509	AEC Regent	O6612457	Short	H28/24R	5/34	10/57
223	OD 7510	AEC Regent	O6612458	Short	H28/24R	5/34	10/57
71	OD 9484	Leyland LT5A	4467	Short	B31F	5/34	10/39
72	OD 9485	Leyland LT5A	4468	Short	B31F	5/34	10/39
73	OD 9486	Leyland LT5A	4471	Short	B31F	5/34	10/39
74	OD 9487	Leyland LT5A	4466	Brush	B31F	5/34	10/39
75	OD 9488	Leyland LT5A	4469	Brush	B31F	5/34	10/39
76	OD 9489	Leyland LT5A	4470	Brush	B31F	5/34	10/39

Notes:

OD 7487-7510 (200-223): These vehicles were replacements for the Torquay Tramways trams and were the first oil engined vehicles in the fleet. They had 8.8 litre engines which were retained throughout their service with Devon General. A few were actually delivered in 1933, but none entered service before 1st January 1934. Several of these vehicles were temporarily converted to run on producer-gas in the early years of World War Two.

OD 7487 (200): Renumbered DR200 1939; rebodied Brush H30/26R 6/49; original body burnt at Torquay.
OD 7488 (201): Renumbered DR201 1939; rebuilt after an accident in 9/47 which necessitated the fitting of a completely new upper saloon; rebuilt again, by Longwell Green incorporating new front windows and tubular frame seats.
OD 7489 (202): Renumbered DR202 1939; rebodied Brush H30/26R 6/49; original body burnt at Torquay.
OD 7490 (203): Renumbered DR203 1939; rebuilt by Portsmouth Aviation 1948; converted to O31/24R incorporating rear destination boxes and side destination boards by Longwell Green 12/54; repainted with red wings and fleetnames for 1960 season.
OD 7491 (204): Renumbered DR204 1939; rebodied Brush H30/26R 6/49; original body burnt at Torquay.
OD 7492 (205): Renumbered DR205 1939; rebuilt by Portsmouth Aviation 1948; converted to O31/24R incorporating rear destination boxes and side destination boards by Longwell Green 1955.
OD 7493-7494 (206-207): Renumbered DR206-207 1939; rebodied Brush H30/26R 6/49; original bodies burnt at Torquay.
OD 7495-7496 (208-209): Renumbered DR208-209 1939; rebuilt 1948.

OD 7497 (210): Renumbered DR210 1939; rebuilt by Portsmouth Aviation 1948; converted to O31/24R incorporating rear destination boxes and side destination boards by Longwell Green 4/55.

OD 7498 (211): Renumbered DR211 1939; rebuilt 1948.

OD 7499-7501 (212-214): Renumbered DR212-214 1939; rebodied Brush H30/26R 6/49; original body burnt at Torquay.

OD 7502 (215): Renumbered DR215 1939; rebuilt 1947.

OD 7503 (216): Renumbered DR216 1939; rebodied Brush H30/26R 6/49; original body burnt at Torquay.

OD 7504 (217): Renumbered DR217 1939; rebuilt 1948.

OD 7505 (218): Renumbered DR218 1939; rebuilt 1951; converted to O31/24R incorporating rear destination boxes and side destination boards by Longwell Green 1955.

OD 7506 (219): Renumbered DR219 1939; rebuilt by Portsmouth Aviation 1948; converted to O31/24R incorporating rear destination boxes and side destination boards by Longwell Green 1955.

OD 7507 (220): Renumbered DR220 1939; rebodied Brush H30/26R 6/49; original body burnt at Torquay.

OD 7508 (221): Renumbered DR221 1939; rebuilt 1948.

OD 7509 (222): Renumbered DR222 1939; rebodied Brush H30/26R 6/49; original body burnt at Torquay.

OD 7510 (223): Renumbered DR223 1939; rebodied Brush H30/26R 6/49; original body burnt at Torquay; fitted with a replacement chassis frame from a London Transport STL class vehicle, believed to have been CXX 192 (STL1443), following an accident 1953.

OD 9484-9489 (71-76): Re-seated to B32F 1938; allocated numbers SK71-76 1939, but probably never carried.

Disposals:

OD 7487 (DR200): Passenger Vehicles Disposals Ltd (dealer), Rugby 10/57; W Norths (PV) Ltd (dealer) Leeds at an unknown date; D Bayliss, Creca (DF) by 7/58; Dennis Higgs & Son Ltd (dealer), Monk Bretton for scrap 1960.

OD 7488 (DR201): Mitchley (dealer), Birmingham 12/56; WG Anderton {Andy's Coaches}, Birmingham (WK) 5/57; withdrawn and scrapped 6/59.

OD 7489 (DR202): Metropolitan Cammell Carriage & Wagon Co Ltd, Birmingham (XWK) as a staff bus 8/57; last licensed 5/66; G Glover, Credition for preservation 1/67; A Blackman, Halifax (preservationist) for spares 6/74.

OD 7490 (DR203): Passenger Vehicles Disposals Ltd (dealer) Dunchurch for scrap 8/61.

OD 7491 (DR204): Transferred to Ancillary Fleet 4/57 (qv).

OD 7492 (DR205): Transferred to Ancillary Fleet 4/61 (qv).

OD 7493 (DR206): Passenger Vehicles Disposals Ltd (dealer) Dunchurch 10/57; Colbro Ltd (dealer), Rothwell at an unknown date; Smiths Luxury Coaches Ltd, Reading (BE) by 10/58; withdrawn 12/60.

OD 7494 (DR207): Passenger Vehicles Disposals Ltd (dealer), Rugby 10/57; W Norths (PV) Ltd (dealer) Leeds at an unknown date; D Bayliss, Creca (DF) by 7/58; Dennis Higgs & Son Ltd (dealer), Monk Bretton for scrap 1960.

OD 7495 (DR208): Mitchley (dealer), Birmingham 8/56.

OD 7496 (DR209): Kirton (dealer) Torquay 8/56.

OD 7497 (DR210): Thomas Bros (Port Talbot) Ltd, Port Talbot (GG) 3/61; named "The Margam Belle"; withdrawn 10/65; G Glover, Crediton for preservation 11/65; Taylor, Tintinhull for preservation 6/87; returned to G Glover, Crediton for preservation 3/95; R Greet, Broadhempston for preservation 9/00; operated as a psv on an irregular basis between 5/01 and 11/03 as R Greet, Broadhempston and between 11/03 and 12/11 as Nostalgic Transport Ltd, Broadhempston (DN); still owned 1/15.

OD 7498 (DR211): Mitchley (dealer), Birmingham 12/56; noted at Malvern 6/58.

OD 7499 (DR212): Passenger Vehicles Disposals Ltd (dealer) Dunchurch 10/57; JW Lloyd & Sons Ltd, Nuneaton (WK) 11/57; withdrawn 10/60; returned to Passenger Vehicles Disposals Ltd (dealer), Dunchurch 1/61; noted derelict at Quedgley, Gloucestershire 4/61.

OD 7500 (DR213): Metropolitan Cammell Carriage and Wagon Co Ltd, Birmingham (XWK) as a staff bus 8/57; last licensed 2/63; Shears & Mitchell, Winkleigh for preservation 8/63; G Glover, Crediton for preservation 1967; D Hoare, Chepstow for preservation 10/74; J Shorland, Exeter for preservation 4/85; still owned 1/15.

OD 7501 (DR214): Passenger Vehicles Disposals Ltd (dealer), Rugby 10/57; W Norths (PV) Ltd (dealer) Leeds at an unknown date; D Bayliss, Creca (DF) by 7/58; Dennis Higgs & Son Ltd (dealer), Monk Bretton for scrap 1960.

OD 7502 (DR215): Transferred to Ancillary Fleet 1953.

OD 7503 (DR216): Passenger Vehicles Disposals Ltd (dealer), Rugby 10/57; JW Lloyd & Sons Ltd, Nuneaton (WK) 1/58; withdrawn 8/58; Superb Coaches (Birmingham) Ltd, Birmingham (WK) 9/58; withdrawn 9/59; R & A Goddard {Outmoor Coaches}, Birmingham (WK) 9/59; withdrawn 3/60; R Bailey (dealer?), Birmingham 1960; last licensed 11/60.

OD 7504 (DR217): Mitchley (dealer), Birmingham 8/56.

OD 7505 (DR218): Passenger Vehicles Disposals Ltd (dealer) Dunchurch for scrap 8/61.

OD 7506 (DR219): Passenger Vehicles Disposals Ltd (dealer) Dunchurch for scrap 8/61; Colbro Ltd (dealer), Rothwell for scrap by 11/61.

OD 7507 (DR220): Metropolitan Cammell Carriage & Wagon Co Ltd, Birmingham (XWK) as a staff bus 8/57; last licensed 12/63; Mitchley (dealer), Birmingham by 2/64; Hunt Bros (dealer), Molesworth for scrap by 10/69; still there minus engine and gearbox 1/86; scrapped c8/86.

OD 7508 (DR221): Mitchley (dealer), Birmingham 12/56.

OD 7509 (DR222): Passenger Vehicles Disposals Ltd (dealer), Rugby 10/57; W Norths (PV) Ltd (dealer), Leeds at an unknown date; Walthamstow Education Committee, Walthamstow (GEX) as a school bus 10/57; Passenger Vehicles Disposals Ltd (dealer) Dunchurch 3/60; unidentified contractor 1960 until 10/63; W Norths (PV) Ltd (dealer), Leeds at an unknown date; unidentified dealer, Doncaster for scrap 11/63.

OD 7510 (DR223): Passenger Vehicles Disposals Ltd (dealer), Rugby 10/57; Colbro Ltd (dealer), Rothwell at an unknown date; Smiths Luxury Coaches Ltd, Reading (BE) by 10/58; withdrawn 12/60.

OD 9484 (71): War Department (GOV) 7/40.

OD 9485 (72): War Department (GOV) 7/40; scrapped at an unknown date.

OD 9486 (73): War Department (GOV) 7/40; Morning Star Motor Services Ltd, Bristol (GL) 1943; Wessex Coaches Ltd, Bristol (GL) 4/48; Chard & District Motor Services Ltd, Chard (SO) 3/52; withdrawn 3/53; T Sheap (showman), Northolt as a living van at an unknown date; last licensed 6/60; L Bibby (dealer), Grays for scrap at an unknown date.

OD 9487 (74): War Department (GOV) 7/40; E Walls, Wigan (LA) by 8/43; C Gray, Wigan (LA) by 1946; rebodied Santus C33F; H Crumpton {Triangle Coaches}, Stourbridge (WO) by 3/48; Don Everall (Stourbridge) Ltd, Stourbridge (WO) 9/53; Don Everall Ltd (dealer), Wolverhampton 11/54; loaned to Walker, Liverpool (LA) for an unknown period; scrapped 10/56.

OD 9488 (75): War Department (GOV) 7/40; Morning Star Motor Services Ltd, Bristol (GL) 1943; rebodied Duple C33F (45796) 1947; Wessex Coaches Ltd, Bristol (GL) 4/48; Wessex Motorways (Bristol) Ltd, Chard (SO) 11/54; returned to Wessex Coaches Ltd, Bristol (GL) 6/58; withdrawn 11/58; Holland Hannen & Cubbitts Ltd (contractor), London SW1 (XLN) at an unknown date; last licensed 3/60; GE Purkis, Kenton for scrap at an unknown date.

OD 9489 (76): War Department (GOV) 7/40; Morning Star Motor Services Ltd, Bristol (GL) 1943; Wessex Coaches Ltd, Bristol (GL) 4/48; Chard & District Motor Services Ltd, Chard (SO) 5/51; withdrawn 1953; unidentified owner, Surrey 1953; W King & Son Ltd, London N1 (LN) 7/53; last licensed 6/54.

1935

New Vehicles:

77	AUO 72	Leyland LT5A	5712	Short	B36F	6/35	-/40
78	AUO 73	Leyland LT5A	5715	Short	B36F	6/35	-/50
79	AUO 74	Leyland LT5A	5716	Short	B36F	6/35	-/50
80	AUO 75	Leyland LT5A	5718	Short	B36F	6/35	-/50
81	AUO 76	Leyland LT5A	5717	Short	B36F	6/35	-/40
82	AUO 77	Leyland LT5A	5714	Short	B36F	6/35	-/50
83	AUO 78	Leyland LT5A	5719	Short	B36F	6/35	-/40
84	AUO 79	Leyland LT5A	5720	Short	B36F	6/35	-/50
85	AUO 80	Leyland LT5A	5713	Short	B36F	6/35	-/50
86	AUO 81	Leyland LT5A	5722	Short	B36F	6/35	-/50
87	AUO 82	Leyland LT5A	5721	Short	B36F	6/35	-/40
88	AUO 83	Leyland LT5A	5723	Short	B36F	6/35	-/50
89	AUO 84	Leyland LT5A	5724	Short	B36F	6/35	-/40
90	AUO 85	Leyland LT5A	5726	Short	B36F	6/35	-/50
91	AUO 86	Leyland LT5A	5727	Short	B36F	6/35	-/50
92	AUO 87	Leyland LT5A	5728	Short	B36F	6/35	-/40
93	AUO 88	Leyland LT5A	5729	Short	B36F	6/35	-/50
94	AUO 89	Leyland LT5A	5725	Short	B36F	6/35	-/40
224	AUO 90	AEC Regent	O6612939	Short	H28/24R	5/35	-/61
225	AUO 91	AEC Regent	O6612940	Short	H28/24R	5/35	-/57
335	AUO 198	AEC Ranger	665054	Harrington	C26D	5/35	-/50
334	AUO 199	AEC Ranger	665053	Harrington	C26D	5/35	-/50
103	AUO 512	Leyland KP2	3954	Mumford	B20F	6/35	-/48

Notes:

AUO 72-89 (77-94): Were petrol engined and known as the "Camels" because they had a large hump over the rear part of the roof which housed the interior luggage rack; allocated numbers SL77-94 1939, but some probably never carried.

AUO 90 (224): Renumbered DR224 1939; rebuilt, receiving larger front and side destination boxes 1948; converted to O31/24R incorporating rear destination boxes and side destination boards by Longwell Green 1955.

AUO 91 (225): Renumbered DR225 1939; rebodied Brush H30/26R 6/49; original old body burnt at Torquay.

AUO 198 (335): Had opening canvas roof; re-seated to C20D 1935; renumbered TCR335 1939; re-seated to C29D 1940; rebuilt by Devon Coachbuilders 1946; renumbered TCT334 1946; back to TCR335 1947.

AUO 199 (334): Had opening canvas roof; re-seated to C20D 1935; renumbered TCR334 1939; re-seated to C29D 1940; rebuilt by Devon Coachbuilders 1946; renumbered TCT335 1946; back to TCR334 1947.

AUO 512 (103): Had a roof luggage rack with access ladder; renumbered M103 1939; after spending much of the war in storage, it was not returned to service but instead was transferred to the Ancillary Fleet (qv).

Disposals:

AUO 72 (77): War Department (GOV) 7/40; Morning Star Motor Services Ltd, Bristol (GL) rebodied Duple C33F (42532) 1946; Wessex Coaches Ltd, Bristol (GL) 4/48; CW Banfield Ltd, London SE17 (LN) 12/55.

AUO 73-75 (78-80): War Department (GOV) 7/40; returned 1943 (qv).

AUO 76 (81): War Department (GOV) 7/40; Barnes, Sidmouth (DN) at an unknown date; Jones, Ystradgynlais (BC) 12/47; withdrawn 12/50; scrapped 4/54.

AUO 77 (82): War Department (GOV) 7/40; returned 1943 (qv).

AUO 78 (83): War Department (GOV) 7/40; WA Noakes {Dothwill Coaches}, Pensnett (ST) 42 re-registered LRF 697 by 7/46; H & H Motorways Ltd {Bunty}, Kenilworth (WK) 6/49; last licensed 10/55.

AUO 79-81 (84-86): War Department (GOV) 7/40; returned 1943 (qv).

AUO 82 (87): War Department (GOV) 7/40; Morning Star Motor Services Ltd, Bristol (GL) rebodied Duple C33F (42716) 1946; Wessex Coaches Ltd, Bristol (GL) 4/48; Arlington Motor Co Ltd (dealer) London SW1 1955; WG Lacey, London SW2 (LN) 11/55; CJ Cook, Biggleswade (BD) 10/56; Barnard & Barnard (dealer) London SE26 10/57.

AUO 83 (88): War Department (GOV) 7/40; returned 1943 (qv).

AUO 84 (89): War Department (GOV) 7/40; returned 1946 (qv).

AUO 85-86 (90-91): War Department (GOV) 7/40; returned 1943 (qv).

AUO 87 (92): War Department (GOV) 7/40; AJ James {Mendip Queen Coaches}, High Littleton (SO) 7/47; becoming James Bros (High Littleton) Ltd {Mendip Queen Coaches}, High Littleton 4/48; F Pow {Berkeley Coaches}, Paulton (SO) 4/51; becoming Exors of F Pow {Berkeley Coaches}, Paulton (SO) 4/56; withdrawn 8/57.

AUO 88 (93): War Department (GOV) 7/40; returned 1943 (qv).

AUO 89 (94): War Department (GOV) 7/40; Pendennis Motors Ltd, Falmouth (CO) 7/45; withdrawn 6/51; AH George {Pelere Motors}, Penryn (CO) 6/51.

AUO 90 (DR224): Passenger Vehicles Disposals Ltd (dealer) Dunchurch for scrap 8/61

AUO 91 (DR225): Passenger Vehicles Disposals Ltd (dealer) Dunchurch for scrap 12/57; Berresford's Motors Ltd, Cheddleton (ST) 20 5/58; withdrawn 7/63; noted in a yard in Clitheroe 1963.

AUO 198 (TCR335): Scrapped 8/49.

AUO 199 (TCR334): Scrapped 8/49.

AUO 512 (M103): Transferred to Ancillary Fleet 1948 (qv).

Vehicle acquired from AG Aggett, Marldon (DN) 24/6/35:

104	JY 3912	Ford BB	BB5310820	Mumford		B20F	7/34	-/38

Previous history:

This vehicle was acquired with the Aggett business; its previous history is detailed in the Vehicles of Acquired Operators section.

Disposal:

JY 3912 (104): AE Thomas, Chagford (DN) as B26F 11/38; Phillips & Co, North Tawton (DN) at an unknown date; withdrawn 12/49.

1936

New Vehicles:

No.	Reg	Chassis	Body No.	Body		Seating	Date In	Date Out
336	AOD 599	Leyland LTB3	9318	Harrington		C26F	5/36	9/48
337	AOD 600	Leyland LTB3	9319	Harrington		C26F	5/36	9/48
338	AOD 601	Leyland LTB3	9320	Harrington		C26F	6/36	11/47
339	AOD 602	Leyland LTB3	9321	Harrington		C26F	6/36	11/47
340	AOD 603	Leyland LTB3	9322	Harrington		C26F	6/36	9/48
341	AOD 604	Leyland LTB3	9323	Harrington		C26F	6/36	11/47
342	AOD 605	Leyland LTB3	9324	Harrington		C26F	6/36	11/47
343	AOD 606	Leyland LTB3	9325	Harrington		C26F	6/36	11/47
344	AOD 607	Leyland LTB3	9326	Harrington		C26F	6/36	11/47
345	AOD 608	Leyland LTB3	9327	Harrington		C26F	6/36	11/47
110	BDV 1	Leyland TS7	8929	Harrington		DP32F	3/36	11/48
111	BDV 2	Leyland TS7	8930	Harrington		DP32F	3/36	-/48
112	BDV 3	Leyland TS7	8931	Harrington		DP32F	3/36	-/48
113	BDV 4	Leyland TS7	8932	Harrington		DP32F	3/36	-/52
114	BDV 5	Leyland TS7	8933	Harrington		DP32F	3/36	-/48
115	BDV 6	Leyland TS7	8934	Harrington		DP32F	3/36	-/48
116	BDV 7	Leyland TS7	8935	Harrington		DP32F	4/36	-/48
117	BDV 8	Leyland TS7	8936	Harrington		DP32F	4/36	-/54
118	BDV 9	Leyland TS7	8937	Harrington		DP32F	4/36	-/52
119	BDV 10	Leyland TS7	8938	Harrington		DP32F	5/36	-/40
95	BDV 11	Leyland LT7	8939	Weymann	C5000	B36F	5/36	-/40
96	BDV 12	Leyland LT7	8940	Weymann	C5001	B36F	5/36	-/40
226	BDV 13	Leyland TD4	9155	Beadle	462	H28/24R	5/36	-/56
227	BDV 14	Leyland TD4	9156	Beadle	463	H28/24R	5/36	-/56
228	BDV 15	Leyland TD4	9157	Beadle	464	H28/25R	5/36	-/56
229	BDV 16	Leyland TD4	9158	Beadle	465	H28/24R	5/36	-/56
250	CTA 61	Leyland LT7	11851	Harrington		B36F	10/36	-/47
251	CTA 62	Leyland LT7	11852	Harrington		B36F	11/36	-/47
252	CTA 63	Leyland LT7	11853	Harrington		B36F	10/36	-/47
253	CTA 64	Leyland LT7	11854	Harrington		B36F	11/36	11/49
254	CTA 65	Leyland LT7	11855	Harrington		B36F	11/36	-/46
255	CTA 66	Leyland LT7	11856	Harrington		B36F	11/36	-/50
256	CTA 67	Leyland LT7	11857	Harrington		B36F	11/36	-/47
257	CTA 68	Leyland LT7	11858	Harrington		B36F	11/36	-/45
263	CTA 74	Leyland LT7	11864	Harrington		B36F	11/36	-/47

Notes:

AOD 599-608 (336-345): Were petrol-engined, normal-control coaches in Grey Cars livery. They had canvas roofs with a back window, which retracted into the luggage locker when the roof was opened.

AOD 599 (336): Renumbered TCL336 1939; stored for most of the war years, although loaned to Bath Tramways during 1943; rebuilt 1946.

AOD 600 (337): Renumbered TCL337 1939; stored for most of the war years, although loaned to Bath Tramways during 1943; rebuilt 1946.

AOD 601 (338): Renumbered TCL338 1939; stored for most of the war years, although loaned to Bath Tramways during 1943; rebuilt 1946.

AOD 602 (339): Renumbered TCL339 1939; stored for most of the war years, although loaned to Bath Tramways during 1943; rebuilt and repainted saxe blue 1945.

AOD 603 (340): Renumbered TCL340 1939; rebuilt 1945.

AOD 604 (341): Renumbered TCL341 1939; rebuilt and repainted saxe blue 1945.

AOD 605 (342): Renumbered TCL342 1939; rebuilt 1946.

AOD 606-608 (343-345): Renumbered TCL343-345 1939; rebuilt by Longwell Green 1946.

BDV 1-10 (110-119): Were "Sun Saloons" with opening roofs and sliding doors.

BDV 1 (110): Renumbered XL110 1939; repainted into Grey Cars livery and renumbered TCL110 1946.

BDV 2 (111): Renumbered XL111 1939; rebuilt by Tiverton Coachworks 1944.

BDV 3 (112): Renumbered XL112 1939; rebuilt by Tiverton Coachworks 1944.

BDV 4 (113): Renumbered XL113 1939; repainted into Grey Cars livery and renumbered TCL113 1947; rebuilt by Lydney 1947.

BDV 5 (114): Renumbered XL114 1939; rebuilt by Tiverton Coachworks 1944.

BDV 6 (115): Renumbered XL115 1939; repainted into Grey Cars livery and renumbered TCL115 1946.
BDV 7 (116): Renumbered XL116 1939; rebuilt by Tiverton Coachworks 1944.
BDV 8 (117): Renumbered XL117 1939.
BDV 9 (118): Renumbered XL118 1939; rebuilt by HTP Motors, Truro, repainted into Grey Cars livery and renumbered TCL118 1947.
BDV 10 (119): Allocated number XL119 1939, but probably never carried. This vehicle appeared on the front cover of the company's timetable for many years.
BDV 11-12 (95-96): Were two further "Camels" with bodies similar to AUO 72-89 (77-94) of 1935; allocated number SL95-96 1939, but probably never carried.
BDV 13-16 (226-229): Renumbered DL226-229 1939; rebodied NCB H30/26R 1945.

CTA 61-108 (250-297): Were the first oil engined saloons in the fleet and were the largest batch (48) of vehicles ever ordered by Devon General, the remainder of which entered service in 1937 (qv). The bodies were very similar to those on 110-119 but without opening roofs, and having folding rather than sliding doors. A destination box was fitted at roof level along the nearside, though neither this side one nor the rear destination indicators were much used. Early in the war, several of these vehicles were on short-term loan to the military authorities.

CTA 61-63 (250-252): Renumbered SL250-252 1939.
CTA 64 (253): Renumbered SL253 1939; rebuilt 1945.
CTA 65 (254): Renumbered SL254 1939.
CTA 66-67 (255-256): Renumbered SL255 1939; rebuilt by Longwell Green 1945.
CTA 68 (257): Renumbered SL257 1939.
CTA 74 (263): Renumbered XL263 1939.

Disposals:

AOD 599-608 (TCL336-345): Bodies scrapped 1949-1950; chassis to AJ Beale (dealer), Exeter at an unknown date.
BDV 1-7 (XL110-116): War Department (GOV) 1940; returned 1943 (qv).
BDV 8 (XL117): War Department (GOV) 7/40; returned 1947 (qv).
BDV 9 (XL118): War Department (GO) 7/40; returned 1943 (qv).
BDV 10 (119): War Department (GOV) 7/40; WG Abbott {Timperley Coachways), Timperley (CH) 3/49; Charles Coppock Ltd (dealer), Sale by 3/58; Faulkners Transport Co (dealer), Broadcut by 5/59; exported to Makalla, Aden 3/61.
BDV 11 (95): War Department (GOV) 7/40; AJ James {Mendip Queen Coaches}, High Littleton (SO) 1946; not operated; Morning Star Motor Services Ltd, Bristol (GL) rebodied Duple C33F (42715) 1946; Wessex Coaches Ltd, Bristol (GL) 4/48; CW Banfield Ltd, London SE17 (LN) 12/55; scrapped 1958
BDV 12 (96): War Department (GOV) 7/40; Pendennis Motors Ltd, Falmouth (CO) by 9/45; WJ George {Pelere Motors}, Penryn (CO) 7/51; withdrawn 7/54.
BDV 13 (DL226): Body scrapped 4/57; chassis to Kirton (dealer), Torquay 6/57.
BDV 14 (DL227): Mitchley (dealer), Birmingham 8/56; W Norths (PV) Ltd (dealer), Leeds at an unknown date; Northern Roadways Ltd, Glasgow (LK) by 6/57.
BDV 15 (DL228): Mitchley (dealer), Birmingham 8/56; W Norths (PV) Ltd (dealer), Leeds at an unknown date; Northern Roadways Ltd, Glasgow (LK) by 6/57; returned to W Norths (PV) Ltd (dealer), Leeds by 2/59.
BDV 16 (DL229): Mitchley (dealer), Birmingham 8/56; Northern Roadways Ltd, Glasgow (LK) by 6/57.
CTA 61 (SL250): Western Engineering & Motor Services Ltd {WEMS), Clevedon (SO) 31 10/48; withdrawn 12/50; scrapped.
CTA 62-63 (SL251-252): Believed exported to Czechoslovakia 1/47.
CTA 64 (SL253): T Carpenter (dealer), Exeter 1950.
CTA 65 (SL254): AJ James {Mendip Queen Coaches}, High Littleton (SO) 10/46; withdrawn 11/47; T Peel, Maltby (WR) by1948.
CTA 66 (SL255): Mitchley (dealer), Birmingham 1951.
CTA 67 (SL256): Believed exported to Czechoslovakia 1/47.
CTA 68 (SL257): Scrapped following an accident 7/45.
CTA 74 (SL263): Believed exported to Czechoslovakia 1/47.

Vehicle acquired from H Fraser & G Rossiter {Teignmouth Motor Car Co}, Teignmouth (DN) 7/2/36:

DV 5335	Commer 6TK	28052	Willowbrook	2382	C20D	6/30	n/a
DV 5336	Commer 6TK	28111	Willowbrook	2394	C20D	6/30	n/a
UO 2380	Karrier H	1054	?		-20-	5/27	n/a

Previous history:
These vehicles were acquired with the Fraser & Rossiter business; their previous histories are detailed in the Vehicles of Acquired Operators section.

Notes:
None of these vehicles operated for Devon General.

Disposal:
DV 5335: WA Potter, Stedham (WS) 1936; last licensed 3/48.
DV 5336: Sold 1936; Romney & Dymchurch ARP as an ambulance (1940?); last licensed 12/40.
UO 2380: Last licensed 1936; no further operator.

1937

New vehicles:

258	CTA 69	Leyland LT7	11859	Harrington		B36F	1/37	-/50
259	CTA 70	Leyland LT7	11860	Harrington		B36F	1/37	-/50
260	CTA 71	Leyland LT7	11861	Harrington		B36F	1/37	11/49
261	CTA 72	Leyland LT7	11862	Harrington		B36F	1/37	11/49
262	CTA 73	Leyland LT7	11863	Harrington		B36F	6/37	-/50
264	CTA 75	Leyland LT7	11865	Harrington		B36F	1/37	-/50
265	CTA 76	Leyland LT7	11866	Harrington		B36F	1/37	-/50
266	CTA 77	Leyland LT7	11867	Harrington		B36F	1/37	-/50
267	CTA 78	Leyland LT7	11868	Harrington		B36F	2/37	-/50
268	CTA 79	Leyland LT7	11869	Harrington		B36F	1/37	-/46
269	CTA 80	Leyland LT7	11870	Harrington		B36F	3/37	-/47
270	CTA 81	Leyland LT7	11871	Harrington		B36F	1/37	-/50
271	CTA 82	Leyland LT7	11872	Harrington		B36F	1/37	11/49
272	CTA 83	Leyland LT7	11873	Harrington		B36F	3/37	-/47
273	CTA 84	Leyland LT7	11874	Harrington		B36F	4/37	-/50
274	CTA 85	Leyland LT7	11875	Harrington		B36F	1/37	11/49
275	CTA 86	Leyland LT7	11876	Harrington		B36F	3/37	-/47
276	CTA 87	Leyland LT7	11877	Harrington		B36F	3/37	-/47
277	CTA 88	Leyland LT7	11878	Harrington		B36F	2/37	-/47
278	CTA 89	Leyland LT7	11879	Harrington		B36F	3/37	11/49
279	CTA 90	Leyland LT7	11880	Harrington		B36F	2/37	-/46
280	CTA 91	Leyland LT7	11881	Harrington		B36F	3/37	11/49
281	CTA 92	Leyland LT7	11882	Harrington		B36F	4/37	-/47
282	CTA 93	Leyland LT7	11883	Harrington		B36F	5/37	11/49
283	CTA 94	Leyland LT7	11884	Harrington		B36F	2/37	-/50
284	CTA 95	Leyland LT7	11885	Harrington		B36F	4/37	-/40
285	CTA 96	Leyland LT7	11886	Harrington		B36F	1/37	-/50
286	CTA 97	Leyland LT7	11887	Harrington		B36F	2/37	10/48
287	CTA 98	Leyland LT7	11888	Harrington		B36F	2/37	-/47
288	CTA 99	Leyland LT7	11889	Harrington		B36F	3/37	-/41
289	CTA 100	Leyland LT7	11890	Harrington		B36F	3/37	11/49
290	CTA 101	Leyland LT7	11891	Harrington		B36F	1/37	-/50
291	CTA 102	Leyland LT7	11892	Harrington		B36F	3/37	-/47
292	CTA 103	Leyland LT7	11893	Harrington		B36F	2/37	-/50
293	CTA 104	Leyland LT7	11894	Harrington		B36F	3/37	11/49
294	CTA 105	Leyland LT7	11895	Harrington		B36F	3/37	-/47
295	CTA 106	Leyland LT7	11896	Harrington		B36F	7/37	-/47
296	CTA 107	Leyland LT7	11897	Harrington		B36F	3/37	-/47
297	CTA 108	Leyland LT7	11898	Harrington		B36F	4/37	-/47
120	CTA 109	Leyland TS7	12213	Harrington		DP32F	1/37	-/40
121	CTA 110	Leyland TS7	12214	Harrington		DP32F	1/37	-/40
230	CTA 111	Leyland TD4	12215	Beadle	560	H30/26R	3/37	-/56
231	CTA 112	Leyland TD4	12216	Beadle	561	H30/26R	3/37	-/56
232	CTA 113	Leyland TD4	12217	Beadle	562	H30/26R	3/37	-/56
233	CTA 114	Leyland TD4	12218	Beadle	563	H30/26R	3/37	-/56
360	CTT 660	Bedford WTB	111538	Birch		B24F	6/37	10/53
361	CTT 661	Bedford WTB	111548	Birch		B24F	6/37	10/53
234	DTT 47	AEC Regent	O6615343	Weymann	M1128	H28/26R	6/37	-/49
235	DTT 48	AEC Regent	O6615344	Weymann	M1127	H28/26R	6/37	-/49

Notes:

Several of the vehicles within the CTA 61-108 (250-297) batch were on short-term loan to the military authorities, early in World War Two.

CTA 69-70 (258-259): Renumbered SL258-259 1939; rebuilt by Longwell Green 1945.
CTA 71 (260): Renumbered SL260 1939; rebuilt by Tiverton Coachworks 1946.
CTA 72-73 (261-262): Renumbered SL261-262 1939; rebuilt by Longwell Green 1945.
CTA 75-76 (264-265): Renumbered SL264-265 1939; rebuilt by Longwell Green 1945.
CTA 77 (266): Renumbered SL266 1939; rebuilt by Mumford 1945.
CTA 78-80 (267-269): Renumbered SL267-269 1939.
CTA 81 (270): Renumbered SL270 1939; rebuilt 1945.
CTA 82 (271): Renumbered SL271 1939; rebuilt by Longwell Green 1945.
CTA 83 (272): Renumbered SL272 1939.
CTA 84 (273): Renumbered SL273 1939; rebuilt by Tiverton Coachworks 1946.
CTA 85-86 (274-275): Renumbered SL274 1939; rebuilt by Longwell Green 1945.
CTA 87 (276): Renumbered SL276 1939.
CTA 88 (277): Renumbered SL277 1939; rebuilt by Longwell Green 1945.
CTA 89 (278): Renumbered SL278 1939; rebuilt by Mumford 1945.
CTA 90 (279): Renumbered SL279 1939.
CTA 91 (280): Renumbered SL280 1939; rebuilt by Tiverton Coachworks 1945.
CTA 92 (281): Renumbered SL281 1939.
CTA 93 (282): Renumbered SL282 1939; rebuilt after an accident 1946.
CTA 94 (283): Renumbered SL283 1939; rebuilt by Longwell Green 1945.
CTA 95 (284): Renumbered SL284 1939.
CTA 96-97 (285-286): Renumbered SL285-286 1939; rebuilt by Longwell Green 1945.
CTA 98-99 (287-288): Renumbered SL287-288 1939.
CTA 100 (289): Renumbered SL289 1939; rebuilt by Longwell Green 1945.
CTA 101 (290): Renumbered SL290 1939; rebuilt 1945.
CTA 102 (291): Renumbered SL291 1939; rebuilt by Longwell Green 1945.
CTA 103 (292): Renumbered SL292 1939; rebuilt by Tiverton Coachworks 1945
CTA 104-105 (293-294): Renumbered SL293-294 1939; rebuilt by Longwell Green 1945.
CTA 106-108 (295-297): Renumbered SL295-297 1939.
CTA 109-110 (120-121): Were "Sun Saloons" with opening roofs and sliding doors; allocated number XL120-121 1939, but probably never carried.
CTA 111-114 (230-233): Renumbered DR230-233 1939; rebodied Strachan H30/26R 1946.
CTT 660-661 (360-361): Originally painted duck-egg blue and cream, with unglazed side windows, but without destination indicators, although "Coastal Cruise" appeared in chromium-plated letters where the indicator would have been. The fleet name was also in chromed letters and the waistband beading was also chromed. Their original duty was the one-time circular route via Torquay Marine Drive; stored when this service was discontinued at the beginning of the war; renumbered M360-361 1939, although no fleet numbers were actually carried until 1946, when they were fitted with doors and glazed with "Solvent" windows; the "Coastal Cruise" lettering was removed and they were repainted red for use as country buses. CTT 661 (M361) lost the chromed fleet name when it was repainted, but CTT 660 (M360) retained this until 1952. Both were later fitted with destination indicators and were re-seated to B20F for use on certain restricted routes, though retaining the distinctive chromium plated beading.
DTT 47-48 (234-235): Had 7.7 litre oil engines and were the first in the fleet to have metal-framed bodies. They had destination indicators which were larger than those used hitherto and of a different style. The front one projected from the steeply raked front of the vehicles and the rear one was placed above the platform; renumbered DR234-235 1939.

Disposals:

CTA 69-70 (SL258-259): Mitchley (dealer), Birmingham at an unknown date.
CTA 71-72 (SL260-261): T Carpenter (dealer), Exeter 11/49.
CTA 73 (SL262): Mitchley (dealer), Birmingham 1951
CTA 75-77 (SL264-266): Mitchley (dealer), Birmingham at an unknown date.
CTA 78 (SL267): T Carpenter (dealer), Exeter 11/49.
CTA 79 (SL268): Effra Sales (dealer), London 1946.
CTA 80 (SL269): Believed exported to Czechoslovakia 1/47.
CTA 81 (SL270): Mitchley (dealer), Birmingham 1951.
CTA 82 (SL271): T Carpenter (dealer), Exeter 11/49.
CTA 83 (SL272): Believed exported to Czechoslovakia 1/47.
CTA 84 (SL273): Mitchley (dealer), Birmingham 1951.

CTA 85 (SL274): T Carpenter (dealer), Exeter 11/49.

CTA 86-87 (SL275-276): Believed exported to Czechoslovakia 1/47.

CTA 88 (SL277): Burnell Bros {Lorna Doone}, Weston-super-Mare (SO) 1947; Western Engineering & Motor Services Ltd {WEMS), Clevedon (SO) 29 1948; WT Edwards & Sons, Joy's Green (GL) 3/50; withdrawn 2/52; SG Taylor & E Whittington {Enterprise Coaches}, Newbury (BE) 2/52; unidentified showman at an unknown date.

CTA 89 (SL278): Converted to a carnival float for Torquay Carnival 1949; T Carpenter (dealer), Exeter 11/49; Pitt Garage (dealer), Tedburn St Mary for scrap by 3/52.

CTA 90 (SL279): AJ James {Mendip Queen Coaches}, High Littleton (SO) 1946; withdrawn 12/47; A Cadman, Low Spennymoor (DM) at an unknown date.

CTA 91 (SL280): Body scrapped 11/49; chassis used for a float for Torquay Carnival 1950; Mitchley (dealer), Birmingham at an unknown date.

CTA 92 (SL281): Believed exported to Czechoslovakia 1/47.

CTA 93 (SL282): T Carpenter (dealer), Exeter 11/49.

CTA 94 (SL283): Mitchley (dealer), Birmingham 1951.

CTA 95 (SL284): War Department (GOV) 1940; AJ James {Mendip Queen Coaches}, High Littleton (SO) 1946; not operated; Morning Star Motor Services Ltd, Bristol (GL) 1946; Wessex Coaches Ltd, Bristol (GL) 4/48; CW Smart {Chew Valley Coaches}, Chew Magna (SO) 5/52; CW Banfield Ltd, London SE17 (LN) 1954; scrapped 1958.

CTA 96 (SL285): Mitchley (dealer), Birmingham 1951; Grice Motors (dealer), West Bromwich by 6/51 for scrap.

CTA 97 (SL286): Used as a seat store at Torquay.

CTA 98 (SL287): Believed exported to Czechoslovakia 1/47.

CTA 99 (SL288): Destroyed during air raid at Plymouth 1941.

CTA 100 SL(289): T Carpenter (dealer), Exeter 11/49.

CTA 101 (SL290): Mitchley (dealer), Birmingham 11/49.

CTA 102 (SL291): AJ James {Mendip Queen Coaches}, High Littleton (SO) (1947?); FA Parker, Doncaster (WR) 9 6/48; renumbered 7, then 1 at unknown dates; re-seated to B33F at an unknown date; withdrawn 6/54; Comberhill Motors (dealer) Wakefield by 8/54; recorded as operating for DW Voy {Newton Aycliffe Motor Service Co}, Darlington (DM) between unknown dates.

CTA 103 (SL292): Mitchley (dealer), Birmingham 1951.

CTA 104 (SL293): T Carpenter (dealer), Exeter 11/49.

CTA 105 (SL294): Western Engineering & Motor Services Ltd {WEMS), Clevedon (SO) 30 10/48; withdrawn 3/50; WT Edwards & Sons, Joy's Green (GL) 10/50; becoming DJ & LW Edwards {WT Edwards & Sons}, Joy's Green (GL) 3/52; unidentified showman 10/52.

CTA 106 (SL295): Believed exported to Czechoslovakia 1/47.

CTA 107 (SL296): AJ James {Mendip Queen Coaches}, High Littleton (SO) (1946?); I Margo, Somersham (HN) 10/48; becoming GH Garrett {Margo's Coaches}, Somersham (HN) 10/50; withdrawn 1/51.

CTA 108 (SL297): Believed exported to Czechoslovakia 1/47.

CTA 109 (120): War Department (GOV) 1940; chassis only to J Boddy & Son, Bridlington (ER) rebodied Burlingham C33F 4/51; G Killick {Yellow Wheel Motors}, Shelley (WR) 12/53; withdrawn 2/55; T Evans, New Tredegar (MH) 4/55; withdrawn 11/60; WA Way & Sons (dealer) Cardiff for scrap by 1/62.

CTA 110 (121): War Department (GOV) 1940; returned 1943 (qv).

CTA 111 (DR230): Mitchley (dealer), Birmingham 8/56; W Norths (PV) Ltd (dealer), Leeds by 3/57; Northern Roadways Ltd, Glasgow (LK) by 6/57; W Norths (PV) Ltd (dealer), Leeds at an unknown date.

CTA 112 (DR231): Mitchley (dealer), Birmingham 8/56; W Norths (PV) Ltd (dealer), Leeds by 3/57; Northern Roadways Ltd, Glasgow (LK) by 6/57; not operated.

CTA 113 (DR232): Mitchley (dealer), Birmingham 8/56; W Norths (PV) Ltd (dealer), Leeds by 3/57; Northern Roadways Ltd, Glasgow (LK) by 6/57.

CTA 114 (DR233): Mitchley (dealer), Birmingham 12/56.

CTT 660 (M360): Mitchley (dealer), Birmingham 3/54.

CTT 661 (M361): Mitchley (dealer), Birmingham 3/54; Len's Fruit Store, Northfield (GWK) as a mobile shop at an unknown date; last licensed 12/56.

DTT 47 (DR234): Body scrapped 3/50; chassis parts used in the 1953 (qv) reconstruction of ETT 995 (DR705). In its rebuilt form this carried the registration of AEC Regal ETT 995, parts of which were also incorporated, but with the chassis number of the Regent DTT 47.

DTT 48 (DR235): Scrapped 3/50.

1938

New vehicles:

405	DUO 317	AEC Regal	O6623025	Harrington	B35F	7/38	-/52
406	DUO 318	AEC Regal	O6623026	Harrington	B35F	6/38	-/40
407	DUO 319	AEC Regal	O6623027	Harrington	B35F	7/38	-/52
408	DUO 320	AEC Regal	O6623028	Harrington	B35F	7/38	-/52
409	DUO 321	AEC Regal	O6623029	Harrington	B35F	7/38	-/52
410	DUO 322	AEC Regal	O6623030	Harrington	B35F	7/38	-/52
411	DUO 323	AEC Regal	O6623031	Harrington	B35F	7/38	-/40
412	DUO 324	AEC Regal	O6623032	Harrington	B35F	7/38	-/40
413	DUO 325	AEC Regal	O6623033	Harrington	B35F	7/38	-/40
414	DUO 326	AEC Regal	O6623034	Harrington	B35F	7/38	-/40
415	DUO 327	AEC Regal	O6623035	Harrington	B35F	6/38	-/52
416	DUO 328	AEC Regal	O6623036	Harrington	B35F	7/38	-/52
417	DUO 329	AEC Regal	O6623037	Harrington	B35F	7/38	-/52
SD298	DUO 330	Dennis Lancet II	175557	Harrington	B35F	7/38	-/50
SD299	DUO 331	Dennis Lancet II	175560	Harrington	B35F	7/38	-/50
SD300	DUO 332	Dennis Lancet II	175564	Harrington	B35F	7/38	-/50
346	ETT 985	AEC Ranger	665093	Harrington	C26F	3/38	-/50
347	ETT 986	AEC Ranger	665094	Harrington	C26F	5/38	-/50
348	ETT 987	AEC Ranger	665095	Harrington	C26F	5/38	-/50
349	ETT 988	AEC Ranger	665096	Harrington	C26F	5/38	-/50
350	ETT 989	AEC Ranger	665097	Harrington	C26F	3/38	-/50
351	ETT 990	AEC Ranger	665098	Harrington	C26F	3/38	-/50
352	ETT 991	AEC Ranger	665099	Harrington	C26F	5/38	-/50
353	ETT 992	AEC Ranger	665100	Harrington	C26F	5/38	-/50
401	ETT 993	AEC Regal	O6622446	Harrington	DP32F	5/38	-/52
402	ETT 994	AEC Regal	O6622447	Harrington	DP32F	5/38	-/52
403	ETT 995	AEC Regal	O6622448	Harrington	DP32F	5/38	-/51
404	ETT 996	AEC Regal	O6622449	Harrington	DP32F	5/38	-/52
236	ETT 997	AEC Regent	O6615436	Weymann	H28/26R	5/38	-/56
237	ETT 998	AEC Regent	O6615437	Weymann	H28/26R	5/38	-/56
238	ETT 999	AEC Regent	O6615438	Weymann	H28/26R	5/38	-/56
450	EUO 192	Bedford WLG	0158716	Birch	B14F	8/38	-/52
451	EUO 193	Bedford WLG	0159116	Birch	B14F	8/38	-/51

Notes:

DUO 317-329 (405-417): Had 7.7 litre oil engines and bodies similar to Leyland LT7s CTA 61-108 (250-297).

DUO 317 (405): Renumbered SR405 1939; temporarily converted to an ambulance for HM Admiralty {Royal Navy} 1939; re-seated to B30F (perimeter seating) during the war; reverted to B35F 1945; rebuilt by Longwell Green 1946.
DUO 318 (406): Allocated number SR406 1939, but probably never carried.
DUO 319 (407): Renumbered SR407 1939; temporarily converted to an ambulance for HM Admiralty {Royal Navy} 1939; re-seated to B30F (perimeter seating) during the war; reverted to B35F and rebuilt by Longwell Green 1946.
DUO 320 (408): Renumbered SR408 1939; temporarily converted to an ambulance for HM Admiralty {Royal Navy} 1939; re-seated to B30F (perimeter seating) during the war; reverted to B35F 1945; rebuilt by Longwell Green 1946.
DUO 321 (409): Renumbered SR409 1939; temporarily converted to an ambulance for HM Admiralty {Royal Navy} 1939; re-seated to B30F (perimeter seating) during the war; reverted to B35F and rebuilt by Longwell Green 1946
DUO 322 (410): Renumbered SR410 1939; temporarily converted to an ambulance for HM Admiralty {Royal Navy} 1939; re-seated to B30F (perimeter seating) during the war; reverted to B35F and rebuilt by Longwell Green 1945.
DUO 323 (411): Allocated number SR411 1939, but probably never carried.
DUO 324 (412): Allocated number SR412 1939, but probably never carried.
DUO 325-326 (413-414): Allocated number SR413-414 1939, but probably never carried.
DUO 327-329 (415-417): Renumbered SR415-417 1939; re-seated to B30F (perimeter seating) during the war; reverted to B35F 1945; rebuilt by Longwell Green 1946.
DUO 330-332 (SD298-300): Were the first vehicles to have fleet number prefix letters and "Gill Sans" style fleetnames, the bodies were similar to DUO 317-329 (SR405-417).

ETT 985-992 (346-353): Were petrol-engined, normal-control coaches with opening canvas roofs, incorporated on an otherwise modern body style and replaced the last of the AEC Mercurys.

ETT 985-986 (346-347): Renumbered TCR 346-347 1939; stored during the war; rebuilt by Longwell Green 1946; re-seated to C27F 1949.
ETT 987 (348): Renumbered TCR 348 1939; stored during the war; rebuilt 1946; re-seated to C27F 1949.
ETT 988-992 (349-353): Renumbered TCR 349-353 1939; stored during the war; rebuilt by Longwell Green 1946; re-seated to C27F 1949.

ETT 993 (401): Delivered in 1937 but did not into service until 5/38 and was a "Sun Saloon" similar to previous examples, with 7.7 litre oil engines; renumbered XR401 1939; rebuilt by Longwell Green 1945; reclassified as 33 seat post-war.
ETT 994-995 (402-403): Delivered in 1937 but did not into service until 5/38 and were "Sun Saloons" similar to previous examples, with 7.7 litre oil engines; renumbered XR402-403 1939; rebuilt by Longwell Green 1946; reclassified as 33 seat post-war.
ETT 996 (404): Delivered in 1937 but did not into service until 5/38 and was a "Sun Saloon" similar to previous examples, with 7.7 litre oil engines; renumbered XR404 1939; rebuilt by Longwell Green 1945; reclassified as 33 seat post-war.
ETT 997-998 (236-237): Had 8.8 litre oil engines; renumbered DR236-237 1939.
ETT 999 (238): Had an 8.8 litre oil engine; renumbered DR238 1939; converted to run on producer-gas during the war, reverting to oil later.
EUO 192-193 (450-451): One-man operated station buses used at Budleigh Salterton and Sidmouth; renumbered M418-419 1939; re-seated to B20F 1947.

Disposals:
DUO 317 (SR405): Body scrapped 1952 and mechanical units used in the construction of 'Light Six' rebuild in 1953 (qv).
DUO 318 (406): Converted to an ambulance for use by HM Admiralty {Royal Navy} 9/39; sold to Admiralty 1941; not traced further.
DUO 319-322 (SR407-410): Bodies scrapped 1952 and mechanical units used in the construction of 'Light Six' rebuilds in 1953 (qv).
DUO 323 (411): Converted to an ambulance for HM Admiralty {Royal Navy} 9/39; sold to Admiralty 1941; not traced further.
DUO 324 (SR412): Converted to an ambulance for HM Admiralty {Royal Navy} 1941; sold to Admiralty 1941; returned 1947 (qv).
DUO 325-326 (413-414): Converted to ambulances for HM Admiralty {Royal Navy} 9/39; sold to Admiralty 1941; not traced further.
DUO 327-329 (SR415-417): Bodies scrapped 1952 and mechanical units used in the construction of 'Light Six' rebuilds in 1953 (qv).
DUO 330 (SD298): Mitchley (dealer), Birmingham 5/51; HF Cheek {Elms Coaches}, Kenton (MX) 3/51; unidentified showman at an unknown date; noted in a scrapyard, Tenterden 1959.
DUO 331 (SD299): Mitchley (dealer), Birmingham 5/51; Grice Bros (dealer) West Bromwich for scrap 6/51.
DUO 332 (SD300): Mitchley (dealer), Birmingham 5/51.
ETT 985-992 (TCR346-353): Mitchley (dealer), Birmingham 1951.
ETT 993 (XR401): Rhondda Transport Co Ltd, Porth (GG) 4 1952; S Davies (dealer), Penygraig for scrap 1954.
ETT 994-995 (XR402-403): Bodies scrapped 1952 and mechanical units used in the construction of 'Light Six' rebuilds in 1953 (qv).
ETT 996 (XR404): Rhondda Transport Co Ltd, Porth (GG) 1 1952; S Davies (dealer), Penygraig for scrap 1954.
ETT 997-999 (DR236-238): Mitchley (dealer), Birmingham 1951.
EUO 192 (M418): Scrapped between 6/52 and 3/53.
EUO 193 (M419): Mitchley (dealer), Birmingham 1/52; L English, Balsall Common (private) at an unknown date; last licensed 12/57.

Vehicle on loan from W Mumford Ltd, Plymouth:

(354)	ACO 521	Bedford WTB	111236	Mumford	C25F	5/37

Notes:

This vehicle is believed to have been on demonstration carrying fleet number 354, during 1938.

1939

New vehicles:

XR420	DDV 420	AEC Regal	O6623300	Harrington		DP32F	5/39	-/52
XR421	DDV 421	AEC Regal	O6623301	Harrington		DP32F	4/39	-/52
XR422	DDV 422	AEC Regal	O6623302	Harrington		DP32F	5/39	-/52
XR423	DDV 423	AEC Regal	O6623303	Harrington		DP32F	4/39	-/52
XR424	DDV 424	AEC Regal	O6623304	Harrington		DP32F	4/39	-/52
XR425	DDV 425	AEC Regal	O6623305	Harrington		DP32F	5/39	-/52
SR426	DDV 426	AEC Regal	O6623306	Harrington		B35F	4/39	-/55
SR427	DDV 427	AEC Regal	O6623307	Harrington		B35F	4/39	-/55
SR428	DDV 428	AEC Regal	O6623308	Harrington		B35F	4/39	-/52
SR429	DDV 429	AEC Regal	O6623309	Harrington		B35F	5/39	-/52
SR430	DDV 430	AEC Regal	O6623310	Harrington		B35F	5/39	-/52
SR431	DDV 431	AEC Regal	O6623311	Harrington		B35F	5/39	-/52
SR432	DDV 432	AEC Regal	O6623312	Harrington		B35F	6/39	-/52
SR433	DDV 433	AEC Regal	O6623313	Harrington		B35F	6/39	-/52
SR434	DDV 434	AEC Regal	O6623314	Harrington		B35F	6/39	-/52
SR435	DDV 435	AEC Regal	O6623315	Harrington		B35F	5/39	-/52
SR436	DDV 436	AEC Regal	O6623316	Harrington		B35F	6/39	-/55
SR437	DDV 437	AEC Regal	O6623317	Harrington		B35F	5/39	-/52
SR438	DDV 438	AEC Regal	O6623318	Harrington		B35F	6/39	-/52
SR439	DDV 439	AEC Regal	O6623319	Harrington		B35F	7/39	-/52
SR440	DDV 440	AEC Regal	O6623320	Harrington		B35F	7/39	-/52
SR441	DDV 441	AEC Regal	O6623321	Harrington		B35F	5/39	-/52
SR442	DDV 442	AEC Regal	O6623322	Harrington		B35F	7/39	-/52
SR443	DDV 443	AEC Regal	O6623323	Harrington		B35F	6/39	-/52
SR444	DDV 444	AEC Regal	O6623324	Harrington		B35F	6/39	-/54
SR445	DDV 445	AEC Regal	O6623325	Harrington		B35F	7/39	-/55
SR446	DDV 446	AEC Regal	O6623326	Harrington		B35F	7/39	-/52
SR447	DDV 447	AEC Regal	O6623327	Harrington		B35F	5/39	-/52
SR448	DDV 448	AEC Regal	O6623328	Harrington		B35F	7/39	-/52
SR449	DDV 449	AEC Regal	O6623329	Harrington		B35F	7/39	-/52
SR450	DDV 450	AEC Regal	O6623330	Harrington		B35F	7/39	-/55
SR451	DDV 451	AEC Regal	O6623331	Harrington		B35F	6/39	-/52
M452	DDV 452	Leyland KPZO4	201468	Weymann	C5419	DP20F	5/39	-/50
M453	DDV 453	Leyland KPZO4	201469	Weymann	C5420	DP20F	5/39	-/50

Notes:

DDV 420-425 (XR420-425): Were "Sun Saloons" with sliding doors, heaters and canvas opening roof sections for use on express duties; reclassified as DP33F post-war.

DDV 420-421 (XR420-421): Rebuilt by Longwell Green 1946.
DDV 422 (XR422): Rebuilt by Longwell Green 1947.
DDV 423 (XR423): Rebuilt by Longwell Green 1948.
DDV 424 (XR424): Rebuilt by Longwell Green 1947.
DDV 425 (XR425): Rebuilt 1947.
DDV 426 (SR426): Rebodied Weymann B35F (C9343) 1948; original body scrapped at Torquay.
DDV 427 (SR427): Rebodied Weymann B35F (C9346) 1948; original body scrapped at Torquay.
DDV 428 (SR428): Rebuilt by Portsmouth Aviation 1948.
DDV 429 (SR429): Rebuilt by Portsmouth Aviation 1947.
DDV 430 (SR430): Rebuilt by Portsmouth Aviation 1948.
DDV 431 (SR431): Rebuilt 1949.
DDV 432-435 (SR432-435): Rebuilt by Portsmouth Aviation 1948.
DDV 436 (SR436): Rebodied Weymann B35F (C9342) 1948; original body scrapped at Torquay.
DDV 437 (SR437): Rebuilt by Portsmouth Aviation 1948.
DDV 438 (SR438): Rebuilt by Portsmouth Aviation 1947.
DDV 439-443 (SR439-443): Rebuilt by Portsmouth Aviation 1948.
DDV 444 (SR444): Rebodied Weymann B35F (C9341) 1948; original body used as seat store for a period before scrapping.
DDV 445 (SR445): Rebodied Weymann B35F (C9345) 1948; original body scrapped at Torquay.
DDV 446 (SR446): Rebuilt 1947.
DDV 447-449 (SR447-449): Rebuilt by Portsmouth Aviation 1948.

DDV 450 (SR450): Rebodied Weymann B35F (C9344) 1948; original body used as seat store for a period before scrapping.

DDV 451 (SR451): Rebuilt by Portsmouth Aviation 1948.

DDV 452-453 (M452-453): Were small capacity buses of traditional design but with superior internal finish. Most of their life was spent at Tiverton.

Disposals:

DDV 420-421 (XR420-421): Bodies scrapped 1952 and mechanical units used in the construction of 'Light Six' rebuilds in 1953 (qv).

DDV 422-423 (XR422-423): Bodies scrapped 1952 and mechanical units used in the construction of 'Light Six' rebuilds in 1954 (qv).

DDV 424 (XR424): Transferred to Ancillary fleet as a hedge-trimmer (qv); mechanical units used in construction of 'Light Six' rebuild DDV 424 (DR721) (see 1954) and Ancillary Fleet recovery vehicle RV2 1954.

DDV 425 (XR425): Body scrapped 1952 and mechanical units used in the construction of 'Light Six' rebuild in 1954 (qv).

DDV 426 (SR426): Enterprise Services (O-JA) 12/55; shipped 1956.

DDV 427 (SR427): Enterprise Services (O-JA) 12/55; shipped 1956.

DDV 428 (SR428): Rhondda Transport Co Ltd, Porth (GG) 5 1952; SJ Davies (dealer), Penygraig 1954.

DDV 429 (SR429): Thomas Bros (Port Talbot) Ltd, Port Talbot (GG) 1952; AMCC (dealer), London E15 1954; RW Toop, WJ Ironside & PW Davis {Bere Regis & District}, Dorchester (DT) 1/55; withdrawn 1957.

DDV 430-432 (SR430-432): Thomas Bros (Port Talbot) Ltd, Port Talbot (GG) 1952; AMCC (dealer), London E15 1954.

DDV 433-434 (SR433-434): Rhondda Transport Co Ltd, Porth (GG) 6-7 1952; SJ Davies (dealer), Penygraig 1954.

DDV 435 (SR435): Thomas Bros (Port Talbot) Ltd, Port Talbot (GG) 1952; AMCC (dealer), London E15 1954.

DDV 436 (SR436): Enterprise Services (O-JA) 12/55; shipped 1956.

DDV 437 (SR437): Rhondda Transport Co Ltd, Porth (GG) 8 1952; SJ Davies (dealer), Penygraig 1954.

DDV 438 (SR438): Thomas Bros (Port Talbot) Ltd, Port Talbot (GG) 1952; AMCC (dealer), London E15 1954, RW Toop, WJ Ironside & PW Davis {Bere Regis & District}, Dorchester (DT) 1/55; withdrawn 1957; Flight Refuelling Services, Tarrant Rushton (XDT) as a staff bus 11/57.

DDV 439-440 (SR439-440): Thomas Bros (Port Talbot) Ltd, Port Talbot (GG) 1952; AMCC (dealer), London E15 1954.

DDV 441 (SR441): Mexborough & Swinton Traction Co Ltd (WR) 86 1952; F Cowley Ltd (dealer) Salford 1954; Eagre Construction Ltd, Scunthorpe (XLI) by 8/54.

DDV 442 (SR442): Mexborough & Swinton Traction Co Ltd (WR) 87 1952; F Cowley Ltd (dealer) Salford 1954; R Armstrong (Bus Proprietors) Ltd, Westerhope (ND) 6/54; fitted with the 1949 Pickering B38F body transferred from AEC Regal CU 4496; withdrawn 4/58; Cubitts (contractor), Newcastle upon Tyne (XND) by 7/58.

DDV 443 (SR443): Thomas Bros (Port Talbot) Ltd, Port Talbot (GG) 1952; AMCC (dealer), London E15 1954.

DDV 444 (SR444): Millbrook Steamboat & Trading Co, Cremyll (CO) 1954; Okeridge Motor Services Ltd, Okehampton (DN) 12/58; withdrawn 7/61; Alexander & Walker (dealer), Bretforton, Worcestershire 7/61.

DDV 445 (SR445): Enterprise Services (O-JA) 12/55; shipped 1956.

DDV 446 (SR446): Body scrapped 1952 and mechanical units used in the construction of 'Light Six' rebuild in 1953 (qv).

DDV 447 (SR447): Mexborough & Swinton Traction Co Ltd (WR) 85 1952; F Cowley Ltd (dealer) Salford 1954; R Armstrong (Bus Proprietors) Ltd, Westerhope (ND) 6/54; withdrawn 4/60; Colvin Smith (Engineers), Gateshead (XDM) -/60; derelict 5/62; scrapped 6/62; body noted derelict in a field near Gateshead 5/62; scrapped 1/63.

DDV 448 (SR448): Rhondda Transport Co Ltd, Porth (GG) 9 1952; SJ Davies (dealer), Penygraig 1954.

DDV 449 (SR449): Rhondda Transport Co Ltd, Porth (GG) 10 1952; SJ Davies (dealer), Penygraig 1954.

DDV 450 (SR450): Enterprise Services (O-JA) 12/55; shipped 1956.

DDV 451 (SR451): Mexborough & Swinton Traction Co Ltd (WR) 88 1952; F Cowley Ltd (dealer) Salford 1954; Sir Alfred McAlpine (Contractor) (X) P752 by4/55 (based at Hooton).

DDV 452-453 (M452-453): Mitchley (dealer), Birmingham 1951.

Footnote to disposals:

The vehicles sold to Thomas Bros and Mexborough & Swinton in 1952 and those sold to Jamaica in 1955 were all repainted in their new liveries before leaving Torquay. The batch for Jamaica received thorough overhauls and numerous modifications, including the provision of large roof racks with ladders, heavy duty springs and tyres, replacement of the rear destination indicators by ventilation louvres and the fitting of a formidable pair of horns under the roof alongside the half-cab. AEC Regals of the 1940, 1946 and 1947 batches also went to Jamaica, as listed below and were similarly treated. All were shipped early in 1956.

1940

New vehicles:

XR454	DOD 454	AEC Regal	O6623459	Weymann	C5584	DP32F	1/40	-/52
XR455	DOD 455	AEC Regal	O6623458	Weymann	C5583	DP32F	1/40	-/52
SR456	DOD 456	AEC Regal	O6623392	Harrington		DP35F	1/40	-/52
SR457	DOD 457	AEC Regal	O6623435	Weymann	C5560	B35F	1/40	-/55
SR458	DOD 458	AEC Regal	O6623436	Weymann	C5561	B35F	1/40	-/52
SR459	DOD 459	AEC Regal	O6623437	Weymann	C5562	B35F	1/40	-/52
SR460	DOD 460	AEC Regal	O6623438	Weymann	C5563	B35F	1/40	-/55
SR461	DOD 461	AEC Regal	O6623439	Weymann	C5564	B35F	1/40	-/55
SR462	DOD 462	AEC Regal	O6623440	Weymann	C5565	B35F	1/40	-/52
SR463	DOD 463	AEC Regal	O6623441	Weymann	C5566	B35F	1/40	-/55
SR464	DOD 464	AEC Regal	O6623442	Weymann	C5567	B35F	1/40	-/55
SR465	DOD 465	AEC Regal	O6623443	Weymann	C5568	B35F	1/40	-/52
SR466	DOD 466	AEC Regal	O6623444	Weymann	C5569	B35F	1/40	-/52
SR467	DOD 467	AEC Regal	O6623445	Weymann	C5570	B35F	1/40	-/55
SR468	DOD 468	AEC Regal	O6623446	Weymann	C5571	B35F	1/40	-/52
SR469	DOD 469	AEC Regal	O6623447	Weymann	C5572	B35F	1/40	-/52
SR470	DOD 470	AEC Regal	O6623448	Weymann	C5573	B35F	1/40	-/53
SR471	DOD 471	AEC Regal	O6623449	Weymann	C5574	B35F	1/40	-/55
SR472	DOD 472	AEC Regal	O6623450	Weymann	C5575	B35F	1/40	-/55
SR473	DOD 473	AEC Regal	O6623451	Weymann	C5576	B35F	1/40	-/55
SR474	DOD 474	AEC Regal	O6623452	Weymann	C5577	B35F	1/40	-/52
SR475	DOD 475	AEC Regal	O6623453	Weymann	C5578	B35F	1/40	-/55
SR476	DOD 476	AEC Regal	O6623454	Weymann	C5579	B35F	1/40	-/52
SR477	DOD 477	AEC Regal	O6623455	Weymann	C5580	B35F	1/40	-/52
SR478	DOD 478	AEC Regal	O6623456	Weymann	C5581	B35F	1/40	-/55
SR479	DOD 479	AEC Regal	O6623457	Weymann	C5582	B35F	1/40	-/55

Notes:

DOD 454-455 (XR454-455): Reclassified as 33 seat post-war.

DOD 456 (SR456): Intended for exhibition on the Harrington stand at the (cancelled) 1939 Commercial Motor Show; was similar to DDV 420-425 (XR420-425) of 1939, with canvas opening roof section, but folding instead of sliding door.

DOD 457 (SR457): Rebodied Weymann B35F (C9337) 1948; original body scrapped at Torquay.

DOD 458 (SR458): Rebuilt by Portsmouth Aviation1948.

DOD 459 (SR459): Rebuilt by Longwell Green 1948.

DOD 460 (SR460): Rebodied Weymann B35F (C9338) 1948; original body scrapped at Torquay.

DOD 461 (SR461): Rebodied Weymann B35F (C9339) 1948; original body scrapped at Torquay..

DOD 462 (SR462): Rebuilt by Longwell Green 1948.

DOD 463 (SR463): Rebodied Weymann B35F (C9407) 1950.

DOD 464 (SR464): Rebodied Weymann B35F (C9340) 1948; original body scrapped at Torquay.

DOD 465 (SR465): Rebuilt by Longwell Green 1948.

DOD 466 (SR466): Rebuilt 1947.

DOD 467 (SR467): Rebodied Weymann B35F (C9335) 1948; original body scrapped at Torquay.

DOD 468 (SR468): Rebuilt by Longwell Green 1948.

DOD 470 (SR470): Rebuilt by Longwell Green 1949.

DOD 471 (SR471): Rebodied Weymann B35F (C9348) 1948; original body scrapped at Torquay.

DOD 472 (SR472): Rebodied Weymann B35F (C9347) 1948; original body scrapped at Torquay.

DOD 473 (SR473): Rebodied Weymann B35F (C9408) 1950.

DOD 474 (SR474): Rebuilt 1947.

DOD 475 (SR475): Rebodied Weymann B35F (C9349) 1948; original body scrapped at Torquay.

DOD 476 (SR476): Rebuilt 1950.

DOD 477 (SR477): Rebuilt 1947.

DOD 478 (SR478): Rebodied Weymann B35F (C9406) 1950.

DOD 479 (SR479): Rebodied Weymann B35F (C9336) 1948; original body scrapped at Torquay.

Disposals:

DOD 454-455 (XR454-455): Bodies scrapped 1952 and mechanical units used in the construction of 'Light Six' rebuilds in 1953 (qv).

DOD 456 (SR456): Rhondda Transport Co Ltd, Porth (GG) 2 1952; SJ Davies (dealer), Penygraig 1954.

DOD 457 (SR457): Enterprise Services (O-JA) 12/55; shipped 1956.

DOD 458 (SR458): Thomas Bros (Port Talbot) Ltd, Port Talbot (GG) 1952; AMCC (dealer), London E15 1954.

DOD 459 (SR459): Thomas Bros (Port Talbot) Ltd, Port Talbot (GG) 6/52; AMCC (dealer), London E15 1954; Edwards Coaches Ltd, Joy's Green (GL) probably for spares 1960.

DOD 460-461 (SR460-461): Enterprise Services (O-JA) 12/55; shipped 1956.

DOD 462 (SR462): Rhondda Transport Co Ltd, Porth (GG) 10/52; SJ Davies (dealer), Penygraig 1954.

DOD 463-464 (SR463-464): Enterprise Services (O-JA) 12/55; shipped 1956.

DOD 465 (SR465): Thomas Bros (Port Talbot) Ltd, Port Talbot (GG) 6/52; AMCC (dealer), London E15 1954.

DOD 466 (SR466): Thomas Bros (Port Talbot) Ltd, Port Talbot (GG) 1/52; AMCC (dealer), London E15 1954; RW Toop, WJ Ironside & PW Davis {Bere Regis & District}, Dorchester (DT) 7/54; Lulworth Camp, Lulworth (XDT) 1/57.

DOD 467 (SR467): Enterprise Services (O-JA) 12/55; shipped 1956.

DOD 468 (SR468): Rhondda Transport Co Ltd, Porth (GG) 10/52; SJ Davies (dealer), Penygraig 1954-1955.

DOD 469 (SR469): Transferred to Ancillary fleet as a hedge-trimmer 1952 (qv); parts later used in the construction of 'Light Six' rebuild in 1954 (qv).

DOD 470 (SR470): GSP (Gradskog Saobraeajnog Preduzeco), Beograd (O-YU) 1/54.

DOD 471-473 (SR471-473): Enterprise Services (O-JA) 12/55; shipped 1956.

DOD 474 (SR474): Thomas Bros (Port Talbot) Ltd, Port Talbot (GG) 7/52; AMCC (dealer), London E15 1954, RW Toop, WJ Ironside & PW Davis {Bere Regis & District}, Dorchester (DT) 7/54; Flight Refuelling Services, Tarrant Rushton (XDT) as a staff bus 11/57. CT Shears, Exeter for preservation 6/64; J Shorland, Exeter for preservation by 11/97; still owned 1/15.

DOD 475 (SR475): Enterprise Services (O-JA) 12/55; shipped 1956.

DOD 476 (SR476): Rhondda Transport Co Ltd, Porth (GG) 1952; Higgins (dealer) London 1957.

DOD 477 (SR477): Thomas Bros (Port Talbot) Ltd, Port Talbot (GG) 1952; AMCC (dealer), London E15 1954; DJ & LW Edwards {WT Edwards & Sons}, Joy's Green (GL) 1/55; Edwards Coaches Ltd, Joy's Green (GL) 7/57; withdrawn 11/57; BE, AM, AP, JD, KJ & R Crowe & P Charles {Peggie's Coaches}, Reading (BE) at an unknown date.

DOD 478-479 (SR478-479): Enterprise Services (O-JA) 12/55; shipped 1956.

Footnote to disposals:

The vehicles sold to Thomas Bros in 1952 and those sold to Jamaica in 1955 were all repainted in their new liveries before leaving Torquay. The batch for Jamaica received thorough overhauls and numerous modifications, including the provision of large roof racks and ladders, heavy duty springs and tyres, replacement of the rear destination indicators by ventilation louvres and the fitting of a formidable pair of horns under the roof alongside the half-cab. AEC Regals of the 1939, 1946 and 1947 batches also went to Jamaica and were similarly treated. All were shipped early in 1956.

Vehicles on loan from East Kent Road Car Co Ltd, Canterbury (KT):

DL301	AJG 31	Leyland Titan TD5	301034	Park Royal	L27/26R	3/39
DL302	AJG 32	Leyland Titan TD5	301035	Park Royal	L27/26R	3/39
DL303	AJG 33	Leyland Titan TD5	301036	Park Royal	L27/26R	4/39
DL304	AJG 34	Leyland Titan TD5	301037	Park Royal	L27/26R	3/39
DL305	AJG 35	Leyland Titan TD5	301038	Park Royal	L27/26R	4/39

Notes:

AJG 31-35 (DL301-305): Previously on loan to Southdown Motor Services Ltd, Brighton (ES) in whose livery they had been painted; all five were repainted into Devon General livery shortly after entering service in 11/40; returned to East Kent 10/43.

1941

Vehicle reacquired from Torquay Corporation Waterworks Department (XDN):

45	OD 2291	Leyland LT5	551	Weymann	C327	DP31F	5/32	n/a

Previous history:

OD 2291 (45): New to Devon General with the same fleet number; did not re-enter service.

Disposals:

OD 2291 (45): AE Thomas, Chagford (DN) 1941; H Butlin (showman), London SW16 at an unknown date; last licensed 11/48.

1942

New vehicle:

DL239	HTA 302	Leyland TD7		307050	Weymann	C7459	H30/26R	9/42 12/56

Notes:

HTA 302 (DL239): Believed to have been originally intended for Newport Corporation; rebuilt, including fitment of a side destination screen 1951.

Disposal:

HTA 302 (DL239): Mitchley (dealer) Birmingham 2/57.

Vehicles on Loan from London Passenger Transport Board, London WC1 (LN):

(306)	GK 1008	AEC Regent	661664	Tilling	H27/25RO	4/30
(307)	GK 1026	AEC Regent	661687	Tilling	H27/25RO	1/31

Note:

These vehicles were on loan from 1/42 until 10/43, retaining London Transport livery and fleet numbers ST932 & 950; did not carry the allocated Devon General fleet numbers 306-307.

1943

New Vehicles:

DG240	HTA 740	Guy Arab I	FD25868	Park Royal	B21017	H30/26R	5/43	12/56
DD241	HTA 881	Daimler CWG5	11383	Duple	34560	H30/26R	6/43	-/44
DD242	HTA 882	Daimler CWG5	11388	Duple	34576	H30/26R	6/43	-/44
DG308	JTA 308	Guy Arab II	FD25955	Weymann	C7899	H30/26R	6/43	-/59
DG309	JTA 309	Guy Arab II	FD25975	Weymann	C7904	H30/26R	7/43	10/58
DG310	JTA 310	Guy Arab II	FD25987	Weymann	C7907	H30/26R	7/43	9/55
DG311	JTA 311	Guy Arab II	FD26047	Weymann	C7920	H30/26R	8/43	-/59
DG312	JTA 312	Guy Arab II	FD26048	Weymann	C7919	H30/26R	7/43	11/58
DG313	JTA 313	Guy Arab II	FD26050	Weymann	C7922	H30/26R	8/43	11/58
DG314	JTA 314	Guy Arab II	FD26087	Weymann	C7926	H30/26R	8/43	-/59
DG315	JTA 315	Guy Arab II	FD26088	Weymann	C7927	H30/26R	8/43	11/58
DG316	JTA 316	Guy Arab II	FD26103	Weymann	C7928	H30/26R	8/43	12/55
DG317	JTA 317	Guy Arab II	FD26107	Weymann	C7929	H30/26R	9/43	11/58
DG243	JTA 543	Guy Arab II	FD26278	Weymann	C7957	H30/26R	12/43	-/59
DG244	JTA 544	Guy Arab II	FD26280	Weymann	C7958	H30/26R	12/43	10/58
DG245	JTA 545	Guy Arab II	FD26281	Weymann	C7959	H30/26R	12/43	9/58

Notes:

These vehicles were all delivered in wartime grey livery.

JTA 308-317 (DG308-317) and JTA 543-545 (DG343-345): Originally had slatted wooden seats which were replaced about 1947 with new blue Vynide seats; extra half-drop windows were fitted at the same time. The 1947 seats from the vehicles that were rebodied in 1951 (see below), were transferred to the new Roe bodies.

HTA 740 (DG240): Had a Gardner 6LW engine; rebuilt 1949.
JTA 308 (DG308): Had a Gardner 5LW engine; modernised with lower radiator and rebodied Roe H31/25R (GO3317) 5/51.
JTA 309 (DG309): Had a Gardner 5LW engine; modernised with lower radiator and rebodied Roe H31/25R (GO3325) 4/51; re-seated to H31/23R 1954.
JTA 310 (DG310): Had a Gardner 5LW engine; rebuilt 1950.
JTA 311 (DG311): Had a Gardner 5LW engine; modernised with lower radiator and rebodied Roe H31/25R (GO3322) 4/51; platform doors fitted by Roe 1953; re-seated to H31/23RD 1954.
JTA 312 (DG312): Had a Gardner 5LW engine; modernised with lower radiator and rebodied Roe H31/25R (G3326) 4/51; platform doors fitted by Roe 1953; re-seated to H31/23RD 1954.
JTA 313 (DG313): Had a Gardner 5LW engine; modernised with lower radiator and rebodied Roe H31/25R (GO3331) 6/51; platform doors fitted by Roe 1953; re-seated to H31/23RD 1954.

JTA 314 (DG314): Had a Gardner 5LW engine; modernised with lower radiator and rebodied Roe H31/25R (GO3318) 4/51; platform doors fitted by Roe 1953.

JTA 315 (DG315): Had a Gardner 5LW engine; modernised with lower radiator and rebodied Roe H31/25R (GO3327) 6/51; platform doors fitted by Roe 1953.

JTA 316 (DG316): Had a Gardner 5LW engine; rebuilt 1950.

JTA 317 (DG317): Had a Gardner 5LW engine; modernised with lower radiator and rebodied Roe H31/25R (GO3328) 6/51; platform doors fitted by Roe 1953; re-seated to H31/23RD 1954.

JTA 543-544 (DG243-244): Had Gardner 5LW engines; modernised with lower radiator and rebodied Roe H31/25R (GO3319-3320) 6/51.

JTA 545 (DG245): Had a Gardner 5LW engine; modernised with lower radiator and rebodied Roe H31/25R (GO3321) 5/51.

Disposals:

HTA 740 (DG240): Mitchley (dealer), Birmingham 12/56.

HTA 881 (DD241): Rhondda Transport Co Ltd, Porth (GG) 193 6/44; rebuilt by Starkey, Rhondda 1948; withdrawn 12/56; Penygraig at an unknown date; Higgins (dealer), London for scrap at an unknown date.

HTA 882 (DD242): Rhondda Transport Co Ltd, Porth (GG) 194 6/44; rebuilt by Starkey, Rhondda 1948; withdrawn 12/56; SJ Davies (dealer), Penygraig at an unknown date; Higgins (dealer), London for scrap at an unknown date.

JTA 308 (DG308): Mitchley (dealer), Birmingham 2/60; Metropolitan Cammell Carriage & Wagon Co Ltd, Birmingham as a staff bus 1960; last licensed 12/65.

JTA 309 (DG309): Mitchley (dealer), Birmingham c2/60; Metropolitan Cammell Carriage & Wagon Co Ltd, Birmingham as a staff bus 1960; last licensed 12/66.

JTA 310 (DG310): Mitchley (dealer), Birmingham for scrap 12/56.

JTA 311 (DG311): Mitchley (dealer), Birmingham c2/60; Metropolitan Cammell Carriage & Wagon Co Ltd, Birmingham as a staff bus 1960; unidentified dealer, Coventry for scrap 6/66; registration void 12/66.

JTA 312-313 (DG312-313): T Bradford/Drew & Sawyer Ltd (dealer), Mitcham 3/60.

JTA 314 (DG314): Mitchley (dealer), Birmingham 2/60; Metropolitan Cammell Carriage & Wagon Co Ltd, Birmingham as a staff bus 4/60; G Glover, Crediton for preservation 11/66; DG314 Preservation Group 10/84; A Blackman Snr, Halifax for preservation 8/05; D Shears, Bideford for preservation 11/14.

JTA 315 (DG315): T Bradford/Drew & Sawyer Ltd (dealer), Mitcham 3/60.

JTA 316 (DG316): Mitchley (dealer), Birmingham 12/56; Kirton (dealer), Torquay for scrap 6/57.

JTA 317 (DG317): T Bradford/Drew & Sawyer Ltd (dealer), Mitcham 3/60.

JTA 543 (DG243): Mitchley (dealer), Birmingham c2/60; Metropolitan Cammell Carriage & Wagon Co Ltd, Birmingham as a staff bus 1960; last licensed 12/66.

JTA 544 (DG244): T Bradford/Drew & Sawyer Ltd (dealer), Mitcham 2/60; Perry (dealer), Mitcham at an unknown date.

JTA 545 (DG245): T Bradford/Drew & Sawyer Ltd (dealer), Mitcham 3/60.

Vehicles reacquired from War Department (GOV)

SL78	AUO 73	Leyland LT5A	5715	Short	B36F	5/35	10/48
SL79	AUO 74	Leyland LT5A	5716	Short	B36F	5/35	11/49
SL80	AUO 75	Leyland LT5A	5718	Short	B36F	5/35	11/49
SL82	AUO 77	Leyland LT5A	5714	Short	B36F	5/35	11/49
SL84	AUO 79	Leyland LT5A	5720	Short	B36F	5/35	11/49
SL85	AUO 80	Leyland LT5A	5713	Short	B36F	5/35	-/50
SL86	AUO 81	Leyland LT5A	5722	Short	B36F	5/35	11/49
SL88	AUO 83	Leyland LT5A	5723	Short	B36F	5/35	11/49
SL90	AUO 85	Leyland LT5A	5726	Short	B36F	5/35	11/49
SL91	AUO 86	Leyland LT5A	5727	Short	B36F	5/35	11/49
SL93	AUO 88	Leyland LT5A	5729	Short	B36F	5/35	11/49
XL110	BDV 1	Leyland TS7	8929	Harrington	B32F	3/36	-/48
XL111	BDV 2	Leyland TS7	8930	Harrington	B32F	2/36	-/48
XL112	BDV 3	Leyland TS7	8931	Harrington	B32F	-/36	-/48
XL113	BDV 4	Leyland TS7	8932	Harrington	B32F	3/36	-/52
XL114	BDV 5	Leyland TS7	8933	Harrington	B32F	-/36	-/48
XL115	BDV 6	Leyland TS7	8934	Harrington	B32F	3/36	-/48
XL116	BDV 7	Leyland TS7	8935	Harrington	B32F	-/36	-/48
XL118	BDV 9	Leyland TS7	8937	Harrington	B32F	4/36	-/52
XL121	CTA 110	Leyland TS7	12214	Harrington	B32F	12/36	-/48

Previous history:
These vehicles were new to Devon General and originally had the same fleet numbers, without the prefixes.

Notes:
AUO 74 (SL79): Rebuilt by Tiverton 1945 before re-entering service.
AUO 77 (SL82): Rebuilt by Tiverton 1945 before re-entering service.
AUO 79-81 (SL84-86): Rebuilt by Tiverton 1945 before re-entering service.
AUO 88 (SL93): Rebuilt by Tiverton 1945 before re-entering service.
BDV 1 (XL110): Repainted in Grey Cars livery and renumbered TCL110 1946.
BDV 4 (XL113): Rebuilt by Mumford, repainted in Grey Cars livery and renumbered TCL113 1947.
BDV 6 (XL115): Repainted in Grey Cars livery and renumbered TCL115 1946.
BDV 9 (XL118): Repainted in Grey Cars livery and renumbered TCL118 1947.

Disposals:
AUO 73 (SL78): Dismantled for spares.
AUO 74 (SL79): T Carpenter (dealer), Exeter 11/49; rear end of body scrapped and front end of chassis to CT Shears, Winkleigh (preservationist) for spares 6/78; still owned 11/97.
AUO 75 (SL80): T Carpenter (dealer), Exeter 11/49; unidentified owner as a caravan at an unknown date (noted at Aldershot).
AUO 77 (SL82): T Carpenter (dealer), Exeter 11/49.
AUO 79 (SL84): T Carpenter (dealer), Exeter 11/49; Pitts Garage (dealer) Tedburn St Mary for scrap by 3/52.
AUO 80 (SL85): T Carpenter (dealer), Exeter 11/49.
AUO 81 (SL86): T Carpenter (dealer), Exeter 11/49; Pitts Garage (dealer) Tedburn St Mary for scrap by 3/52.
AUO 83 (SL88): T Carpenter (dealer), Exeter 11/49.
AUO 85 (SL90): T Carpenter (dealer), Exeter 11/49; unidentified owner as a caravan at an unknown date (noted at Aldershot).
AUO 86 (SL91): T Carpenter (dealer), Exeter 11/49.
AUO 88 (SL93): T Carpenter (dealer), Exeter 11/49.
BDV 1 (TCL110): Body scrapped; chassis to Ribble Motor Services Ltd, Preston (LA) 11/48; fitted with 7.4 litre diesel engine; rebodied Burlingham (3767) B35F 1949; to service as 2705 1949; renumbered 214 1951; withdrawn 1960; Millburn Motors Ltd (dealer), Preston 7/61; R Campion {Princess Bus Service} Clonmel (EI) 9/62; becoming Phelan, Clonmel (EI) 5/69; unknown contractor, Clonmel (XEI) by 9/69; Transport Museum Society of Ireland, Dublin for preservation 11/69; believed scrapped by 4/85.
BDV 2 (XL111): Body scrapped; chassis to Ribble Motor Services Ltd, Preston (LA) 11/48; fitted with 7.4 litre diesel engine; rebodied Burlingham (3768) B35F 1949; to service as 2707 1949; renumbered 216 1951; withdrawn 1960; Millburn Motors Ltd (dealer), Preston 7/61; Kaye, Goodfellow & Co Ltd (contractor), Manchester (XLA) 2/62; Alex Findlay & Co Ltd (contractor), Motherwell (XLK) by 6/62.
BDV 3 (XL112): Body scrapped; chassis to Ribble Motor Services Ltd, Preston (LA) 12/48; fitted with 7.4 litre diesel engine; rebodied Burlingham (3771) B35F 1949; to service as 2711 1949; renumbered 216 1951; withdrawn 1960; Millburn Motors Ltd (dealer), Preston 7/61; Lindale Garage (dealer); Grange-over-Sands at an unknown date; W Goodacre & Sons Ltd (carpet manufacturers) Kendal (XWT) 12/63.
BDV 4 (TCL113): Mitchley (dealer), Birmingham 1/52; RH & Mrs WM Jacques, Castle Bromwich (WK) by 5/52.
BDV 5 (XL114): Body scrapped; chassis to Ribble Motor Services Ltd, Preston (LA) 11/48; fitted with 7.4 litre diesel engine; rebodied Burlingham (3775) B35F 1949; to service as 2708 1949; renumbered 217 1951; withdrawn 1960; Millburn Motors Ltd (dealer), Preston 7/61; F Parkinson Ltd (contractor), Blackpool (XLA) at an unknown date; still owned 1967.
BDV 6 (TCL115): Body scrapped; chassis to Ribble Motor Services Ltd, Preston (LA) 1948; fitted with 7.4 litre diesel engine; rebodied Burlingham B35F 1949; to service as 2710 1949; renumbered 218 1951; withdrawn 1960; Millburn Motors Ltd (dealer), Preston 7/61; Beighton Construction Co Ltd, Whittington Moor (XDE) 5/66.
BDV 7 (XL116): Body scrapped; chassis to Ribble Motor Services Ltd, Preston (LA) 11/48; fitted with 7.4 litre diesel engine; rebodied Burlingham B35F 1949; to service as 2709 1949; renumbered 219 1951; withdrawn 1960; Millburn Motors Ltd (dealer), Preston 7/61; Kaye, Goodfellow & Co Ltd (contractor), Manchester (XLA) 2/62.
BDV 9 (TCL118): Mitchley (dealer), Birmingham 1952; not traced further.
CTA 110 (XL121): Body scrapped; chassis to Ribble Motor Services Ltd, Preston (LA) 1948; fitted with 7.4 litre diesel engine; rebodied Burlingham B35F 1949; to service as 2706 1949;

renumbered 215 1951; withdrawn 1960; Millburn Motors Ltd (dealer), Preston 7/61; Kaye, Goodfellow & Co Ltd (contractor), Manchester (XLA) 2/62; Alex Findlay & Co Ltd (contractor), Motherwell (XLK) by 6/62.

1944

New Vehicles:

DG246	JTA 546	Guy Arab II	FD26401	Weymann	C7982	H30/26R	3/44	-/59
DG247	JTA 547	Guy Arab II	FD26403	Weymann	C7983	H30/26R	4/44	-/59
DG248	JTA 548	Guy Arab II	FD26404	Weymann	C7984	H30/26R	2/44	-/59
DG249	JTA 549	Guy Arab II	FD26451	Weymann	C7992	H30/26R	3/44	10/58

Notes:

JTA 546-549 (DG246-249): Had Gardner 5LW engine with slatted wooden seats, which were replaced about 1947 with new blue Vynide seats; extra half-drop windows were fitted at the same time. The 1947 seats were transferred to the new Roe bodies in 1951 (see below).

JTA 546 (DG246): Delivered in grey livery; modernised with lower radiator and rebodied Roe H31/25R (GO3329) 5/51
JTA 547 (DG247): Modernised with lower radiator and rebodied Roe H31/25R (GO3323) 6/51.
JTA 548 (DG248): Modernised with lower radiator and rebodied Roe H31/25R (GO3330) 5/51.
JTA 549 (DG249): Modernised with lower radiator and rebodied Roe H31/25R (GO3332) 5/51.

Disposals:

JTA 546 (DG246): Mitchley (dealer), Birmingham 2/60; Metropolitan Cammell Carriage & Wagon Co Ltd, Birmingham (XWK) as a staff bus 4/60.
JTA 547 (DG247): Mitchley (dealer), Birmingham 3/60; Metropolitan Cammell Carriage & Wagon Co Ltd, Birmingham (XWK) as a staff bus 4/60; unidentified (dealer), Coventry for scrap 6/66.
JTA 548 (DG248): Mitchley (dealer), Birmingham 2/60; Metropolitan Cammell Carriage & Wagon Co Ltd, Birmingham (XWK) as a staff bus 4/60; last licensed 12/67.
JTA 549 (DG249): T Bradford/Drew & Sawyer Ltd (dealer), Mitcham 3/60.

Vehicles acquired from Rhondda Transport Co Ltd, Porth (GG) 6/44:

DG318	ETX 832	Guy Arab I	FD25468	Weymann	C7337	H30/26R	8/42	-/59
DG319	ETX 833	Guy Arab I	FD25477	Weymann	C7341	H30/26R	8/42	-/59

Notes:

These vehicles were received in exchange for Daimler CWG5 HTA 881-882 (DD241-242) of 1943 and had been new to Rhondda as 176-177. Before entering service with Devon General, windows were fitted into the previously unglazed emergency exits at the rear of the upper deck.

ETX 832 (DG318): Had a Gardner 5LW engine; fitted with new roof domes 1947; modernised with lower radiator and rebodied Roe H31/25R (GO3324) 5/51; fitted with platform doors by Roe 1953; re-seated to H31/23RD 1954.
ETX 833 (DG319): Had a Gardner 5LW engine; fitted with new roof domes 1947; modernised with lower radiator and rebodied Roe H31/25R (GO3315) 4/51; fitted with platform doors by Roe 1953; re-seated to H31/23RD 1954.

Disposals:

ETX 832 (DG318): Mitchley (dealer), Birmingham 4/60; Baileys Coaches (Birmingham) Ltd, Birmingham (WK) 2/61; F Cowley Ltd (dealer) Salford 9/65.
ETX 833 (DG319): Mitchley (dealer), Birmingham 4/60; Baileys Coaches (Birmingham) Ltd, Birmingham (WK) 4/60; withdrawn 9/64.

1945

New Vehicles:

DG320	GTT 420	Guy Arab II	FD27914	Park Royal	B30978	H30/26R	11/45	10/58
DG321	GTT 421	Guy Arab II	FD27917	Park Royal	B30979	H30/26R	11/45	10/58
DG322	GTT 422	Guy Arab II	FD27923	Park Royal	B30980	H30/26R	11/45	10/57
DG323	GTT 423	Guy Arab II	FD28013	Park Royal	B30998	H30/26R	12/45	10/58
DG324	GTT 424	Guy Arab II	FD28014	Park Royal	B30999	H30/26R	12/45	10/58
DG325	GTT 425	Guy Arab II	FD28020	Park Royal	B31000	H30/26R	12/45	10/58

Notes:

GTT 420-423 (DG320-323): Had Gardner 6LW engines and were built to 'relaxed' utility specification with upholstered seats; rebuilt by Longwell Green 1956.

GTT 424-425 (DG324-325): Had Gardner 6LW engines and were built to 'relaxed' utility specification with upholstered seats; rebuilt by Longwell Green 1955.

Disposals:

GTT 420-421 (DG320-321): AMCC (dealer), London E15 10/59.

GTT 422 (DG322): Transferred to Ancillary Fleet 10/57 (qv).

GTT 423-424 (DG323-324): A Whitelegg (showman), Devonport 10/59.

GTT 425 (DG325): AMCC (dealer), London E15 10/59.

1946

New Vehicles:

DR328	HTT 328	AEC Regent III	O961220	Weymann	M3055	H30/26R	12/46	-/60
DR332	HTT 332	AEC Regent III	O961224	Weymann	M3054	H30/26R	12/46	-/60
SR480	HTT 480	AEC Regal	O6624806	Weymann	C9046	B35F	7/46	-/53
SR481	HTT 481	AEC Regal	O6624807	Weymann	C9047	B35F	7/46	-/53
SR482	HTT 482	AEC Regal	O6624808	Weymann	C9048	B35F	7/46	-/53
SR483	HTT 483	AEC Regal	O6624809	Weymann	C9049	B35F	7/46	-/53
SR484	HTT 484	AEC Regal	O6624810	Weymann	C9050	B35F	7/46	-/52
SR485	HTT 485	AEC Regal	O6624811	Weymann	C9051	B35F	7/46	-/53
SR486	HTT 486	AEC Regal	O6624812	Weymann	C9052	B35F	7/46	-/52
SR487	HTT 487	AEC Regal	O6624813	Weymann	C9053	B35F	7/46	-/52
SR488	HTT 488	AEC Regal	O6624814	Weymann	C9054	B35F	8/46	-/53
SR489	HTT 489	AEC Regal	O6624815	Weymann	C9055	B35F	8/46	-/53
SR490	HTT 490	AEC Regal	O6624816	Weymann	C9056	B35F	8/46	-/53
SR491	HTT 491	AEC Regal	O6624817	Weymann	C9057	B35F	8/46	-/53
SR492	HTT 492	AEC Regal	O6624818	Weymann	C9058	B35F	8/46	-/53
SR493	HTT 493	AEC Regal	O6624819	Weymann	C9059	B35F	9/46	-/53
SR494	HTT 494	AEC Regal	O6624820	Weymann	C9060	B35F	9/46	-/53
SR495	HTT 495	AEC Regal	O6624821	Weymann	C9061	B35F	10/46	-/53
SR496	HTT 496	AEC Regal	O6624822	Weymann	C9062	B35F	10/46	-/53
SR497	HTT 497	AEC Regal	O6624823	Weymann	C9063	B35F	10/46	-/53
SR498	HTT 498	AEC Regal	O6624824	Weymann	C9064	B35F	11/46	-/52
SR499	HTT 499	AEC Regal	O6624825	Weymann	C9065	B35F	10/46	-/53
SR500	HTT 500	AEC Regal	O6624826	Weymann	C9066	B35F	11/46	-/53
SR501	HTT 501	AEC Regal	O6624827	Weymann	C9067	B35F	11/46	-/53
SR502	HTT 502	AEC Regal	O6624828	Weymann	C9068	B35F	12/46	-/52
SR503	HTT 503	AEC Regal	O6624829	Weymann	C9069	B35F	11/46	-/53
SR504	HTT 504	AEC Regal	O6624830	Weymann	C9070	B35F	12/46	-/52
SR505	HTT 505	AEC Regal	O6624831	Weymann	C9071	B35F	12/46	-/55
SR506	HTT 506	AEC Regal	O6624832	Weymann	C9072	B35F	12/46	-/55
SR507	HTT 507	AEC Regal	O6625079	Weymann	C9073	B35F	12/46	-/55
SR508	JTT 508	AEC Regal	O6624833	Weymann	C9167	B35F	12/46	-/53

Notes:

HTT 328 (DR328): Had chassis of London RT class specification.

HTT 332 (DR332): Had chassis of London RT class specification.

HTT 491 (SR491): Loaned to South Wales Transport Ltd, Swansea (GG) from 7/53; returned 8/53.

HTT 494 (SR494): Re-seated for "standee" experiments in 1952, becoming first B28F and finally B27F being licensed for 22 standees; this configuration was retained until sale.

HTT 495 (SR495): Loaned to South Wales Transport Ltd, Swansea (GG) from 7/53; returned 8/53.

HTT 497 (SR497): Loaned to South Wales Transport Ltd, Swansea (GG) from 7/53; returned 8/53.

HTT 503 (SR503) Completely rebuilt following a serious accident early in its career. The chassis was returned to AEC for straightening and only the rear half of the body was of any further use.

HTT 505 (SR505): Loaned to South Wales Transport Ltd, Swansea (GG) from 7/53; returned 8/53.

Disposals:

HTT 328 (DR328): Passenger Vehicles Disposals Ltd, (dealer) Dunchurch 6/60 ; WA Dawson, location unknown, Co Durham at an unknown date; CF Cantello, Birmingham (WK) 10,60; Bird's Commercial Motors Ltd (dealer), Stratford-upon-Avon 9/63; scrapped by 1970.

HTT 332 (DR332): Passenger Vehicles Disposals Ltd (dealer) Dunchurch 6/60; CB Green & TH Griffin {G & G Coaches}, Leamington Spa (WK) 10/60; withdrawn 10/62; Passenger Vehicles Disposals Ltd (dealer) Dunchurch 10/62.
HTT 480 (SR480): Thomas Bros (Port Talbot) Ltd (GG) 4/53; AMCC (dealer), London E15 1959.
HTT 481 (SR481): Millbrook Steamboat & Trading Co, Cremyll (CO) 11/53; Okeridge Motor Services Ltd, Okehampton (DN) 12/58; withdrawn 7/61; Alexander & Walker (dealer), Bretforton 7/61.
HTT 482-483 (SR482-483): GSP (Gradskog Saobraeajnog Preduzeco), Beograd (O-YU) 1/54.
HTT 484 (SR484): Leicester City Transport, Leicester (LE) 195 7/52; re-seated to B29F 1954 and to B34F 1955; withdrawn 12/63; R Irvine {Tiger Coaches} (dealer), Salsburgh 9/62.
HTT 485 (SR485): GSP (Gradskog Saobraeajnog Preduzeco), Beograd (O-YU) 1/54.
HTT 486 (SR486): Leicester City Transport, Leicester (LE) 196 7/52; re-seated to B34F 1956; withdrawn 5/62; R Irvine {Tiger Coaches} (dealer), Salsburgh 9/62.
HTT 487 (SR487): Leicester City Transport, Leicester (LE) 197 7/52; withdrawn 8/57; Leicester Education Department (XLE) 8/57; A Coombes and others, Aylesbeare for preservation 2/65; renamed 487 Group by 1/93; R Greet, Broadhempston for preservation 1995; operated as a psv on an irregular basis between 5/01 and 11/03 as R Greet, Broadhempston and between 11/03 and 12/11 as Nostalgic Transport Ltd, Broadhempston (DN); still owned 1/15.
HTT 488-497 (SR488-497): GSP (Gradskog Saobraeajnog Preduzeco), Beograd (O-YU) 1/54.
HTT 498 (SR498): Leicester City Transport, Leicester (LE) 198 7/52; withdrawn 8/62; R Irvine {Tiger Coaches} (dealer), Salsburgh 9/62.
HTT 499 (SR499): GSP (Gradskog Saobraeajnog Preduzeco), Beograd (O-YU) 1/54.
HTT 500 (SR500): Thomas Bros (Port Talbot) Ltd (GG) 1953; AMCC (dealer), London E15 1959; Homeworthy Guaranteed Furniture Ltd, London N18 (XLN) rebodied as a van 1959; unidentified dealer for scrap, London E17 5/67.
HTT 501 (SR501): Thomas Bros (Port Talbot) Ltd (GG) 4/53; AMCC (dealer), London E15 1959.
HTT 502 (SR502): Leicester City Transport, Leicester (LE) 199 7/52; to B34F 1956; withdrawn 1/64; Colbro Ltd (dealer), Rothwell 5/64.
HTT 503 (SR503): GSP (Gradskog Saobraeajnog Preduzeco), Beograd (O-YU) 1/54.
HTT 504 (SR504): Leicester City Transport, Leicester (LE) 200 7/52; re-seated to B29F 1954 and to B34F 1955; withdrawn 12/63; R Irvine {Tiger Coaches} (dealer), Salsburgh 9/62; unidentified contractor, Fort William by 7/65.
HTT 505-507 (SR505-507): Enterprise Services (O-JA) 11/55; shipped 1/56.
JTT 508 (SR508): Thomas Bros (Port Talbot) Ltd (GG) 4/53; AMCC (dealer), London E15 11/59.

Footnote to disposals:
The vehicles sold to Thomas Bros and those sold to Jamaica in 1955 were all repainted in their new liveries before leaving Torquay. The batch for Jamaica received thorough overhauls and numerous modifications, including the provision of large roof racks and ladders, heavy duty springs and tyres, replacement of the rear destination indicators by ventilation louvres and the fitting of a formidable pair of horns under the roof alongside the half-cab. AEC Regals of the 1939 and 1940 batches also went to Jamaica and were similarly treated. All were shipped early in 1956.

Vehicle reacquired from War Department (GOV) 12/46
| SL84 | AUO 84 | Leyland LT5A | 5724 | Short | B36F | 6/35 | n/a |
| XL117 | BDV 8 | Leyland TS7 | 8936 | Harrington | B32F | 4/36 | 8/53 |

Previous history
AUO 84 (SL84): New to Devon General as 84 (qv); did not re-enter service.
BDV 8 (XL117): New to Devon General as 117 (qv).

Notes:
BDV 8 (TCL117): Rebuilt by Tiverton, repainted in Grey Cars livery and renumbered TCL117 1947.

Disposals:
AUO 84 (SL84): Morning Star Motor Services Ltd, Bristol (GL) 1946; rebodied Duple C33F (49585) 1947; Wessex Coaches Ltd, Bristol (GL) 4/48; Arlington Motor Co Ltd (dealer) London SW1 1955; CW Banfield Ltd, London SE17 (LN) 12/55; scrapped 1958.
BDV 8 (TCL117): AJ Beale (dealer), Exeter 1954; Marston Coaches (Oxford) Ltd, Marston (OX) by 3/54; withdrawn 7/55.

1947

New Vehicles:

DR326	HTT 326	AEC Regent III	O961218	Weymann	M3053	H30/26R	2/47	-/60
DR327	HTT 327	AEC Regent III	O961219	Weymann	M3048	H30/26R	2/47	-/60
DR329	HTT 329	AEC Regent III	O961221	Weymann	M3052	H30/26R	2/47	-/60
DR330	HTT 330	AEC Regent III	O961222	Weymann	M3051	H30/26R	2/47	-/60
DR331	HTT 331	AEC Regent III	O961223	Weymann	M3049	H30/26R	2/47	-/60
DR333	HTT 333	AEC Regent III	O961230	Weymann	M3050	H30/26R	2/47	-/60

Notes:

These vehicles had chassis to London Transport RT class specification.

Disposals:

HTT 326 (DR326): Passenger Vehicles Disposals Ltd (dealer) Dunchurch 6/60; John Laing & Son Ltd (contractor), London NW7 (XLN) by 9/60; AH Ralph, Whittlesford, Cambridgeshire use and date unknown; last licensed 2/61; sold via General Auctions, London SW18 9/63.

HTT 327 (DR327): Passenger Vehicles Disposals Ltd (dealer) Dunchurch 6/60; John Laing & Son Ltd (contractor), London NW7 (XLN) by 9/60; CF Hill, (dealer?) London SW1 at an unknown date, last licensed 8/63; Clapham Commercials (dealer), London SW9 8/63.

HTT 329 (DR329): Passenger Vehicles Disposals Ltd (dealer) Dunchurch 6/60; Holloway Bros (London) Ltd, London SW1 (XLN) as staff bus at an unknown date; last licensed 1/63.

HTT 330 (DR330): Passenger Vehicles Disposals Ltd (dealer) Dunchurch 6/60; John Laing & Son Ltd (contractor), London NW7 (XLN) by 9/60; last licensed 12/60.

HTT 331 (DR331): Passenger Vehicles Disposals Ltd (dealer) Dunchurch 6/60; Goldhanger Fruit Farms, Tollesbury (XEX) 5/61; Martin (dealer?), London N16 at an unknown date.

HTT 333 (DR333): Passenger Vehicles Disposals Ltd (dealer) Dunchurch 6/60; Browns Blue Coaches Ltd, Markfield (LE) 9/61; fitted with platform doors; R Armstrong (Bus Proprietors) Ltd, Westerhope (ND) 3/63; withdrawn after an accident 1964; scrapped 1/65.

Vehicle on loan from Leyland Motors Ltd:

CVA 430	Leyland PD2		EX1	Alexander	3008	H30/26R	7/46

Notes:

CVA 430: This vehicle was on demonstration for a short period during 1947.

Vehicle reacquired from HM Admiralty {Royal Navy} (GOV) 9/47:

SR412	DUO 324	AEC Regal	O6623032	Harrington		B35F	7/38	-/52

Notes:

DUO 324 (SR412): New to Devon General as 412; rebuilt before re-entering service.

Disposals:

DUO 324 (SR412): Rhondda Transport Co Ltd, Porth (GG) 3 1952; S Davies (dealer), Penygraig for scrap 1954.

1948

New vehicles:

SR509	HUO 509	AEC Regal	O6625519	Weymann	C9195	B35F	3/48	-/57
SR510	HUO 510	AEC Regal	O6625520	Weymann	C9188	B35F	2/48	-/57
SR511	HUO 511	AEC Regal	O6625521	Weymann	C9194	B35F	3/48	-/57
SR512	HUO 512	AEC Regal	O6625522	Weymann	C9189	B35F	2/48	-/57
SR513	HUO 513	AEC Regal	O6625523	Weymann	C9192	B35F	2/48	-/57
SR514	HUO 514	AEC Regal	O6625524	Weymann	C9191	B35F	2/48	-/57
SR515	HUO 515	AEC Regal	O6625525	Weymann	C9193	B35F	3/48	-/57
SR516	HUO 516	AEC Regal	O6625526	Weymann	C9190	B35F	3/48	-/57
SR517	HUO 517	AEC Regal	O6625527	Weymann	C9198	B35F	4/48	-/57
SR518	HUO 518	AEC Regal	O6625528	Weymann	C9197	B35F	3/48	-/57
SR519	HUO 519	AEC Regal	O6625529	Weymann	C9199	B35F	5/48	-/57
SR520	HUO 520	AEC Regal	O6625530	Weymann	C9196	B35F	3/48	-/57
SR521	HUO 521	AEC Regal	O6625531	Weymann	C9226	B35F	11/48	-/58
SR522	HUO 522	AEC Regal	O6625532	Weymann	C9204	B35F	6/48	-/57
SR523	HUO 523	AEC Regal	O6625533	Weymann	C9201	B35F	5/48	-/57

SR524	HUO 524	AEC Regal	O6625534	Weymann	C9203	B35F	6/48	-/59
SR525	HUO 525	AEC Regal	O6625535	Weymann	C9205	B35F	6/48	-/59
SR526	HUO 526	AEC Regal	O6625536	Weymann	C9202	B35F	5/48	-/59
SR527	HUO 527	AEC Regal	O6625537	Weymann	C9219	B35F	10/48	-/58
SR528	HUO 528	AEC Regal	O6625538	Weymann	C9216	B35F	10/48	-/58
SR529	HUO 529	AEC Regal	O6625539	Weymann	C9208	B35F	6/48	-/58
SR530	HUO 530	AEC Regal	O6625540	Weymann	C9206	B35F	6/48	-/59
SR531	HUO 531	AEC Regal	O6625541	Weymann	C9221	B35F	10/48	-/58
SR532	HUO 532	AEC Regal	O6625542	Weymann	C9213	B35F	9/48	-/58
SR533	HUO 533	AEC Regal	O6625543	Weymann	C9200	B35F	11/48	-/59
SR534	HUO 534	AEC Regal	O6625544	Weymann	C9207	B35F	6/48	-/59
SR535	HUO 535	AEC Regal	O6625545	Weymann	C9227	B35F	11/48	-/58
SR536	HUO 536	AEC Regal	O6625546	Weymann	C9209	B35F	7/48	-/58
SR537	HUO 537	AEC Regal	O6625547	Weymann	C9220	B35F	10/48	-/58
SR538	HUO 538	AEC Regal	O6625548	Weymann	C9215	B35F	10/48	-/58
SR539	HUO 539	AEC Regal	O6625549	Weymann	C9225	B35F	11/48	-/59
SR540	HUO 540	AEC Regal	O6625550	Weymann	C9211	B35F	9/48	-/58
SR541	HUO 541	AEC Regal	O6625551	Weymann	C9224	B35F	11/48	-/58
SR542	HUO 542	AEC Regal	O6625552	Weymann	C9223	B35F	11/48	-/59
SR543	HUO 543	AEC Regal	O6625553	Weymann	C9210	B35F	9/48	-/59
SR544	HUO 544	AEC Regal	O6625554	Weymann	C9222	B35F	10/48	-/58
SR545	HUO 545	AEC Regal	O6625555	Weymann	C9214	B35F	9/48	-/58
SR546	HUO 546	AEC Regal	O6625556	Weymann	C9217	B35F	10/48	-/58
SR547	HUO 547	AEC Regal	O6625557	Weymann	C9218	B35F	10/48	-/59
SR548	HUO 548	AEC Regal	O6625558	Weymann	C9212	B35F	9/48	-/59
DR549	JUO 549	AEC Regent III	O9611224	Weymann	M3273	H30/26R	5/48	-/60
DR550	JUO 550	AEC Regent III	O9611225	Weymann	M3278	H30/26R	6/48	-/60
DR551	JUO 551	AEC Regent III	O9611226	Weymann	M3268	H30/26R	6/48	-/60
DR552	JUO 552	AEC Regent III	O9611227	Weymann	M3279	H30/26R	5/48	-/60
DR553	JUO 553	AEC Regent III	O9611228	Weymann	M3285	H30/26R	7/48	-/60
DR554	JUO 554	AEC Regent III	O9611229	Weymann	M3271	H30/26R	3/48	-/60
DR555	JUO 555	AEC Regent III	O9611230	Weymann	M3269	H30/26R	3/48	-/60
DR556	JUO 556	AEC Regent III	O9611231	Weymann	M3280	H30/26R	5/48	-/60
DR557	JUO 557	AEC Regent III	O9611232	Weymann	M3275	H30/26R	3/48	-/60
DR558	JUO 558	AEC Regent III	O9611233	Weymann	M3270	H30/26R	5/48	-/60
DR559	JUO 559	AEC Regent III	9612E1234	Weymann	M3276	H30/26R	5/48	-/60
DR560	JUO 560	AEC Regent III	9612E1235	Weymann	M3282	H30/26R	5/48	-/60
DR561	JUO 561	AEC Regent III	9612E1236	Weymann	M3283	H30/26R	5/48	-/60
DR562	JUO 562	AEC Regent III	9612E1237	Weymann	M3274	H30/26R	3/48	-/60
DR563	JUO 563	AEC Regent III	9612E1238	Weymann	M3277	H30/26R	5/48	-/60
DR564	JUO 564	AEC Regent III	9612E1239	Weymann	M3281	H30/26R	4/48	-/60
DR565	JUO 565	AEC Regent III	9612E1240	Weymann	M3272	H30/26R	6/48	-/60
DR566	JUO 566	AEC Regent III	9612E1241	Weymann	M3284	H30/26R	6/48	-/60
TCB600	JUO 600	Bedford OB	63393	Duple	47690	C29F	3/48	-/58
TCB601	JUO 601	Bedford OB	65082	Duple	47691	C29F	3/48	-/58
TCB602	JUO 602	Bedford OB	69859	Duple	47692	C29F	3/48	-/58
TCB603	JUO 603	Bedford OB	71117	Duple	47693	C29F	3/48	-/58
TCB604	JUO 604	Bedford OB	71224	Duple	47694	C29F	3/48	-/58
TCB605	JUO 605	Bedford OB	71454	Duple	47695	C29F	3/48	-/54
TCB606	JUO 606	Bedford OB	73118	Duple	47696	C29F	3/48	-/54
TCB607	JUO 607	Bedford OB	75437	Duple	47698	C29F	6/48	-/58
TCB608	JUO 608	Bedford OB	76097	Duple	47697	C29F	6/48	-/54
TCB609	JUO 609	Bedford OB	76253	Duple	47699	C29F	6/48	-/58

Notes:

HUO 509-548 (SR509-548): Were delivered in two distinct batches; the chassis for the second twenty being stored at Torwood Street Garage whilst the first twenty were being delivered. The first batch were similar to HTT 480-507 (SR480-507) of 1947 except that a rear indicator display showing the route number was incorporated into the rear dome, this becoming a standard fitting for single deckers. The second batch differed from the first in having "Solvent" instead of half-drop windows and side destination indicators.

JUO 600-609 (TCB600-609): Were all originally in Grey Cars livery.

JUO 600 (TCB600): Repainted red and renumbered SB600 5/52; reseated to C20F 10/53.
JUO 601 (TCB601): Repainted red and renumbered SB601 5/53; reseated to C20F 10/53.
JUO 602 (TCB602): Repainted red and renumbered SB602 10/53.
JUO 603 (TCB603): Repainted red and renumbered SB603 10/53; reseated to C24F 5/56.
JUO 604 (TCB604): Repainted red and renumbered SB604 12/54; reseated to C24F 6/56.
JUO 607 (TCB607): Repainted red and renumbered SB607 4/53.

Disposals:

HUO 509 (SR509): W Norths (PV) Ltd (dealer) Leeds 10/57; not traced further.
HUO 510 (SR510): Passenger Vehicle Disposals Ltd (dealer), Rugby 10/57; Colbro Ltd (dealer) Rothwell at an unknown date; Double Two Shirt Co Ltd, Wakefield (XWR) as a staff bus 3/60; CT Shears, Winkleigh for preservation 8/69; J Corah & B Beard, Newton Abbot for preservation 10/72; Rexquote Ltd, Bishops Lydeard (SO) as a preserved vehicle 11/97; moved to Norton Fitzwarren by 4/02; becoming Quantock Motor Services Ltd, Wiveliscombe (SO) 3/04; A Blackman Snr, Halifax for preservation 8/09; P Platt, Dawlish Warren for preservation 8/14.
HUO 511 (SR511): W Norths (PV) Ltd (dealer) Leeds 11/57; Goodyer (contractor), Horsforth as an office by 8/60; scrapped by 8/75.
HUO 512 (SR512): Passenger Vehicle Disposals Ltd (dealer), Rugby 10/57; Colbro Ltd (dealer), Rothwell at an unknown date.
HUO 513 (SR513): W Norths (PV) Ltd (dealer) Leeds 10/57; not traced further.
HUO 514 (SR514): Passenger Vehicle Disposals Ltd (dealer), Rugby 10/57; GP Holder {Charlton-on-Otmoor Services}, Charlton-on-Otmoor (OX) 1957; withdrawn 1961; returned to Passenger Vehicle Disposals Ltd (dealer), Rugby by 4/62.
HUO 515 (SR515): W Norths (PV) Ltd (dealer) Leeds 10/57; not traced further.
HUO 516 (SR516): PVD (dealer), Marton, Rugby 10/57; JW Lloyd & Sons, Nuneaton (WK) 11/57; withdrawn 10/61; Askin (dealer) Barnsley for scrap by 7/62.
HUO 517 (SR517): W Norths (PV) Ltd (dealer) Leeds 10/57; Fleet, Mansfield (XNG) by 5/61.
HUO 518 (SR518): Passenger Vehicle Disposals Ltd (dealer), Rugby 10/57; Colbro Ltd (dealer) Rothwell at an unknown date; Miller (contractor), Wakefield (XWR) 1960; not operated; returned to Colbro Ltd (dealer) Rothwell at an unknown date.
HUO 519 (SR519): W Norths (PV) Ltd (dealer) Leeds 10/57; Northern Driving School, Bradford (XWR) at an unknown date; Marshall & Rushworth (contractor), Elland (XWR) 1961.
HUO 520 (SR520): Passenger Vehicle Disposals Ltd (dealer), Rugby 10/57; Miller (contractor), Wakefield (XWR) 1960.
HUO 521 (SR521): Percy D Sleeman Ltd (dealer), London W5 3/58; not traced further.
HUO 522 (SR522): Passenger Vehicle Disposals Ltd (dealer), Rugby 10/57; Colbro Ltd (dealer), Rothwell at an unknown date.
HUO 523 (SR523): W Norths (PV) Ltd (dealer) Leeds 10/57; Clugston (contractor), Scunthorpe (XLI) by 1960.
HUO 524 (SR524): Transport (Passenger Equipment) Ltd (dealer), Macclesfield 5/59; scrapped by 2/61.
HUO 525 (SR525): Percy D Sleeman Ltd (dealer), London W5 3/58; PVT (dealer), London SW18 at an unknown date; W & C French (contractor), Buckhurst Hill (XEX) 1163 2/59.
HUO 526 (SR526): Transport (Passenger Equipment) Ltd (dealer), Macclesfield 5/59; scrapped by 2/61.
HUO 527 (SR527): Percy D Sleeman Ltd (dealer), London W5 3/58; R & R Russell Developments (contractor), Rickmansworth (XHT) by10/59.
HUO 528 (SR528): Percy D Sleeman Ltd (dealer), London W5 3/58; not traced further.
HUO 529 (SR529): Percy D Sleeman Ltd (dealer), London W5 3/58; Kyle Stewart (contractor) London NW6 (XLN) at an unknown date.
HUO 530 (SR530): Transport (Passenger Equipment) Ltd (dealer), Macclesfield 5/59; scrapped by 2/61.
HUO 531-532 (SR531-532): Percy D Sleeman Ltd (dealer), London W5 3/58; not traced further.
HUO 533-534 (SR533-534): Transport (Passenger Equipment) Ltd (dealer), Macclesfield 5/59; scrapped by 2/61.
HUO 535 (SR535): Percy D Sleeman Ltd (dealer), London W5 3/58; AG Linfield (growers), Thatcham (XBE) 1960.
HUO 536-537 (SR536-537): Transport (Passenger Equipment) Ltd (dealer), Macclesfield 5/59; scrapped by 2/61.
HUO 538 (SR538): Percy D Sleeman Ltd (dealer), London W5 3/58; Henley Ltd, Hendon (XMX) as a staff bus by 5/59.
HUO 539 (SR539): Transport (Passenger Equipment) Ltd (dealer), Macclesfield 5/59; scrapped by 2/61.
HUO 540 (SR540): Percy D Sleeman Ltd (dealer), London W5 3/58.
HUO 541 (SR541): Percy D Sleeman Ltd (dealer), London W5 3/58; R & R Russell Developments (contractor), Rickmansworth (XHT) by10/59.
HUO 542-543 (SR542-543): Transport (Passenger Equipment) Ltd (dealer), Macclesfield 5/59; scrapped by 2/61.

HUO 544 (SR544): Percy D Sleeman Ltd (dealer), London W5 3/58; not traced further.
HUO 545 (SR545): Percy D Sleeman Ltd (dealer), London W5 3/58; PVT (dealer) London SW18; W & C French (contractor), Buckhurst Hill (XEX) 11/62; Baynham (dealer), London E1 for scrap 8/65.
HUO 546 (SR546): Percy D Sleeman Ltd (dealer), London W5 3/58; not traced further.
HUO 547 (SR547): Transport (Passenger Equipment) Ltd (dealer), Macclesfield 5/59; Emmanuel Church, Flixton (XLA) 8/60; not traced further.
HUO 548 (SR548): Transport (Passenger Equipment) Ltd (dealer), Macclesfield 5/59; scrapped by 2/61.
JUO 549 (DR549): Passenger Vehicle Disposals Ltd (dealer), Dunchurch 6/60; Service Engineers (dealer), Newcastle upon Tyne c6/60; hired to Bedlington & District Luxury Coaches Ltd, Ashington (ND) 8/60; Arthur Robinson (contractor), Middlesbrough (XNR) 1960.
JUO 550 (DR550): Passenger Vehicle Disposals Ltd (dealer), Dunchurch 6/60; John Laing & Son Ltd (contractor), London NW7 (XLN) 926 by 8/60; sold via General Auction (dealer) London SW18 6/64; Blamire (dealer), Bradford for scrap 8/64.
JUO 551 (DR551): Passenger Vehicle Disposals Ltd (dealer), Dunchurch 6/60; JE Morris & Sons (Bearwood) Ltd, Smethwick (ST) 7/60; withdrawn 5/61; Don Everall Ltd (dealer), Wolverhampton 5/61;
JUO 552 (DR552): Passenger Vehicle Disposals Ltd (dealer), Dunchurch 6/60; JE Morris & Sons (Bearwood) Ltd, Smethwick (ST) 7/60; withdrawn 6/64; F Cowley Ltd (dealer), Dunchurch 6/64.
JUO 553 (DR553): Passenger Vehicle Disposals Ltd (dealer), Dunchurch 6/60; Val de Travers Ltd, London (GLN) as lorry 2/64; still in use 6/70.
JUO 554 (DR554): Western Welsh Omnibus Co Ltd, Cardiff (GG) 1554 5/60; Charles Coppock Ltd (dealer), Sale 11/60; Warners Motors Ltd, Tewkesbury (GL) 1/61; fitted with platform doors and to service 7/61; withdrawn 3/70; Martin & Sons Ltd (dealer) Weaverham 1970.
JUO 555 (DR555): Passenger Vehicle Disposals Ltd (dealer), Dunchurch 6/60; Service Engineers (dealer), Newcastle upon Tyne c6/60; hired to Bedlington & District Luxury Coaches Ltd, Ashington (ND) 8/60; Bell (contractor), Newcastle upon Tyne (XND) 1960; withdrawn 1963; Jackson (dealer) Bradford for scrap 6/67.
JUO 556 (DR556): Western Welsh Omnibus Co Ltd, Cardiff (GG) 1556 5/60; Charles Coppock Ltd (dealer), Sale 12/60; Warners Motors Ltd, Tewkesbury (GL) 1/61; licensed 6/61; withdrawn 11/69; Martin & Sons Ltd (dealer) Weaverham 1/70.
JUO 557 (DR557): Western Welsh Omnibus Co Ltd, Cardiff (GG) 1557 5/60; Jones (dealer), Cardiff 10/60; Llynfi Motor Services Ltd, Maesteg (GG) for spares by 6/61; scrapped by 8/61.
JUO 558 (DR558): Passenger Vehicle Disposals Ltd (dealer), Dunchurch 6/60; Llynfi Motor Services Ltd, Maesteg (GG) 65 6/60; withdrawn 12/63; reinstated 7/64; withdrawn 11/65; believed scrapped 5/70.
JUO 559 (DR559): Western Welsh Omnibus Co Ltd, Cardiff (GG) 1559 5/60; Charles Coppock Ltd (dealer), Sale 11/60; Bedlington & District Luxury Coaches Ltd, Ashington (ND) 3/61; withdrawn 1/63; Hancock & Turner (dealer), Tynemouth for scrap 4/63.
JUO 560 (DR560): Western Welsh Omnibus Co Ltd, Cardiff (GG) 1560 5/60; Charles Coppock Ltd (dealer), Sale 12/60; Warners Motors Ltd, Tewkesbury (GL) 1/61; withdrawn 2/67; dismantled for spares.
JUO 561 (DR561): Western Welsh Omnibus Co Ltd, Cardiff (GG) 1561 5/60; Charles Coppock Ltd (dealer), Sale 12/60; AH Kearsey Ltd, Cheltenham (GL) 67A 5/61; Passenger Vehicle Sales (London) Ltd (dealer), Upminster 10/66; PVS Contracts, Upminster (XLN) 74 10/66; withdrawn after an accident 7/68; Poole Lane Autos (dealer), Highwood for scrap 1/69.
JUO 562 (DR562): Western Welsh Omnibus Co Ltd, Cardiff (GG) 1562 5/60; Charles Coppock Ltd (dealer), Sale 12/60; W Norths (PV) Ltd (dealer), Leeds 1/61; RB Talbott {Barry's Coaches}, Moreton-in-Marsh (GL) 4/61; fitted with platform doors at an unknown date; R Kime & EH Jackson {Richard Kime & Co}, Folkingham (KN) 10/66; Yeates (dealer), Loughborough 4/68; scrapped 1968.
JUO 563 (DR563): Passenger Vehicle Disposals Ltd (dealer), Dunchurch 6/60; Culling & Sons (Norwich) Ltd, Claxton (NK) 7/60; unidentified dealer for scrap 12/69.
JUO 564 (DR564): Western Welsh Omnibus Co Ltd, Cardiff (GG) 1564 5/60; Charles Coppock Ltd (dealer), Sale 12/60; AH Kearsey Ltd, Cheltenham (GL) 61A 5/61; licensed 5/61; withdrawn 2/67; unidentified dealer, Staverton for scrap 1/69.
JUO 565 (DR565): Western Welsh Omnibus Co Ltd, Cardiff (GG) 1565 5/60; Charles Coppock Ltd (dealer), Sale 11/60; Wessex Coaches Ltd, Bristol (GL) 5/61; used at Wylfa Power Station, Anglesey; withdrawn 5/63; scrapped at Wylfa 10/64.
JUO 566 (DR566): Western Welsh Omnibus Co Ltd, Cardiff (GG) 1566 5/60; Charles Coppock Ltd (dealer), Sale 11/60; Wessex Coaches Ltd, Bristol (GL) 5/61 used at Wylfa Power Station, Anglesey; out of use and derelict by 5/68; scrapped at Wylfa at an unknown date.

JUO 600 (SB600): Percy D Sleeman Ltd (dealer) London W5 10/58; JJ Kavanagh & Son, Kilkenny (EI) at an unknown date; Harris (dealer), Dublin 3/64.

JUO 601 (SB601): Percy D Sleeman Ltd (dealer) London W5 10/58; West Street Motors (dealer), Pease Pottage 8/59.

JUO 602-603 (SB602-603): Percy D Sleeman Ltd (dealer) London W5 10/58; not traced further, possibly exported.

JUO 604 (SB604): Percy D Sleeman Ltd (dealer) London W5 10/58; C Collier, Abertillery (MH) 2/59; withdrawn 2/61

JUO 605 (TCB605): Greenslades Tours Ltd, Exeter (DN) 3/54; AMCC (dealer), London E15 1958; Efstathios Kyriakou & Sons Ltd, Limassol (O-CY), re-registered TAV 704 7/59; withdrawn 12/71.

JUO 606 (TCB606): Greenslades Tours Ltd, Exeter (DN) 3/54; AMCC (dealer), London E15 1958; Efstathios Kyriakou & Sons Ltd, Limassol (O-CY), re-registered TAY 31 10/59; Hamboullas, Limassol (O-CY) 2/60; Shiakli, Evdhimou (O-CY) 5/60; Osman, Kato Polemidhia (O-CY) 7/66; Djemal, Limassol (O-CY) 3/69; rebodied by unknown builder FB32F 10/69; Christodoulou, Vatili (O-CY) 9/71; reseated to FB34F 12/71; Atil, Elea (O-CY) 4/72; Pavlides (dealer), Nicosia 6/72.

JUO 607 (SB607): Percy D Sleeman Ltd (dealer) London W5 10/58; not traced further.

JUO 608 (TCB608): Greenslades Tours Ltd, Exeter (DN) 3/54; AMCC (dealer), London E15 1958; TK Roberts & JAC Davies {Brechfa Express}, Felingwm (CR) 11/58; EW Bonnell {Bonnell's Blue Line Coaches}, Pwll (CR) 7/59; withdrawn 7/63; Gwyn Williams & Sons Ltd, Lower Tumble (CR) 6 9/66; D Jones {Ffoshelig Coaches}, Newchurch (CR) 2/68; used as a storeshed from 10/69; N Robertson, Sible Hedingham for preservation 5/71; Piper (dealer), Great Yeldham for scrap late 1975 or early 1976.

JUO 609 (TCB609): Percy D Sleeman Ltd (dealer) London W5 10/58; not traced further.

Vehicle acquired from Greenslades Tours Ltd, Exeter (DN) 1/48:

M610	EFJ 548	Bedford WTB	7890	Tiverton	B20F	11/38	12/50

Previous history:

EFJ 548 (M610): New to Greenslades and was acquired along with their Witheridge area stage services.

Disposals:

EFJ 348 (M610): Mitchley (dealer), Birmingham 5/51; collected 12/51.

1949

New Vehicles:

TCR611	JOD 611	AEC Regal III	9621A532	Duple	45336	C32F	4/49	-/52
TCR612	JOD 612	AEC Regal III	9621A533	Duple	45337	C32F	4/49	-/52
TCR613	JOD 613	AEC Regal III	9621A534	Duple	45338	C32F	4/49	-/52
TCR614	JOD 614	AEC Regal III	9621A535	Duple	45339	C32F	4/49	-/52
TCR615	JOD 615	AEC Regal III	9621A336	Duple	45340	C32F	4/49	-/52
TCR616	JOD 616	AEC Regal III	9621A337	Duple	45341	C32F	4/49	-/52
TCR617	JOD 617	AEC Regal III	9621A338	Duple	45342	C32F	4/49	-/52
TCR618	JOD 618	AEC Regal III	9621A339	Duple	45347	C32F	4/49	-/52
TCR619	JOD 619	AEC Regal III	9621A326	Duple	45343	C32F	4/49	-/52
TCR620	JOD 620	AEC Regal III	9621A327	Duple	45344	C32F	5/49	-/52
TCR621	JOD 621	AEC Regal III	9621A328	Duple	45345	C32F	5/49	-/52
TCR622	JOD 622	AEC Regal III	9621A329	Duple	45346	C32F	5/49	-/52
DR567	KOD 567	AEC Regent III	9612E2477	Weymann	M3780	H30/26R	7/49	-/61
DR568	KOD 568	AEC Regent III	9612E2478	Weymann	M3777	H30/26R	7/49	-/61
DR569	KOD 569	AEC Regent III	9612E2479	Weymann	M3779	H30/26R	7/49	-/61
DR570	KOD 570	AEC Regent III	9612E2480	Weymann	M3778	H30/26R	7/49	-/61
DR571	KOD 571	AEC Regent III	9612E2481	Weymann	M3782	H30/26R	7/49	-/61
DR572	KOD 572	AEC Regent III	9612E2482	Weymann	M3786	H30/26R	8/49	-/61
DR573	KOD 573	AEC Regent III	9612E2483	Weymann	M3781	H30/26R	7/49	-/61
DR574	KOD 574	AEC Regent III	9612E2484	Weymann	M3785	H30/26R	7/49	-/61
DR575	KOD 575	AEC Regent III	9612E2485	Weymann	M3784	H30/26R	7/49	-/61
DR576	KOD 576	AEC Regent III	9612E2486	Weymann	M3783	H30/26R	8/49	-/61
DR577	KOD 577	AEC Regent III	9612E2487	Weymann	M3788	H30/26R	8/49	-/61
DR579	KOD 579	AEC Regent III	9612E2489	Weymann	M3789	H30/26R	8/49	-/61
DR585	KOD 585	AEC Regent III	9612E2495	Weymann	M3787	H30/26R	8/49	-/61
DR586	KOD 586	AEC Regent III	9612E2496	Weymann	M3790	H30/26R	8/49	-/61

Notes:

JOD 611-622 (TCR611-622): Were in Grey Cars livery and had an upswept rear, to clear the ramps on the River Dart ferry; although delivered in 1948 they did not enter service until 1949 (as listed above).

JOD 618 (TCR618): Operated with 'TC' fleet number prefix for a period.

KOD 573 (DR573): Received a replacement upper saloon after being driven under a low bridge at speed 1956.

Disposals:

JOD 611 (TCR611): Western Welsh Omnibus Co Ltd, Cardiff (GG) 524 11/52; licensed 3/53; withdrawn 1959; Charles Coppock Ltd (dealer), Sale 1959; WL Jones, Cwmavon (GG) 4/59; David Jones & Son (Port Talbot) Ltd, Pantdu (GG) 3/60; returned to WL Jones, Cwmavon (GG) 9/65; not used; William Press & Son Ltd (contractor), London N17 (XLN) by 6/66; not licensed.

JOD 612 (TCR612): Western Welsh Omnibus Co Ltd, Cardiff (GG) 525 11/52; licensed 3/53; withdrawn 1959; Pioneer Motors (Kenfig Hill) Ltd, Kenfig Hill (GG) 3/59; withdrawn 8/64; William Press & Son Ltd (contractor), London N17 (XLN) by 5/65; last licensed 9/66; Donald Martindale Ltd (dealer) Chorley for scrap by 1/67.

JOD 613 (TCR613): Western Welsh Omnibus Co Ltd, Cardiff (GG) 526 11/52; licensed 3/53; David Jones & Son (Port Talbot) Ltd, Pantdu (GG) 3/59; withdrawn 3/63; scrapped 9/63.

JOD 614 (TCR614): Western Welsh Omnibus Co Ltd, Cardiff (GG) 527 11/52; licensed 3/53; David Jones & Son (Port Talbot) Ltd, Pantdu (GG) 3/59; scrapped 8/64.

JOD 615 (TCR615): Western Welsh Omnibus Co Ltd, Cardiff (GG) 528 11/52; licensed 3/53; David Jones & Son (Port Talbot) Ltd, Pantdu (GG) 3/59; Thomas Bros (Port Talbot) Ltd (GG) 1965; not operated; Way (dealer) Cardiff for scrap 9/65.

JOD 616 (TCR616): Western Welsh Omnibus Co Ltd, Cardiff (GG) 529 11/52; licensed 3/53; Jones (dealer), Cardiff, minus engine, for scrap 3/59.

JOD 617 (TCR617): Western Welsh Omnibus Co Ltd, Cardiff (GG) 530 11/52; licensed 3/53; Pioneer Motors (Kenfig Hill) Ltd, Kenfig Hill (GG) 3/59; withdrawn 5/61.

JOD 618 (TCR618): Western Welsh Omnibus Co Ltd, Cardiff (GG) 531 11/52; licensed 2/53; repainted in red and ivory dual-purpose livery between 9/59 and 1/60; Passenger Vehicle Disposals Ltd (dealer), Dunchurch 5/61; Banbury Buildings, Ryton (XOX) 1/62; last licensed 2/64.

JOD 619 (TCR619): Western Welsh Omnibus Co Ltd, Cardiff (GG) 532 11/52; licensed 3/53; repainted in red and ivory dual-purpose livery between 9/59 and 1/60; Passenger Vehicle Disposals Ltd (dealer), Dunchurch 5/61; loaned to DW Cook, Warmsworth (WR) 6/61; returned to Passenger Vehicle Disposals Ltd 7/61; Banbury Buildings, Ryton (XOX) 1/62; last licensed 3/64.

JOD 620 (TCR620): Western Welsh Omnibus Co Ltd, Cardiff (GG) 533 11/52; licensed 1/53; repainted in red and ivory dual-purpose livery between 9/59 and 1/60; Passenger Vehicle Disposals Ltd (dealer), Dunchurch 5/61; Hoy, Saunderton (XBK) by 8/67; Thame Youth Club, Thame (XOX) 11/67; out of use from 9/68.

JOD 621 (TCR621): Western Welsh Omnibus Co Ltd, Cardiff (GG) 534 11/52; licensed 3/53; repainted in red and ivory dual-purpose livery between 9/59 and 1/60; Passenger Vehicle Disposals Ltd (dealer), Dunchurch 5/61; WP Simon {Riduna Buses}, Alderney (CI) re-registered AY 101 1962; withdrawn 1967.

JOD 622 (TCR622): Western Welsh Omnibus Co Ltd, Cardiff (GG) 535 11/52; licensed 3/53; repainted in red and ivory dual-purpose livery between 9/59 and 1/60; Passenger Vehicle Disposals Ltd (dealer), Dunchurch 5/61; JA Dickson, Stoke Mandeville (BK) 6/61; Allison's Coaches Ltd, Heddenham (BK) by 7/63; Luton Commercial Motors (dealer), Luton by7/63.

KOD 567 (DR567): Passenger Vehicle Disposals Ltd (dealer), Dunchurch 4/61; Bee-Line Roadways (Tees-Side) Limited; West Hartlepool (DM) 7/61; withdrawn 2/64; Yuill (Contractor) West Hartlepool (XDM) 1964; Monte (dealer), Fencehouses for scrap 11/71.

KOD 568 (DR568): Passenger Vehicle Disposals Ltd (dealer), Dunchurch 6/61; Bee-Line Roadways (Tees-Side) Limited; West Hartlepool (DM) 7/61; returned to PVD Ltd (dealer), Dunchurch 9/61; Warners Motors Ltd, Tewkesbury (GL) 11/61; fitted with platform doors at an unknown date; withdrawn 1/70; Martin & Sons Ltd (dealer), Weaverham 1/70.

KOD 569 (DR569): Passenger Vehicle Disposals Ltd (dealer), Dunchurch 7/61; CF Cantello, Birmingham (WK) 8/61; F Cowley Ltd (dealer), Dunchurch 3/64.

KOD 570 (DR570): Passenger Vehicle Disposals Ltd (dealer), Dunchurch 5/61; JE Morris & Sons (Bearwood) Ltd, Smethwick (ST) 5/61; withdrawn 2/64; F Cowley Ltd (dealer), Dunchurch 3/64.

KOD 571 (DR571): Passenger Vehicle Disposals Ltd (dealer), Dunchurch 6/61; EG Palmer {Fordham & District Coaches}, Fordham (CM) 6/61.

KOD 572 (DR572): Passenger Vehicle Disposals Ltd (dealer), Dunchurch 7/61; Bee-Line Roadways (Tees-Side) Limited; West Hartlepool (DM) 7/61; returned to Passenger Vehicle Disposals Ltd (dealer), Dunchurch 9/61; Warners Motors Ltd, Tewkesbury (GL) 2/62; withdrawn 1/70; Martin & Sons Ltd (dealer), Weaverham 1/70.

KOD 573 (DR573): Passenger Vehicle Disposals Ltd (dealer), Dunchurch 6/61; Bee-Line Roadways (Tees-Side) Limited; West Hartlepool (DM) 7/61; withdrawn 9/63; Yuill (Contractor) West Harlepool (XDM) 1963; Monte (dealer), Fencehouses for scrap 11/71.

KOD 574 (DR574): Passenger Vehicle Disposals Ltd (dealer), Dunchurch 8/61; Bee-Line Roadways (Tees-Side) Limited; West Hartlepool (DM) 9/61; withdrawn 1/64; Yuill (Contractor) West Harlepool (XDM) 1/64;

KOD 575 (DR575): Passenger Vehicle Disposals Ltd (dealer), Dunchurch 6/61; P Shapiro Ltd, Hainault (XEX) as a staff bus 8/61; sold by 1966.

KOD 576 (DR576): Passenger Vehicle Disposals Ltd (dealer), Dunchurch 7/61; Bee-Line Roadways (Tees-Side) Limited; West Hartlepool (DM) 7/61; withdrawn 1964; Val de Travers Ltd, London (XLN) 591 rebodied as a tar-boiler lorry by 6/64; still in use 6/70.

KOD 577 (DR577): Passenger Vehicle Disposals Ltd (dealer), Dunchurch 8/61; EG Palmer {Fordham & District Coaches}, Fordham (CM) 12/61.

KOD 579 (DR579): Passenger Vehicles Disposals Ltd (dealer), Dunchurch 7/61; Bee-Line Roadways (Tees-Side) Limited; West Hartlepool (DM) 9/61; withdrawn 9/63; Yuill (Contractor) West Harlepool (XDM) 9/63.

KOD 585 (DR585): Passenger Vehicle Disposals Ltd (dealer), Dunchurch 5/61; A & P McConnachie, Campbeltown (AL) 6/61; G Glover, Crediton (DN) for preservation 1/67; c/o West of England Transport Museum, Winkleigh; G & M Brown, Newton Abbot (DN) for preservation 9/72; R Greet, Ipplepen for preservation 1973; loaned to N Robertson, Bristol for preservation 10/81; R Greet, Broadhempston for preservation by 9/92; operated as a psv on an irregular basis between 5/01 and 11/03 as R Greet, Broadhempston and between 11/03 and 12/11 as Nostalgic Transport Ltd, Broadhempston (DN); still owned 1/15.

KOD 586 (DR586): Passenger Vehicle Disposals Ltd (dealer), Dunchurch 8/61; Bee-Line Roadways (Tees-Side) Limited; West Hartlepool (DM) 9/61; withdrawn 2/64; Yuill (Contractor) West Harlepool (XDM) 2/64.

Vehicle on loan from Metropolitan Cammell Weymann Motor Bodies Ltd, Birmingham:

KOC 242	Leyland TC40	494307	MCCW	L3	B40F	11/49

Notes:

On demonstration and operated in service for three days during 11/49 in blue & cream livery.

1950

New Vehicles:

DR578	KOD 578	AEC Regent III	9612E2488	Weymann	M3799	H30/26R	3/50	-/62
DR580	KOD 580	AEC Regent III	9612E2490	Weymann	M3796	H30/26R	3/50	-/62
DR581	KOD 581	AEC Regent III	9612E2491	Weymann	M3802	H30/26R	3/50	-/62
DR582	KOD 582	AEC Regent III	9612E2492	Weymann	M3794	H30/26R	3/50	-/62
DR583	KOD 583	AEC Regent III	9612E2493	Weymann	M3793	H30/26R	3/50	-/62
DR584	KOD 584	AEC Regent III	9612E2494	Weymann	M3791	H30/26R	3/50	-/62
DR587	KOD 587	AEC Regent III	9612E2497	Weymann	M3792	H30/26R	3/50	-/62
DR588	KOD 588	AEC Regent III	9612E2498	Weymann	M3800	H30/26R	3/50	-/62
DR589	KOD 589	AEC Regent III	9612E2499	Weymann	M3801	H30/26R	3/50	-/62
DR590	KOD 590	AEC Regent III	9612E2500	Weymann	M3795	H30/26R	3/50	-/62
DR591	KOD 591	AEC Regent III	9612E2501	Weymann	M3797	H30/26R	3/50	-/62
DR592	KOD 592	AEC Regent III	9612E2502	Weymann	M3798	H30/26R	3/50	-/62
TCR623	LTA 623	AEC Regal III	9621A773	Duple	55181	C32F	5/50	4/58
TCR624	LTA 624	AEC Regal III	9621A774	Duple	55177	C32F	5/50	4/58
TCR625	LTA 625	AEC Regal III	9621A775	Duple	55178	C32F	5/50	4/58
TCR626	LTA 626	AEC Regal III	9621A776	Duple	55179	C32F	5/50	5/58
TCR627	LTA 627	AEC Regal III	9621A777	Duple	55180	C32F	5/50	5/58
TCR628	LTA 628	AEC Regal III	9621A778	Duple	55183	C32F	5/50	5/58
TCR629	LTA 629	AEC Regal III	9621A779	Duple	55182	C32F	5/50	5/58
TCR630	LTA 630	AEC Regal III	9621A780	Duple	55184	C32F	5/50	5/58
TCR631	LTA 631	AEC Regal III	9621A781	Duple	55185	C32F	5/50	5/58
TCR632	LTA 632	AEC Regal III	9621A782	Duple	55186	C32F	5/50	5/58
TCR633	LTA 633	AEC Regal III	9621A783	Duple	55188	C32F	5/50	6/58
TCR634	LTA 634	AEC Regal III	9621A784	Duple	55187	C32F	5/50	6/58

SR593	LUO 593	AEC Regal III	6821A448	Weymann	C9393	B35F	5/50	4/62
SR594	LUO 594	AEC Regal III	6821A449	Weymann	C9392	B35F	5/50	4/62
SR595	LUO 595	AEC Regal III	6821A450	Weymann	C9389	B35F	5/50	4/62
SR596	LUO 596	AEC Regal III	6821A451	Weymann	C9391	B35F	5/50	4/62
SR597	LUO 597	AEC Regal III	6821A452	Weymann	C9390	B35F	5/50	4/62

Notes:

KOD 578, 580, 584, 587-592 (DR578, 580, 584, 587-592): Delivered in 1949 and stored over the winter, entering service in 3/50 on Exeter city services.

LUO 593-597 (SR593-597): Had bodies similar to those on HUO 509-548 (SR509-548) with "Solovent" windows and also incorporated improved seating and suspension.

LTA 623-634 (TCR623-634): Were in Grey Cars livery and had an upswept rear, to clear the ramps on the River Dart ferry.

Disposals:

KOD 578 (DR578): Passenger Vehicles Disposals Ltd (dealer), Dunchurch 6/62; F Smith, Long Itchington (WK) 7/62; withdrawn 6/64.

KOD 580 (DR580): Passenger Vehicles Disposals Ltd (dealer), Dunchurch 6/62; CB Green & TH Griffin {G & G Coaches} Leamington Spa (WK) 8/62; becoming G & G Coaches (Leamington) Ltd, Leamington Spa (WK) 5/65; Toon (dealer) Coalville for scrap 5/67.

KOD 581 (DR581): Passenger Vehicles Disposals Ltd (dealer), Dunchurch 6/62; W & EH Gibson {Gibson Bros} Barlestone (LE) 51 7/62; becoming Gibson Bros (Barlestone) Ltd, Barlestone (LE) 51 c7/64; withdrawn 6/67.

KOD 582 (DR582): Passenger Vehicles Disposals Ltd (dealer), Dunchurch 6/62; Service Coaches Ltd, Bebside (ND) 9/62; W Norths (PV) Ltd (dealer), Sherburn in Elmet by 5/64.

KOD 583 (DR583): Passenger Vehicles Disposals Ltd (dealer), Dunchurch 6/62; G & B Margo {Bexleyheath Transport}, Bexleyheath (KT) 22 7/62; withdrawn 8/64; Higgins (dealer), London SE15 8/64.

KOD 584 (DR584): Passenger Vehicles Disposals Ltd (dealer), Dunchurch 7/62; TD Edmunds, Rassau (MH) 7/62; withdrawn 5/64; scrapped 11/65.

KOD 587 (DR587): Passenger Vehicles Disposals Ltd (dealer), Dunchurch 5/62; Drewitt (contractor), Bournemouth (XHA) 6/62.

KOD 588 (DR588): Passenger Vehicles Disposals Ltd (dealer), Dunchurch 5/62; W Davies {Marino Coaches}, Ferryhill (DM) 6/62; Basey (dealer) Langley Moor for scrap 7/63.

KOD 589 (DR589): Passenger Vehicles Disposals Ltd (dealer), Dunchurch 6/62; G & B Margo {Bexleyheath Transport}, Bexleyheath (LN) 21 7/62; scrapped 11/64.

KOD 590 (DR590): Passenger Vehicles Disposals Ltd (dealer), Dunchurch 5/62; WA, MA & A Stacey {Hylton Castle Coaches}, Sunderland (DM) 6/62; withdrawn 6/64.

KOD 591 (DR591): Passenger Vehicles Disposals Ltd (dealer), Dunchurch 7/62; Weeks {Valdene Coaches}, Sutton Valence (KT) 8/62; Elm Park Coaches, Romford (LN) 10/64; scrapped 2/66.

KOD 592 (DR592): Passenger Vehicles Disposals Ltd (dealer), Dunchurch 6/62; Browns Blue Coaches Ltd, Markfield (LE) 7/62; fitted with platform doors; W & EH Gibson (Gibson Bros), Barlestone (LE) 54 3/63; Gibson Bros (Barlestone) Ltd, Barlestone (LE) 54 c7/64; withdrawn 4/68; Alf Moseley & Son Ltd (dealer), Loughborough 2=1968.

LTA 623 (TCR623): Greenslades Tours Ltd, Exeter (DN) 4/58; AG Bowerman Ltd {Bowerman's Tours}, Taunton (SO) 1/61; withdrawn 10/64; unidentified showman 10/64; noted Norwich 12/66.

LTA 624 (TCR624): Greenslades Tours Ltd, Exeter (DN) 4/58; AG Bowerman Ltd {Bowerman's Tours}, Taunton (SO) 9/60; withdrawn 1964; unidentified showman 1964; noted Wanstead Flats 3/64.

LTA 625 (TCR625): Greenslades Tours Ltd, Exeter (DN) 4/58; Philip & Son (Shipbuilders and Engineers), Dartmouth (XDN) 12/60; Riverside Building & Construction Co Ltd, Dartmouth (XDN) by 12/63; withdrawn after accident 4/64.

LTA 626 (TCR626): Greenslades Tours Ltd, Exeter (DN) 5/58; AMCC (dealer) London E15 11/63; Lansdowne Luxury Coaches Ltd, London E11 (LN) 8/64; withdrawn 3/65; Homeworthy Guaranteed Furniture, London N18 (GLN) rebodied as a van by 11/65; still in use 5/68.

LTA 627 (TCR627): Greenslades Tours Ltd, Exeter (DN) 5/58; AG Bowerman Ltd {Bowerman's Tours}, Taunton (SO) 10/60; withdrawn 6/64; Dyer (contractor), Weston-super-Mare (XSO) 7/64; Penfold (dealer), Hewish for scrap 3/66.

LTA 628 (TCR628): Greenslades Tours Ltd, Exeter (DN) 5/58; W & LR Hard {W Hard & Sons} {The Avon} South Brent (DN) as C33F 10/60; becoming LR Hard {The Avon}, South Brent (DN) 6/65; RW Jefferies {Moorland Heather Coaches}, Chagford (DN) 9/66; withdrawn 12/69; GW Glover, Crediton for preservation 1/70; G & M Brown, Newton Abbot for preservation 12/72; R Greet, Ipplepen for preservation 1973; for sale 3/74; scrapped 1974.

LTA 629 (TCR629): Greenslades Tours Ltd, Exeter (DN) 5/58; GW Glover, Crediton for preservation 4/66; D Sayer, Halifax for preservation 1/73; G Bedford, Scarborough for preservation 11/79; Grey Cars Ltd, Torquay (DN) 1/88; Devon General Ltd, Exeter (DN) 8/88; not operated GM Goodwin, Ilfracombe (DN) 1/89; DN Dean {Classique Saloon Luxury Coaches}, Paisley (SC) named "Fiona" 3/92; C Cowdery, East Markham for preservation 5/08; current 1/15.
LTA 630 (TCR630): Greenslades Tours Ltd, Exeter (DN) 5/58; AMCC (dealer) London E15 4/66; Homeworthy Guaranteed Furniture, London N18 (GLN) rebodied as a van 4/66.
LTA 631 (TCR631): Greenslades Tours Ltd, Exeter (DN) 5/58; WJ Down {Otter Coaches}, Ottery St Mary (DN) 9/60; Rowe (dealer), Exeter for scrap 5/65.
LTA 632 (TCR632): Greenslades Tours Ltd, Exeter (DN) 5/58; AMCC (dealer) London E15 12/60; LF Everson {RE Everson} Wix (EX) 6/61; FAE Mann {Everson's Coaches}; Dovercourt (EX) (1963?); AC Peck {Cedric Coaches}, Wivenhoe (EX) 20 2/65; Cedric Contracts Ltd, Wivenhoe (XEX) 20 9/65; used as a store by 6/68; scrapped at Wivenhoe 8/70.
LTA 633 (TCR633): Greenslades Tours Ltd, Exeter (DN) 5/58; AMCC (dealer) London E15 11/63; Homeworthy Guaranteed Furniture, London N18 (GLN) rebodied as a van by 2/64.
LTA 634 (TCR634): Greenslades Tours Ltd, Exeter (DN) 5/58; AMCC (dealer) London E15 5/61; J Navarro {Transportes Guanarteme}, Las Palmas, Gran Canaria (O-IC) 16 re-registered GC 18719 10/61; rebuilt to DP30C; still in use 6/71.
LUO 593 (SR593): Mitchley (dealer), Birmingham 5/62; CN & S Butter & PR Managh, Childs Ercall (SH) 9/62; withdrawn 5/68; West of England Transport Collection, Winkleigh for preservation 6/68; used for spares at 5/71; scrapped 12/73.
LUO 594 (SR594): Mitchley (dealer), Birmingham 5/62; MRQ Construction Ltd (contractor), Oldham (XLA) by 10/65; Hartwood Finance Ltd (dealer), Barnsley for scrap 4/67.
LUO 595 (SR595): Mitchley (dealer), Birmingham 5/62; CN & S Butter & PR Managh, Childs Ercall (SH) 10/62; withdrawn 4/66; G Glover, Crediton for preservation 3/67; N Robertson, Torquay for preservation 1969; moved subsequently to Chelmsford, Sible Hedingham, Bristol; West of England Transport Collection, Winkleigh for preservation 6/76; loaned to West of Yorkshire Transport Collection, Halifax for preservation by 4/78; D Hoare, Chepstow for preservation 3/80 (at West of England Transport Collection, Winkleigh); P Soan, Exeter for preservation c7/84; A Blackman Jnr, Halifax for preservation 9/04; M Izzard, Winchcombe for preservation by 9/13.
LUO 596 (SR596): Mitchley (dealer), Birmingham 5/62; noted at Antwerp Docks 5/63.
LUO 597 (SR597): Mitchley (dealer), Birmingham 5/62.

Vehicle on loan from ACV Sales Ltd, Southall:

| un-regd | AEC Regal IV | U137523 | Park Royal | B34353 | B38F | -/50 |

Notes:

This vehicle arrived on trade plates c5/50 and was briefly examined only. It was later registered VMK 271 for use as a demonstrator in 10/50.

Vehicle on loan from City of Oxford Motor Services Ltd, Oxford (OX):

| OFC 403 | AEC Regent III | 9612A4388 | Weymann | M4550 | H30/26R | 10/49 |

Notes:

OFC 403: This vehicle was City of Oxford H403 and was 8ft 0in wide; operated for several weeks in 1950.

Vehicle on loan from Leyland Motors Ltd:

| MTA 747 | Leyland PD2/12 | 502429 | Leyland | | H30/26R | 9/50 |

Notes:

MTA 747: This vehicle was first registered for use by Devon General and was on demonstration from 9/50, returned at an unknown date.

1951

New Vehicles:

SL635	MTT 635	Leyland PSU1/9	502625	Willowbrook	50826	B43F	3/51	-/63
SL636	MTT 636	Leyland PSU1/9	502622	Willowbrook	50827	B43F	3/51	-/63
SL637	MTT 637	Leyland PSU1/9	502623	Willowbrook	50828	B43F	3/51	-/63
SL638	MTT 638	Leyland PSU1/9	502624	Willowbrook	50830	B43F	3/51	-/63
SL639	MTT 639	Leyland PSU1/9	502626	Willowbrook	50829	B43F	5/51	-/63
DL640	MTT 640	Leyland PD2/1	511256	Leyland		L27/26R	6/51	-/64

DL641	MTT 641	Leyland PD2/1	511258	Leyland		L27/26R	6/51	-/64
DL642	MTT 642	Leyland PD2/1	511259	Leyland		L27/26R	6/51	-/64
DL643	MTT 643	Leyland PD2/1	511261	Leyland		L27/26R	6/51	-/64
DL644	MTT 644	Leyland PD2/1	511257	Leyland		L27/26R	6/51	-/64
DL645	MTT 645	Leyland PD2/1	511260	Leyland		L27/26R	6/51	-/64
DR646	MTT 646	AEC Regent III	9613A2586	Weymann	M4477	H30/26R	3/51	-/64
DR647	MTT 647	AEC Regent III	9613A2587	Weymann	M4486	H30/26R	3/51	-/64
DR648	MTT 648	AEC Regent III	9613A2588	Weymann	M4481	H30/26R	3/51	-/64
DR649	MTT 649	AEC Regent III	9613A2589	Weymann	M4490	H30/26R	3/51	-/61
DR650	MTT 650	AEC Regent III	9613A2590	Weymann	M4478	H30/26R	3/51	-/64
DR651	MTT 651	AEC Regent III	9613A2591	Weymann	M4483	H30/26R	3/51	-/64
DR652	MTT 652	AEC Regent III	9613A2592	Weymann	M4482	H30/26R	3/51	-/64
DR653	MTT 653	AEC Regent III	9613A2593	Weymann	M4485	H30/26R	3/51	-/64
DR654	MTT 654	AEC Regent III	9613A2594	Weymann	M4484	H30/26R	3/51	-/64
DR655	MTT 655	AEC Regent III	9613A2595	Weymann	M4488	H30/26R	3/51	-/64
DR656	MTT 656	AEC Regent III	9613A2596	Weymann	M4487	H30/26R	3/51	-/64
DR657	MTT 657	AEC Regent III	9613A2597	Weymann	M4489	H30/26R	3/51	-/64
DR658	MTT 658	AEC Regent III	9613A2598	Weymann	M4480	H30/26R	3/51	-/64
DR659	MTT 659	AEC Regent III	9613A2599	Weymann	M4479	H30/26R	3/51	-/64

Notes:

Fleet number prefixes were removed on repaint from 2/62.

MTT 635 (SL635): Rebuilt 1958.
MTT 636 (SL636): Rebuilt 5/60.
MTT 637-639 (SL637-639): Rebuilt 1958.
MTT 640-645 (DL640-645): Originally intended for route 3 (Exeter-Tiverton) but the lowbridge restriction on that route was soon removed and they were transferred elsewhere.
MTT 646-659 (DR646-659): Were the first 8ft 0in wide vehicles in the fleet.
MTT 646-651 (DR646-651): Fitted with platform doors by Weymann in 1955; renumbered DRD646-651 1957.

Disposals:

MTT 635 (SL635): Transport (Passenger Equipment) Ltd (dealer), Macclesfield 4/63; Great Yarmouth Corporation (NK) 15 5/63; withdrawn 1964; Dublin Hire Coaches (dealer), Dublin 3/65; Barry, Cobh (EI) by 1/65; re-registered VZB 225 at an unknown date; O'Sullivan, Kildorrery (EI) 4/68.
MTT 636 (SL636): Transport (Passenger Equipment) Ltd (dealer), Macclesfield 4/63; Great Yarmouth Corporation (NK) 16 5/63; withdrawn 1963; M & P Phillipson {Dearneways}, Goldthorpe (WR) 48 4/64; S Twell (dealer), Ingham for scrap 1/67.
MTT 637 (SL637): Transport (Passenger Equipment) Ltd (dealer), Macclesfield 4/63; M & P Phillipson {Dearneways}, Goldthorpe (WR) 43 7/63; W Norths (PV) Ltd (dealer), Sherburn in Elmet 7/66.
MTT 638 (SL638): Transport (Passenger Equipment) Ltd (dealer), Macclesfield 4/63; Ezra Laycock Ltd, Barnoldswick (WR) 68 4/63; scrapped 8/65.
MTT 639 (SL639): Transport (Passenger Equipment) Ltd (dealer), Macclesfield 4/63; TW Holme {Regency Coaches}, Salford (LA) 7/63; M & P Phillipson {Dearneways}, Goldthorpe (WR) 44 10/63; Millburn Motors Ltd (dealer), Preston 4/66.
MTT 640 (DL640): Transport (Passenger Equipment) Ltd (dealer), Macclesfield 7/64; Pearson (contractor), Hetton-le-Hole (XDM) 7/64; withdrawn 11/75; A Hazell & D Godley, Exeter for preservation 11/75; A Hazell, Northlew for preservation 11/95; A Hazell {Carmel Coaches}, Northlew (DN) as preserved vehicle 5/11; retained by A Hazell, Nortlew for preservation 11/14; still owned 1/15.
MTT 641 (DL641): Transport (Passenger Equipment) Ltd (dealer), Macclesfield 5/64; Pearson (contractor), Hetton-le-Hole (XDM) 7/64; Lister PVS (Bolton) Ltd (dealer), Bolton 12/75; Carlton Metals (dealer), Barnsley for scrap 7/76.
MTT 642 (DL642): Transport (Passenger Equipment) Ltd (dealer), Macclesfield 5/64; Pearson (contractor), Hetton-le-Hole (XDM) 7/64; Lister PVS (Bolton) Ltd (dealer), Bolton 12/75; Carlton Metals (dealer), Barnsley for scrap 7/76.
MTT 643 (643): Transport (Passenger Equipment) Ltd (dealer), Macclesfield 5/64; Pearson (contractor), Hetton-le-Hole (XDM) 7/64; Lister PVS (Bolton) Ltd (dealer), Bolton 12/75; Carlton Metals (dealer), Barnsley for scrap 7/76.

MTT 644 (DL644): Transport (Passenger Equipment) Ltd (dealer), Macclesfield 5/64; Pearson (contractor), Hetton-le-Hole (XDM) 7/64; Lister PVS (Bolton) Ltd (dealer), Bolton 12/75; Carlton Metals (dealer), Barnsley for scrap 7/76.

MTT 645 (DL645): Transport (Passenger Equipment) Ltd (dealer), Macclesfield 5/64; Pearson (contractor), Hetton-le-Hole (XDM) 7/64; Lister PVS (Bolton) Ltd (dealer), Bolton 12/75; Carlton Metals (dealer), Carlton for scrap 7/76.

MTT 646 (646): Transport (Passenger Equipment) Ltd (dealer), Macclesfield 4/64; CJ Smith & Sons Ltd {Bluebell}, March (CM) 5/64; LV Morris, Harlow (EX) 5/66; sold for scrap 1967.

MTT 647 (DRD647): Transport (Passenger Equipment) Ltd (dealer), Macclesfield 4/64; B Marfleet, Binbrook (LI) 6/64; P Sheffield, Cleethorpes (LI) for spares 3/66; sold 1966.

MTT 648 (DRD648): Transport (Passenger Equipment) Ltd (dealer), Macclesfield 4/64; A & BM Foster, Ellesmere Port (CH) 5/64; withdrawn 11/67; G Glover, Crediton for preservation 12/67 (c/o West of England Transport Collection, Winkleigh); Lister PVS (Bolton) Ltd (dealer), Bolton 8/74; G Jamieson {Dunscroft Commercials} (dealer), Dunscroft for scrap 8/74.

MTT 649 (649): Transport (Passenger Equipment) Ltd (dealer), Macclesfield 4/64; Baileys Coaches (Birmingham) Ltd, Birmingham (WK) 9/64; returned to Transport (Passenger Equipment) Ltd (dealer), Macclesfield 3/67; Martin & Sons Ltd (dealer), Weaverham 4/67.

MTT 650 (DRD650): Transport (Passenger Equipment) Ltd (dealer), Macclesfield 4/64; Baileys Coaches (Birmingham) Ltd, Birmingham (WK) 9/64; returned to Transport (Passenger Equipment) Ltd (dealer), Macclesfield 12/67; Wombwell Diesels Co Ltd (dealer), Wombwell 1/68; Chris Hoyle & Son Ltd (dealer), Wombwell for scrap 1/68.

MTT 651 (DRD651): Transport (Passenger Equipment) Ltd (dealer), Macclesfield 4/64; Lamcote Motors (Radcliffe) Ltd, Radcliffe-on-Trent (NG) 4/64; returned to Transport (Passenger Equipment) Ltd (dealer), Macclesfield for scrap 12/68.

MTT 652 (DR652): Transport (Passenger Equipment) Ltd (dealer), Macclesfield 5/64; James (Invincible Coaches), Tamworth (ST) 12/64; returned to Transport (Passenger Equipment) Ltd (dealer), Macclesfield 1/65; Chris Hoyle & Son Ltd (dealer), Wombwell for scrap 2/65.

MTT 653 (653): Transport (Passenger Equipment) Ltd (dealer), Macclesfield 5/64; Hoyle (dealer) Wombwell for scrap 10/64.

MTT 654 (DR654): Transport (Passenger Equipment) Ltd (dealer), Macclesfield 5/64; James {Invincible Coaches}, Tamworth (ST) 4/65; withdrawn 12/65.

MTT 655 (DR655): Transport (Passenger Equipment) Ltd (dealer), Macclesfield 5/64; Chris Hoyle & Son Ltd (dealer), Wombwell for scrap 10/64.

MTT 656 (656): Transport (Passenger Equipment) Ltd (dealer), Macclesfield 5/64; Chris Hoyle & Son Ltd (dealer), Wombwell for scrap 10/64.

MTT 657 (DR657): Transport (Passenger Equipment) Ltd (dealer), Macclesfield 6/64; S & JR Cubbins, (dealer) Farnworth for scrap 11/64.

MTT 658 (658): Transport (Passenger Equipment) Ltd (dealer), Macclesfield 5/64; S & JR Cubbins (dealer), Farnworth for scrap 11/64.

MTT 659 (DR659): Transport (Passenger Equipment) Ltd (dealer), Macclesfield 5/64; Chris Hoyle & Son Ltd (dealer), Wombwell for scrap 1965.

1952

New Vehicles:

DR660	NTT 660	AEC Regent III	9613A7154	Weymann	M5511	H30/26R	7/52	2/65
DR661	NTT 661	AEC Regent III	9613A7155	Weymann	M5514	H30/26R	7/52	2/65
DR662	NTT 662	AEC Regent III	9613A7156	Weymann	M5515	H30/26R	7/52	2/65
DR663	NTT 663	AEC Regent III	9613A7157	Weymann	M5509	H30/26R	7/52	2/65
DR664	NTT 664	AEC Regent III	9613A7158	Weymann	M5516	H30/26R	7/52	2/65
DR665	NTT 665	AEC Regent III	9613A7159	Weymann	M5519	H30/26R	7/52	4/65
DR666	NTT 666	AEC Regent III	9613A7160	Weymann	M5521	H30/26R	7/52	2/65
DR667	NTT 667	AEC Regent III	9613A7161	Weymann	M5508	H30/26R	7/52	10/64
DR668	NTT 668	AEC Regent III	9613A7162	Weymann	M5518	H30/26R	7/52	4/65
DR669	NTT 669	AEC Regent III	9613A7163	Weymann	M5520	H30/26R	7/52	2/65
DR670	NTT 670	AEC Regent III	9613A7164	Weymann	M5510	H30/26R	7/52	4/65
DR671	NTT 671	AEC Regent III	9613A7165	Weymann	M5506	H30/26R	7/52	2/65
DR672	NTT 672	AEC Regent III	9613A7166	Weymann	M5517	H30/26R	7/52	4/65
DR673	NTT 673	AEC Regent III	9613A7167	Weymann	M5513	H30/26R	7/52	2/65
DR674	NTT 674	AEC Regent III	9613A7168	Weymann	M5507	H30/26R	7/52	4/65
DR675	NTT 675	AEC Regent III	9613A7169	Weymann	M5512	H30/26R	7/52	4/65
DR676	NTT 676	AEC Regent III	9613A7170	Weymann	M5522	H30/26R	7/52	4/65
DR677	NTT 677	AEC Regent III	9613A7171	Weymann	M5504	H30/26R	7/52	4/65
DR678	NTT 678	AEC Regent III	9613A7172	Weymann	M5505	H30/26R	7/52	2/65

Notes:

Fleet number prefixes were removed on repaint from 2/62.

Disposals:

NTT 660 (DR660): Transport (Passenger Equipment) Ltd (dealer), Macclesfield 4/65; TD Edmunds, Rassau (MH) 4/65; becoming Edmunds Omnibus Services Ltd, Rassau (MH) 6/66; G Glover, Crediton for preservation 1/67; G & M Brown, Newton Abbot for preservation 10/71; R Greet, Ipplepen for preservation 1973; Jamieson (dealer) Teigngrace for scrap 6/80.

NTT 661 (661): Transport (Passenger Equipment) Ltd (dealer), Macclesfield 4/65; TD Edmunds, Rassau (MH) 4/65; becoming Edmunds Omnibus Services Ltd, Rassau (MH) 6/66; P Platt, Exeter for preservation 12/66; moved to Dawlish Warren 9/11; still owned 1/15.

NTT 662 (662): Transport (Passenger Equipment) Ltd (dealer), Macclesfield 4/65; R Askin (dealer), Barnsley for scrap 6/65.

NTT 663 (DR663): Transport (Passenger Equipment) Ltd (dealer), Macclesfield 5/65; loaned to Bedlington & District Luxury Coaches Ltd, Ashington (ND) 6/65; returned to Transport (Passenger Equipment) Ltd (dealer), Macclesfield 8/65; James (Invincible Coaches), Tamworth (ST) 8/65; sold by 6/67.

NTT 664 (DR664): Transport (Passenger Equipment) Ltd (dealer), Macclesfield 5/65; T Burrows & Sons Ltd, Wombwell (WR) 104 7/65; Yorkshire Traction Co Ltd, Barnsley (WR) 10/66; not operated; F Cowley Ltd (dealer), Salford 10/66; scrapped.

NTT 665 (DR665): Transport (Passenger Equipment) Ltd (dealer), Macclesfield 5/65; Bedlington & District Luxury Coaches Ltd, Ashington (ND) 6/65; returned to Transport (Passenger Equipment) Ltd (dealer), Macclesfield 8/66.

NTT 666 (666): Transport (Passenger Equipment) Ltd (dealer), Macclesfield 5/65; Chris Hoyle & Son Ltd (dealer), Wombwell for scrap by 7/65.

NTT 667 (DR667): Transferred to Ancillary Fleet 10/64 (qv).

NTT 668 (DR668): Transport (Passenger Equipment) Ltd (dealer), Macclesfield 7/65; Chris Hoyle & Son Ltd (dealer), Wombwell 6/65.

NTT 669 (669): Transport (Passenger Equipment) Ltd (dealer), Macclesfield 5/65; T Burrows & Sons Ltd, Wombwell (WR) 105 6/65; to service 8/65; Yorkshire Traction Co Ltd, Barnsley (WR) 10/66; not operated; F Cowley Ltd (dealer), Salford 10/66; A Barraclough (dealer), Carlton 11/66.

NTT 670 (670): Transport (Passenger Equipment) Ltd (dealer), Macclesfield 6/65; H Thomas (Motors) Ltd, Chorlton-cum-Hardy (LA) 7/65; "Top Ten Club", Penkridge (XST) 1/66.

NTT 671 (DR671): Transport (Passenger Equipment) Ltd (dealer), Macclesfield 4/65; TD Edmunds, Rassau (MH) 5/65; becoming Edmunds Omnibus Services Ltd, Rassau (MH) 6/66; withdrawn 2/68; returned to Transport (Passenger Equipment) Ltd (dealer), Macclesfield 10/68; Chris Hoyle & Son Ltd (dealer), Wombwell 11/68.

NTT 672 (DR672): Transport (Passenger Equipment) Ltd (dealer), Macclesfield 6/65; T Burrows & Sons Ltd, Wombwell (WR) 106 6/65; to service 9/65; Yorkshire Traction Co Ltd, Barnsley (WR) 10/66; not operated; F Cowley Ltd (dealer), Salford 10/66.

NTT 673 (673): Transport (Passenger Equipment) Ltd (dealer), Macclesfield 6/65; T Burrows & Sons Ltd, Wombwell (WR) 107 10/65; fitted with platform doors at an unknown date; Yorkshire Traction Co Ltd, Barnsley (WR) 10/66; not operated; F Cowley Ltd (dealer), Salford 10/66.

NTT 674 (DR674): Transport (Passenger Equipment) Ltd (dealer), Macclesfield 5/65; Chris Hoyle & Son Ltd (dealer), Wombwell for scrap 5/65.

NTT 675 (DR675): Transport (Passenger Equipment) Ltd (dealer), Macclesfield 6/65; but written off in an accident on the way to Macclesfield; Chris Hoyle & Son Ltd (dealer), Wombwell for scrap 6/65.

NTT 676 (DR676): Transport (Passenger Equipment) Ltd (dealer), Macclesfield 7/65.

NTT 677 (DR677): Transport (Passenger Equipment) Ltd (dealer), Macclesfield 6/65; Foster Wheeler John Brown Ltd (contractor), Tilbury (1965?).

NTT 678 (DR678): Transport (Passenger Equipment) Ltd (dealer), Macclesfield 5/65; Chris Hoyle & Son Ltd (dealer), Wombwell for scrap 5/65.

Vehicles acquired from Leicester City Transport (LE) 7/52:

DR101	DJF 324	AEC Regent II	O6617518	Park Royal	B31753	H30/26R	2/46	-/60
DR102	DJF 325	AEC Regent II	O6617519	Park Royal	B31757	H30/26R	2/46	-/60
DR103	DJF 326	AEC Regent II	O6617513	Park Royal	B31758	H30/26R	2/46	-/60
DR104	DJF 327	AEC Regent II	O6617521	Park Royal	B31762	H30/26R	2/46	-/60
DR105	DJF 328	AEC Regent II	O6617522	Park Royal	B31763	H30/26R	3/46	-/60
DR106	DJF 330	AEC Regent II	O6617526	Park Royal	B31765	H30/26R	3/46	-/60

Previous history:
>DJF 324-328 (DR101-105): New as Leicester 211-215.
>DJF 330 (DR106): New as Leicester 217.

Notes:
>These vehicles were acquired in exchange for six 1946 AEC Regals (qv) and operated initially in Leicester livery.

>DJF 324-328 (DR101-105): Renumbered DR698-702 1952-1953.
>DJF 330 (DR106): Renumbered DR703 1952-1953.

Diisposals:
>DJF 324 (DR698): Passenger Vehicle Disposals Ltd (dealer), Dunchurch 6/60; Sir Alfred McAlpine & Son (contractor), Hooton (XCH) 1960; Mitchell Construction Co (contractor), Peterborough (XSP) 12/60.
>DJF 325 (DR699): Passenger Vehicle Disposals Ltd (dealer), Dunchurch 6/60; Chivers (contractor), Devizes (XWI) L356 9/60; Southern Counties Trading Co (dealer), Havant 12/64; Wallington Commercials (dealer), Fareham for scrap 1966.
>DJF 326 (DR700): Passenger Vehicle Disposals Ltd (dealer), Dunchurch 6/60; Chivers (contractor), Devizes (XWI) 9/60; Southern Counties Trading Co (dealer), Havant 12/64; Wallington Commercials (dealer), Fareham for scrap 1966.
>DJF 327-328 (DR701-702): Transferred to Ancillary Fleet 7/60 (qv).
>DJF 330 (DR703): Transferred to Ancillary Fleet 7/60 (qv).

Vehicles acquired from Mrs WA Hart, Budleigh Salterton (DN) 17/3/52:

OD 8725	Commer B50	56034	Tiverton		B20F	3/34	n/a
OD 8726	Commer B50	56033	Tiverton		B20F	3/34	n/a
AYC 106	Albion PK115	25002D	Harrington		C27C	4/35	n/a
BTT 186	Commer B3	63010	Tiverton		B20F	3/35	n/a
DTA 499	Albion PK115	25012H	Tiverton		B30F	1/37	n/a

Previous history:
>These vehicles were acquired with the Hart business; their previous histories are detailed in the Vehicles of Acquired Operators section.

Disposals:
>OD 8725: Kirton (dealer), Torquay (1952?); chicken house at Starpitten Corner, Torquay at an unknown date; still there 4/63.
>OD 8726: Kirton (dealer), Torquay (1952?); chicken house at Starpitten Corner, Torquay at an unknown date.
>AYC 106: Kirton (dealer), Torquay (1952?); not traced further.
>BTT 186: Kirton (dealer), Torquay (1952?); not traced further.
>DTA 499: Kirton (dealer), Torquay (1952?); not traced further.

Vehicle acquired from-Balls Bus Service Ltd, Newton Abbot (DN) 21/10/52:

FTT 800	Bedford OWB	21332	Duple	38863	B30F	8/44	n/a

Previous history:
>This vehicle was acquired with Balls' stage services; its previous history is detailed in the Vehicles of Acquired Operators section.

Disposal:
>FTT 800: Mitchley (dealer), Birmingham 1953; R Clarke, Handsworth (GWK) as a mobile shop at an unknown date.

Vehicles on loan from City of Oxford Motor Services, Oxford (OX):

H138	HFC 951	AEC Regent	O6616589	Weymann	C5421	H28/24R	6/39
H139	HFC 952	AEC Regent	O6616592	Weymann	C5422	H28/24R	6/39
H133	HFC 953	AEC Regent	O6616593	Weymann	C5423	H28/24R	6/39
H135	HFC 954	AEC Regent	O6616590	Park Royal	B5691	H28/24R	6/39
H136	HFC 955	AEC Regent	O6616591	Park Royal	B5692	H28/24R	6/39
H145	HFC 956	AEC Regent	O6616594	Park Royal	B5693	H28/24R	6/39

Notes:
These vehicles were on loan from 7/52 to 8/52 allocated to Kingsteignton depot to cover additional services for the Royal Agricultural Show held near Newton Abbot and retained their COMS fleet numbers as listed.

1953
New Vehicles:

DR679	NTT 679	AEC Regent III	9613S7173	Weymann	M5523	H30/26R	1/53	4/65
TCR680	NUO 680	AEC Regal IV	9822S1624	Willowbrook	53094	C41F	6/53	3/61
TCR681	NUO 681	AEC Regal IV	9822S1625	Willowbrook	53096	C41F	6/53	3/61
TCR682	NUO 682	AEC Regal IV	9822S1626	Willowbrook	53095	C41F	6/53	3/61
TCR683	NUO 683	AEC Regal IV	9822S1627	Willowbrook	53097	C41F	6/53	6/61
TCR684	NUO 684	AEC Regal IV	9822S1628	Willowbrook	53098	C41F	6/53	4/61
TCR685	NUO 685	AEC Regal IV	9822S1629	Willowbrook	53099	C41F	6/53	6/61
TCR686	NUO 686	AEC Regal IV	9822S1630	Willowbrook	53100	C41F	6/53	7/61
TCR687	NUO 687	AEC Regal IV	9822S1631	Willowbrook	53101	C41F	6/53	7/61
TCR688	NUO 688	AEC Regal IV	9822S1632	Willowbrook	53102	C41F	6/53	6/61
TCR689	NUO 689	AEC Regal IV	9822S1633	Willowbrook	53103	C41F	6/53	3/62
TCR690	NUO 690	AEC Regal IV	9822S1634	Willowbrook	53104	C41F	6/53	3/62
TCR691	NUO 691	AEC Regal IV	9822S1635	Willowbrook	53105	C41F	6/53	3/62

Notes:
NTT 679 (DR679): Fitted with the prototype Aurora body, exhibited at the 1952 Commercial Motor Show in London Transport style Devon General livery; repainted into standard livery prior to entry into service.
NUO 680-691 (TCR680-691): Were 30ft long x 7ft 6in wide and in Grey Cars livery.
NUO 682 (TCR682): Repainted in Townsend livery following the acquisition of the Townsend's Coaches business in 1954; repainted back into Grey Cars livery 1958.

Disposals:
NTT 679 (DR679): Transport (Passenger Equipment) Ltd (dealer), Macclesfield 5/65; TD Edmunds, Rassau (MH) 7/65; becoming Edmunds Omnibus Services Ltd, Rassau (MH) 6/66; withdrawn 12/66; D Drinnan, Exeter for preservation 2/67; R Greet, Broadhempston for preservation 6/93; ; operated as a psv on an irregular basis between 5/01 and 11/03 as R Greet, Broadhempston and between 11/03 and 12/11 as Nostalgic Transport Ltd, Broadhempston (DN); still owned 1/15.
NUO 680 (TCR680): Greenslades Tours Ltd, Exeter (DN) 3/61; withdrawn 1963; Lansdowne Luxury Coaches Ltd (dealer), Frating 1/64; HAC Claireaux {CJ Partridge & Son}, Hadleigh (WF) 1/64; Blackwell (dealer), Earls Colne 4/66; in use as a storeshed by 7/73; S Gilkes, Chislehurst for preservation 7/85; S Gilkes & Rudkin, Chislehurst for preservation 8/85; unidentified preservation group Horsham 1/88; D Rollinson (Bus Centre) Ltd (dealer), Carlton for scrap 2/88.
NUO 681 (TCR681): Greenslades Tours Ltd, Exeter (DN) 3/61; withdrawn 1964; Lansdowne Luxury Coaches Ltd (dealer), Frating 11/64; Lefkaritis Bros Ltd, Larnarca (O-CY) 12/64; re-registered TCM 598 2/65; withdrawn 6/71; derelict until destroyed by fire 7/84.
NUO 682 (TCR682): Greenslades Tours Ltd, Exeter (DN) 3/61; withdrawn 1965; Lansdowne Luxury Coaches Ltd (dealer), Frating 11/65; Lefkaritis Bros Ltd, Larnarca (O-CY) 12/65; re-registered TCU 654 2/66; withdrawn by 10/72; derelict until destroyed by fire 7/84.
NUO 683 (TCR683): Greenslades Tours Ltd, Exeter (DN) 6/61; withdrawn 1964; Lansdowne Luxury Coaches Ltd (dealer), Frating 11/64; Vines Luxury Coaches Ltd, Great Bromley (EX) 11/64; Shaw & Kilburn (dealer), London W3 10/67; RW Denyer {Denyer Bros}, Brentwood (EX) 5/68; not operated; noted there derelict 7/73; still there 3/01.
NUO 684 (TCR684): Greenslades Tours Ltd, Exeter (DN) 4/61; withdrawn 1963; AG Bowerman Ltd {Bowerman's Tours}, Taunton (SO) 3/64; Kingdom's Tours Ltd {Tivvy Coaches}, Tiverton (DN) 1/65; DP Gourd, Bishopsteignton (DN) 4/67; A, J & K Millman, Buckfastleigh (DN) 4/68; EJ Deeble & Son, Upton Cross (CO) 3/69; Ninestones Riding School, Liskeard (XCO) by 3/75; D Sayer, Halifax for preservation 7/79; Wombwell Diesels Co Ltd (dealer), Wombwell for scrap 10/80.
NUO 685 (TCR685): Greenslades Tours Ltd, Exeter (DN) 6/61; withdrawn 1964; Lansdowne Luxury Coaches Ltd (dealer), Frating 11/64; AC Peck {Cedric Coaches}, Wivenhoe (EX) 11/64; EJ Deeble & Son, Upton Cross (CO) 6/66; RK & RE Webber {Webber Bros}, Blisland (CO) 5/71; withdrawn 8/71; returned to EJ Deeble & Son, Upton Cross (CO) 8/72.

NUO 686 (TCR686): Greenslades Tours Ltd, Exeter (DN) 7/61; withdrawn 1963; AG Bowerman Ltd {Bowerman's Tours}, Taunton (SO) 3/64; Kingdom's Tours Ltd {Tivvy Coaches}, Tiverton (DN) 1/65; Ascough (dealer), Dublin 2/66; Richardson's Fertilisers, Belfast (XAM) 5/66.

NUO 687 (TCR687): Greenslades Tours Ltd, Exeter (DN) 7/61; withdrawn 1965; Lansdowne Luxury Coaches Ltd (dealer), Frating 11/65; Lefkaritis Bros Ltd, Larnaca (O-CY) 12/65; re-registered TCU 656 2/66; withdrawn by10/72, derelict until destroyed by fire 7/84.

NUO 688 (TCR688): Greenslades Tours Ltd, Exeter (DN) 6/61; withdrawn 1963; SG Parnell {Seatax Coaches} Paignton (DN) 10/63; Dawlish Coaches Ltd, Dawlish (DN) 3/65; withdrawn 9/65; Lansdowne Luxury Coaches Ltd (dealer), Frating 9/65; M Ascough (dealer), Dublin 2/66; Cronin's Coaches Ltd, Cork (EI) by 8/67; re-registered MPI 624; withdrawn by 1973.

NUO 689 (TCR689): Greenslades Tours Ltd, Exeter (DN) 3/62; withdrawn 1964; Lansdowne Luxury Coaches Ltd (dealer), Frating 12/64; Vines Luxury Coaches Ltd, Great Bromley (EX) 12/64; Shaw & Kilburn (dealer), London W3 9/67; loaned to County Coaches, (Brentwood) Ltd, Brentwood (EX) 10/67; RW Denyer {Denyer Bros}, Stondon Massey (EX) 5/68; withdrawn 5/70; still there derelict 3/01.

NUO 690 (TCR690): Greenslades Tours Ltd, Exeter (DN) 3/62; not operated; AG Bowerman Ltd {Bowerman's Tours}, Taunton (SO) 5/62; Kingdom's Tours Ltd {Tivvy Coaches}, Tiverton (DN) 1/65; Dawlish Coaches Ltd {Tomlinson's}, Dawlish (DN) 1/66; DC Venner, Witheridge (DN) 3/66; LJ Hubber {Streamline Coaches}, Newquay (CO) 5/66; HG Brown & G Davies {Truronian Coaches}, Truro (CO) 5/68; withdrawn 6/70; Cornish Gliding & Flying Club, Perranporth (XCO) as a clubhouse by 8/72; J Orchard & Son (dealer), St Day for scrap 4/79.

NUO 691 (TCR691): Greenslades Tours Ltd, Exeter (DN) 3/62; withdrawn 1966; Lansdowne Luxury Coaches Ltd (dealer), Frating 4/66; Lefkaritis Bros Ltd, Larnaca (O-CY) 4/66; not operated; derelict until destroyed by fire 7/84.

Rebuilt vehicles:

DR714	DDV 420	AEC Rebuild	O6623300	Weymann	M6200	H32/26R	9/53	3/63
DR715	DDV 421	AEC Rebuild	O6623301	Weymann	M6190	H32/26R	7/53	3/63
DR716	DDV 446	AEC Rebuild	O6623326	Weymann	M6196	H32/26R	9/53	3/63
DR717	DOD 454	AEC Rebuild	O6623459	Weymann	M6193	H32/26R	7/53	3/63
DR718	DOD 455	AEC Rebuild	O6623458	Weymann	M6185	H32/26R	7/53	3/63
DR706	DUO 317	AEC Rebuild	O6623025	Weymann	M6195	H32/26R	9/53	3/63
DR707	DUO 319	AEC Rebuild	O6623027	Weymann	M6201	H32/26R	10/53	3/63
DR708	DUO 320	AEC Rebuild	O6623028	Weymann	M6198	H32/26R	9/53	3/63
DR709	DUO 321	AEC Rebuild	O6623029	Weymann	M6192	H32/26R	7/53	3/63
DR710	DUO 322	AEC Rebuild	O6623030	Weymann	M6199	H32/26R	9/53	3/63
DR711	DUO 327	AEC Rebuild	O6623035	Weymann	M6197	H32/26R	9/53	3/63
DR712	DUO 328	AEC Rebuild	O6623036	Weymann	M6189	H32/26R	7/53	3/63
DR713	DUO 329	AEC Rebuild	O6623037	Weymann	M6194	H32/26R	10/53	3/63
DR704	ETT 994	AEC Rebuild	O6622447	Weymann	M6191	H32/26R	7/53	3/63
DR705	ETT 995	AEC Rebuild	O6615343	Saunders-Roe	648	H30/26R	2/53	3/63

Notes:

With the exception of ETT 995 (see below), these vehicles were constructed from reconditioned Regent chassis frames acquired from ACV Sales Ltd, incorporating the engines and other parts from pre-war Regal chassis, the identities of which were retained and bodied as listed above. They were known as the 'Light Sixes' and it was originally intended to re-register them from NUO 680 upwards with fleet numbers DR680 etc. However these registrations were instead allocated to new Grey Cars Regal IV coaches (NUO 680-691) and an Ancillary Fleet van (NUO 692). The reconditioned chassis frames incorporated into these vehicles are unidentified, but are known to include those of RD 4773 (ex Reading Corporation) and BLH 718 (ex London Transport STL655). These vehicles were associated with Route 12 (Newton Abbot–Torquay–Brixham) until replaced by Atlanteans in 1959, when they became more widely scattered, although even then they rarely penetrated into the Exeter area or beyond

DUO 317 (DR706): Used as a driver trainer at Torquay for many years, although still used on passenger service.

ETT 995 (DR705): Was rebuilt incorporating the chassis frame from DTT 47 (DR234) and other parts from ETT 995 (XR403), which was then bodied by Saunders-Roe. It was delivered with fleet number DR681 and registered NUO 681 2/53, but was renumbered DR705 before entering service, and licensed as ETT 995. For a time the chassis number was shown as O6622448 (that of ETT 995) on the PSV licence.

Tram 38. In 1923 Torquay Tramways purchased two of these large Brush built bogie cars seating seventy-six. These cars had vestibule platforms yet retaining open-tops and, in company with a number of other cars, passed to Plymouth when the Torquay system closed in 1934. (The Omnibus Society)

T 8188 (1). Torquay Tramways began motor bus operations in response to the then competing, Devon General in 1920. The opening fleet consisting of eight of these AEC YC type, all of which had similar thirty-two seat bodies by Brush, a manufacturer who had already featured as a tramcar supplier. (The Omnibus Society)

TA 1006 (14). The following year, 1921, saw the delivery of six of these London General type AEC K type double-deckers. They only had a relatively short time in Devon, being traded in part exchange for newer vehicles in 1926 and then found their way into the London General Omnibus Co fleet, as additions to their K Class. (The Omnibus Society)

DV 9220 (184). Intended for use on 'express services' were ten of these AEC Regals delivered in 1931, the first of many to see service with Devon General. Their Park Royal bodies originally had seating for only twenty six, although later increased to thirty-two. (The Omnibus Society)

OD 1831 (36). During the 1930s single-deck orders comprised almost exclusively of AEC and Leyland models, this Leyland LT5 with Weymann body being one of the 1932 intake. Although their four cylinder engines were barely adequate for the hilly Devon General routes, many of this type were purchased in this period. (GHF Atkins, courtesy Simon J Butler)

OD 2260 (190). The first of many AEC Regent double-deckers to enter service were three with Brush lowbridge bodies new in 1931. Unlike other fleets in the area, lowbridge bodied double-deckers were always outnumbered by highbridge examples in the Devon General fleet. These three also had a short life in Devon, being sold off in 1937 and subsequently rebodied as coaches. (The Omnibus Society)

GC 4843-4844 (303-304). When the Grey Cars coach business was acquired from Timpson's, amongst the vehicles acquired were eighteen of these fine bonneted Harrington bodied AEC Mercury canvas-roofed coaches dating from 1930 and 1931. (Arthur Ingram)

OD 7487 (200). Replacements for the Torquay tramway system which closed in 1934, were twenty four of these AEC Regents with Short bodies, seen here in original pre-war condition. All were rebuilt and/or rebodied in the post-war period, some lasting after conversion to open-top, until replacement in the early 1960s. (Arthur Ingram)

OD 7491 (DR204). From the same batch as the vehicle in the previous photo, this one is seen in the post-war period after being rebodied by Brush in 1949. It went on to give another eight years service with Devon General before ending up as an ancillary vehicle. (The Omnibus Society, XLM Collection)

AOD 605 (342). Continuing the tradition of bonneted petrol engined coaches for touring work, 1936 saw the purchase of ten of these twenty-six seat Leyland Tigress coaches, which like earlier Grey Cars vehicles had bodies by Harrington with canvas opening roofs. (Roy Marshall Collection, Leyland Motors)

This line-up represents three examples from the largest single order ever placed by Devon General, for forty-eight Leyland LT7s with Harrington bodies delivered in 1936-1937, with CTA 84 (SL273) nearest the camera. They are depicted here in wartime, complete with headlight masks and white edging on wings and rear bodywork. (The Omnibus Society, CF Klapper)

CTT 660 (M360). This Bedford WTB with Birch body is the first of a pair new in 1937, originally delivered in a special livery with unglazed side windows for operation on a Torquay circular route which ran along the town's Marine Drive. After World War Two they were rebuilt as 'normal' buses, in which form this one is seen in service during the 1950s. (The Omnibus Society, RF Mack)

EUO 192 (M418). A second pair of Birch bodied Bedfords were taken into stock the following year, 1938, but this time based on the 2 ton WLG chassis. Originally used as small capacity station buses at Budleigh Salterton and Sidmouth, they were later re-seated to B20F as seen here. (The Omnibus Society, Surfleet)

DOD 468 (SR468). This AEC Regal with Weymann body is a representative of the final batch of single-deckers delivered to pre-war standards. It is seen here in the post-war period after, in company with several others from the same batch, it had been rebuilt by Longwell Green. (The Omnibus Society, AB Cross)

ETX 832 (DG318). This Guy Arab I, originally with utility bodywork, was one of a pair exchanged with Rhondda Transport for a pair of utility Daimler CWG5s new to Devon General in 1944. Like a number of other Guy Arabs new to Devon General these two were modernised with a lower mounted radiator and rebodied by Roe in 1954, as seen here. (The Omnibus Society, AB Cross)

GTT 425 (DG325). Unlike earlier wartime Guy Arabs, the 1945 Park Royal bodied batch retained their original Park Royal bodies through to withdrawal towards the end of the 1950s, albeit having been rebuilt by Longwell Green in the post-war period. This batch were notable in being delivered with the more powerful Gardner 6LW engine, which was much more suitable for the Devon hills. (The Omnibus Society)

HTT 332 (DR332). The first double-deck deliveries to post-war standards were eight AEC Regent III with chassis to London Transport RT specification, easily recognisable by their much lower bonnet line. The Weymann bodywork was similar to their post-war standard, of which many other examples were to follow. (The Omnibus Society, XLM Collection)

HTT 484 (SR484). The first post-war AEC Regal single-deckers, delivered towards the end of 1946, had chassis of similar specification to the final pre-war deliveries, but the Weymann bodywork was to a more austere design than the earlier vehicles. This vehicle was one of six exchanged with Leicester City Transport for double-deckers of similar vintage in 1952. (The Omnibus Society, XLM Collection)

HUO 538 (SR538). 1948 saw the delivery of a further batch of forty Regal/Weymann single-deckers, which were the last of this type to enter service. Because of a surplus of single-deckers in the 1950s this batch had a shorter than usual lifespan with the company. (The Omnibus Society, XLM Collection)

JOD 620 (TCR620). Twelve of these handsome AEC Regal III coaches with Duple coach bodies arrived in 1949, replacing pre-war coaches that had returned to service following the end of hostilities. This batch had a very short life with Devon General, as the whole batch were sold on to Western Welsh in 1952. (The Omnibus Society, AB Cross)

JUO 558 (DR558). The next double-deckers to arrive following the RT type AEC Regent III, were the first of several batches of standard Regent III/Weymann vehicles in 1948. (The Omnibus Society, Roy Marshall)

JUO 608 (TCB608). The first new coaches to enter service after the war were a batch of Bedford OB/ Duple Vistas of which this is an example that arrived in 1948. They were originally painted in Grey Cars livery, but following the arrival of newer coaches in the 1950s, were painted red and downgraded to bus work. (The Omnibus Society, AB Cross)

MTT 636 (SL636). The underfloor engined single-decker first appeared in the fleet in 1951, when five of these 7ft 6in wide Leyland PSU1/9s entered service. They were also the first Willowbrook bodied vehicles bought new, this manufacturer subsequently became a regular supplier of bodies during the 1950s and 1960s. (The Omnibus Society, Roy Marshall)

MTT 643 (DL643). Also purchased in 1951, alongside further AEC Regent III/Weymann double-deckers, were six of these Leyland bodied Leyland PD2/1s, intended for a particular route that required higher capacity vehicles but which had a height restriction. These were the only PD2s purchased new. (The Omnibus Society, Roy Marshall Collection)

DUO 327 (DR711). During 1953 and 1954 a total of twenty rebuilt vehicles entered service which were constructed from reconditioned second-hand AEC chassis frames, fitted with units from pre-war Regent and Regal chassis. Nineteen of the resultant chassis were fitted with new lightweight bodies by Weymann similar to this example. (The Omnibus Society)

DJF 330 (DR106). Six of these ex Leicester City Transport Regent II with Park Royal bodies of this 'relaxed utility' style, dating from early 1946, were acquired in exchange for six Regal/Weymann single-deckers in 1952. As seen here, they entered service still carrying Leicester livery. (The Omnibus Society, AB Cross)

PDV 693 (TCR693). The underfloor engined AEC Regal IV first entered the fleet in 1953, however this example dates from the following year and was one of six with Park Royal coach bodies in Grey Cars livery. Devon General continued to purchase 7ft 6in wide coaches throughout the 1950s as these were more suitable for the narrow roads on some tour routes. (The Omnibus Society, Peter Yeomans)

JOD 639 (TC737). When the Townsend of Torquay business was acquired in 1954, four Dennis Lancet IIIs with Dutfield bodies entered the fleet. Dennis was a manufacturer whose products had not featured in the Devon General fleet since 1926, apart from a batch of three earlier Lancet IIs bought in 1938. (The Omnibus Society)

ROD 750 (TCR750). By 1955 the AEC Regal IV had been superseded on the home market by the lighter Reliance. This example, one of two, was fitted with a Weymann Fanfare coach body of a style quite popular for a few years with several BET Group operators. (The Omnibus Society, Peter Yeomans)

TTT 790 (SC790). Another type to have a brief spell of popularity was the Beadle-Commer chassisless model, in this case with the less common, Beadle bus body dating from 1956. Until 1958 Devon General was unusual in specifying off-side cab doors for its underfloor engined single-deckers, as demonstrated by this vehicle. (The Omnibus Society, Roy Marshall)

XTA 845 (TCC845). Six further Beadle-Commer vehicles were delivered in 1958, but these had the quite stylish Rochester coach body and were in Grey Cars livery. The Rootes TS3 engines which powered these vehicles, although quite lively, was renowned for being noisy, which tended to somewhat lessen their appeal as a front-line coach. (The Omnibus Society, Peter Yeomans)

UO 2720 (19). Devon General operated the Fleet Cars business as a subsidiary following acquisition in 1924. Existing vehicles were replaced by a fleet of new Lancia coaches, capable of being driven at highly illegal speeds! This example with its open canvas roof, dating from 1927, demonstrates coaching style of a different era in this view, complete with its smartly attired driver. (The Omnibus Society)

Disposals:

DDV 420-421 (DR714-715): Transport (Passenger Equipment) Ltd (dealer), Macclesfield 10/63; S & JR Cubbins (dealer), Farnworth for scrap 1/64.

DDV 446 (DR716): Transport (Passenger Equipment) Ltd (dealer), Macclesfield 6/63; Berresford Motors Ltd, Cheddleton (ST) 50 7/63; withdrawn 1/65; Rush Green Motors (dealer), Codicote as an office 1967 ; W Hulme, Bristol for preservation by 11/08; moved to Yatton by 10/09; still at Rush Green Motors 1/15.

DDV 454-455 (DR717-718): Transport (Passenger Equipment) Ltd (dealer), Macclesfield 11/63; S & JR Cubbins (dealer), Farnworth for scrap 1/64.

DUO 317 (DR706): Transport (Passenger Equipment) Ltd (dealer), Macclesfield by 10/63; S & JR Cubbins (dealer), Farnworth for scrap 1/64.

DUO 319 (DR707): Transport (Passenger Equipment) Ltd (dealer), Macclesfield 8/63; S & JR Cubbins (dealer), Farnworth for scrap 1/64.

DUO 320 (DR708): Transport (Passenger Equipment) Ltd (dealer), Macclesfield 10/63; S & JR Cubbins (dealer), Farnworth for scrap 1/64.

DUO 321 (DR709): Transport (Passenger Equipment) Ltd (dealer), Macclesfield 8/63; S & JR Cubbins (dealer), Farnworth for scrap 1/64.

DUO 322 (DR710): Transport (Passenger Equipment) Ltd (dealer), Macclesfield 5/63; S & JR Cubbins (dealer), Farnworth for scrap 1/64.

DUO 327 (DR711): Transport (Passenger Equipment) Ltd (dealer), Macclesfield 9/63; S & JR Cubbins (dealer), Farnworth for scrap 1/64.

DUO 328 (DR712): Transport (Passenger Equipment) Ltd (dealer), Macclesfield 10/63; S & JR Cubbins (dealer), Farnworth for scrap 1/64.

DUO 329 (DR713): Transport (Passenger Equipment) Ltd (dealer), Macclesfield 9/63; S & JR Cubbins (dealer), Farnworth for scrap 1/64.

ETT 994 (DR704): Transport (Passenger Equipment) Ltd (dealer), Macclesfield by 10/63; Foster Wheeler John Brown Ltd (contractor), Tilbury 11/63.

ETT 995 (DR705): Transport (Passenger Equipment) Ltd (dealer), Macclesfield 11/63; Foster Wheeler John Brown Ltd (contractor), Tilbury 12/63; West of England Transport Collection, Winkleigh for preservation 8/68; S Cope, Longton for preservation 9/04; still owned 1/15.

Vehicle on loan from Leyland Motors Ltd:

OTC 738	Leyland PSUC1/1	515176	Saunders-Roe	B44F	6/52

Notes:

OTC 738: This vehicle was on demonstration during 6/53 and again from 7/53 until 8/53.

1954

New Vehicles:

TC743	POD 908	Bedford SBG	29139	Burlingham	4792	C36F	5/54	-/58
TCR692	PDV 692	AEC Regal IV	9822S1786	Park Royal	B37246	C41F	7/54	3/62
TCR693	PDV 693	AEC Regal IV	9822S1787	Park Royal	B37247	C41F	7/54	3/62
TCR694	PDV 694	AEC Regal IV	9822S1788	Park Royal	B37248	C41F	7/54	3/62
TCR695	PDV 695	AEC Regal IV	9822S1789	Park Royal	B37249	C41F	7/54	3/62
TCR696	PDV 696	AEC Regal IV	9822S1790	Park Royal	B37250	C41F	7/54	3/62
TCR697	PDV 697	AEC Regal IV	9822S1791	Park Royal	B37251	C41F	7/54	3/62
DR724	PDV 724	AEC Regent III	9613S8090	Weymann	M6462	H32/26RD	5/54	6/66
DR725	PDV 725	AEC Regent III	9613S8091	Weymann	M6454	H32/26RD	5/54	6/66
DR726	PDV 726	AEC Regent III	9613S8092	Weymann	M6453	H32/26RD	5/54	7/66
DR727	PDV 727	AEC Regent III	9613S8093	Weymann	M6459	H32/26RD	5/54	7/66
DR728	PDV 728	AEC Regent III	9613S8094	Weymann	M6455	H32/26RD	5/54	7/66
DR729	PDV 729	AEC Regent III	9613S8095	Weymann	M6460	H32/26RD	5/54	7/66
DR730	PDV 730	AEC Regent III	9613S8096	Weymann	M6463	H32/26RD	5/54	7/66
DR731	PDV 731	AEC Regent III	9613S8097	Weymann	M6461	H32/26RD	5/54	7/66
DR732	PDV 732	AEC Regent III	9613S8098	Weymann	M6458	H32/26RD	5/54	7/66
DR733	PDV 733	AEC Regent III	9613S8099	Weymann	M6452	H32/26RD	5/54	6/66
DR734	PDV 734	AEC Regent III	9613S8100	Weymann	M6456	H32/26RD	5/54	7/66
DR735	PDV 735	AEC Regent III	9613S8101	Weymann	M6457	H32/26RD	5/54	7/66

Notes:

Fleet number prefixes were removed on repaint from 2/62.

PDV 692-697 (TCR692-697): Were 30ft long x 7ft 6in wide and in Grey Cars livery.

PDV 724-735 (DR724-735): Renumbered DRD724-735 1957.
POD 908 (TC743): Ordered by Townsend, Torquay prior to takeover, but delivered direct to Devon
General in Townsend's grey and maroon livery; repainted into Grey Cars livery and
renumbered TCB743 1958

Disposals:
POD 908 (TC743): Percy D Sleeman Ltd (dealer), London W5 10/58; RT Tucker {Tomitax Coaches},
Melksham (WI) 6/59; withdrawn 5/68
PDV 692 (TCR692): Greenslades Tours Ltd, Exeter, (DN) 3/62; withdrawn 1965; Lansdowne Luxury
Coaches Ltd (dealer), Frating 11/65; Lefkaritis Bros Ltd, Larnarca (O-CY) 12/65; re-
registered TCU 655 2/66; withdrawn by 10/72; derelict until destroyed by fire 7/84.
PDV 693 (TCR693): Greenslades Tours Ltd, Exeter, (DN) 3/62; withdrawn 1965; Lansdowne Luxury
Coaches Ltd (dealer), Frating 12/65; Lefkaritis Bros Ltd, Larnarca (O-CY) 4/66; not operated;
derelict until destroyed by fire 7/84.
PDV 694 (TCR694): Greenslades Tours Ltd, Exeter, (DN) 3/62; withdrawn 1965; Lansdowne Luxury
Coaches Ltd (dealer), Frating 11/65; Lefkaritis (dealer), Larnarca (O-CY) 12/65; re-registered
TCU 658 2/66; withdrawn by 10/72; derelict until destroyed by fire 7/84.
PDV 695 (TCR695): Greenslades Tours Ltd, Exeter, (DN) 3/62; withdrawn 1965; Lansdowne Luxury
Coaches Ltd (dealer), Frating 11/65; Lefkaritis Bros Ltd, Larnarca (O-CY) 12/65; re-
registered TCU 657 2/66; withdrawn by 10/72; derelict until destroyed by fire 7/84.
PDV 696 (TCR696): Greenslades Tours Ltd, Exeter, (DN) 3/62; withdrawn 1966; Lansdowne Luxury
Coaches Ltd (dealer), Frating 4/66; Lefkaritis Bros Ltd, Larnarca (O-CY) 4/66; not operated;
derelict until destroyed by fire 7/84.
PDV 697 (TCR697): Greenslades Tours Ltd, Exeter, (DN) 3/62; withdrawn 1965; Lansdowne Luxury
Coaches Ltd (dealer), Frating 11/65; Lefkaritis Bros Ltd, Larnarca (O-CY) 12/65, re-
registered TCU 659 2/66; withdrawn by 10/72; derelict until destroyed by fire 7/84.
PDV 724 (724): Transport (Passenger Equipment) Ltd (dealer), Macclesfield 6/66; R Wesley & Sons,
Stoke Goldington (BK) 7/66; RJO & BR Watts {Prospect Coaches}, Stourbridge (WO) 6/72;
Lister PVS (Bolton) Ltd (dealer), Bolton 1/74; G Jameson {Dunscroft Commercials} (dealer),
Dunscroft 1/74.
PDV 725 (725): Transport (Passenger Equipment) Ltd (dealer), Macclesfield 7/66; Leon Motor Services
Ltd, Finningley (NG) 67 6/66; Transport (Passenger Equipment) Ltd (dealer), Macclesfield
1970; Wallace Driving School, Nottingham (XNG) 5/70.
PDV 726 (726): Transport (Passenger Equipment) Ltd (dealer), Macclesfield 7/66; F Cowley Ltd (dealer)
Salford 1966; Executors of Samuel Ledgard, Armley (WR) 9/66; to service 12/66; withdrawn
10/67; West Yorkshire Road Car Co Ltd, Harrogate (WR) 10/67; not operated; H & C
Transport Ltd, Garston (HT) 1/68; not operated; F Cowley Ltd (dealer), Dunchurch 12/69; R
Askin (dealer), Barnsley 12/69 (collected direct).
PDV 727 (727): Transport (Passenger Equipment) Ltd (dealer), Macclesfield 7/66; LJ & WB Ede {Roselyn
Coaches}, Par (CO) 9/66; G Jameson {Dunscroft Commercials} (dealer), Dunscroft by 4/74.
PDV 728 (728): Transport (Passenger Equipment) Ltd (dealer), Macclesfield 7/66; Hutfield's Coaches
(Gosport) Ltd (HA) 8/66; Grayline Coaches, Gosport (HA) at an unknown date; G Jameson
{Dunscroft Commercials} (dealer), Dunscroft 4/74.
PDV 729 (729): Transport (Passenger Equipment) Ltd (dealer), Macclesfield 7/66; Hutfield's Coaches
(Gosport) Ltd (HA) 8/66; scrapped following an accident 6/67.
PDV 730 (730): Transport (Passenger Equipment) Ltd (dealer), Macclesfield 7/66; JJ Longstaff & Sons
Ltd, Mirfield (WR) 8/66; withdrawn 11/69.
PDV 731 (731): Transport (Passenger Equipment) Ltd (dealer), Macclesfield 7/66; Leon Motor Services
Ltd, Finningley (NG) 69 8/66; A & HA Scutt, Owston Ferry (LI) 6/70; Mawle (farmer), West
Butterwick use and date unknown; J Sykes (dealer), Carlton for scrap 11/81.
PDV 732 (732): Transport (Passenger Equipment) Ltd (dealer), Macclesfield 7/66; F Cowley Ltd (dealer)
Salford 1966; Executors of Samuel Ledgard, Armley (WR) 9/66; to service 12/66; withdrawn
10/67; West Yorkshire Road Car Co Ltd, Harrogate (WR) 10/67; not operated; H & C
Transport Ltd, Garston (HT) 1/68; W Martin & Son, Weaverham (XCH) 5/71; A Barraclough
(dealer), Carlton for scrap 8/71.
PDV 733 (733): Transport (Passenger Equipment) Ltd (dealer), Macclesfield 7/66; W Stonier & Sons Ltd,
Goldenhill (ST) 11 7/66; withdrawn 1/71; W Norths (PV) Ltd (dealer), Sherburn in Elmet 1/71;
sold by 12/72.
PDV 734 (734): Transport (Passenger Equipment) Ltd (dealer), Macclesfield 7/66; Leon Motor Services
Ltd, Finningley (NG) 68 9/66; unidentified showman/dealer, Sandtoft 6/70.

PDV 735 (735): Transport (Passenger Equipment) Ltd (dealer), Macclesfield 7/66; AM & Mrs E Parkin {Luxicoaches}, Borrowash (DE) 13 7/66; withdrawn 12/72; Paul Sykes Organisation Ltd (dealer), Carlton 1/73.

Rebuilt vehicles:

DR719	DDV 422	AEC Rebuild	O6623302	Weymann	M6465	H32/26R	-/54	4/63
DR720	DDV 423	AEC Rebuild	O6623303	Weymann	M6464	H32/26R	-/54	3/63
DR721	DDV 424	AEC Rebuild	O6623304	Weymann	M6467	H32/26R	-/54	4/63
DR722	DDV 425	AEC Rebuild	O6623305	Weymann	M6468	H32/26R	-/54	3/63
DR723	DOD 469	AEC Rebuild	O6623447	Weymann	M6466	H32/26R	-/54	4/63

Notes:

These were further 'Light Six' lightweight rebuilds on reconditioned Regent chassis acquired from ACV Sales Ltd, using parts of the pre-war Regal chassis, the registration and chassis numbers of which were retained. They were bodied as listed above. These vehicles were distinguishable from the earlier lightweights by having deeper front mudgards and a ventilator set in the front dome over the front windows.

Disposals:

DDV 422 (DR719): Transport (Passenger Equipment) Ltd (dealer), Macclesfield 8/63; Berresfords Motors Ltd, Cheddleton (ST) 8/63.

DDV 423 (DR720): Transferred to Ancillary Fleet 3/63 (qv).

DDV 424 (DR721): Transport (Passenger Equipment) Ltd (dealer), Macclesfield 6/63; Berresfords Motors Ltd, Cheddleton (ST) 49 9/63; Transport (Passenger Equipment) Ltd (dealer), Macclesfield 6/66; Chris Hoyle & Son Ltd (dealer), Wombwell for scrap 6/66.

DDV 425 (DR722): Transport (Passenger Equipment) Ltd (dealer), Macclesfield 8/63; Berresfords Motors Ltd, Cheddleton (ST) 54 12/63; withdrawn 2/68.

DOD 469 (DR723): Transport (Passenger Equipment) Ltd (dealer), Macclesfield 8/63. Berresfords Motors Ltd, Cheddleton (ST) 55 2/64; withdrawn 9/67.

Vehicles on loan from ACV Sales Ltd:

7194 H	AEC Regent III	U163996	Park Royal	B36807	H32/28R	8/53
50 AMC	AEC Monocoach	U163452	Park Royal	B36802	B44F	7/53

Notes:

7194 H: Was on demonstration and operated in service during 1954.
50 AMC: Was on demonstration and operated in service during 1954.

Vehicle on loan from Guy Motors Ltd, Wolverhampton:

LJW 336	Guy Arab LUF	LUF71567	Saunders-Roe	B44F	-/53

Notes:

LJW 336: Had a Gardner 5HLW engine, was on demonstration and operated in service during 1954.

Vehicle on loan from John C Beadle (Coachbuilders) Ltd, Dartford:

RKR 120	Beadle Commer	JCB317	Beadle	C35C	10/53

Notes:

RKR 120: Had a Rootes TS3 engine, was on demonstration and operated in service during 1954.

Vehicles acquired from AE Townsend, Torquay (DN) 1/4/54:

TC736	JOD 638	Dennis Lancet III	393J3	Dutfield		C33F	6/48	-/57
TC737	JOD 639	Dennis Lancet III	439J3	Dutfield		C33F	7/48	-/57
TC738	KOD 116	Dennis Lancet III	608J3	Dutfield		C33F	6/49	-/57
TC739	KOD 117	Dennis Lancet III	620J3	Dutfield		C33F	5/49	-/57
TC740	MTA 567	TSM K6---	9619	Dutfield		FC33F	9/50	-/58
TC741	NTT 246	Bedford SB	5851	Duple	1006/497	C33F	11/51	-/58
TC742	OUO 587	Bedford SB	16254	Duple	1030/17	C35F	3/53	-/58

Notes:

These vehicles were acquired with the Townsend business; their previous histories are detailed in the Vehicles of Acquired Operators section.

A Bedford SBG on order at the time of the takeover, was delivered direct to Devon General as POD 908 (TC743) see above.

Townsend's grey and maroon livery was retained until 1958 when MTA 567 (TC740), NTT 246 (TC741) and OUO 587 (TC742) were repainted in Grey Cars livery, the remaining vehicles retained Townsend livery until withdrawal.

NTT 246 (TC741): Renumbered TCB741 1958
OUO 587 (TC742): Renumbered TCB742 1958

Disposals:
JOD 638 (TC736): F Cowley Ltd (dealer), Salford 10/57; Dew (contractor), Oldham (XLA) 68 at an unknown date; last licensed 11/62; R Askin (dealer), Barnsley for scrap 1962.

JOD 639 (TC737): F Cowley Ltd (dealer), Salford 10/57; Dew (contractor), Oldham (XLA) 69 at an unknown date; last licensed 12/61; S & JR Cubbins (dealer), Farnworth for scrap 5/62.

KOD 116 (TC738): F Cowley Ltd (dealer), Salford 10/57; Dew (contractor), Oldham (XLA) 67 at an unknown date, last licensed 1/62; S & JR Cubbins (dealer), Farnworth for scrap 5/62.

KOD 117 (TC739): "Lest We Forget", location unknown as an ambulance/invalid chair carrier 8/57; withdrawn 12/65.

MTA 567 (TC740): Percy D Sleeman Ltd (dealer), London W5 10/58; Wizard Fireworks Ltd, London E1 (XLN) 10/58; last licensed 11/61; AC Pond (dealer), Ipswich at an unknown date.

NTT 246 (TCB741): Percy D Sleeman Ltd (dealer), London W5 10/58; CM Perkins, Woodley (BE) 10/58; withdrawn 4/64; Nadder Valley Coaches Ltd, East Knowle (WI) 6/65; withdrawn 3/66; Dawlish Coaches Ltd, Dawlish (DN) 5/66; withdrawn 9/67; Southgate Coaches, London N11 (LN) 9/67; withdrawn 4/69.

OUO 587 (TCB742): Percy D Sleeman Ltd (dealer), London W5 10/58; L & D Pailthorpe {Grove Vale Coaches}, London SE22 (LN) 1/59; GT Marsh {Ansell's Coaches}, London SE5 (LN) 4/61; Tourist Coachways Ltd, Hounslow (MX) 1/64; Marchwood Motorways Ltd, Totton (HA) 9/65; withdrawn following accident 4/66.

Vehicles acquired from Balls Tours Ltd, Newton Abbot (DN) 9/54:

SB746	JDV 789	Bedford OB		67110	Mulliner	T170	B31F	12/47	n/a
SC745	KTT 44	Commer Commando		17A1113	Whitson		C29F	10/48	n/a
SB744	LTT 44	Bedford OB		115870	Mulliner	T485	B28F	9/49	n/a
TC747	LUO 444	Commer Avenger		23A0146	Harrington	643	C32F	12/49	-/57
TC748	MOD 44	Commer Avenger		23A0564	Heaver		C33C	5/51	-/57

Previous history:
These vehicles were acquired with the Balls Tours Ltd business; their previous histories are detailed in the Vehicles of Acquired Operators section.

Notes:
JDV 789 (SB 746) Not used by Devon General; stored until sale.
KTT 44 (SC 745): Not used by Devon General; stored until sale.
LTT 44 (SB744): Re-seated to B24F 1956.
LUO 444 (TC747): Repainted into Grey Cars livery.
MOD 44 (TC748): Repainted into Grey Cars livery.

Disposals:
JDV 789 (SB 746): Mitchley (dealer), Birmingham 8/56; not traced further.

KTT 44 (SC 745): Mitchley (dealer), Birmingham 8/56; AV Pugh {Castle Coaches}, Birmingham (WK) 7/57; R Bailey {Jubilee Coaches}, Sutton Coldfield (WK) 1958; GG Hewitt {Georgina Coaches}, Birmingham (WK) 9/58; Don Everall (dealer) Wolverhampton 8/59.

LTT 44 (SB744): Mitchley (dealer), Birmingham 9/56; Hall Green Coachways, Birmingham (WK) by 6/58; Jones Coachways Ltd, Market Drayton (SH) 69 2/59; sold to unknown owner as mobile shop by 9/62.

LUO 444 (TC747): F Cowley Ltd (dealer) Salford 10/57; AA Pitcher Ltd {Tantivy Motors}, St Helier, Jersey (CI) 12, re-registered J   991 re-seated to C35F 4/58; withdrawn 12/72; unidentified owner for preservation, Sandtoft by 5/73; Wombwell Diesels Co Ltd (dealer), Wombwell 7/73; noted in a garden at Wombwell 2/74; returned to Wombwell Diesels Co Ltd (dealer), Wombwell by 4/77; scrapped post-3/82.

MOD 44 (TC748): Millbrook Steamboat & Trading Co, Cremyll (CO) 10/57; Barnard & Barnard (dealer) London SE26 by 2/59.

1955

New Vehicles:

TCR749	ROD 749	AEC Reliance	MU3RV640	Weymann	M7016	C37F	5/55	2/64
TCR750	ROD 750	AEC Reliance	MU3RV641	Weymann	M7017	C37F	5/55	2/64
DR760	ROD 760	AEC Regent V	MD3RV031	MCCW		H33/26RD	12/55	9/68
DR770	ROD 770	AEC Regent V	MD3RV041	MCCW		H33/26R	12/55	10/68
DR771	ROD 771	AEC Regent V	MD3RV042	MCCW		H33/26R	12/55	4/68
DR772	ROD 772	AEC Regent V	MD3RV043	MCCW		H33/26R	12/55	10/68
DR773	ROD 773	AEC Regent V	MD3RV044	MCCW		H33/26R	12/55	5/68
DR774	ROD 774	AEC Regent V	MD3RV045	MCCW		H33/26R	12/55	9/68
DR775	ROD 775	AEC Regent V	MD3RV046	MCCW		H33/26R	12/55	5/68
DR776	ROD 776	AEC Regent V	MD3RV047	MCCW		H33/26R	12/55	12/68
DR778	ROD 778	AEC Regent V	MD3RV049	MCCW		H33/26R	12/55	4/68
DR779	ROD 779	AEC Regent V	MD3RV050	MCCW		H33/26R	12/55	12/68

Notes:

Fleet number prefixes were removed on repaint from 2/62.

ROD 749-750 (TCR749-750): Had 30ft 0in x 8ft 0in Fanfare style bodies for extended tours and were in Grey Cars livery.
ROD 760 (DR760): Renumbered DRD760 1957.

Disposals:

ROD 749 (TCR749): Greenslades Tours Ltd, Exeter (DN) 3/64; Lansdowne Luxury Coaches Ltd (dealer), Frating 2/68; Vines Luxury Coaches Ltd, Great Bromley (EX) 6/68; Luton Commercial Motors (dealer), Dunstable 9/68; MW Smaller {Mick Smaller's Luxury Coaches}, Barton-on-Humber (LI) 1 11/68; subsequently used by Smaller as a non-PSV at Anchor Steelworks, Scunthorpe at an unknown date; withdrawn 11/70.
ROD 750 (TCR750): Greenslades Tours Ltd, Exeter (DN) 3/64; Lansdowne Luxury Coaches Ltd (dealer), Frating 2/68; believed exported.
ROD 760 (760): Transport (Passenger Equipment) Ltd (dealer), Macclesfield 9/68; GC Brown, Warboys (CM) 9/68.
ROD 770 (770): Transport (Passenger Equipment) Ltd (dealer), Macclesfield 11/68; Stevensons of Uttoxeter Ltd, Spath (ST) for spares 12/68; Wombwell Diesels Co Ltd (dealer), Wombwell for scrap 12/68.
ROD 771 (771): Transport (Passenger Equipment) Ltd (dealer), Macclesfield 7/68; loaned to GH & GE Ellis, Buckley (FT) 9/68; returned to Transport (Passenger Equipment) Ltd (dealer), Macclesfield 12/68; A Pickersgill & Laverack (dealer), Carlton for scrap 3/69.
ROD 772 (772): Transport (Passenger Equipment) Ltd (dealer), Macclesfield 2/69; A Pickersgill & Laverack (dealer), Carlton for scrap 3/69.
ROD 773-774 (773-774): Transport (Passenger Equipment) Ltd (dealer), Macclesfield 1/69; S & JR Cubbins (dealer), Farnworth for scrap 1/69.
ROD 775 (775): Transport (Passenger Equipment) Ltd (dealer), Macclesfield 2/69; Service Coaches Ltd, Bebside (ND) 4/69; Willoughby (dealer), Ashington for scrap 9/72.
ROD 776 (776): Transport (Passenger Equipment) Ltd (dealer), Macclesfield 2/69; Service Coaches Ltd, Bebside (ND) 4/69; withdrawn 5/70.
ROD 778 (778): Transport (Passenger Equipment) Ltd (dealer), Macclesfield 5/68; Wombwell Diesels Co Ltd (dealer), Wombwell 11/68; Chris Hoyle & Son Ltd (dealer), Wombwell for scrap 11/68.
ROD 779 (779): Transport (Passenger Equipment) Ltd (dealer), Macclesfield 2/69; Ashington and District Luxury Coaches Ltd, Bedlington (ND) 6/69; Hancock & Turner (dealer), Bedlington for scrap 1/70.

Vehicle acquired from HD Gourd & Sons, Bishopsteignton (DN) 1/55:

ETG 295	Bedford WTB		20016	Willmott	C20F	8/39	n/a

Previous history:

ETG 295: New to DT & EA Stephens, Cwmavon (GG); E Thomas {Morning Star}, Nelson (GG) at an unknown date; RJW Welsford & WH Johnson {Johnson's Motors}, Rushden (NO) by 8/47; from whom it was acquired by Gourd at an unknown date; acquired with the Gourd stage services; not used by Devon General.

Disposal:

ETG 295: Kirton (dealer), Torquay for scrap 6/57.

Vehicle on loan from Leyland Motors Ltd, Leyland:

STF 90	Leyland Lowloader	530001	Saunders-Roe	H37/24R	4/54

Notes:

STF 90: On demonstration during 3/55.

Vehicle on loan from ACV Sales Ltd, Southall:

88 CMV	Crossley Regent V	CMD3RV001	Park Royal	B37223	H33/28R	10/54

Notes:

88 CMV: On demonstration during 1955.

1956

New vehicles:

TCC751	ROD 751	Beadle-Commer	JCB647	Beadle	C41F	3/56	2/64
TCC752	ROD 752	Beadle-Commer	JCB648	Beadle	C41F	3/56	2/64
TCC753	ROD 753	Beadle-Commer	JCB649	Beadle	C41F	3/56	2/64
TCC754	ROD 754	Beadle-Commer	JCB650	Beadle	C41F	3/56	2/64
TCC755	ROD 755	Beadle-Commer	JCB651	Beadle	C41F	4/56	2/64
TCC756	ROD 756	Beadle-Commer	JCB652	Beadle	C41F	4/56	2/64
SC757	ROD 757	Beadle-Commer	JCB653	Beadle	B40F	6/56	10/63
SC758	ROD 758	Beadle-Commer	JCB654	Beadle	B40F	6/56	2/67
SC759	ROD 759	Beadle-Commer	JCB655	Beadle	B40F	6/56	2/67
DR761	ROD 761	AEC Regent V	MD3RV032	MCCW	H33/26RD	1/56	4/68
DR762	ROD 762	AEC Regent V	MD3RV033	MCCW	H33/26RD	1/56	4/68
DR763	ROD 763	AEC Regent V	MD3RV034	MCCW	H33/26RD	2/56	4/68
DR764	ROD 764	AEC Regent V	MD3RV035	MCCW	H33/26RD	2/56	5/68
DR765	ROD 765	AEC Regent V	MD3RV036	MCCW	H33/26RD	2/56	5/68
DR766	ROD 766	AEC Regent V	MD3RV037	MCCW	H33/26RD	2/56	3/68
DR767	ROD 767	AEC Regent V	MD3RV038	MCCW	H33/26RD	2/56	4/68
DR768	ROD 768	AEC Regent V	MD3RV039	MCCW	H33/26RD	2/56	4/68
DR769	ROD 769	AEC Regent V	MD3RV040	MCCW	H33/26RD	3/56	9/68
DR777	ROD 777	AEC Regent V	MD3RV048	MCCW	H33/26R	1/56	4/68
DR780	TTT 780	AEC Regent V	MD3RV218	MCCW	H33/26RD	7/56	4/68
DR781	TTT 781	AEC Regent V	MD3RV219	MCCW	H33/26RD	7/56	4/68
DR782	TTT 782	AEC Regent V	MD3RV220	MCCW	H33/26RD	7/56	4/68
DR783	TTT 783	AEC Regent V	MD3RV221	MCCW	H33/26RD	7/56	7/68
DR784	TTT 784	AEC Regent V	MD3RV222	MCCW	H33/26RD	7/56	1/71
DR785	TTT 785	AEC Regent V	MD3RV223	MCCW	H33/26RD	7/56	1/71
DR786	TTT 786	AEC Regent V	MD3RV224	MCCW	H33/26RD	7/56	1/71
DR787	TTT 787	AEC Regent V	MD3RV225	MCCW	H33/26RD	7/56	1/71
DR788	TTT 788	AEC Regent V	MD3RV226	MCCW	H33/26RD	7/56	10/69
DR789	TTT 789	AEC Regent V	MD3RV227	MCCW	H33/26RD	7/56	10/69
SC790	TTT 790	Beadle-Commer	JCB686	Beadle	B40F	6/56	2/67
SC791	TTT 791	Beadle-Commer	JCB687	Beadle	B40F	6/56	2/67
SC792	TTT 792	Beadle-Commer	JCB688	Beadle	B40F	6/56	10/66

Notes:

Fleet number prefixes were removed on repaint from 2/62.

ROD 751-754 (TCC751-754): Were 30ft long x 7ft 6in wide, had Rootes TS3 engines and bodywork of similar style to the 1953-1954 Regal IV coaches. They were originally in Townsend's livery, being repainted into Grey Cars livery 1958

ROD 755-756 (TCC755-756): Were 30ft long x 7ft 6in wide and in Grey Cars livery, had Rootes TS3 engines and bodywork of similar style to the 1953-1954 Regal IV coaches.

ROD 757-759 (SC757-759): Had Rootes TS3 engines and were 7ft 6in wide.

ROD 761-769 (DR761-769): Renumbered DRD761-769 1957.

TTT 780-789 (DR780-789): Renumbered DRD780-789 1957.

TTT 790-792 (SC790-792): Had Rootes TS3 engines and were 7ft 6in wide.

Disposals:

ROD 751 (TCC751): Transport (Passenger Equipment) Ltd (dealer), Macclesfield 4/64; HFJ Cheek {Starline}, North Harrow (MX) 5/64; Inns of Court & Gainsford Boys Club, London WC2 (XLN) by 5/70; Luton Commercial Motors (dealer), Dunstable by 9/70; Weaton Commercials (dealer), London SW1 for scrap 10/70.

ROD 752 (TCC752): Transport (Passenger Equipment) Ltd (dealer), Macclesfield 5/64; HFJ Cheek {Starline}, North Harrow (MX) 6/64; Luton Commercial Motors (dealer), Dunstable 1970; J Thorpe {Link-Line Coaches}, London NW10 (LN) 1970; not operated; Alf Moseley & Son Ltd (dealer), Loughborough by 10/70; Cedric Contracts Ltd, Wivenhoe (XEX) 1/71; scrapped 5/71.

ROD 753 (TCC753): Percy D Sleeman Ltd (dealer), London W5 3/64; Ronsway Coaches Ltd, Hemel Hempstead (HT) 3/64; T Murray, Corby (NO) 9/64; Alf Moseley & Son Ltd (dealer) Loughborough 9/65; Nadder Valley Coaches Ltd, East Knoyle (WI) 3/66; HFJ Cheek {Starline}, North Harrow (MX) 6/68; Luton Commercial Motors (dealer), Dunstable 1/72; Mark Autos (dealer), London W4 1/72.

ROD 754 (TCC754): Transport (Passenger Equipment) Ltd (dealer), Macclesfield 5/64; WJ Hall, Blackwood (MH) 8/64; withdrawn 3/67; derelict on premises of Marshall (dealer), Nantyglo 1967.

ROD 755 (TCC755): Percy D Sleeman Ltd (dealer), London W5 3/64; JS Thorpe {Link-Line Coaches}, London NW10 (LN) 3/64; JS Teague, Burnt Oak (MX) 6/65; J, J & H Jones, Leighton Buzzard as a car transporter 9/66.

ROD 756 (TCC756): Percy D Sleeman Ltd (dealer), London W5 3/64; JJ & ML Jones {Audawn Coaches} Corringham (EX) 3/64; RG & A Salmons, Corringham (EX) 10/65; JS Thorpe {Link-Line Coaches}, London NW10 (LN) 5/66; Luton Commercial Motors (dealer), Dunstable 6/66; JG Motors, Linslade (XBK) as racing car transporter 7/66; J Markey, London (XLN) as racing car transporter 1968; Newbridge Racing, Romsey (XHA) as racing car transporter by 4/73.

ROD 757 (SC757): Broken up after collision with Western National Omnibus Co Ltd, Exeter (DN) Bristol LS6G VDV 749 (2206) 10/63; remains to T Carpenter (dealer), Exeter 11/63.

ROD 758 (SC758): Transport (Passenger Equipment) Ltd (dealer), Macclesfield 3/67; G Pooley {Pamela Coaches}, Long Sutton (HD) 3/68; withdrawn 9/70; scrapped 1/76.

ROD 759 (SC759): Transport (Passenger Equipment) Ltd (dealer), Macclesfield 2/67; Wombwell Diesels Co Ltd (dealer), Wombwell for scrap 9/69.

ROD 761 (761): Transport (Passenger Equipment) Ltd (dealer), Macclesfield 5/68; Stephens {Crew Mini Cabs}, Crewe (CH) 8/68; Martin & Sons Ltd (dealer), Weaverham 3/69; WE Robinson {Streamline Coaches}, Wigan (LA) 3/69; returned to Martin & Sons Ltd (dealer), Weaverham 6/73.

ROD 762 (762): Transport (Passenger Equipment) Ltd (dealer), Macclesfield 5/68; F Smith, Long Itchington (WK) 8/68; Mellor's Coaches Ltd, Goxhill (LI) 2/72; withdrawn 6/75.

ROD 763 (763): Transport (Passenger Equipment) Ltd (dealer), Macclesfield 5/68; R Bailey {Jubilee Coaches}, Marston Green (WK) 5/68; K Wren & CE Ellis {Ellren Coaches}, Water Orton (WK) 2/70; Lister PVS (Bolton) Ltd (dealer), Bolton 3/71; Paul Sykes Organisation Ltd (dealer), Barnsley for scrap 5/71.

ROD 764 (764): Transport (Passenger Equipment) Ltd (dealer), Macclesfield 9/68; P & O Lloyd Ltd, Bagillt (FT) 9/68, withdrawn 7/71; Paul Sykes Organisation Ltd (dealer), Barnsley for scrap 1974.

ROD 765 (765): Transport (Passenger Equipment) Ltd (dealer), Macclesfield 9/68; Red Rover Omnibus Ltd, Aylesbury (BK) 9 10/68; renumbered 109 4/77; withdrawn 1/78; Moseley Group (PSV) Ltd (dealer), Loughborough 1/78; sold for use as a mobile commentary post at Atnho, Near Banbury 2/78; S Gilkes, Chislehurst for preservation 3/88; A Blackman Jnr, Halifax for preservation 8/90; moved to Newton Abbot by 8/07; M Wright, Cottingham for preservation 8/13.

ROD 766 (766): Transport (Passenger Equipment) Ltd (dealer), Macclesfield 5/68; FB Ellis, Llangefni (AY) 9/68; unknown dealer, Carlton for scrap 9/72.

ROD 767 (767): Transport (Passenger Equipment) Ltd (dealer), Macclesfield 5/68; Reliance Motor Services (Newbury) Ltd (BE) 125 7/68; Peskett (dealer), Grayshott 12/77; Norwich Playbus (XNK) 3/78; painted yellow and named 'Rod the Bus'; CJ Shears & P Platt, , Winkleigh for preservation project 11/96; G Davies, Llanelli as spares for preservation 11/96; South Wales Transport Preservation Trust for spares by10/11.

ROD 768 (768): Transport (Passenger Equipment) Ltd (dealer), Macclesfield 7/68; (loaned to?) F Smith, Long Itchington (WK) 8/68; returned to Transport (Passenger Equipment) Ltd (dealer), Macclesfield 8/68; Lamcote Motors (Radcliffe) Ltd, Radcliffe-on-Trent (NG) 1/69; A Pickersgill & Laverack (dealer) Barnsley for scrap 8/71; J Sykes (dealer), Blackerhill for scrap 1971.

ROD 769 (769): Transport (Passenger Equipment) Ltd (dealer), Macclesfield 1968; Hadleys Ltd, Quarry Bank (ST) 12/68; withdrawn 10/73.

ROD 777 (777): Transport (Passenger Equipment) Ltd (dealer), Macclesfield 2/69; P Sheffield, Cleethorpes (LI) 10/69; Wombwell Diesels Co Ltd (dealer), Wombwell 11/69; Chris Hoyle & Son Ltd (dealer), Wombwell for scrap 11/69.

TTT 780 (780): Transport (Passenger Equipment) Ltd (dealer), Macclesfield 7/68; Stevensons of Uttoxeter Ltd, Spath (ST) 3 9/68; renumbered 3A 10/77; converted to tree-lopper/towing vehicle 12/77; renumbered 05 2/81; G Bloor (dealer) Spath for scrap 6/82.

TTT 781 (781): Transport (Passenger Equipment) Ltd (dealer), Macclesfield 7/68; Reliance Motor Services (Newbury) Ltd (BE) 126 7/68; Peskett (dealer), Grayshott 12/77; Page, Ascot (XBE) as promotional vehicle at an unknown date; West of England Transport Collection, Winkleigh for preservation by 4/88; R Greet, Broadhempston for preservation 6/96; R Cooper, Burnley for preservation 10/98; L Blackman, Halifax for preservation 8/03; A Blackman, Halifax (WY) 4/06; moved to Luddendenfoot by 9/14; still owned 1/15.

TTT 782 (782): Transport (Passenger Equipment) Ltd (dealer), Macclesfield 7/68; PW Cherry & Sons, Beverley (EY) 8/68; withdrawn 1970; Transport (Passenger Equipment) Ltd (dealer), Macclesfield 11/69; Wombwell Diesels Co Ltd (dealer), Wombwell 11/69; Chris Hoyle & Son Ltd (dealer), Wombwell for scrap 2/70.

TTT 783 (783): Transport (Passenger Equipment) Ltd (dealer), Macclesfield 7/68; Hadleys Ltd, Quarry Bank (ST) 8/68; Ward (dealer), Middlestown 7/74.

TTT 784-785 (784-785): Western National Omnibus Co Ltd, Exeter (DN) 784 1/71; not used; W Norths (PV) Ltd (dealer), Sherburn in Elmet 4/71; unidentified dealer for scrap by 8/72.

TTT 786 (786): Western National Omnibus Co Ltd, Exeter (DN) 786 1/71; not used; W Norths (PV) Ltd (dealer), Sherburn in Elmet 4/71; unidentified dealer for scrap 12/75.

TTT 787 (787): Western National Omnibus Co Ltd, Exeter (DN) 787 1/71; not used; Rundle (dealer), Plymouth for scrap 5/71.

TTT 788 (788): Transport (Passenger Equipment) Ltd (dealer), Macclesfield 10/69; Bedlington & District Luxury Coaches Ltd, Ashington (ND) 1/70; Hancock & Turner (dealer), Lynmouth for scrap by 11/72.

TTT 789 (789): Transport (Passenger Equipment) Ltd (dealer), Macclesfield 10/69; JD Andrew Ltd; Sheffield (WY) 2/70; G & G Coaches (Leamington) Ltd, Leamington Spa (WK) 7/71; withdrawn 10/72; F & JI Smith, Long Itchington (WK) 12/72; R Catherall, Southam (WK) 7/75; withdrawn 7/75; Sherman (dealer) Coventry c1/76; still there 1/82; chassis to R Holladay, Aylesbeare as spares for preservation project by 12/95 for spares; remains scrapped 4/97.

TTT 790 (SC790): Transport (Passenger Equipment) Ltd (dealer), Macclesfield 3/67; Clynnog & Trevor Motor Co Ltd, Trefor (CN) 11/67; withdrawn 1971; sold by 12/71.

TTT 791 (SC791): Transport (Passenger Equipment) Ltd (dealer), Macclesfield 1967; Clynnog & Trevor Motor Co Ltd, Trefor (CN) 4/68; withdrawn 1970; sold by 5/70.

TTT 792 (SC792): Transport (Passenger Equipment) Ltd (dealer), Macclesfield 1967; Clynnog & Trevor Motor Co Ltd, Trefor (CN) 7/67; Mason & Nicholson (contractor), Porthmadog (XCN) 1/71; noted in use as site hut, Criccieth 1973; scrapped by 8/76.

1957

New Vehicles:

SR793	VDV 793	AEC Reliance	MU3RA1410	Weymann	M8016	B41F	7/57	1/71
SR794	VDV 794	AEC Reliance	MU3RA1411	Weymann	M8023	B41F	7/57	4/69
SR795	VDV 795	AEC Reliance	MU3RA1412	Weymann	M8022	B41F	7/57	4/69
SR796	VDV 796	AEC Reliance	MU3RA1420	Weymann	M8020	B41F	7/57	4/69
SR797	VDV 797	AEC Reliance	MU3RA1414	Weymann	M8021	B41F	7/57	4/69
SR798	VDV 798	AEC Reliance	MU3RA1415	Weymann	M8018	B41F	7/57	1/71
SR799	VDV 799	AEC Reliance	MU3RA1421	Weymann	M8017	B41F	7/57	1/71
SR800	VDV 800	AEC Reliance	MU3RA1423	Weymann	M8019	B41F	7/57	4/69
SR801	VDV 801	AEC Reliance	MU3RA1418	Weymann	M8011	B41F	7/57	4/69
SR802	VDV 802	AEC Reliance	MU3RA1419	Weymann	M8014	B41F	7/57	4/69
SR803	VDV 803	AEC Reliance	MU3RA1413	Weymann	M8012	B41F	7/57	4/69
SR804	VDV 804	AEC Reliance	MU3RA1416	Weymann	M8013	B41F	7/57	4/69
SR805	VDV 805	AEC Reliance	MU3RA1422	Weymann	M8010	B41F	7/57	4/69
SR806	VDV 806	AEC Reliance	MU3RA1417	Weymann	M8015	B41F	7/57	4/69
DR807	VDV 807	AEC Regent V	MD3RV311	MCCW		H33/26R	7/57	1/71
DR808	VDV 808	AEC Regent V	MD3RV312	MCCW		H33/26R	7/57	1/71
DR809	VDV 809	AEC Regent V	MD3RV313	MCCW		H33/26R	7/57	1/71
DR810	VDV 810	AEC Regent V	MD3RV314	MCCW		H33/26R	7/57	1/71

DR811	VDV 811	AEC Regent V	MD3RV315	MCCW		H33/26R	7/57	1/71
DR812	VDV 812	AEC Regent V	MD3RV316	MCCW		H33/26R	7/57	1/71
DR813	VDV 813	AEC Regent V	MD3RV317	MCCW		H33/26R	7/57	1/71
DR814	VDV 814	AEC Regent V	MD3RV318	MCCW		H33/26R	7/57	1/71
DR815	VDV 815	AEC Regent V	MD3RV319	MCCW		H33/26R	7/57	1/71
DR816	VDV 816	AEC Regent V	MD3RV320	MCCW		H33/26R	7/57	1/71
DR817	VDV 817	AEC Regent V	MD3RV321	MCCW		H33/26R	7/57	1/71
DR818	VDV 818	AEC Regent V	MD3RV322	MCCW		H33/26R	7/57	1/71
DR819	VDV 819	AEC Regent V	MD3RV323	MCCW		H33/26R	7/57	1/71

Notes:

Fleet number prefixes were removed on repaint from 2/62.

VDV 801-806 (SR801-806): Had opening roof hatches.

Disposals:

VDV 793 (793): Western National Omnibus Co Ltd, Exeter 793 1/71; withdrawn 11/72; unidentified dealer 2/73; Solway Pre-Cast Concrete, Creetown (XKK) 8/74; sold for scrap 1981.

VDV 794 (794): Transport (Passenger Equipment) Ltd (dealer), Macclesfield 5/69; Premier Travel Ltd, Cambridge (CM) 201 9/69; unidentified dealer, Bury St Edmunds 2/78; Askin (dealer), Barnsley 9/78.

VDV 795 (795): Transport (Passenger Equipment) Ltd (dealer), Macclesfield 5/69; Premier Travel Ltd, Cambridge (CM) 203 10/69; withdrawn 11/74.

VDV 796 (796): Transport (Passenger Equipment) Ltd (dealer), Macclesfield 5/69; Premier Travel Ltd, Cambridge (CM) 199 7/69; withdrawn 2/77; P Platt, Exeter (preservationist) as spares for VDV 798 6/77; moved to Dawlish Warren 9/11; still owned 1/15.

VDV 797 (797): Transport (Passenger Equipment) Ltd (dealer), Macclesfield 5/69; Premier Travel Ltd, Cambridge (CM) 197 7/69; withdrawn 1976. Thetford ATC, Thetford (XNK) 9/76.

VDV 798 (798): Western National Omnibus Co Ltd, Exeter 798 1/71; withdrawn 11/72; W Norths (PV) Ltd (dealer) Sherburn in Elmet 4/71; TI & WG Richards, Moylgrove (PE) 7/71; West of England Transport Collection, Winkleigh for preservation 12/75; 798 Group, Exeter for preservation by 4/88; P Platt, Exeter for preservation by 10/07; moved to Dawlish Warren 9/11; still owned 1/15.

VDV 799 (799): Western National Omnibus Co Ltd, Exeter 799 1/71; withdrawn 11/72; Rundle (dealer), Plymouth for scrap 2/73.

VDV 800 (800): Transport (Passenger Equipment) Ltd (dealer), Macclesfield 5/69; Premier Travel Ltd, Cambridge (CM) 204 10/69; withdrawn 11/73.

VDV 801 (801): Western National Omnibus Co Ltd, Exeter 801 1/71; withdrawn 11/72; Rundle (dealer), Plymouth for scrap 2/73.

VDV 802 (802): Transport (Passenger Equipment) Ltd (dealer), Macclesfield 5/69; Brown & Jackson (contractor), Fleetwood (XLA) 9/69; Transport (Passenger Equipment) Ltd (dealer), Macclesfield 7/73; Wombwell Diesels Co Ltd (dealer) Wombwell for scrap 8/73.

VDV 803 (803): Transport (Passenger Equipment) Ltd (dealer), Macclesfield 5/69; Premier Travel Ltd, Cambridge (CM) 200 9/69; withdrawn 8/75.

VDV 804 (804): Transport (Passenger Equipment) Ltd (dealer), Macclesfield 10/69; Premier Travel Ltd, Cambridge (CM) 205 1/70; withdrawn 1975; Harris (dealer), Hunstanton for scrap 1976.

VDV 805 (805): Transport (Passenger Equipment) Ltd (dealer), Macclesfield 5/69; Premier Travel Ltd, Cambridge (CM) 198 7/69; withdrawn 7/75.

VDV 806 (806): Transport (Passenger Equipment) Ltd (dealer), Macclesfield 5/69; Premier Travel Ltd, Cambridge (CM) 202 2/69; withdrawn 10/74;Smith (dealer), Thriplow for scrap 1974.

VDV 807 (807): Western National Omnibus Co Ltd, Exeter 807 1/71; withdrawn 1/71; W Norths (PV) Ltd (dealer) Sherburn in Elmet 4/71; unidentified dealer for scrap 5/73.

VDV 808 (808): Western National Omnibus Co Ltd, Exeter 808 1/71; withdrawn 2/71; Rundle (dealer), Plymouth for scrap 6/71.

VDV 809 (809): Western National Omnibus Co Ltd, Exeter 809 1/71; withdrawn 2/71; W Norths (PV) Ltd (dealer) Sherburn in Elmet 4/71; Queensway Coaches Ltd, Liverpool (LA) 10/71; withdrawn 10/73.

VDV 810 (810): Western National Omnibus Co Ltd, Exeter 810 1/71; withdrawn 2/71; W Norths (PV) Ltd (dealer) Sherburn in Elmet 4/71; Queensway Coaches Ltd, Liverpool (LA) 10/71; withdrawn 10/73.

VDV 811 (811): Western National Omnibus Co Ltd, Exeter 811 1/71; withdrawn 2/71; W Norths (PV) Ltd (dealer) Sherburn in Elmet 4/71; Queensway Coaches Ltd, Liverpool (LA) 10/71; withdrawn 8/73.

VDV 812 (812): Western National Omnibus Co Ltd, Exeter 812 1/71; withdrawn 2/71; W Norths (PV) Ltd (dealer) Sherburn in Elmet 4/71; Queensway Coaches Ltd, Liverpool (LA) 10/71; used for spares by 1/72; scrapped 5/73.

VDV 813 (813): Western National Omnibus Co Ltd, Exeter 813 1/71; withdrawn 2/71; W Norths (PV) Ltd (dealer) Sherburn in Elmet 4/71; Queensway Coaches Ltd, Liverpool (LA) 10/71; withdrawn 5/73.

VDV 814 (814): Western National Omnibus Co Ltd, Exeter 814 1/71;withdrawn 2/71; W Norths (PV) Ltd (dealer) Sherburn in Elmet 4/71; Graham, Torquay (XDN) as a mobile café 8/71; Summer Schools of Foreign Languages (Torbay) Ltd, Torquay (XDN) 4/72; Students International Service Ltd, Torquay (XDN) 5/73; D Hoare (dealer), Chepstow 8/77; Hartwood Exports (Machinery) Ltd (dealer), Barnsley for scrap 11/77.

VDV 815 (815): Western National Omnibus Co Ltd, Exeter 815 1/71; withdrawn 2/71; W Norths (PV) Ltd (dealer) Sherburn in Elmet 4/71; Queensway Coaches Ltd, Liverpool (LA) 10/71; withdrawn 5/73.

VDV 816 (816): Western National Omnibus Co Ltd, Exeter 816 1/71; withdrawn 2/71; W Norths (PV) Ltd (dealer) Sherburn in Elmet 4/71; Calderstone Hospital Management Committee, Whalley (XLA) as a playbus 1973; Lancashire Area Health Authority (XLA) 4/74; unidentified dealer, Carlton for scrap 8/80.

VDV 817 (817): Western National Omnibus Co Ltd, Exeter 817 1/71; withdrawn 2/71; P Platt, Exeter for preservation 5/71; moved to Dawlish Warren 9/11; still owned 1/15.

VDV 818 (818): Western National Omnibus Co Ltd, Exeter 818 1/71; withdrawn 2/71; W Norths (PV) Ltd (dealer) Sherburn in Elmet 9/71; Queensway Coaches Ltd, Liverpool (LA) 10/71; CT Shears & P Platt, Winkleigh (XDN) 7/73; converted to O33/26R; RM Holladay {Red Bus Services}, Clyst Honiton (DN) 10/92; moved to Aylesbeare (DN) 8/94; R Greet, Broadhempston for preservation by 5/01; operated as a psv on an irregular basis between 5/01 and 11/03 as R Greet, Broadhempston and between 11/03 and 12/11 as Nostalgic Transport Ltd, Broadhempston (DN); DJ Shears, Northam (DN) 11/14.

VDV 819 (819): Western National Omnibus Co Ltd, Exeter 819 1/71; withdrawn 2/71; W Norths (PV) Ltd (dealer) Sherburn in Elmet 9/71; Queensway Coaches Ltd, Liverpool (LA) 10/71; CY Shears, Winkleigh for preservation 7/73; converted to open-top; G Jameson {Dunscroft Commercials} (dealer), Dunscroft for scrap 12/76.

Vehicles acquired from Falkland Garages Ltd, Torquay (DN) 6/57:

TCB820	MOD 363	Bedford SB	2181	Duple	56906	C33F	7/51	9/57
TCB821	NDV 44	Bedford SB	9600	Duple	1020/7	C33F	5/52	9/58
TCB822	BEN 500	Bedford SB	10157	Yeates	326	C35F	3/53	9/58
TCB823	SUO 826	Bedford SBG	37378	Duple	1055/300	C36F	5/55	9/58

Previous history:

These vehicles were acquired with the Falkland business; their previous histories are detailed in the Vehicles of Acquired Operators section.

Notes:

BEN 500 (TCB822): Repainted into Grey Cars livery 1958.
MOD 363 (TCB 820): Retained its brown and cream Falkland livery until sold.
NDV 44 (TCB 821): Repainted into Grey Cars livery 1958.
SUO 826 (TCB 823): Repainted into Grey Cars livery 1958.

Disposals:

BEN 500 (TCB822): Percy D Sleeman Ltd (dealer), London W5 10/58; Supreme Coaches Ltd, Hadleigh (EX) 6/59; RGH Webb & AJ Smithers {Globe Taxis}, Witney (OX) 12/60; BK, Leighton Buzzard (XBD) as a staff bus by 11/64.
MOD 363 (TCB 820): Millbrook Steamboat & Trading Co Ltd, Cremyll (CO) 10/57; Waters, Old Byfleet (SR) 12/61; Carter & Blewitt, Boxted (XEX) as a staff bus 1/66.
NDV 44 (TCB 821): Percy D Sleeman Ltd (dealer), London W5 10/58; Smith's Coaches (Buntingford) Ltd (HT) by 2/59; Corvedale Motor Co Ltd, Ludlow (SH) 3/64; Soudley Valley Coaches Ltd, Soudley (GL) 10/64; IW Williams, Deiniolen (CN) 8/71; withdrawn 8/74.
SUO 826 (TCB 823): Percy D Sleeman Ltd (dealer), London W5 10/58; WF Carter & Sons Ltd {Alpha Coaches}, Maidenhead (BE) 12/58; RA Robertson, Strathglass (IV) 6/66; Highland Omnibuses Ltd, Inverness (IV) 8/67; not used; A MacIntyre, Castlebay, Barra (IV) 8/67.

Vehicle on loan from Albion Motors Ltd, Glasgow:

NSG 298	Albion MR9N		82000C	Alexander	4819	B31F	7/55

Notes:

      NSG 298: On demonstration during 1957.

Vehicle on loan from ACV Sales Ltd, Southall:

	60 MMD	AEC Bridgemaster	MB3RA003	Crossley		H41/31R	7/57	

Notes:

      60 MMD: On demonstration during 1957.

1958

New Vehicles:

TCR850	XDV 850	AEC Reliance	MU3RV2075	Willowbrook	58102	C41F	6/58	3/66
TCR851	XDV 851	AEC Reliance	MU3RV2076	Willowbrook	58108	C41F	6/58	3/66
TCR852	XDV 852	AEC Reliance	MU3RV2077	Willowbrook	58104	C41F	6/58	3/66
TCR853	XDV 853	AEC Reliance	MU3RV2078	Willowbrook	58109	C41F	6/58	3/66
TCR854	XDV 854	AEC Reliance	MU3RV2079	Willowbrook	58103	C41F	6/58	3/66
TCR855	XDV 855	AEC Reliance	MU3RV2080	Willowbrook	58106	C41F	6/58	1/67
TCR856	XDV 856	AEC Reliance	MU3RV2081	Willowbrook	58110	C41F	6/58	1/67
TCR857	XDV 857	AEC Reliance	MU3RV2082	Willowbrook	58105	C41F	6/58	12/66
TCR858	XDV 858	AEC Reliance	MU3RV2083	Willowbrook	58107	C41F	6/58	12/66
TCR859	XDV 859	AEC Reliance	MU3RV2084	Willowbrook	58111	C41F	6/58	12/66
SR824	XTA 824	AEC Reliance	MU3RV1767	Weymann	M8381	B41F	2/58	1/71
SR825	XTA 825	AEC Reliance	MU3RV1768	Weymann	M8380	B41F	2/58	1/71
SR826	XTA 826	AEC Reliance	MU3RV1769	Weymann	M8382	B41F	2/58	1/71
SR827	XTA 827	AEC Reliance	MU3RV1770	Weymann	M8383	B41F	2/58	1/71
SR828	XTA 828	AEC Reliance	MU3RV1771	Weymann	M8390	B41F	2/58	1/71
SR829	XTA 829	AEC Reliance	MU3RV1772	Weymann	M8389	B41F	2/58	1/71
SR830	XTA 830	AEC Reliance	MU3RV1773	Weymann	M8388	B41F	2/58	1/71
SR831	XTA 831	AEC Reliance	MU3RV1774	Weymann	M8393	B41F	2/58	1/71
SR832	XTA 832	AEC Reliance	MU3RV1775	Weymann	M8392	B41F	3/58	1/71
SR833	XTA 833	AEC Reliance	MU3RV1776	Weymann	M8385	B41F	3/58	1/71
SR834	XTA 834	AEC Reliance	MU3RV1777	Weymann	M8391	B41F	3/58	1/71
SR835	XTA 835	AEC Reliance	MU3RV1778	Weymann	M8386	B41F	3/58	1/71
SR836	XTA 836	AEC Reliance	MU3RV1779	Weymann	M8387	B41F	3/58	1/71
SR837	XTA 837	AEC Reliance	MU3RV1780	Weymann	M8384	B41F	3/58	1/71
SN838	XTA 838	Albion NS3N	82050G	Willowbrook	58005	B31F	10/58	1/71
SN839	XTA 839	Albion NS3N	82050H	Willowbrook	58006	B31F	9/58	1/71
SN840	XTA 840	Albion NS3N	82050C	Willowbrook	58002	B31F	10/58	1/71
SN841	XTA 841	Albion NS3N	82050D	Willowbrook	58003	B31F	10/58	1/71
SN842	XTA 842	Albion NS3N	82050E	Willowbrook	58004	B31F	10/58	1/71
SN843	XTA 843	Albion NS3N	82050F	Willowbrook	58001	B31F	9/58	1/71
TCC844	XTA 844	Beadle-Commer	JCB754	Beadle		C41F	4/58	2/66
TCC845	XTA 845	Beadle-Commer	JCB755	Beadle		C41F	4/58	2/66
TCC846	XTA 846	Beadle-Commer	JCB756	Beadle		C41F	4/58	2/66
TCC847	XTA 847	Beadle-Commer	JCB757	Beadle		C41F	4/58	2/66
TCC848	XTA 848	Beadle-Commer	JCB789	Beadle		C41F	4/58	2/66
TCC849	XTA 849	Beadle-Commer	JCB790	Beadle		C41F	4/58	2/66

Notes:

      Fleet number prefixes were removed on repaint from 2/62.

      XDV 850-859 (TCR850-859): Were 30ft long x 7ft 6in wide, had "Viking" style bodies and were in Grey Cars livery. In 1962 they were cosmetically restyled to match the later Viscount bodies.

      XTA 838-843 (SN838-843): Were one-man buses for restricted routes to replace the Bedford OBs.

      XTA 839 (SN839): Exhibited at the 1958 Commercial Motor Show.

      XTA 844-849 (TCC844-849): Were 30ft long x 7ft 6in wide, had Rootes TS3 engines with "Rochester" style bodies and were in Grey Cars livery.

Disposals:

XDV 850 (850): Greenslades Tours Ltd, Exeter (DN) 3/66, licensed 4/66; withdrawn 1968, Lansdowne Luxury Coaches Ltd (dealer), Frating 4/68; Culling & Son (Norwich) Ltd, Norwich (NK) 5/71; withdrawn 10/74; Partridge (dealer) Hadleigh 6/75; DJ Green (dealer), Stock for scrap 4/76.

XDV 851 (851): Greenslades Tours Ltd, Exeter (DN) 3/66, licensed 4/66, withdrawn 1968, Lansdowne Luxury Coaches Ltd (dealer), Frating 11/68; Vines Luxury Coaches Ltd, Great Bromley (EX) 5/69; Grenville Motors Ltd, Camborne (CO) 6/70; P Platt, Exeter for preservation 6/83; S Hookins, Bampton for preservation 12/83; returned to P Platt, Exeter for preservation 9/05; S Blackman, Halifax for preservation 10/05; CT Shears, Winkleigh for preservation by 8/07; C & R Gibbons (preservationist), Hastings as spares for restoration of 253 BKM 9/10; still owned 1/15.

XDV 852 (852): Greenslades Tours Ltd, Exeter (DN) 3/66, licensed 4/66; Lansdowne Luxury Coaches Ltd (dealer), Frating 11/68; Vines Luxury Coaches Ltd, Great Bromley (EX) 6/69; licensed 4/71; Lansdowne Luxury Coaches Ltd (dealer), Frating 7/71.

XDV 853 (853): Greenslades Tours Ltd, Exeter (DN) 3/66, licensed 4/66; withdrawn 1968, Lansdowne Luxury Coaches Ltd (dealer), Frating 11/68; Vines Luxury Coaches Ltd, Great Bromley (EX) 10/70; not operated; Grenville Motors Ltd, Camborne (CO) 10/70; withdrawn 5/74; scrapped by 3/77.

XDV 854 (854): Greenslades Tours Ltd, Exeter (DN) 3/66, licensed 4/66; withdrawn 1968, Lansdowne Luxury Coaches Ltd (dealer), Frating 11/68; Vines Luxury Coaches Ltd, Great Bromley (EX) 6/69; licensed 4/71; Lansdowne Luxury Coaches Ltd (dealer), Frating 7/71; Clapton Park Angling Society, London E9 (XLN) 8/73; unidentified owner, London E2 5/78 and scrapped at an unknown date.

XDV 855 (855): Greenslades Tours Ltd, Exeter (DN) 1/67, licensed 4/67; withdrawn 1/70, W Norths (PV) Ltd (dealer), Sherburn in Elmet 1/70; Cooper & Wood, Wakefield (XWR) 5/70; renamed Bacal Construction (Northern) Ltd by 11/70; unidentified owner, Coxhoe as a mobile shop by10/76.

XDV 856 (856): Greenslades Tours Ltd, Exeter (DN) 1/67, licensed 4/67; withdrawn 1/70; W Norths (PV) Ltd (dealer), Sherburn in Elmet 1/70; Bacal Construction (Northern) Ltd, Wakefield (XWR) 11/70; Warren and Taylor, Farnworth as a car transporter by 8/74; withdrawn 1/76.

XDV 857 (857): Greenslades Tours Ltd, Exeter (DN) 12/66, licensed 4/67; withdrawn 1/70, W Norths (PV) Ltd (dealer), Sherburn in Elmet 1/70; Invicta Bridge, Hoveringham (XNG) 3/70; G Jones {Carlton Metals} (dealer), Carlton for scrap 2/78.

XDV 858 (858): Greenslades Tours Ltd, Exeter (DN) 12/66, licensed 4/67; withdrawn 1/70, W Norths (PV) Ltd (dealer), Sherburn in Elmet 1/70; DE & DS Bannatyne {Bannatyne Motors}, Blackwaterfoot, Arran (BU) 3/70; Allander Coaches Ltd, Milngavie (SC) 2/74; not operated; used for spares by 7/74; remains to RW Dunsmore (dealer), Larkhall for scrap by 6/75.

XDV 859 (859): Greenslades Tours Ltd, Exeter (DN) 12/66, withdrawn 1969; W Norths (PV) Ltd (dealer), Sherburn in Elmet 6/69; Allenways Ltd, Birmingham (XWK) 6/69; returned to W Norths (PV) Ltd (dealer), Sherburn in Elmet 1/71; sold for scrap 8/71.

XTA 824 (824): Western National Omnibus Co Ltd, Exeter (DN) 824 1/71; withdrawn 11/72; Rundle (dealer), Plymouth for scrap 2/73.

XTA 825 (825): Western National Omnibus Co Ltd, Exeter (DN) 825 1/71; withdrawn 1/73; W Norths (PV) Ltd (dealer), Sherburn in Elmet 5/73; Geest, Spalding (XLI) 9/73.

XTA 826 (826): Western National Omnibus Co Ltd, Exeter (DN) 826 1/71; withdrawn 11/72. Rundle (dealer), Plymouth for scrap 2/73.

XTA 827 (827): Western National Omnibus Co Ltd, Exeter (DN) 827 1/71; withdrawn 1/73; W Norths (PV) Ltd (dealer), Sherburn in Elmet 10/73; Eagre Construction (contractor), Scunthorpe (XLI) 10/73; DJ Green (dealer) Tilehurst 7/75; M Plunkett, London (preservationist) 7/75; Anderson, Darvills Hill Farm, Speen for use as a chicken hut (in exchange for TSM B10A2 UF 6805) by 4/76; S Gilkes, Chislehurst for preservation 1/88; Ward Jones Commercials (dealer), High Wycombe (for scrap?) 2/92.

XTA 828 (828): Western National Omnibus Co Ltd, Exeter (DN) 828 1/71; withdrawn 1/73; Rundle (dealer), Plymouth for scrap 12/73.

XTA 829 (829): Western National Omnibus Co Ltd, Exeter (DN) 829 1/71; withdrawn 1/73; W Norths (PV) Ltd (dealer), Sherburn in Elmet 5/73; Geest, Spalding (XLI) 9/73; returned to W Norths (PV) Ltd (dealer), Sherburn in Elmet 1975; unidentified dealer for scrap 6/75.

XTA 830 (830): Western National Omnibus Co Ltd, Exeter (DN) 830 1/71; withdrawn 1/73; W Norths (PV) Ltd (dealer), Sherburn in Elmet 10/73; Eagre Construction (contractor), Scunthorpe (XLI) 1/74; DJ Green (dealer), Tilehurst 6/75.

XTA 831 (831): Western National Omnibus Co Ltd, Exeter (DN) 831 1/71; withdrawn 1/73; W Norths (PV) Ltd (dealer), Sherburn in Elmet 5/73; Geest, Spalding (XLI) 9/73.

XTA 832 (832): Western National Omnibus Co Ltd, Exeter (DN) 832 1/71; withdrawn 1/73; dismantled for spares 1973; body shell to Butlins, Minehead (XSO) 5/73.

XTA 833 (833): Western National Omnibus Co Ltd, Exeter (DN) 833 1/71; withdrawn 1/73; W Norths (PV) Ltd (dealer), Sherburn in Elmet 5/73; Geest, Spalding (XLI) 9/73; returned to W Norths (PV) Ltd (dealer), Sherburn in Elmet 6/75; unidentified dealer for scrap 6/75.

XTA 834 (834): Western National Omnibus Co Ltd, Exeter (DN) 834 1/71; withdrawn 1/73; W Norths (PV) Ltd (dealer), Sherburn in Elmet 5/73; Geest, Spalding (XLI) 9/73.

XTA 835 (835): Western National Omnibus Co Ltd, Exeter (DN) 835 1/71; withdrawn 1/73; Rundle (dealer), Plymouth for scrap 12/73.

XTA 836 (836): Western National Omnibus Co Ltd, Exeter (DN) 836 1/71; withdrawn 1/73; Rundle (dealer), Plymouth for scrap 1/74.

XTA 837 (837): Western National Omnibus Co Ltd, Exeter (DN) 837 1/71; withdrawn 1/73; W Norths (PV) Ltd (dealer), Sherburn in Elmet 10/73; McCullough, Birtley (XDM) 12/73.

XTA 838 (838): Western National Omnibus Co Ltd, Exeter (DN) 838 1/71; withdrawn 2/71; PD Monk & AC Allday, Fowey (CO) 5/71; withdrawn 12/72; B & D Rees {Celtic Services}, St Just (CO) 3/75; withdrawn 8/78; CB Knubley {Brutonian Coaches}, Bruton (SO) 10/78; not operated; RM Holladay {Red Bus Services}, Kenton (DN) for spares 8/83.

XTA 839 (839): Western National Omnibus Co Ltd, Exeter (DN) 839 1/71; withdrawn 2/71; PD Monk & AC Allday, Fowey (CO) 2/71; PA Newton, Chulmleigh (DN) 4/72; A & AR Turner, Chulmleigh (DN) 9/72; withdrawn 2/76; T Whitfield (dealer), Kentisbeare 1976; N Mitchell, Exeter for preservation 8/76; A Hazell, Wellington for preservation 1978 or early 1979; R Holladay, Kenton for preservation 6/81; R Holladay, Starcross (DN) 8/82; moved to Clyst Honiton (DN) by 10/84; to Aylesbeare (DN) 8/94; to Broadclyst (DN) 4/97; R Wilson, Bovey Tracey for preservation 8/98; F Taylor, Polegate for preservation 12/01; W Hulme, Yatton for preservation 6/09; still owned 1/15.

XTA 840 (840): Western National Omnibus Co Ltd, Exeter (DN) 840 1/71; withdrawn 2/72. W Norths (PV) Ltd (dealer), Sherburn in Elmet 6/72; Yuill (contractor) Hartlepool (XDM) 7/72; withdrawn by 8/73; Spence (dealer), Scotton for scrap by 11/73.

XTA 841 (841): Western National Omnibus Co Ltd, Exeter (DN) 841 1/71; withdrawn 2/72. W Norths (PV) Ltd (dealer), Sherburn in Elmet 6/72; Yuill (contractor) Hartlepool (XDM) 7/72.

XTA 842 (842): Western National Omnibus Co Ltd, Exeter (DN) 842 1/71; withdrawn 6/71; W Norths (PV) Ltd (dealer), Sherburn in Elmet 6/72; Yuill (contractor) Hartlepool (XDM) 7/72; withdrawn by 8/73; Spence (dealer), Scotton for scrap 11/73.

XTA 843 (843): Western National Omnibus Co Ltd, Exeter (DN) 843 1/71; withdrawn 2/72; W Norths (PV) Ltd (dealer), Sherburn in Elmet 6/72; Yuill (contractor) Hartlepool (XDM) B18 7/72; Spence (dealer), Scotton for scrap 11/73.

XTA 844 (844): Transport (Passenger Equipment) Ltd (dealer), Macclesfield 3/66; P McCabe, Douglas Water (LK) 7/66; Chapman, Airdrie (LK) 4/73; SMT Sales & Service Co Ltd (dealer), Glasgow 6/73.

XTA 845 (845): Transport (Passenger Equipment) Ltd (dealer), Macclesfield 3/66; John Beuken & Co, Fauldhouse (WL) 1/67; withdrawn by 1/71.

XTA 846 (846): Transport (Passenger Equipment) Ltd (dealer), Macclesfield 3/66; Heseltine, Featherstone (WR) 11/66; Allenways, Birmingham (WK) 4/69; W Norths (PV) Ltd (dealer), Sherburn in Elmet 12/69; unidentified dealer, Royston for scrap by 10/70.

XTA 847 (847): Transport (Passenger Equipment) Ltd (dealer), Macclesfield 3/66; WE Jones, Llanerchymedd (AY) 4/66; AW Lewis, Carreglefn (AY) 10/72; withdrawn 6/74.

XTA 848 (848): Transport (Passenger Equipment) Ltd (dealer), Macclesfield 3/66; EW Thomas, Upper Llandwrog (CN) 6/66; withdrawn 1973.

XTA 849 (849): Transport (Passenger Equipment) Ltd (dealer), Macclesfield 3/66; Clynnog & Trevor Omnibus Co Ltd, Trefor (CN) 5/66; withdrawn 2/74; Transport (Passenger Equipment) Ltd (dealer), Macclesfield 1974.

Vehicle on loan from Albion Motors Ltd, Glasgow:

330 CTD	Albion MR9N		82004E	Alexander	4896	B31F	7/57

Notes:

330 CTD: On demonstration during 5/58.

1959

New Vehicles:

TCR889	889 ADV	AEC Reliance	2MU3RV2348	Willowbrook	59365	C41F	5/59	12/66
TCR890	890 ADV	AEC Reliance	2MU3RV2349	Willowbrook	59366	C41F	5/59	12/66
TCR891	891 ADV	AEC Reliance	2MU3RV2350	Willowbrook	59367	C41F	5/59	12/66
TCR892	892 ADV	AEC Reliance	2MU3RV2351	Willowbrook	59368	C41F	5/59	12/66
TCR893	893 ADV	AEC Reliance	2MU3RV2352	Willowbrook	59369	C41F	5/59	12/66

TCR894	894 ADV	AEC Reliance	2MU3RV2353	Willowbrook	59370	C41F	5/59	12/66
SR860	860 ATA	AEC Reliance	2MU3RV2127	Willowbrook	59291	B41F	3/59	1/71
SR861	861 ATA	AEC Reliance	2MU3RV2128	Willowbrook	59292	B41F	3/59	1/71
SR862	862 ATA	AEC Reliance	2MU3RV2129	Willowbrook	59293	B41F	3/59	1/71
SR863	863 ATA	AEC Reliance	2MU3RV2130	Willowbrook	59294	B41F	3/59	1/71
SR864	864 ATA	AEC Reliance	2MU3RV2131	Willowbrook	59295	B41F	3/59	1/71
SR865	865 ATA	AEC Reliance	2MU3RV2132	Willowbrook	59296	B41F	3/59	1/71
SR866	866 ATA	AEC Reliance	2MU3RV2133	Willowbrook	59297	B41F	3/59	1/71
SR867	867 ATA	AEC Reliance	2MU3RV2134	Willowbrook	59298	B41F	3/59	1/71
SR868	868 ATA	AEC Reliance	2MU3RV2135	Willowbrook	59299	B41F	3/59	1/71
SR869	869 ATA	AEC Reliance	2MU3RV2136	Willowbrook	59300	B41F	3/59	7/67
SR870	870 ATA	AEC Reliance	2MU3RV2137	Willowbrook	59301	B41F	3/59	1/71
SR871	871 ATA	AEC Reliance	2MU3RV2138	Willowbrook	59302	B41F	3/59	1/71
DL872	872 ATA	Leyland PDR1/1	590593	MCCW		H44/34F	7/59	1/71
DL873	873 ATA	Leyland PDR1/1	590615	MCCW		H44/34F	6/59	1/71
DL874	874 ATA	Leyland PDR1/1	590616	MCCW		H44/34F	7/59	1/71
DL875	875 ATA	Leyland PDR1/1	590617	MCCW		H44/34F	6/59	1/71
DL876	876 ATA	Leyland PDR1/1	590592	MCCW		H44/34F	6/59	1/71
DL877	877 ATA	Leyland PDR1/1	590627	MCCW		H44/34F	6/59	1/71
DL878	878 ATA	Leyland PDR1/1	590668	MCCW		H44/34F	6/59	1/71
DL879	879 ATA	Leyland PDR1/1	590676	MCCW		H44/34F	6/59	1/71
DL880	880 ATA	Leyland PDR1/1	590677	MCCW		H44/34F	6/59	1/71
DL881	881 ATA	Leyland PDR1/1	590659	MCCW		H44/34F	7/59	1/71
DL882	882 ATA	Leyland PDR1/1	590689	MCCW		H44/34F	7/59	1/71
DL883	883 ATA	Leyland PDR1/1	590687	MCCW		H44/34F	7/59	1/71
DL884	884 ATA	Leyland PDR1/1	590688	MCCW		H44/34F	7/59	1/71
DL885	885 ATA	Leyland PDR1/1	590755	MCCW		H44/34F	7/59	1/71
DL886	886 ATA	Leyland PDR1/1	590754	MCCW		H44/34F	7/59	1/71
DL887	887 ATA	Leyland PDR1/1	590765	MCCW		H44/34F	7/59	1/71
DL888	888 ATA	Leyland PDR1/1	590766	MCCW		H44/34F	7/59	1/71

Notes:

Fleet number prefixes were removed on repaint from 2/62.

889-894 ADV (TCR889-894): Were 30ft long x 7ft 6in wide and had Viking style bodywork in Grey Cars livery. In 1962 they were cosmetically restyled to match the later Viscount bodies.
872-874 ATA (DL872-874): Re-seated to H44/32F 1960.
875 ATA (DL875): Fitted with a turbocharger at an unknown date; re-seated to H44/32F 1960; turbocharger removed 1966; fitted with a Willowbrook roof following an accident.
876-880 ATA (DL876-880): Re-seated to H44/32F 1960.
881 ATA (DL881): Re-seated to H44/32F 1959; fitted with a turbocharger at an unknown date, which was removed in 1966.
882-888 ATA (DL882-888): Re-seated to H44/32F 1960.

Disposals:

889 ADV (889): Greenslades Tours, Ltd, Exeter (DN) 12/66; to service 4/67; withdrawn 1970; W Norths (PV) Ltd (dealer), Sherburn in Elmet 12/70; Glen Tours (Baildon) Ltd, Baildon 28 9/71; licensed 12/71; Connor & Graham Ltd, Essington (EY) 47 5/73; withdrawn 11/75; CHC Phillips {Phillips Coach Co}, Shiptonthorpe by 5/78; not operated; Blackett (dealer) Butterknowle for scrap by 6/86.
890 ADV (890): Greenslades Tours, Ltd, Exeter (DN) 12/66; to service 4/67; Western National Omnibus Co Ltd, Exeter (DN) 437 7/70; renumbered 1237 7/71, withdrawn 5/80; G Sharman, Cobham for preservation 8/80; G Brazier, Staines for preservation by 10/90; M Gibbons, Weybridge for preservation c3/93; S Morris, Wiveliscombe for preservation by 8/96; Rexquote Ltd, Bishops Lydeard (SO) 4/97; moved to Norton Fitzwarren by 3/02; Quantock Motor Services Ltd, Wiveliscombe (SO) for preservation 3/04; AK Cotton, Saltash (CO) for preservation 7/11; still owned 1/15.
891 ADV (891): Greenslades Tours, Ltd, Exeter (DN) 12/66; to service 4/67; withdrawn 1970; W Norths (PV) Ltd (dealer), Sherburn in Elmet 12/70; DE & DS Bannatyne (Bannatyne Motors), Blackwaterfoot, Arran (BU) 2/71; licensed 3/71; Grangemouth Celtic Amateur Football Club Supporters Club, Glasgow (XLK) 12/73; Allander Coaches, Milngavie (SC) 11/76; not operated.

892 ADV (892): Greenslades Tours, Ltd, Exeter (DN) 12/66; to service 4/67; withdrawn 1970; W Norths (PV) Ltd (dealer), Sherburn in Elmet 12/70; Glen Tours (Baildon) Ltd, Baildon (WR) 26 6/71; withdrawn 8/73; Twell (dealer), Ingham for scrap by1/75.

893 ADV (893): Court Garages, Torquay (DN) 10/66; returned to Devon General 10/68 (qv).

894 ADV (894): Court Garages, Torquay (DN) 10/66; returned to Devon General 10/68 (qv).

860 ATA (860): Western National Omnibus Co Ltd, Exeter (DN) 860 1/71; withdrawn 10/74; W Norths (PV) Ltd (dealer), Sherburn in Elmet 2/75; sold for scrap 3/76.

861 ATA (861): Western National Omnibus Co Ltd, Exeter (DN) 861 1/71; withdrawn 10/74; W Norths (PV) Ltd (dealer), Sherburn in Elmet 2/75; sold for scrap 10/75.

862 ATA (862): Western National Omnibus Co Ltd, Exeter (DN) 862 1/71; withdrawn 10/74; W Norths (PV) Ltd (dealer), Sherburn in Elmet 2/75; Martin & Sons Ltd (dealer), Weaverham by 7/75; Adlington, Chorley (XLA) 7/75; sold by 5/76.

863 ATA (863): Western National Omnibus Co Ltd, Exeter (DN) 863 1/71; withdrawn 10/74; W Norths (PV) Ltd (dealer), Sherburn in Elmet 2/75; sold for scrap 10/75.

864 ATA (864): Western National Omnibus Co Ltd, Exeter (DN) 864 1/71; withdrawn 8/74; W Norths (PV) Ltd (dealer), Sherburn in Elmet 2/75; Lyjon (Site Transport Management Services), Ellesmere Port (XLA) 3/75; Pemberton, Capenhurst (XLA) 3/77, not used, sold for scrap by 12/83.

865 ATA (865): Western National Omnibus Co Ltd, Exeter (DN) 865 1/71; withdrawn 8/74; W Norths (PV) Ltd (dealer), Sherburn in Elmet 2/75; Adlington, Chorley (XLA) 1/75; Martin Bus & Coach Sales Ltd (dealer), Middlewich 7/75.

866 ATA (866): Western National Omnibus Co Ltd, Exeter (DN) 866 1/71; withdrawn 8/74; W Norths (PV) Ltd (dealer), Sherburn in Elmet 2/75; Saunders, Redditch (XMW) 2/75.

867-868 ATA (867-868): Western National Omnibus Co Ltd, Exeter (DN) 867-868 1/71; withdrawn 1/77; Thornton (dealer) Cundy Cross 1/77; G Jameson {Dunscroft Commercials} (dealer), Dunscroft for scrap 2/77.

869 ATA (869): Dismantled for spares 7/67, following an accident in 12/66.

870 ATA (870): Western National Omnibus Co Ltd, Exeter (DN) 870 1/71; withdrawn after an accident 2/74; Rundle (dealer), Plymouth for scrap 4/74.

871 ATA (871): Western National Omnibus Co Ltd, Exeter (DN) 871 1/71; withdrawn after an accident 10/76; scrapped by Western National at Torquay 1/77.

872 ATA (872): Western National Omnibus Co Ltd, Exeter (DN) 872 1/71; withdrawn 12/82; S Gilkes, Chislehurst for preservation 10/82; Gilkes and Fleming, Chislehurst for preservation 5/89; Wealden (dealer), Five Oak Green by 7/92; WW Hulme {Rubicon Classis Travel}, Bristol (GL) by 6/99; retained for preservation 2/08; moved to Yatton by 10/09; Stagecoach Devon Ltd, Exeter (DN) for preservation 11/11; still owned 1/15.

873 ATA (873): Western National Omnibus Co Ltd, Exeter (DN) 873 1/71; withdrawn 2/81; D Rollinson (Bus Centre) Ltd (dealer), Carlton for scrap 3/81.

874 ATA (874): Western National Omnibus Co Ltd, Exeter (DN) 874 1/71; withdrawn 3/82; 874 Group (R Cooper), Little Stoke for preservation 5/82; LC Munden & Son Ltd, Bristol (AV) 5/83; SS Bryant & KT Henderson, Easton-In-Gordano (AV) by 11/87; Wacton Trading/Coach Sales (dealer), Bromyard 11/89; Mannaquin World, Heaton Moor (XGM) 11/89; burnt out 11/97; JA Ashall, Manchester (GM) 11/97 for spares; scrapped by 3/98.

875 ATA (875): Western National Omnibus Co Ltd, Exeter (DN) 875 1/71; withdrawn 2/81; D Rollinson (Bus Centre) Ltd (dealer), Carlton for scrap 2/81.

876 ATA (876): Western National Omnibus Co Ltd, Exeter (DN) 876 1/71; withdrawn 3/81; D Rollinson (Bus Centre) Ltd (dealer), Carlton for scrap 3/81.

877-878 ATA (877-878): Western National Omnibus Co Ltd, Exeter (DN) 877-878 1/71; withdrawn 2/81; D Rollinson (Bus Centre) Ltd (dealer), Carlton for scrap 2/81.

879 ATA (879): Western National Omnibus Co Ltd, Exeter (DN) 879 1/71; withdrawn 5/81; M Parton & Allen (dealer), Carlton for scrap 5/81.

880 ATA (880): Western National Omnibus Co Ltd, Exeter (DN) 880 1/71; withdrawn 3/82; CF Booth Ltd (dealer), Rotherham for scrap 4/82.

881 ATA (881): Western National Omnibus Co Ltd, Exeter (DN) 881 1/71; withdrawn 12/82; Western National Ltd 881 1/83; North Devon Ltd, Barnstaple (DN) 881 6/84; not operated; D Hoare (as dealer), Chepstow 8/84; S Gilkes, Chislehurst for preservation 3/85; S Gilkes & Fleming, Chislehurst for preservation 9/85; S Gilkes, Fleming & Rayner, Chislehurst for preservation 1/88; S Gilkes & Rayner, Chislehurst for preservation 5/89; T Wigley (dealer), Carlton 3/91.

882 ATA (882): Western National Omnibus Co Ltd, Exeter (DN) 882 1/71; withdrawn 12/82; Cole, Shiphay (XDN) 12/82; scrapped by 3/84

883 ATA (883): Western National Omnibus Co Ltd, Exeter (DN) 883 1/71; repainted into NBC poppy red livery 5/73; withdrawn 3/82; CF Booth Ltd (dealer), Rotherham for scrap 4/82.

884 ATA (884): Western National Omnibus Co Ltd, Exeter (DN) 884 1/71; withdrawn 2/81; D Rollinson (Bus Centre) Ltd (dealer), Carlton for scrap 3/81.

885 ATA (885): Western National Omnibus Co Ltd, Exeter (DN) 885 1/71; withdrawn 2/81; D Rollinson
(Bus Centre) Ltd (dealer), Carlton 2/81; SC & DN Rutherford {Earnside Coaches}, Glenfarg
(TE) 9/81; Toft Hill Farm, Perth (XTE) 6/83; J Stewart, Glencarse (TE) c6/83; re-registered
WTS 715A 6/89; used as a storeshed from 1994.
886-888 ATA (886-888): Western National Omnibus Co Ltd, Exeter (DN) 886-888 1/71; withdrawn 2/81;
D Rollinson (Bus Centre) Ltd (dealer), Carlton for scrap 2/81.

1960

New Vehicles:

DL895	895 DTT	Leyland PDR1/1	592467	Roe	GO5044	H44/31F	5/60	1/71
DL896	896 DTT	Leyland PDR1/1	592471	Roe	GO5049	H44/31F	4/60	1/71
DL897	897 DTT	Leyland PDR1/1	592472	Roe	GO5062	H44/31F	6/60	1/71
DL898	898 DTT	Leyland PDR1/1	592481	Roe	GO5061	H44/31F	6/60	1/71
DL899	899 DTT	Leyland PDR1/1	592482	Roe	GO5060	H44/31F	6/60	1/71
DL900	900 DTT	Leyland PDR1/1	592491	Roe	GO5058	H44/31F	6/60	1/71
DL901	901 DTT	Leyland PDR1/1	592492	Roe	GO5056	H44/31F	6/60	1/71
DL902	902 DTT	Leyland PDR1/1	592493	Roe	GO5064	H44/31F	6/60	1/71
DL903	903 DTT	Leyland PDR1/1	592517	Roe	GO5059	H44/31F	6/60	1/71
DL904	904 DTT	Leyland PDR1/1	592518	Roe	GO5051	H44/31F	4/60	1/71
DL905	905 DTT	Leyland PDR1/1	592519	Roe	GO5052	H44/31F	4/60	1/71
DL906	906 DTT	Leyland PDR1/1	592530	Roe	GO5053	H44/31F	5/60	1/71
DL907	907 DTT	Leyland PDR1/1	592572	Roe	GO5055	H44/31F	5/60	1/71
DL908	908 DTT	Leyland PDR1/1	592597	Roe	GO5050	H44/31F	4/60	1/71
DL909	909 DTT	Leyland PDR1/1	592598	Roe	GO5045	H44/31F	4/60	1/71
DL910	910 DTT	Leyland PDR1/1	592599	Roe	GO5048	H44/31F	4/60	1/71
DL911	911 DTT	Leyland PDR1/1	592606	Roe	GO5042	H44/31F	4/60	1/71
DL912	912 DTT	Leyland PDR1/1	592607	Roe	GO5047	H44/31F	4/60	1/71
DL913	913 DTT	Leyland PDR1/1	592608	Roe	GO5063	H44/31F	6/60	1/71
DL914	914 DTT	Leyland PDR1/1	592645	Roe	GO5054	H44/31F	6/60	1/71
DL915	915 DTT	Leyland PDR1/1	592669	Roe	GO5043	H44/31F	4/60	1/71
DL916	916 DTT	Leyland PDR1/1	592670	Roe	GO5046	H44/31F	4/60	1/71
DL917	917 DTT	Leyland PDR1/1	600097	Roe	GO5057	H44/31F	6/60	1/71

Notes:

Fleet number prefixes were removed on repaint from 2/62.

Disposals:

895 DTT (895): Western National Omnibus Co Ltd, Exeter (DN) 895 1/71; withdrawn 1/80; dismantled for
spares at Newton Road depot by T Carpenter (dealer), Exeter 1980.
896 DTT (896): Western National Omnibus Co Ltd, Exeter (DN) 896 1/71; withdrawn 12/81; CF Booth Ltd
(dealer), Rotherham for scrap 3/82.
897 DTT (897): Western National Omnibus Co Ltd, Exeter (DN) 897 1/71; withdrawn 12/80; Ensign Bus
Co Ltd (dealer) 11/82; C Meynell (dealer) Carlton for scrap 11/82.
898 DTT (898): Western National Omnibus Co Ltd, Exeter (DN) 898 1/71; withdrawn 5/81; T Wigley
(dealer), Carlton for scrap 5/81.
899 DTT (899): Western National Omnibus Co Ltd, Exeter (DN) 899 1/71; withdrawn 2/81; D Rollinson
(Bus Centre) Ltd (dealer), Carlton for scrap 3/81.
900 DTT (900): Western National Omnibus Co Ltd, Exeter (DN) 900 1/71; repainted in Great Western
Railway chocolate and cream livery with GWR monograms for the 75th anniversary of the
first GWR bus service with Western National fleet names 6/78; withdrawn 2/81; Wood
(dealer), Crediton 2/81; scrapped 7/81.
901 DTT (901): Western National Omnibus Co Ltd, Exeter (DN) 901 1/71; withdrawn 1/81; D Rollinson
(Bus Centre) Ltd (dealer), Carlton for scrap 2/81.
902 DTT (902): Western National Omnibus Co Ltd, Exeter (DN) 902 1/71; repainted into NBC poppy red
livery 2/73; withdrawn 1/80; dismantled for spares at Newton Road depot by T Carpenter
(dealer), Exeter 5/80.
903 DTT (903): Western National Omnibus Co Ltd, Exeter (DN) 903 1/71; withdrawn 1/80; dismantled for
spares at Newton Road depot by T Carpenter (dealer), Exeter 1980.
904 DTT (904): Western National Omnibus Co Ltd, Exeter (DN) 904 1/71; withdrawn 12/81; CF Booth Ltd
(dealer), Rotherham for scrap 3/82.
905 DTT (905): Western National Omnibus Co Ltd, Exeter (DN) 905 1/71; withdrawn 2/81; D Rollinson
(Bus Centre) Ltd (dealer), Carlton for scrap 3/81.

906 DTT (906): Western National Omnibus Co Ltd, Exeter (DN) 906 1/71; withdrawn 2/81; D Rollinson (Bus Centre) Ltd (dealer), Carlton for scrap 2/81.

907 DTT (907): Western National Omnibus Co Ltd, Exeter (DN) 907 1/71; withdrawn 12/82; Western National Ltd, Exeter (DN) 907 1/83; North Devon Ltd, Barnstaple (DN) 907 6/84; not operated; D Hoare (dealer), Chepstow 8/84; R Knight, Steyning for preservation for spares 4/85; Wigley (dealer), Carlton 4/85.

908 DTT (908): Western National Omnibus Co Ltd, Exeter (DN) 908 1/71; withdrawn 5/81; M Parton & Allen (dealer), Carlton for scrap 5/81.

909 DTT (909): Western National Omnibus Co Ltd, Exeter (DN) 909 1/71; Devon General Ltd, Exeter (DN) 909 1/83; withdrawn 1983; Hartwood Exports (Machinery) Ltd (dealer), Barnsley 2/84; T Thornton & P Lloyd (dealer), Cundy Cross for scrap 2/84.

910 DTT (910): Western National Omnibus Co Ltd, Exeter (DN) 910 1/71; withdrawn 1/80; dismantled for spares at Newton Road depot by T Carpenter (dealer), Exeter 5/80.

911 DTT (911): Western National Omnibus Co Ltd, Exeter (DN) 911 1/71; withdrawn 12/80; D Rollinson (Bus Centre) Ltd (dealer), Carlton 3/81; SC & DN Rutherford {Earnside Coaches}, Glenfarg (TE) 4/81; C Inverarity, Crensley Farm, Liff (XTE) 6/82; out of use 7/91; M Roulston, Glasgow for preservation c2/97; re-registered ESL 876 6/99; scrapped by 11/99.

912 DTT (912): Western National Omnibus Co Ltd, Exeter (DN) 912 1/71; withdrawn 6/81; Passenger Vehicle Spares (Barnsley) Ltd (dealer), Carlton for scrap 5/81.

913 DTT (913): Western National Omnibus Co Ltd, Exeter (DN) 913 1/71; Western National, Exeter (DN) 913 1/83; withdrawn 1983; North Devon Ltd, Barnstaple (DN) 913 5/83; not operated; D Hoare (dealer), Chepstow 8/84; R Knight, Steyning for preservation 4/85; loaned to RM Holladay {Red Bus Services}, Aylesbeare (DN) 12/95; withdrawn after an accident 3/96; E Jacobs {ESJ Coaches}, St Stephens (CO) 1/98; moved to Hatt (CO) by 7/03; T Bennett, Sherborne for preservation 12/03; still owned 1/15.

914 DTT (914): Western National Omnibus Co Ltd, Exeter (DN) 914 1/71; withdrawn 1/80; broken up for spares at WNOC by T Carpenter (dealer), Exeter 1980.

915 DTT (915): Western National Omnibus Co Ltd, Exeter (DN) 915 1/71; Devon General Ltd, Exeter (DN) 915 1/83; withdrawn 1983; Hartwood Exports (Machinery) Ltd (dealer), Barnsley for scrap 2/84

916 DTT (916): Western National Omnibus Co Ltd, Exeter (DN) 916 1/71; withdrawn 2/81; D Rollinson (Bus Centre) Ltd (dealer), Carlton 2/81.

917 DTT (917): Western National Omnibus Co Ltd, Exeter (DN) 917 1/71; withdrawn 1/80; dismantled for spares at Newton Road depot by T Carpenter (dealer), Exeter c5/80.

Vehicle on loan from ACV Sales Ltd, Southall:

WJU 407	AEC Reliance	2MU3RA3076	Willowbrook	60594	C41F	10/60

Notes:

WJU 407: Had a Viscount style body and also had Duple Group body number CF6; on demonstration during 10/60.

1961

New Vehicles:

DL918	918 GTA	Leyland PDR1/1	602568	Roe	GO5257	H44/31F	5/61	1/71
DL919	919 GTA	Leyland PDR1/1	602569	Roe	GO5260	H44/31F	5/61	1/71
DL920	920 GTA	Leyland PDR1/1	602570	Roe	GO5258	H44/31F	5/61	1/71
DL921	921 GTA	Leyland PDR1/1	602593	Roe	GO5254	H44/31F	4/61	1/71
DL922	922 GTA	Leyland PDR1/1	602594	Roe	GO5256	H44/31F	5/61	1/71
DL923	923 GTA	Leyland PDR1/1	602622	Roe	GO5255	H44/31F	5/61	1/71
DL924	924 GTA	Leyland PDR1/1	602623	Roe	GO5259	H44/31F	5/61	1/71
DL925	925 GTA	Leyland PDR1/1	602642	MCCW		CO44/31F	5/61	1/71
DL926	926 GTA	Leyland PDR1/1	602643	MCCW		CO44/31F	5/61	1/71
DL927	927 GTA	Leyland PDR1/1	602644	MCCW		CO44/31F	5/61	1/71
DL928	928 GTA	Leyland PDR1/1	602664	MCCW		CO44/31F	5/61	1/71
DL929	929 GTA	Leyland PDR1/1	602665	MCCW		CO44/31F	5/61	1/71
DL930	930 GTA	Leyland PDR1/1	602666	MCCW		CO44/31F	6/61	1/71
DL931	931 GTA	Leyland PDR1/1	602728	MCCW		CO44/31F	6/61	1/71
DL932	932 GTA	Leyland PDR1/1	602729	MCCW		CO44/31F	6/61	1/71
DL933	933 GTA	Leyland PDR1/1	602730	MCCW		CO44/31F	6/61	1/71
TCR934	934 GTA	AEC Reliance	2MU3RV3090	Willowbrook	60669	C41F	6/61	5/69
TCR935	935 GTA	AEC Reliance	2MU3RV3091	Willowbrook	60670	C41F	6/61	5/69
TCR936	936 GTA	AEC Reliance	2MU3RV3092	Willowbrook	60671	C41F	6/61	6/70

TCR937	937 GTA	AEC Reliance	2MU3RV3093	Willowbrook	60672	C41F	6/61	10/70
TCR938	938 GTA	AEC Reliance	2MU3RV3094	Willowbrook	60673	C41F	6/61	10/70
TCR939	939 GTA	AEC Reliance	2MU3RV3095	Willowbrook	60674	C41F	6/61	10/70
TCR940	940 GTA	AEC Reliance	2MU3RV3096	Willowbrook	60675	C41F	6/61	10/70
TCR941	941 GTA	AEC Reliance	2MU3RV3097	Willowbrook	60676	C41F	6/61	7/70
TCR942	942 GTA	AEC Reliance	2MU3RV3098	Willowbrook	60677	C41F	6/61	7/70

Notes:

Fleet number prefixes were removed on repaint from 2/62.

921 GTA (DL921): Fitted with a turbocharger soon after delivery, which was removed 1966.
924 GTA (DL924): Fitted with a turbocharger at an unknown date, which was removed 1966.

925-933 GTA (DL925-933): These vehicles were designed for use in the Torbay area and had removable roofs. These roofs were stored while the vehicles were operating in open-top form, on special racks constructed from the chassis of AEC Regent II DJF 327-328 & 330 (DR701-703) (see 1952), each rack carrying three roofs. They were named after famous West Country 'Sea Dogs' and were painted in a "reversed" livery of ivory with two red bands and red lettering. Wheels were initially painted ivory, but changed to red in 1962. Their names (see below) were carried both inside and across the front and back outside, with some also having a picture of their namesakes inside. No advertisement displays were carried.

DL925 Admiral Blake	DL928 Sir Humphrey Gilbert	DL931 Sir Thomas Howard
DL926 Sir Francis Drake	DL929 Sir Richard Grenville	DL932 Earl Howe
DL927 Sir Martin Frobisher	DL930 Sir John Hawkins	DL933 Sir Walter Raleigh

934-940 GTA (TCR934-940): Had Viscount style bodies in Grey Cars livery and were 7ft 6in wide.

934 GTA (TCR934): Also had Duple Group body number CF87.
935 GTA (TCR935): Also had Duple Group body number CF92.
936-939 GTA (TCR936-939): Also had Duple Group body numbers CF98-101.
940 GTA (TCR940): Also had Duple Group body number CF105.

941-942 GTA (TCR941-942): Had Viscount style bodies in Grey Cars livery and were 8ft 0in wide for use on extended tours.

934-935 GTA (TCR934-935): Also had Duple Group body numbers CF106-107.

Disposals:

918 GTA (918): Western National Omnibus Co Ltd, Exeter (DN) 918 1/71; repainted into NBC poppy red livery 10/72; withdrawn 3/82; CF Booth Ltd (dealer), Rotherham for scrap 4/82.
919 GTA (919): Western National Omnibus Co Ltd, Exeter (DN) 919 1/71; repainted into NBC poppy red livery 11/72; withdrawn 12/81; CF Booth Ltd (dealer), Rotherham for scrap 3/82.
920 GTA (920): Western National Omnibus Co Ltd, Exeter (DN) 920 1/71; North Devon Ltd, Barnstaple (DN) 920 1/83; re-registered ADV 435A 4/86; withdrawn 1986; S Gilkes, Chislehurst for preservation 11/86; S Gilkes, Rayner & Fleming, Chislehurst for preservation 12/86; used for spares following accident by 12/87; D Rollinson (Bus Centre) Ltd (dealer), Carlton for scrap 1/88.
921 GTA (921): Western National Omnibus Co Ltd, Exeter (DN) 921 1/71; withdrawn 8/82; Ensign (dealer), Purfleet 11/82; Meynell (dealer) Carlton 11/82; G Jones {Carlton Metals} (dealer), Carlton 1/83.
922 GTA (922): Western National Omnibus Co Ltd, Exeter (DN) 922 1/71; withdrawn 1/80; dismantled for spares at Newton Road depot by T Carpenter (dealer), Exeter 5/80.
923 GTA (923): Western National Omnibus Co Ltd, Exeter (DN) 923 1/71; withdrawn 2/81; D Rollinson (Bus Centre) Ltd (dealer), Carlton 3/81.
924 GTA (924): Western National Omnibus Co Ltd, Exeter (DN) 924 1/71; withdrawn 6/81; Passenger Vehicle Spares (Barnsley) Ltd (dealer), Carlton for scrap 5/81.
925 GTA (925): Western National Omnibus Co Ltd, Exeter (DN) 925 1/71; Western National, Exeter DN) 925 1/83; North Devon Ltd, Barnstaple (DN) 925 5/83; re-registered ADV 299A 7/85; P Platt, Exeter for preservation 8/91; Abacus Carriage Services Ltd {Leisurelink}, Horley (SR) 12/92; moved to Newhaven (ES) 7/96; Metrobus Ltd, Orpington (LN), 7/97; Vintage Yellow Buses Ltd, Bournemouth (DT) 9/97; re-registered MSJ 499 5/98; Bournemouth Transport Ltd, Bournemouth (DT) 245 6/01; J Hawkins, Kingswear for preservation 6/06; re-seated to

O44/31F by 2/10; R McAllister {Devon Classic Vehicle Hire}, Paignton (DN) 5/10; returned to J Hawkins, Kingswear for preservation 5/11; still owned 1/15.

926 GTA (926): Western National Omnibus Co Ltd, Exeter (DN) 926 1/71; Amalgamated Passenger Transport Ltd (dealer), Bracebridge Heath by 4/82; East Yorkshire Motor Services Ltd, Kingston-on-Hull (EY) 902 4/82; renumbered 626 10/86; Scarborough and District Motor Services Ltd, Scarborough (NY) 626 1/88; re-registered NKH 396A 3/90; Passenger Vehicle Spares (Barnsley) Ltd (dealer), Carlton 6/90.

927 GTA (927): Western National Omnibus Co Ltd, Exeter (DN) 927 1/71; Amalgamated Passenger Transport Ltd (dealer), Bracebridge Heath 6/82; loaned to Lincolnshire Road Car Co Ltd, Lincoln (LI) 927 during 1982 and 1983 summer seasons; loaned to Hastings & District Transport Ltd (ES) for 1984 summer season; Ribble Motor Services Ltd, Preston (LA) 1927 11/84; re-registered ABV 669A 2/90; Cumberland Motor Services Ltd, Whitehaven (CA) 1927 5/90; withdrawn 11/90; Stagecoach (North West) Ltd, Whitehaven (CA) 1927 5/91; Fife Scottish Omnibuses Ltd, Kirkcaldy (FE) 669 3/92; renumbered 1102 8/92 and to 15869 1/03; Roulston, Glasgow for preservation 5/03; First Glasgow (No 1) Ltd, Glasgow (SC) 39989 3/04; M Roulston, Glasgow for preservation by 9/06; T Wigley (dealer), Carlton 5/07; DL Hoare, Chepstow (CS) 7/07; S Cope, Longton for preservation 11/09; R Anderson, London for preservation 10/10; re-registered 724 XUW by 4/11; Western Greyhound Ltd, Summercourt (CO) 6/12; probably retained by M Howarth, Newquay following sale of Western Greyhound business 12/14.

928 GTA (928): Western National Omnibus Co Ltd, Exeter (DN) 928 1/71; Devon General Ltd, Exeter (DN) 928 1/83; East Yorkshire Motor Services Ltd, Kingston-on-Hull (EY) 905 10/83; Lincolnshire Road Car Co Ltd, Lincoln (LI) 2353 2/84; re-registered AFE 387A 5/86; Passenger Vehicle Spares (Barnsley) Ltd (dealer), Carlton 4/87; possibly to London Bus Export Co (dealer), Chepstow (1987?); Quay West Beach Resort, Goodrington (XDN) 7/88; S Gilkes, Chislehurst for preservation by 9/90; M Arnold, Crawley for preservation 11/91; reverted to original registration 928 GTA 3/92; Abacus Carriage Services Ltd {Leisurelink}, Horley (SR) 4/93; loaned to Cardiff branch 8/93; returned by 2/94; Metrobus Ltd, Orpington (LN) 7/97; Vintage Yellow Buses Ltd, Bournemouth (DT) 248 by 9/97; Bournemouth Transport Ltd, Bournemouth (DT) 248 6/01; Lampar (dealer), Bournemouth 2001; Dorset Heritage Transport Services Ltd (DT) 6/02; Somerbus Ltd, Paulton (SO) 5/03; T Bennett, Sherborne for preservation 8/05; still owned 1/15.

929 GTA (929): Western National Omnibus Co Ltd, Exeter (DN) 929 1/71; Devon General Ltd, Exeter 929 1/83; Amalgamated Passenger Transport Ltd (dealer), Bracebridge Heath 1983; Lincolnshire Road Car Co Ltd, Lincoln (LI) 3354 10/83; withdrawn by 9/86; re-registered AFE 388A 5/86; Passenger Vehicle Spares (Barnsley) Ltd (dealer), Carlton 4/87.

930 GTA (930): Western National Omnibus Co Ltd, Exeter (DN) 930 1/71; Devon General Ltd, Exeter 930 1/83; Lincolnshire Road Car Co Ltd, Lincoln (LI) 10/83; not operated; East Yorkshire Motor Services Ltd, Kingston-on-Hull (EY) for spares 2/84; GP Ripley (dealer), Carlton for scrap 2/85.

931 GTA (931): Western National Omnibus Co Ltd, Exeter (DN) 931 1/71; Western National Ltd, Exeter (DN) 931 1/83; East Yorkshire Motor Services Ltd, Kingston-on-Hull (EY) 903 2/83; renumbered 631 10/86; Scarborough & District Motor Services Ltd, Scarborough (NY) 631 1/88; re-registered NAT 747A 5/89; Wombwell Diesels Co Ltd (dealer), Wombwell 8/89; P Cammack, Liverpool for preservation 9/89; reverted to original registration 931 GTA 9/91; S Gardner, Preston for preservation 10/96; W Hulme, Bristol (GL) 4/99; retained for preservation from an unknown date; moved to Yatton by10/09; operated as Rubicon Classic, Bristol (GL) from 4/09 until c10/09; still owned 1/15.

932 GTA (932): Western National Omnibus Co Ltd, Exeter (DN) 932 1/71; Devon General Ltd, Exeter 932 1/83; East Yorkshire Motor Services Ltd, Kingston-on-Hull (EY) 904 1/83; renumbered 632 10/86; Scarborough & District Motor Services Ltd, Scarborough (NY) 632 1/88; R Follwell, Stapleford for preservation 9/89; operated as Follwell & Owen {Midland Heritage}, Cotes Heath (ST) from 4/11; moved to Stableford (ST) by 1/14; T Bennett, Sherborne for preservation by 12/14.

933 GTA (933): Western National Omnibus Co Ltd, Exeter (DN) 933 1/71; PD Wright {Pullman Coaches}, Norwich (NK) 5/82; Holman Bros (Coaches) Ltd {Crouch End Coaches}, London N22 (LN) 3/83; London Cityrama Ltd, London SW8 (LN) 4/85; sold for scrap 1/89.

934 GTA (934): Greenslades Tours Ltd, Exeter (DN) 5/69; Western National Omnibus Co Ltd, Exeter (DN) 1238 7/71; withdrawn 10/73; C Pugsley, Yeo Vale (DN) 12/73; L Wadman, {SW Coaches}, Throwleigh (DN) 5/74; withdrawn 8/77; Robinson {Spreyton Garage}, Spreyton (XDN) for conversion to a caravan by 3/79; not carried out; sold 1983.

935 GTA (935): Greenslades Tours Ltd, Exeter (DN) 5/69; repainted in a white and ivy green livery 1971; Western National Omnibus Co Ltd, Exeter (DN) 1239 7/71; withdrawn 10/73; C Pugsley, Yeo Vale (DN) 12/73; L Wadman {SW Coaches}, Throwleigh (DN) 5/74; licensed 6/74; withdrawn

11/77; believed sold by 5/94; M Sherwood, Paignton for preservation 10/95; M Sherwood {Grey Line Tours}, Paignton (DN) as preserved vehicle 11/96; Wright, Egmanton (NG) as preserved vehicle 10/97; retained for preservation from 12/03; W Hulme, Yatton for preservation by 10/12.

936 GTA (936): Western National Omnibus Co Ltd, Exeter (DN) 436 6/70; renumbered 1236 7/71; W Norths (PV) Ltd (dealer), Sherburn in Elmet 10/73; Wylie Coaches, Thorne (WR) 3/74; Team Lockside, Castleford (motor cycle transporter/caravan) by 3/80; disused on site of Calder Gravel Ltd, Brighouse (XWY) by 1984; sold by 1/94.

937 GTA (937): Greenslades Tours Ltd, Exeter (DN) 10/70; numbered 406 6/71; Western National Omnibus Co Ltd, Exeter (DN) 1240 10/71; withdrawn 10/73; W Norths (PV) Ltd (dealer), Sherburn in Elmet 11/73; Simmons & Hawker Ltd, Feltham (XMX) 2/74; Windsor, Slough & Eton Athletic Club, Windsor (XBE) by 12/77; unidentified owner 5/81; left at premises of Rounds, Reading; to farm at Hurst, near Wokingham 6/81; Lister PVS (Bolton) Ltd (dealer), Bolton for scrap 8/87.

938 GTA (938): Greenslades Tours Ltd, Exeter (DN) 1241 10/70, numbered 407 6/71; Western National Omnibus Co Ltd, Exeter (DN) 10/71; withdrawn 7/73; Rundle (dealer), Plymouth for scrap after an accident 12/73.

939 GTA (939): Greenslades Tours Ltd, Exeter (DN) 10/70, numbered 408 6/71; AJ Beale (dealer), Exeter 3/73; J Hoare & Sons Ltd {The Ivy Coaches}, Ivybridge (DN) 3/73; Tally Ho! Coaches Ltd, Kingsbridge (DN) 3/76; withdrawn 8/76; Dudley Coles (contractor), Plymouth (DN) 8/76; sold by 10/92.

940 GTA (940): Greenslades Tours Ltd, Exeter (DN) 10/70, numbered 409 6/71; AJ Beale (dealer), Exeter 3/73; J Hoare & Sons Ltd {The Ivy Coaches}, Ivybridge (DN) 2/73; Tally Ho! Coaches Ltd, Kingsbridge (DN) 3/76; withdrawn 9/76; E Beckett (dealer), Carlton for scrap 8/77.

941 GTA (941): Greenslades Tours Ltd, Exeter (DN) 7/70, numbered 410 6/71; AJ Beale (dealer), Exeter 3/73; Millbay Laundries, Plymouth (XDN) 3/73; West of England Transport Collection, Winkleigh for spares 1/77; RS Brown {Shaftesbury & District Motor Services}, Motcombe (DT) for spares 5/77.

942 GTA (942): Greenslades Tours Ltd, Exeter (DN) 7/70, numbered 411 6/71; Exeter City Architects Department, Exeter (XDN) V32/00 as a mobile office 12/72; plated as a goods vehicle 7/73; subsequently used as an immobile office; P Platt, Exeter for preservation 10/87; I Trotter & T Bartlett, Bruton for preservation 12/89; A Williams, Huddersfield for preservation 4/95; A Hardwick (dealer), Carlton for scrap 9/97.

1962

New Vehicles:

943	943 HTT	AEC Regent V	MD3RV558	Weymann	M176	H33/26R	5/62	1/71
944	944 HTT	AEC Regent V	MD3RV559	Weymann	M177	H33/26R	5/62	1/71
945	945 HTT	AEC Regent V	MD3RV560	Weymann	M178	H33/26R	5/62	1/71
946	946 HTT	AEC Regent V	MD3RV561	Weymann	M173	H33/26R	5/62	1/71
947	947 HTT	AEC Regent V	MD3RV562	Weymann	M172	H33/26R	5/62	1/71
948	948 HTT	AEC Regent V	MD3RV563	Weymann	M174	H33/26R	5/62	1/71
949	949 HTT	AEC Regent V	MD3RV564	Weymann	M175	H33/26R	5/62	1/71
SR950	950 HTT	AEC Reliance	2MU3RV3943	Marshall	B3042	B41F	4/62	1/71
SR951	951 HTT	AEC Reliance	2MU3RV3944	Marshall	B3045	B41F	4/62	1/71
SR952	952 HTT	AEC Reliance	2MU3RV3945	Marshall	B3039	B41F	4/62	1/71
SR953	953 HTT	AEC Reliance	2MU3RV3946	Marshall	B3040	B41F	4/62	1/71
SR954	954 HTT	AEC Reliance	2MU3RV3947	Marshall	B3041	B41F	4/62	1/71
SR955	955 HTT	AEC Reliance	2MU3RV3948	Marshall	B3043	B41F	4/62	1/71
SR956	956 HTT	AEC Reliance	2MU3RV3949	Marshall	B3044	B41F	4/62	1/71
SN957	957 HTT	Albion NS3AN	82065D	Harrington	2585	B31F	3/62	1/71
SN958	958 HTT	Albion NS3AN	82065E	Harrington	2586	B31F	5/62	1/71
SN959	959 HTT	Albion NS3AN	82065F	Harrington	2587	B31F	5/62	1/71
TCR960	960 HTT	AEC Reliance	2MU3RV3934	Willowbrook	61764	C41F	5/62	11/69
TCR961	961 HTT	AEC Reliance	2MU3RV3935	Willowbrook	61761	C41F	5/62	1/70
TCR962	962 HTT	AEC Reliance	2MU3RV3936	Willowbrook	61765	C41F	5/62	1/70
TCR963	963 HTT	AEC Reliance	2MU3RV3937	Willowbrook	61766	C41F	5/62	10/70
TCR964	964 HTT	AEC Reliance	2MU3RV3938	Willowbrook	61767	C41F	5/62	1/71
TCR965	965 HTT	AEC Reliance	2MU3RV3939	Willowbrook	61762	C41F	5/62	1/71
TCR966	966 HTT	AEC Reliance	2MU3RV3940	Willowbrook	61760	C41F	6/62	1/71
TCR967	967 HTT	AEC Reliance	2MU3RV3941	Willowbrook	61763	C41F	6/62	1/71
TCR968	968 HTT	AEC Reliance	2MU3RV3942	Willowbrook	61768	C41F	6/62	1/71

Notes:

Fleet number prefixes were removed on repaint.

960-968 HTT (TCR960-968): Had 7ft 6in wide Viscount style bodies in Grey Cars livery.

960 HTT (TCR 960): Also had Duple Group body number CF233.
961 HTT (TCR 961): Also had Duple Group body number CF221.
962 HTT (TCR 962): Also had Duple Group body number CF154.
963 HTT (TCR 963): Also had Duple Group body number CF238.
964 HTT (TCR 964): Also had Duple Group body number CF241.
965 HTT (TCR 965): Also had Duple Group body number CF222.
966 HTT (TCR 966): Also had Duple Group body number CF220.
967 HTT (TCR 967): Also had Duple Group body number CF223.
968 HTT (TCR 968): Also had Duple Group body number CF243.

Disposals:

943 HTT (943): Western National Omnibus Co Ltd, Exeter (DN) 943 1/71; loaned to Hants & Dorset Motor Services Ltd, Bournemouth (HA) 9/74; returned and withdrawn 11/74; W Norths (PV) Ltd (dealer), Sherburn in-Elmet 2/75; Wakefield Metropolitan District Council (XWY) as a playbus 10/76; P Platt, Exeter as spares for preservation project 5/81; J Sykes (dealer), Carlton for scrap 1981.

944 HTT (944): Western National Omnibus Co Ltd, Exeter (DN) 944 1/71; withdrawn 10/74; Western Welsh Omnibus Co Ltd, Cardiff (GG) for spares 1/75; Jones (dealer), Cardiff for scrap 5/75.

945 HTT (945): Western National Omnibus Co Ltd, Exeter (DN) 945 1/71; withdrawn 6/74; Cornwall County Council, Truro (XCO) as a road safety exhibition 1/75; unidentified dealer, St Day for scrap 8/78.

946 HTT (946): Western National Omnibus Co Ltd, Exeter (DN) 946 1/71; withdrawn 10/74; Sadler (dealer), Grimsby for scrap 11/74.

947 HTT (947): Western National Omnibus Co Ltd, Exeter (DN) 947 1/71; withdrawn 10/74; Western Welsh Omnibus Co Ltd, Cardiff (GG) for spares 1/75; Jones (dealer), Cardiff for scrap 5/75.

948 HTT (948): Western National Omnibus Co Ltd, Exeter (DN) 948 1/71; withdrawn 10/74; W Norths (PV) Ltd (dealer), Sherburn in-Elmet 2/75.

949 HTT (949): Western National Omnibus Co Ltd, Exeter (DN) 949 1/71; withdrawn 10/72; W Norths (PV) Ltd (dealer), Sherburn in-Elmet 10/72; PVS (dealer), Canvey 3/74; Ensign Bus Co Ltd (dealer), Hornchurch 7/74; Hexagona Discotecas, Valencia (O-E) 3/74; awaiting scrapping 10/77.

950 HTT (950): Western National Omnibus Co Ltd, Exeter (DN) 950 1/71; withdrawn 6/75; scrapped by Western National at Torquay 1/77.

951 HTT (951): Western National Omnibus Co Ltd, Exeter (DN) 951 1/71; withdrawn 6/74; Martin & Sons Ltd (dealer), Weaverham 10/74; Whitton Albion AFC, Northwich (XCH) by 4/76; T Goodwin (dealer), Carlton 10/76.

952 HTT (952): Western National Omnibus Co Ltd, Exeter (DN) 952 1/71; withdrawn 1/77; Thornton (dealer), Cundy Cross 1/77; G Jameson {Dunscroft Commercials} (dealer), Dunscroft for scrap 2/77.

953 HTT (953): Western National Omnibus Co Ltd, Exeter (DN) 953 1/71; withdrawn 11/74; sold 10/74; Martin & Sons Ltd (dealer), Weaverham 11/74.

954 HTT (954): Western National Omnibus Co Ltd, Exeter (DN) 954 1/71; withdrawn 11/74; Rundle (dealer), Plymouth for scrap 11/74.

955 HTT (955): Western National Omnibus Co Ltd, Exeter (DN) 955 1/71; withdrawn 10/74; Martin & Sons Ltd (dealer), Weaverham 11/74.

956 HTT (956): Western National Omnibus Co Ltd, Exeter (DN) 956 1/71; withdrawn 6/74; sold 10/74; N Harvey & Sons, Mousehole (CO) 10/74; Fyffes-Munro Horticultural Sundries, Penzance (XCO) by 4/77; LJ & WB Ede {Roselyn Coaches}, Par (CO) for spares 7/83; scrapped by 9/83

957 HTT (957): Western National Omnibus Co Ltd, Exeter (DN) 957 1/71; withdrawn 4/72; W Norths (PV) Ltd (dealer), Sherburn in-Elmet 7/72; Camm & Co, Chesterfield (XDE) 7/73; returned to W Norths (PV) Ltd (dealer), Sherburn in-Elmet 3/75: unidentified dealer for scrap 7/76.

958 HTT (958): Western National Omnibus Co Ltd, Exeter (DN) 958 1/71; withdrawn 4/72; W Norths (PV) Ltd (dealer), Sherburn in-Elmet 7/72; Armoride, Earby (XWR) 1973; Sinclair, Whitefield (XGM) 9/75; unknown owner as a mobile caravan 1976.

959 HTT (959): Western National Omnibus Co Ltd, Exeter (DN) 959 1/71; withdrawn 5/73; W Norths (PV) Ltd (dealer), Sherburn in-Elmet 5/73; Pearson, Stainton-in-Cleveland (XCD) by 10/73.

960 HTT (960): Greenslades Tours, Exeter (DN) 1/70; renumbered 422 6/71; LJ & WB Ede {Roselyn Coaches}, Par (CO) 3/73; licensed 4/73; Tally Ho! Coaches Ltd, Kingsbridge (DN) 10/75;

withdrawn 8/77; West of England Transport Collection (P Platt?), Winkleigh for preservation 11/77; S Wren, Beddau & D Rockey, Exeter for preservation 3/83; kept at West of England Transport Collection, Winkleigh; S Wren, Pontypridd for preservation 8/78; still owned 1/15.

961 HTT (961): Greenslades Tours, Exeter 1/70; renumbered 423 6/71; AJ Beale (dealer), Exeter 3/73; Millbay Laundries, Plymouth (XDN) 3/73; West of England Transport Collection, Winkleigh for preservation 12/76; later used for spares for 960 HTT 11/77; remains to CF Booth Ltd (dealer), Rotherham for scrap 1/78.

962 HTT (962): Greenslades Tours, Exeter 1/70; renumbered 424 6/71; LJ & WB Ede {Roselyn Coaches}, Par (CO) 3/73; licensed 4/73; WG & CS Peake {El Peake}, Pontypool (GT) 8/75; Way (dealer) Cardiff by 10/78; Passenger Vehicle Spares (Barnsley) Ltd (dealer), Carlton 10/79.

963 HTT (963): Greenslades Tours, Exeter 10/70; renumbered 425 6/71; LJ & WB Ede {Roselyn Coaches}, Par (CO) 3/73; licensed 4/73; HG Brown & G Davies {Truronian Coaches}, Truro (CO) 11/73; withdrawn 7/76; Cornwall County Council (Weare Comprehensive School), Saltash (XCO) 7/76; Willis (Central Garage) Ltd, Bodmin (CO) by 11/80; licensed fitted with bus seats 3/81; sold for scrap 1989.

964 HTT (964): Western National Omnibus Co Ltd, Exeter (DN) 964 1/71; Greenslades Tours, Exeter (DN) 5/71; numbered 426 6/71; Blackbrooker (dealer) London SE11 9/74; G Jones {S Jones & Son}, Bancyfelin (DD) 1974; D Lansdown {CH Lansdown & Sons}, Tockington (AV) 4/75; withdrawn 8/76; DJ Green (dealer), Weymouth 1976; Haywards Heath Grammar School, Haywards Heath (XWS) 1976; IE Thomas, West Ewell (SR) 2/78; JC Rettalick & RC Kernutt {Surreyways}, Godalming (SR) 7/78; not operated; moved to Guildford 12/79.

965 HTT (965): Western National Omnibus Co Ltd, Exeter (DN) 965 1/71; Greenslades Tours, Exeter 5/71; renumbered 427 6/71; Dawlish Coaches Ltd {Tomlinson's}, Dawlish (DN) 10/74 (having been on loan from 8/74); licensed 11/74 to 1/77; Mitchell's (Perranporth) Ltd, Perranporth (CO) 6/77.

966 HTT (966): Western National Omnibus Co Ltd, Exeter (DN) 966 1/71; Greenslades Tours, Exeter 5/71; renumbered 428 6/71; Blackbrooker (dealer) London SE11 9/74;

967 HTT (967): Western National Omnibus Co Ltd, Exeter (DN) 967 1/71; Greenslades Tours, Exeter 5/70; renumbered 429 6/71; Blackbrooker (dealer) London SE11 9/74; G Jones {S Jones & Son}, Bancyfelin (DD) 1974; Moseley (Gloucester) Ltd (dealer), Cinderford 4/75; LE Evans, Yate (AV) 5/75; withdrawn 2/76; RS Brown {Shaftesbury & District Motor Services}, Motcombe (DT) 3/76; entered service 5/76; M Light & RS Brown {Shaftesbury & District Motor Services}, Motcombe (DT) 10/77; withdrawn 9/79; RS Brown, Motcombe for preservation 9/80; P Morley, Dunster for preservation 10/81; P Platt, Exeter (preservationist) for spares 1/86; Wigley (dealer), Carlton for scrap 2/87.

968 HTT (968): Western National Omnibus Co Ltd, Exeter (DN) 968 1/71; Greenslades Tours, Exeter 5/71; renumbered 430 6/71; RK & RE Webber {Webber Bros}, Blisland (CO) 5/73; WT Moyle, Newquay (CO) 3/75; withdrawn 8/78.

1963

New vehicles:

969	969 MDV	AEC Regent V	MD3RV566	MCCW		H33/26F	6/63	1/71
970	970 MDV	AEC Regent V	MD3RV567	MCCW		H33/26F	6/63	1/71
971	971 MDV	AEC Regent V	MD3RV568	MCCW		H33/26F	6/63	1/71
972	972 MDV	AEC Regent V	MD3RV569	MCCW		H33/26F	6/63	1/71
973	973 MDV	AEC Regent V	MD3RV570	MCCW		H33/26F	6/63	1/71
974	974 MDV	AEC Regent V	MD3RV571	MCCW		H33/26F	6/63	1/71
975	975 MDV	AEC Regent V	MD3RV572	MCCW		H33/26F	6/63	1/71
976	976 MDV	AEC Regent V	MD3RV573	MCCW		H33/26F	6/63	1/71
977	977 MDV	AEC Regent V	MD3RV574	MCCW		H33/26F	6/63	1/71
978	978 MDV	AEC Regent V	MD3RV575	MCCW		H33/26F	6/63	1/71
979	979 MDV	AEC Regent V	MD3RV576	MCCW		H33/26F	6/63	1/71
980	980 MDV	AEC Regent V	MD3RV577	MCCW		H33/26F	6/63	1/71
981	981 MDV	AEC Regent V	MD3RV578	MCCW		H33/26F	6/63	1/71
982	982 MDV	AEC Regent V	MD3RV579	MCCW		H33/26F	6/63	1/71
983	983 MDV	AEC Regent V	MD3RV580	MCCW		H33/26F	6/63	1/71
984	984 MDV	AEC Regent V	MD3RV581	MCCW		H33/26F	6/63	1/71
985	985 MDV	AEC Reliance	2MU3RV4418	Marshall	B3061	B41F	4/63	1/71
986	986 MDV	AEC Reliance	2MU3RV4419	Marshall	B3056	B41F	4/63	1/71
987	987 MDV	AEC Reliance	2MU3RV4420	Marshall	B3057	B41F	4/63	1/71
988	988 MDV	AEC Reliance	2MU3RV4421	Marshall	B3059	B41F	4/63	1/71
989	989 MDV	AEC Reliance	2MU3RV4422	Marshall	B3058	B41F	4/63	1/71

990	990 MDV	AEC Reliance	2MU3RV4423	Marshall	B3060	B41F	4/63	1/71
991	991 MDV	AEC Reliance	2MU3RV4424	Marshall	B3062	B41F	4/63	1/71

Disposals:

969 MDV (969): Western National Omnibus Co Ltd, Exeter (DN) 969 1/71; withdrawn 7/75; W Norths (PV) Ltd (dealer), Sherburn in Elmet 4/76; unidentified dealer, Carlton by 12/77.

970 MDV (970): Western National Omnibus Co Ltd, Exeter (DN) 970 1/71; withdrawn 8/75; sold 4/76; WO Blythin {Gold Star Coachways}, St Asaph (CL) 4/76; not used; Cattell, Rhuddlan (XDD) by 8/78; returned to WO Blythin {Gold Star Coachways}, St Asaph (CL) 6/79; withdrawn by 8/80; used as seat store by 10/82; J Partridge, Bristol for preservation 10/82; P Platt, Exeter for preservation 1983; T Wigley (dealer), Carlton for scrap 1/84.

971 MDV (971): Western National Omnibus Co Ltd, Exeter (DN) 971 1/71; withdrawn 10/75; sold 4/76; WO Blythin {Gold Star Coachways}, St Asaph (CL) by 8/76; not used; Lister PVS (Bolton) Ltd (dealer), Bolton 5/79; CF Booth Ltd (dealer), Rotherham for scrap 5/79.

972 MDV (972): Western National Omnibus Co Ltd, Exeter (DN) 972 1/71; withdrawn 10/75; WO Blythin {Gold Star Coachways}, St Asaph (CL) 4/76; not operated; J Eagles, W Crawford & F Hughes, Mold (CL) 10/77; Paul Sykes Organisation Ltd (dealer), Barnsley 1981.

973 MDV (973): Western National Omnibus Co Ltd, Exeter (DN) 973 1/71; withdrawn 10/75; W Norths (PV) Ltd (dealer), Sherburn in Elmet 6/76; sold 6/77.

974 MDV (974): Western National Omnibus Co Ltd, Exeter (DN) 974 1/71; withdrawn 9/75; Martin's Bus & Coach Sales Ltd (dealer), Middlewich 3/76.

975 MDV (975): Western National Omnibus Co Ltd, Exeter (DN) 975 1/71; withdrawn 9/75; Martin's Bus & Coach Sales Ltd (dealer), Middlewich 3/76; T Goodwin (dealer), Carlton 12/76; (Boswell?) Bros (dealer), Cundy Cross for scrap 1/77.

976 MDV (976): Western National Omnibus Co Ltd, Exeter (DN) 976 1/71; withdrawn 8/75; DJ Green (dealer), Weymouth 3/76; Hounslow Evangelical Church, Hounslow (XLN) 4/76; unidentified dealer 12/78; snack bar, London NW1 5/79; unidentified dealer, Gospel Oak, London 2/83.

977 MDV (977): Western National Omnibus Co Ltd, Exeter (DN) 977 1/71; withdrawn 8/75; WO Blythin {Gold Star Coachways}, St Asaph (CL) 4/76; not licensed; Office Cleaning Services, London WC1 (XLN) by 6/78; Office Cleaning Services, Cardiff (XSG) 9/78; Ensign Bus Co Ltd (dealer), Grays 12/78; MJL International, location unknown (O-F) 2/79.

978 MDV (978): Western National Omnibus Co Ltd, Exeter (DN) 978 1/71; withdrawn 8/75; W Norths (PV) Ltd (dealer), Sherburn in Elmet, 6/76; sold 6/77.

979 MDV (979): Western National Omnibus Co Ltd, Exeter (DN) 979 1/71; withdrawn 9/75; sold 4/76; WO Blythin {Gold Star Coachways}, St Asaph (CL) 4/76; licensed 11/77; Taylor {Alpha Coaches}, Bootle (MY) 7/82; Beauside Ltd {Alpha}, Bootle (MY) by 7/84; Lister PVS (Bolton) Ltd(dealer), Bolton 9/84; Borg, London N9 (XLN) 4/85; returned to Lister PVS (Bolton) Ltd (dealer), Bolton 8/85; Bedayn, Lafayette, CA (O-USA) 9/85, still owned 2/00, sold by 9/09.

980 MDV (980): Western National Omnibus Co Ltd, Exeter (DN) 980 1/71; withdrawn 9/75; W Norths (PV) Ltd (dealer), Sherburn in Elmet, 6/76.

981 MDV (981): Western National Omnibus Co Ltd, Exeter (DN) 981 1/71; withdrawn 9/75; sold 4/76; Omnibus Promotions (dealer), London by 9/76; unidentified owner, Neu Isenburg (O-D) as a publicity shop by 9/76; upper deck reduced in height; Creativ Marketing, Scheyem (O-D) by 10/05.

982 MDV (982): Western National Omnibus Co Ltd, Exeter (DN) 982 1/71; withdrawn 9/75; sold 4/76; WO Blythin {Gold Star Coachways}, St Asaph (CL) 4/76; unidentified dealer, Carlton for scrap 2/79.

983 MDV (983): Western National Omnibus Co Ltd, Exeter (DN) 983 1/71; withdrawn 3/75; W Norths (PV) Ltd (dealer), Sherburn in Elmet, 6/76.

984 MDV (984): Western National Omnibus Co Ltd, Exeter (DN) 984 1/71; withdrawn 10/75; W Norths (PV) Ltd (dealer), Sherburn in Elmet, 6/76.

985 MDV (985): Western National Omnibus Co Ltd, Exeter (DN) 985 1/71; withdrawn 9/75; Martin's Bus & Coach Sales Ltd (dealer), Middlewich 11/75; G Jones {Carlton Metals} (dealer), Carlton for scrap by 12/75.

986 MDV (986): Western National Omnibus Co Ltd, Exeter (DN) 986 1/71; withdrawn 9/75; Martin's Bus & Coach Sales Ltd (dealer), Middlewich 11/75; G Jones {Carlton Metals} (dealer), Carlton by 12/75; scrapped 2/76.

987 MDV (987): Western National Omnibus Co Ltd, Exeter (DN) 987 1/71; South Wales Transport Co Ltd, Swansea (WG) for spares 9/75.

988 MDV (988): Western National Omnibus Co Ltd, Exeter (DN) 988 1/71; South Wales Transport Co Ltd, Swansea (WG) for spares 9/75; Martin's Bus & Coach Sales Ltd (dealer), Middlewich 11/75; Goodwin (dealer) Carlton, for scrap 11/76.

989 MDV (989): Western National Omnibus Co Ltd, Exeter (DN) 989 1/71; South Wales Transport Co Ltd, Swansea (WG) for spares 9/75.

990 MDV (990): Western National Omnibus Co Ltd, Exeter (DN) 990 1/71; withdrawn 9/75; Martin's Bus & Coach Sales Ltd (dealer), Middlewich 9/75; South Wales Transport Co Ltd, Swansea (WG) for spares 9/75.

991 MDV (991): Western National Omnibus Co Ltd, Exeter (DN) 991 1/71; withdrawn 7/75; Martin's Bus & Coach Sales Ltd (dealer), Middlewich 9/75; 1st Endon Scout Group, Endon (XST) by 4/76; Wacton Trading/Coach Sales (dealer) Bromyard 10/88; S Gilkes, Chislehurst for preservation 2/89; 991 Group, Winkleigh for preservation 2/90; CT Shears & P Platt, Winkleigh (preservationists) for spares by 8/07; still owned 1/15.

Vehicle on loan from Dodge Bros (Britain) Ltd, Kew:

2498 PK	Dodge S306	S306/SPEC/643	Weymann	M671	B42F	9/62

Notes:

2498 PK: On demonstration during 5/63.

Vehicle on loan from Transport Vehicles (Daimler) Ltd

4559 VC	Daimler CRG6LX	60065	NCME	5875	H43/33F	10/62

Notes

4559 VC: On demonstration and used in service from 6/63 until 7/63.

1964

New vehicles:

1	1 RDV	AEC Reliance	2MU3RA4971	Harrington	2850	C41F	4/64	1/71
2	2 RDV	AEC Reliance	2MU3RA4972	Harrington	2851	C41F	4/64	1/71
3	3 RDV	AEC Reliance	2MU3RA4973	Harrington	2852	C41F	4/64	1/71
4	4 RDV	AEC Reliance	2MU3RA4974	Harrington	2853	C41F	4/64	1/71
5	5 RDV	AEC Reliance	2MU3RA4975	Harrington	2854	C41F	4/64	1/71
6	6 RDV	AEC Reliance	2MU3RA4976	Harrington	2855	C41F	4/64	1/71
7	7 RDV	AEC Reliance	2MU3RA4977	Harrington	2856	C41F	4/64	1/71
8	8 RDV	AEC Reliance	2MU3RA4978	Harrington	2857	C41F	4/64	1/71
9	9 RDV	AEC Reliance	2U3RA4967	Marshall	B3249	B53F	6/64	1/71
10	10 RDV	AEC Reliance	2U3RA4968	Marshall	B3250	B53F	6/64	1/71
11	11 RDV	AEC Reliance	2U3RA4969	Marshall	B3251	B53F	6/64	1/71
12	12 RDV	AEC Reliance	2U3RA4970	Marshall	B3252	B53F	6/64	1/71
13	13 RDV	AEC Reliance	2MU3RA4962	Willowbrook	75701	B41F	4/64	1/71
14	14 RDV	AEC Reliance	2MU3RA4963	Willowbrook	75702	B41F	4/64	1/71
15	15 RDV	AEC Reliance	2MU3RA4964	Willowbrook	75703	B41F	4/64	1/71
16	16 RDV	AEC Reliance	2MU3RA4965	Willowbrook	75704	B41F	4/64	1/71
17	17 RDV	AEC Reliance	2MU3RA4966	Willowbrook	75705	B41F	5/64	1/71
501	501 RUO	AEC Regent V	2D3RA1463	Willowbrook	75467	H39/30F	4/64	1/71
502	502 RUO	AEC Regent V	2D3RA1464	Willowbrook	75468	H39/30F	4/64	1/71
503	503 RUO	AEC Regent V	2D3RA1465	Willowbrook	75469	H39/30F	4/64	1/71
504	504 RUO	AEC Regent V	2D3RA1466	Willowbrook	75470	H39/30F	4/64	1/71
505	505 RUO	AEC Regent V	2D3RA1467	Willowbrook	75471	H39/30F	4/64	1/71
506	506 RUO	AEC Regent V	2D3RA1468	Willowbrook	75472	H39/30F	4/64	1/71
507	507 RUO	AEC Regent V	2D3RA1469	Willowbrook	75473	H39/30F	4/64	1/71
508	508 RUO	AEC Regent V	2D3RA1470	Willowbrook	75474	H39/30F	4/64	1/71

Notes:

1-8 RDV (1-8): Delivered late 1963, but did not enter service until 4/64 and had special 31ft 5in long x 7ft 6in wide Cavalier 315 style bodies in Grey Cars livery.

9-12 RDV (9-12): Were the first 36ft long x 8ft 2½ in wide vehicles in the fleet; re-seated to B51F before entering service.

13-17 RDV (13-17): Also had Duple Group body number CF648-652.

501-508 RUO (501-508): Also had Duple Group body numbers CF640-647.

Disposals:

1 RDV (1): Western National Omnibus Co Ltd, Exeter (DN) 1 1/71; Greenslades Tours Ltd, Exeter. (DN) 5/71; renumbered 431 6/71; withdrawn 1975; DE & BJ Allmey, Eastcote (LN) 5/75; withdrawn 12/79; loaned to West of England Transport Collection, Winkleigh from 12/79 and repainted in Grey Cars livery, for preservation 1981; P Platt, Exeter for preservation 3/91; moved Dawlish Warren 9/11; current 1/15.

2 RDV (2): Western National Omnibus Co Ltd, Exeter (DN) 2 1/71; Greenslades Tours Ltd, Exeter. (DN) 5/71; renumbered 432 6/71; withdrawn 1975; FJ & JA Fry {Fry's Tours}, Tintagel (CO) 4/75; withdrawn by 3/83; P Platt (preservationist), Exeter for spares 10/84; R Greet (preservationist), Broadhempston for spares 5/04; still owned 1/15.

3 RDV (3): Western National Omnibus Co Ltd, Exeter (DN) 3 1/71; Greenslades Tours Ltd, Exeter. (DN) 5/71; renumbered 433 6/71; withdrawn 1975; WLG Sherrin, Carhampton (SO) 7/75; withdrawn 7/78; P & Mrs GL Baird {Prestwood Travel}, Prestwood (BK) 9/78; Ward Jones (dealer), High Wycombe by8/83; sold for scrap by 2/85.

4 RDV (4): Western National Omnibus Co Ltd, Exeter (DN) 4 1/71; Greenslades Tours Ltd, Exeter. (DN) 5/71; renumbered 434 6/71; withdrawn 1975; DC Venner {Scarlet Coaches}, Minehead (SO) 7/75; DE & BJ Allmey, Pinner (LN) 11/77; withdrawn 6/81; Dawlish Coaches Ltd {Tomlinson's}, Dawlish (DN) re-registered TSV 850 4/85; R Huckle, Sutton Coldfield for preservation and reverted to original registration (4 RDV) 1/94; B Heywood & K Prosser {A Line Coaches}, Bedworth (WK) by 12/94; not operated; P Platt, Exeter for preservation 3/04; R Greet, Broadhempston for preservation 5/04; still owned 12/13; re-seated to C40F at an unknown date.

5 RDV (5): Western National Omnibus Co Ltd, Exeter (DN) 5 1/71; Greenslades Tours Ltd, Exeter. (DN) 5/71; renumbered 435 6/71; withdrawn 1975; RK & RE Webber {Webber Bros}, Blisland (CO) 4/75; Educational Holidays Guernsey Ltd {Island Coachways}, St Peter Port, Guernsey (CI) 7/81; re-registered 6769 5/82; Wacton Trading/Coach Sales (dealer), Bromyard 12/84; Truscott, Roche for preservation 12/84; D Rundle, Falmouth for preservation 1/99; Falmouth Coaches Ltd {King Harry}, Falmouth (CO) 7/02; converted to recovery vehicle by 12/03; re-registered YCV 365B 10/05.

6 RDV (6): Western National Omnibus Co Ltd, Exeter (DN) 6 1/71; Greenslades Tours Ltd, Exeter. (DN) 5/71; renumbered 436 6/71; renumbered 294 5/75; withdrawn 1975; RK & RE Webber {Webber Bros}, Blisland (CO) for spares 4/75; scrapped at Blisland by 5/78.

7 RDV (7): Western National Omnibus Co Ltd, Exeter (DN) 7 1/71; Greenslades Tours Ltd, Exeter. (DN) 5/71; renumbered 437 6/71; withdrawn 1975; SEJ Ridler {Dulverton Motors}, Dulverton (H) 5/75; licensed 7/75; T Greenslade, Bathealton (XSO) c7/80; moved to Nether Stowey (XSO) at an unknown date; sold by 10/92; R Warren, Martock for preservation 3/02; for sale 1/15.

8 RDV (8): Western National Omnibus Co Ltd, Exeter (DN) 8 1/71; Greenslades Tours Ltd, Exeter. (DN) 5/71; renumbered 438 6/71; withdrawn 1975; SEJ Ridler {Dulverton Motors}, Dulverton (SO) 5/75; licensed 7/75; Dawlish Coaches Ltd {Tomlinson's}, Dawlish (DN) 7/80; re-registered BDV 175B by 5/88; SC Glover, Exeter as a mobile caravan 8/88.

9 RDV (9): Western National Omnibus Co Ltd, Exeter (DN) 9 1/71; reseated to B49F 3/74; withdrawn 4/80; West of England Transport Collection, Winkleigh 7/80; C Jeavons, Kingswinford for preservation 1/82; S Cope, Longton for preservation 10/98; P Platt, Dawlish Warren for preservation 9/11; R Morgan & D Chick, Solihull for preservation 1/12; still owned 1/15.

10 RDV (10): Western National Omnibus Co Ltd, Exeter (DN) 10 1/71; reseated to B49F 3/74; withdrawn 4/80; W Norths (PV) Ltd (dealer), Sherburn in Elmet 8/80; M Parton & Allen (dealer), Carlton for scrap 8/80.

11 RDV (11): Western National Omnibus Co Ltd, Exeter (DN) 11 1/71; reseated to B49F 3/74; withdrawn 4/80; CF Booth Ltd (dealer), Rotherham for scrap 8/80.

12 RDV (11): Western National Omnibus Co Ltd, Exeter (DN) 12 1/71; reseated to B49F 4/74; to B50F 8/76 and back to B49F 1977; withdrawn 1980; Kinross Plant & Construction Co Ltd (contractor), Kinross (XTE) 8/80; withdrawn 10/81.

13 RDV (13): Western National Omnibus Co Ltd, Exeter (DN) 13 (as B39F) 1/71; withdrawn 9/77; Finlay (dealer), Birdwell by 12/77; Kennedy's Catering, Morley (XWY) 2/78; Hartwood Exports (Machinery) Ltd (dealer), Barnsley 8/79; D Rollinson (Bus Centre) Ltd (dealer), Carlton 12/79.

14 RDV (14): Western National Omnibus Co Ltd, Exeter (DN) 14 (as B39F) 1/71; withdrawn 9/77; Finlay (dealer), Birdwell by 12/77; D Rollinson (Bus Centre) Ltd (dealer), Carlton 2/79.

15 RDV (15): Western National Omnibus Co Ltd, Exeter (DN) 15 1/71; reseated to B39F 1975; withdrawn 9/77; unidentified dealer, Totnes for scrap 1/78.

16 RDV (16): Western National Omnibus Co Ltd, Exeter (DN) 16 1/71; withdrawn 9/77; Finlay (dealer), Birdwell by 12/77; D Rollinson (Bus Centre) Ltd (dealer), Carlton 2/79.

17 RDV (17): Western National Omnibus Co Ltd, Exeter (DN) 17 1/71; reseated to B39F 8/73; withdrawn 9/77; A Finlay (dealer), Birdwell by 11/77; Kennedy's Catering, Morley (XWY) 11/77; Hartwood Exports (Machinery) Ltd (dealer), Barnsley 8/79; D Rollinson (Bus Centre) Ltd (dealer), Carlton 12/79.

501 RUO (501): Western National Omnibus Co Ltd, Exeter (DN) 501 1/71; withdrawn 11/79; CF Booth Ltd (dealer), Rotherham 7/80; scrapped 9/80.

502 RUO (502): Western National Omnibus Co Ltd, Exeter (DN) 502 1/71; withdrawn 5/80; CF Booth Ltd (dealer), Rotherham 7/80; scrapped 9/80.

503 RUO (503): Western National Omnibus Co Ltd, Exeter (DN) 503 1/71; withdrawn 6/80; G Bailey, Banstead for preservation 8/80; West of England Transport Collection (CT Shears), Winkleigh for preservation 4/82; R Greet, Broadhempston for preservation 5/95; P Platt, Exeter for preservation 3/10; moved to Dawlish Warren 9/11; R McAllister, Paignton for preservation by 11/11; Devon General Omnibus Trust for preservation 10/13; still owned 1/15.

504 RUO (504): Western National Omnibus Co Ltd, Exeter (DN) 504 1/71; withdrawn 5/80; parts removed by T Carpenter (dealer), Exeter at Torquay depot 5/80; W Norths (PV) Ltd (dealer), Sherburn in Elmet 8/80; Whiting (dealer), Carlton 8/80.

505 RUO (505): Western National Omnibus Co Ltd, Exeter (DN) 505 1/71; withdrawn 5/80; CF Booth Ltd (dealer), Rotherham 7/80; West of England Transport Collection, Winkleigh for preservation 8/80; S Gilkes, Chiselhurst for preservation 8/85; Hewitts Farm, Chelsfield (XLN) as roadside advertisement hoarding 8/85; unidentified dealer for scrap after being vandalised 1988.

506 RUO (506): Western National Omnibus Co Ltd, Exeter (DN) 506 1/71; withdrawn 1/79; dismantled for spares at Newton Road depot by T Carpenter (dealer), Exeter 8/80.

507 RUO (507): Western National Omnibus Co Ltd, Exeter (DN) 507 1/71; rebuilt as O39/30F in reversed livery and named 'Prince Regent' 3/76; withdrawn 11/78; PAS Marshall {Obsolete Fleet}, London W1 (LN) DRO1 12/78; DL Hoare, Chepstow for preservation 10/81; DL Hoare {Chepstow Classic Buses}, Chepstow (GT) 4/98; rebuilt to O36/22FT by 7/03; still owned 1/15.

508 RUO (508): Western National Omnibus Co Ltd, Exeter (DN) 508 1/71; rebuilt as O39/30F in reversed livery and named 'Regency Princess' 3/76; withdrawn 11/78; PAS Marshall {Obsolete Fleet}, London W1 (LN) 12/78; West of England Transport Collection, Winkleigh for preservation 10/81; Corlett & Brown {Sundekkers}, San Diego, CA (O-USA) 9/83; Subby's Double Decker, Chula Vista, CA (O-USA) 1985, re-registered 3K70640; Price Breakers. Chula Vista, CA (O-USA) c5/92; returned to Subby's Double Decker, Chula Vista, CA (O-USA) c10/92; unknown owner, Julian, CA (O-USA) c10/93; noted out of use 8/00; Big Red Double Decker Bus Tours, Arroyo Grande, CA (O-USA) c2004, re-registered LON-BUS by 5/05; R Chapman, Atascadero, CA (O-USA) c7/08.

Vehicle on loan from Guy Motors (Europe) Ltd, Wolverhampton:

888 DUK	Guy Arab V		FD75320	Strachan	52097	H41/31F	11/63

Notes:

888 DUK: This vehicle had a Gardner 6LW engine and was on demonstration and used in service during 9/64.

Vehicle on loan from Leyland Motors Ltd:

SGD 669	Leyland PDR1/1		623350	Alexander	9080	H44/34F	1/63

Notes:

SGD 669: This vehicle was on demonstration and used in service during 11/64.

1965

New vehicles:

18	CTT 18C	AEC Reliance	2MU3RA5511	Park Royal	B51691	B41F	5/65	1/71
19	CTT 19C	AEC Reliance	2MU3RA5512	Park Royal	B51692	B41F	5/65	1/71
20	CTT 20C	AEC Reliance	2MU3RA5513	Park Royal	B51693	B41F	5/65	1/71
21	CTT 21C	AEC Reliance	2MU3RA5514	Park Royal	B51694	B41F	5/65	1/71
22	CTT 22C	AEC Reliance	2MU3RA5515	Park Royal	B51695	B41F	5/65	1/71
23	CTT 23C	AEC Reliance	2MU3RA5516	Park Royal	B51696	B41F	5/65	1/71
509	CTT 509C	AEC Regent V	2D3RA1648	Park Royal	B51593	H40/29F	5/65	1/71
510	CTT 510C	AEC Regent V	2D3RA1649	Park Royal	B51594	H40/29F	5/65	1/71
511	CTT 511C	AEC Regent V	2D3RA1650	Park Royal	B51595	H40/29F	5/65	1/71
512	CTT 512C	AEC Regent V	2D3RA1651	Park Royal	B51596	H40/29F	5/65	1/71
513	CTT 513C	AEC Regent V	2D3RA1652	Park Royal	B51597	H40/29F	5/65	1/71
514	CTT 514C	AEC Regent V	2D3RA1653	Park Royal	B51598	H40/29F	5/65	1/71
515	CTT 515C	AEC Regent V	2MD3RA610	Willowbrook	76760	H33/26F	5/65	1/71
516	CTT 516C	AEC Regent V	2MD3RA611	Willowbrook	76759	H33/26F	5/65	1/71
517	CTT 517C	AEC Regent V	2MD3RA612	Willowbrook	76762	H33/26F	5/65	1/71
518	CTT 518C	AEC Regent V	2MD3RA613	Willowbrook	76758	H33/26F	5/65	1/71
519	CTT 519C	AEC Regent V	2MD3RA614	Willowbrook	76761	H33/26F	6/65	1/71
520	CTT 520C	AEC Regent V	2MD3RA615	Willowbrook	76763	H33/26F	6/65	1/71

Notes:

CTT 18-23C (18-23): Re-seated to B39F from 1969 onwards.
CTT 515C (515): Also had Duple Group body number CF938.
CTT 516C (516): Also had Duple Group body number CF937.
CTT 517C (517): Also had Duple Group body number CF940.
CTT 518C (518): Also had Duple Group body number CF936.
CTT 519C (519): Also had Duple Group body number CF939.
CTT 520C (520): Also had Duple Group body number CF941.

Disposals:

CTT 18C (18): Western National Omnibus Co Ltd, Exeter (DN) 18 1/71; withdrawn 7/77; DJ Green (dealer), Weymouth 8/77; Askin (dealer), Barnsley 8/77; Goodwin (dealer), Carlton for scrap 8/77.

CTT 19C (19): Western National Omnibus Co Ltd, Exeter (DN) 19 1/71; withdrawn 7/77; DJ Green (dealer), Weymouth 8/77; G Jones {Carlton Metals} (dealer), Carlton 8/77.

CTT 20C (20): Western National Omnibus Co Ltd, Exeter (DN) 20 1/71; withdrawn 9/77; DJ Green (dealer), Weymouth 9/77; St Peters Scout Group, Bushey Heath (XHT) 9/77; Bushey Heath Youth Club, Bushey Heath (XHT) 12/77; Dumfries & Galloway Students Association, Dumfries (XDG) 11/80.

CTT 21C (21): Western National Omnibus Co Ltd, Exeter (DN) 21 1/71; withdrawn 9/77; DJ Green (dealer), Weymouth 9/77; Our Ladies' School, Dartford (XLN) 9/77; withdrawn 10/83.

CTT 22C (22): Western National Omnibus Co Ltd, Exeter (DN) 22 1/71; reseated to B39F by 12/71; withdrawn 9/77; unidentified contractor, Nuneaton 10/77; still owned 9/79.

CTT 23C (23): Western National Omnibus Co Ltd, Exeter (DN) 23 1/71; withdrawn 9/77; DJ Green (dealer), Weymouth 9/77; All Saints School, Wyke Regis (XDT) 9/77; Stanbridge & Crichel Bus Co Ltd, Stanbridge (DT) 7/80; licensed 10/80; N Robertson, Bristol for preservation 8/82; R Follwell, Stableford for preservation 11/96; D Wright, Fenton 10/14; Fee, Sandbach for preservation 1/15.

CTT 509C (509): Western National Omnibus Co Ltd, Exeter (DN) 509 1/71; withdrawn 8/77; PDS (dealer), Exeter 9/77; LJ & WB Ede (Roselyn Coaches}, Par (CO) 10/77; scrapped 8/84.

CTT 510C (510): Western National Omnibus Co Ltd, Exeter (DN) 510 1/71; withdrawn 8/80; D Tyler, Newton Abbot for preservation 4/81; Wacton Trading/Coach Sales (dealer), Bromyard 12/85; F Woolley, Llanedwen (GD) 2/86; not operated; RD Paterson {Sully PSV/HGV Driving School}, Sully (XSG) as a driver trainer by 6/86; withdrawn 6/92; noted in Chepstow possibly as a caravan 1997; S Whitfield, Leintwardine as a caravan 6/06; still there 1/15.

CTT 511C (511): Western National Omnibus Co Ltd, Exeter (DN) 511 1/71; withdrawn 4/80; CF Booth Ltd (dealer) Rotherham for scrap 8/80.

CTT 512C (512): Western National Omnibus Co Ltd, Exeter (DN) 512 1/71; withdrawn 11/78; British Double Deckers (dealer), Wootton 5/79; Lyons Tetley, London W4 (XLN) as a playbus 7/79; National Playbus Association 2/80; Trent Motor Traction Co Ltd, Derby (DE) in lieu of payment following recovery from low bridge accident, 1986; West of England Transport Collection, Winkleigh as spares for preservation projects 6/87; rebuilt as open-top by 10/88; Wigley (dealer), Carlton for scrap 1990.

CTT 513C (513): Western National Omnibus Co Ltd, Exeter (DN) 513 1/71; withdrawn 10/80; G Wareham, Yarnton for preservation 4/81; CT Shears, Exeter for preservation 11/81; P Platt, Exeter for preservation 1/06; moved to Dawlish Warren 7/11; still owned 1/15.

CTT 514C (514): Western National Omnibus Co Ltd, Exeter (DN) 514 1/71; withdrawn 10/80; Crust, Burgh Heath as a mobile catering vehicle 6/81; unidentified dealer, Mitcham by 12/87.

CTT 515C (515): Western National Omnibus Co Ltd, Exeter (DN) 515 1/71; withdrawn 12/77; Ensign Bus Co Ltd (dealer), Grays 12/77.

CTT 516C (516): Western National Omnibus Co Ltd, Exeter (DN) 516 1/71; withdrawn 7/77; DJ Green (dealer), Weymouth 8/77; Jones (Carlton Metals) (dealer), Carlton 8/77;

CTT 517C (517): Western National Omnibus Co Ltd, Exeter (DN) 517 1/71; Ensign Bus Co Ltd (dealer), Grays 12/77.

CTT 518C (518): Western National Omnibus Co Ltd, Exeter (DN) 518 1/71; withdrawn 11/78 DJ Green (dealer), Weymouth 12/78; Devon General Regent Preservation Group, Guildford for preservation 1/79; becoming 518 Preservation Group, New Malden for preservation by 12/92; G Yarnell, S Powell & R Morgan, Sawley for preservation 1/00; A Blackman Jnr, Halifax for preservation 9/02; P Platt, Exeter for preservation 3/07; T Bennett, Sherborne for preservation 10/09; still owned 1/15.

CTT 519C (519): Western National Omnibus Co Ltd, Exeter (DN) 519 1/71; withdrawn 1/78; DJ Green (dealer), Weymouth 1/78; Aerosol Research & Development, Farlington (XHA) 1/78; damaged in fire 4/79; C Doe (dealer), Chichester 5/79; R & W Motor Spares (dealer), Chichester for scrap 1/80.

CTT 520C (520): Western National Omnibus Co Ltd, Exeter (DN) 520 1/71; withdrawn 1/78; DJ Green (dealer), Weymouth 1/78; Aerosol Research and Development, Farlington (XHA) 1/78; damaged in fire 4/79; C Doe (dealer), Chichester 5/79; R & W Motor Spares (dealer), Chichester for scrap 1/80.

Vehicle on loan from Leyland Motors Ltd:

KTD 551C	Leyland PDR1/1		L23296	Park Royal	B52907	H44/33F	1/65

Notes:

KTD 551C: This vehicle was on demonstration and used in service during 11/65.

1966

New Vehicles:

24	EOD 24D	AEC Reliance	2U3RA6023	Harrington	3207	C49F	3/66	1/71
25	EOD 25D	AEC Reliance	2U3RA6024	Harrington	3208	C49F	4/66	1/71
26	EOD 26D	AEC Reliance	2U3RA6025	Harrington	3209	C49F	4/66	1/71
27	EOD 27D	AEC Reliance	2U3RA6026	Harrington	3210	C49F	4/66	1/71
28	EOD 28D	AEC Reliance	2U3RA6027	Harrington	3211	C49F	5/66	1/71
29	EOD 29D	AEC Reliance	2U3RA6028	Harrington	3212	C49F	5/66	1/71
30	EOD 30D	AEC Reliance	2U3RA6029	Harrington	3213	C49F	5/66	1/71
31	EOD 31D	AEC Reliance	2U3RA6030	Harrington	3214	C49F	5/66	1/71
521	EOD 521D	AEC Regent V	2D3RA1802	MCW		H34/25F	7/66	1/71
522	EOD 522D	AEC Regent V	2D3RA1803	MCW		H34/25F	7/66	1/71
523	EOD 523D	AEC Regent V	2D3RA1804	MCW		H34/25F	7/66	1/71
524	EOD 524D	AEC Regent V	2D3RA1805	MCW		H34/25F	7/66	1/71
525	EOD 525D	AEC Regent V	2D3RA1806	MCW		H34/25F	7/66	1/71
526	EOD 526D	Leyland PDR1/1	L45024	Willowbrook	78172	H44/31F	6/66	1/71
527	EOD 527D	Leyland PDR1/1	L45025	Willowbrook	78177	H44/31F	6/66	1/71
528	EOD 528D	Leyland PDR1/1	L45040	Willowbrook	78173	H44/31F	6/66	1/71
529	EOD 529D	Leyland PDR1/1	L45041	Willowbrook	78174	H44/31F	6/66	1/71
530	EOD 530D	Leyland PDR1/1	L60050	Willowbrook	78175	H44/31F	6/66	1/71
531	EOD 531D	Leyland PDR1/1	L60051	Willowbrook	78176	H44/31F	6/66	1/71

Notes:

EOD 24-31D (24-31): Had 36ft long x 8ft 2½in wide Grenadier 36 style bodies and were in Grey Cars livery.

EOD 521-525D (521-525): Body frames constructed at Weymann, Addlestone, but completed by MCW; had O.680 engines and low ratio differentials specifically for the Paignton Foxholes service.

EOD 526D (526): Also had Duple Group body number CF1154.

EOD 527D (527): Also had Duple Group body number CF1159.

EOD 528-531D (528-531): Also had Duple Group body numbers CF1155-1158.

Disposals:

EOD 24D (24): Western National Omnibus Co Ltd, Exeter (DN) 24 1/71; Greenslades Tours 5/71; renumbered 464 6/71 and 264 1/75; withdrawn 1975; Paul Sykes Organisation Ltd (dealer), Barnsley 12/75; RI Davies & Son Ltd, Tredegar (GT) 3/76; Stonnis Ltd, Tredegar (GT) 2/77; JN Baker Ltd, Weston-super-Mare (AV) 5/77; withdrawn 7/77; Wilkins Coaches (Cymmer) Ltd, Cymmer (WG) 9/77; disused by 7/82; scrapped at Pantdu 3/83.

EOD 25D (25): Western National Omnibus Co Ltd, Exeter (DN) 25 1/71; Greenslades Tours 5/71; renumbered 465 6/71 and 265 1/75; withdrawn 1975; Paul Sykes Organisation Ltd (dealer), Barnsley 12/75; J Nicholls, Tredegar (GT) 1/76; withdrawn 8/76; Arlington Motor Co Ltd (dealer), Enfield by 12/78; RA Jefferies {R & J Coaches}, Southall (LN) for spares 1979; DE Allmey, Eastcote (LN) for spares 1979; Wombwell Diesels Co Ltd (dealer), Wombwell for scrap 3/79.

EOD 26D (26): Western National Omnibus Co Ltd, Exeter (DN) 26 1/71; Greenslades Tours Ltd, Exeter (DN) 5/71; renumbered 466 6/71 and 266 1/75; withdrawn 1975; Paul Sykes Organisation Ltd (dealer), Barnsley 12/75; RI Davies & Son Ltd, Tredegar (GT) 2/76; DM Nicholls {Broad Oak Coaches} Garway (HW) 11/76; withdrawn 2/78; Vincent Greenhous (Hereford) Ltd (dealer), Hereford 8/78; Eardington Tours Ltd {Bridgnorth Coach Co}, Eardington (SH) by 12/78; licensed 4/79; W Hall, Rock End (ST) 4/80; Martin's Bus & Coach Sales Ltd (dealer), Middlewich for scrap 5/83.

EOD 27D (27): Western National Omnibus Co Ltd, Exeter (DN) 27 1/71; Greenslades Tours Ltd, Exeter (DN) 5/71; renumbered 467 6/71 and 267 1/75; withdrawn 1975; Paul Sykes Organisation

Ltd (dealer), Barnsley 12/75; RI Davies & Son Ltd, Tredegar (GT) 2/76; Stonnis Ltd, Tredegar (GT) 2/77; JN Baker Ltd, Weston-super-Mare (AV) 5/77; withdrawn 7/77; Wilkins Coaches (Cymmer) Ltd, Cymmer (WG) 9/77; disused by 7/82; scrapped at Pantdu 3/83.

EOD 28D (28): Western National Omnibus Co Ltd, Exeter (DN) 28 1/71; Greenslades Tours Ltd, Exeter (DN) 5/71; renumbered 468 6/71 and 268 1/75; withdrawn 1975; Paul Sykes Organisation Ltd (dealer), Barnsley 12/75; RI Davies & Son Ltd, Tredegar (GT) 3/76; Stonnis Ltd, Tredegar (GT) 2/77; JN Baker Ltd, Weston-super-Mare (AV) 5/77; withdrawn 7/77; CE Smith, Ingham (LI) 12/78; withdrawn 4/80.

EOD 29D (29): Western National Omnibus Co Ltd, Exeter (DN) 29 1/71; Greenslades Tours Ltd, Exeter (DN) 5/71; renumbered 469 6/71 and 269 1/75; withdrawn 1975; Paul Sykes Organisation Ltd (dealer), Barnsley 12/75; RI Davies & Son Ltd, Tredegar (GT) 2/76; Stonnis Ltd, Tredegar (GT) 2/77; Wilkins Coaches (Cymmer) Ltd, Cymmer (WG) 9/77; licensed 6/78; withdrawn 1982; scrapped at Pantdu 3/83.

EOD 30D (30): Western National Omnibus Co Ltd, Exeter (DN) 30 1/71; Greenslades Tours Ltd, Exeter (DN) 5/71; renumbered 470 6/71 and 270 1/75; withdrawn 1975; Paul Sykes Organisation Ltd (dealer), Barnsley 12/75; RI Davies & Son Ltd, Tredegar (GT) 2/76; Stonnis Ltd, Tredegar (GT) 2/77; Wilkins Coaches (Cymmer) Ltd, Cymmer (WG) 9/77; withdrawn 1982; scrapped at Pantdu 3/83.

EOD 31D (31): Western National Omnibus Co Ltd, Exeter (DN) 31 1/71; Greenslades Tours 5/71; renumbered 471 6/71 and 271 1/75; withdrawn 1975; Paul Sykes Organisation Ltd (dealer), Barnsley 2/76; RI Davies & Son Ltd, Tredegar (GT) 3/76; not operated; WA & J Howells Ltd, Ynysddu (GT) 5/76; licensed 8/76; A Ward {Websters Coaches}, Hognaston (DE) 16 4/77; Barraclough (dealer), Carlton 11/79.

EOD 521D (521): Western National Omnibus Co Ltd, Exeter (DN) 521 1/71; withdrawn 11/78; DJ Green (dealer), Weymouth 12/78; E Beckett (dealer), Carlton for scrap at an unknown date.

EOD 522D (522): Western National Omnibus Co Ltd, Exeter (DN) 522 1/71; withdrawn 3/78; chassis used for storing open-top roofs; renumbered 9882 at an unknown date; Western National Ltd, Exeter (DN) 9882 1/83; not traced further.

EOD 523D (523): Western National Omnibus Co Ltd, Exeter (DN) 523 1/71; withdrawn 5/79; British Double Deckers (dealer), Wootton 5/79; "Mr B", Ely Inn, Wroughton (XWI) as a mobile café 3/81; burnt out 8/81.

EOD 524D (524): Western National Omnibus Co Ltd, Exeter (DN) 524 1/71; withdrawn 11/78; DJ Green (dealer), Weymouth 12/78; Language Tours, Torquay (XDN) 12/78; EF Languages School Ltd, Torquay (XDN) 3/80; Ironside Travel Ltd {Davis Coaches}, Sevenoaks (KT) 1983; West of England Transport Collection, Winkleigh for preservation 2/84; C Jeavons and R Folwell, Kingswinford for preservation 10/84; R Follwell, A Newbold & R Morgan, Newcastle under Lyme for preservation by3/95; R Follwell & R Morgan for preservation by 5/99; D Chick & R Morgan, Solihull for preservation by 9/04; current 1/15.

EOD 525D (525): Western National Omnibus Co Ltd, Exeter (DN) 525 1/71; withdrawn 11/78; DJ Green (dealer), Weymouth 12/78; Hexagon Group, Kirkby (XMY) 8/79; Cantril Farm Community Group, Liverpool (XMY) 3/81; Liverpool Community Transport, Liverpool (XMY) 5/83; Parkside Welfare Community, Newton le Willows (XMY) 9/84; Morgan (dealer) Warrington 2/85; Bold Colliery Miners Club, St Helens (XMY) 1985; scrapped 6/86.

EOD 526D (526): Western National Omnibus Co Ltd, Exeter (DN) 526 1/71; withdrawn 1982; Devon General Ltd, Exeter (DN) 526 1/83; withdrawn 1983; Passenger Vehicle Spares (Barnsley) Ltd (dealer), Carlton 1/84; Hartwood Exports (Machinery) Ltd (dealer), Barnsley 2/84; T Thornton & P Lloyd (dealer), Cundy Cross for scrap 2/84.

EOD 527D (527): Western National Omnibus Co Ltd, Exeter (DN) 527 1/71; Devon General Ltd, Exeter (DN) 527 1/83; withdrawn 1984; Hartwood Exports (Machinery) Ltd (dealer), Barnsley 2/84; T Thornton & P Lloyd (dealer), Cundy Cross for scrap 2/84.

EOD 528D (528-531): Western National Omnibus Co Ltd, Exeter (DN) 528 1/71; Devon General Ltd, Exeter (DN) 528 1/83; withdrawn 1983; Hartwood Exports (Machinery) Ltd (dealer), Barnsley 2/84; T Thornton & P Lloyd (dealer), Cundy Cross for scrap 2/84.

EOD 529-531D (529-531): Western National Omnibus Co Ltd, Exeter (DN) 529-531 1/71;Devon General Ltd, Exeter (DN) 529-531 1/83; withdrawn 1984; Hartwood Exports (Machinery) Ltd (dealer), Barnsley 2/84; T Thornton & P Lloyd (dealer), Cundy Cross for scrap 2/84.

1967

New Vehicles:

32	HOD 32E	AEC Reliance	2U3RA1454	Duple Northern 175/8	C49F	4/67	1/71
33	HOD 33E	AEC Reliance	2U3RA1455	Duple Northern 175/9	C49F	4/67	1/71
34	HOD 34E	AEC Reliance	2U3RA1456	Duple Northern 175/7	C49F	4/67	1/71
35	HOD 35E	AEC Reliance	2U3RA1457	Duple Northern 178/6	C49F	4/67	1/71

36	HOD 36E	AEC Reliance	2U3RA1458	Duple Northern	175/5	C49F	4/67	1/71
37	HOD 37E	AEC Reliance	2U3RA1459	Duple Northern	175/4	C49F	5/67	1/71
38	HOD 38E	AEC Reliance	2U3RA1460	Duple Northern	175/3	C49F	5/67	1/71
39	HOD 39E	AEC Reliance	2U3RA1461	Duple Northern	178/2	C49F	5/67	1/71
40	HOD 40E	AEC Reliance	2MU3RA6462	Marshall	B3847	B41F	3/67	1/71
41	HOD 41E	AEC Reliance	2MU3RA6463	Marshall	B3848	B41F	3/67	1/71
42	HOD 42E	AEC Reliance	2MU3RA6464	Marshall	B3849	B41F	3/67	1/71
43	HOD 43E	AEC Reliance	2MU3RA6465	Marshall	B3850	B41F	3/67	1/71
44	HOD 44E	AEC Reliance	2MU3RA6466	Marshall	B3851	B41F	3/67	1/71

Notes:

HOD 32-39E (32-39): Were 36ft long x 8ft 2½ wide with Duple 'Commander' style bodywork in Grey Cars livery; repainted into white with grey band livery by 1/70.

HOD 40-44E (404-44): Were 30ft 6in long x 8ft 0in wide.

Disposals:

HOD 32E (32): Western National Omnibus Co Ltd, Exeter (DN) 32 1/71; Greenslades Tours Ltd, Exeter (DN) 5/71; renumbered 472 6/71; renumbered 272 1/75; Midland Red Omnibus Co Ltd (dealer), Birmingham 4/76; Paul Sykes Organisation Ltd (dealer), Barnsley 4/76; Doagh Flaxing & Spinning Co Ltd, Doagh (XAM) 6/76; sold for scrap by 6/84.

HOD 33E (33): Western National Omnibus Co Ltd, Exeter (DN) 33 1/71; Greenslades Tours Ltd, Exeter (DN) 5/71; renumbered 473 6/71; renumbered 273 1/75; Midland Red Omnibus Co Ltd (dealer), Birmingham 4/76; Paul Sykes Organisation Ltd (dealer), Barnsley 4/76; Morlais Services Ltd, Merthyr Tydfil (MG) 6/76; withdrawn 4/78; Mrs IFK Tanner & M Allpress, Sibford Gower (OX) 8/78; withdrawn 11/80; Turner, Banbury (OX); J Sykes (dealer), Carlton 10/83; Diamond Drum Majorettes, Royston (XSY) 1984; returned to J Sykes (dealer), Carlton for scrap 9/85..

HOD 34E (34): Western National Omnibus Co Ltd, Exeter (DN) 34 1/71; Greenslades Tours Ltd, Exeter (DN) 5/71; renumbered 474 6/71; renumbered 274 1/75; Midland Red Omnibus Co Ltd (dealer), Birmingham 4/76; Paul Sykes Organisation Ltd (dealer), Barnsley 4/76; A Simpson, Keswick (CA) 5/76; Moseley (Durham) Ltd (dealer), Durham 6/78; hired to Gardiner Bros, Spennymoor (A) 6/78 until late 1978; S & N Motors Ltd (dealer), Bishopbriggs 8/79; J Cosgrove {Tay Valley Coaches}, Invergowrie (TE) 10/79; unidentified private owner, Dundee 11/79; Thompson (dealer), Carnoustie by 5/81; scrapped 6/81.

HOD 35E (35): Western National Omnibus Co Ltd, Exeter (DN) 35 1/71; Greenslades Tours Ltd, Exeter (DN) 5/71; renumbered 475 6/71; renumbered 275 1/75; Midland Red Omnibus Co Ltd (dealer), Birmingham 4/76; Paul Sykes Organisation Ltd (dealer), Barnsley 4/76; W Irvine, Law (SC) 5/76; returned to Paul Sykes Organisation Ltd (dealer) 10/76; Askin (dealer) Barnsley for scrap 4/78.

HOD 36E (36): Western National Omnibus Co Ltd, Exeter (DN) 36 1/71; Greenslades Tours Ltd, Exeter (DN) 5/71; renumbered 476 6/71; renumbered 276 1/75; Midland Red Omnibus Co Ltd (dealer), Birmingham 4/76; Paul Sykes Organisation Ltd (dealer), Barnsley 4/76; Morlais Services Ltd, Merthyr Tydfil (MG) 6/76; withdrawn 4/78; Harris Coaches (Pengam) Ltd, Fleur-de-Lys (SG) 4/78; although licensed, purchase was not completed and not operated by Harris; returned to Morlais 5/78; Mrs IFK Tanner & M Allpress, Sibford Gower (OX) 8/78; withdrawn 9/79; reinstated by Tanner, Sibford Gower (OX) 4/80; Kiss of Life public house, Wath (XNY) by 11/83; G Jones {Carlton Metals} (dealer), Carlton by 12/84.

HOD 37E (37): Western National Omnibus Co Ltd, Exeter (DN) 37 1/71; Greenslades Tours Ltd, Exeter (DN) 5/71; renumbered 477 6/71; renumbered 277 1/75; used as a seatstore by 4/76; GE Haywood {George's Coaches}, Coventry (WM) 6/76; withdrawn 10/76; Paul Sykes Organisation Ltd (dealer), Barnsley 11/76; TH & TH Jones {Caelloi Motors}, Pwllheli (GD) 9/78; withdrawn 9/80; GP Ripley (dealer), Carlton for scrap 3/84.

HOD 38E (38): Western National Omnibus Co Ltd, Exeter (DN) 38 1/71; Greenslades Tours Ltd, Exeter (DN) 5/71; renumbered 478 6/71; renumbered 278 1/75; Midland Red Omnibus Co Ltd (dealer), Birmingham 4/76; Paul Sykes Organisation Ltd (dealer), Barnsley 4/76; W Irvine, Law (SC) 5/76; Worldwide Coaches (Scotland) Ltd, Lanark (SC) 6/76; JS Whiteford {Nationwide Coaches}, Lanark (SC) 3/78; not operated; still owned 1981; sold (for scrap?) by 1993.

HOD 39E (39): Western National Omnibus Co Ltd, Exeter (DN) 39 1/71; Greenslades Tours Ltd, Exeter (DN) 5/71; renumbered 479 6/71; renumbered 279 1/75; Midland Red Omnibus Co Ltd (dealer), Birmingham 4/76; Paul Sykes Organisation Ltd (dealer), Barnsley 4/76; James Gibson & Sons {Gibson's Motor Service}, Moffat (DG) 5/76; withdrawn after an accident 1/77; IE Thomas, West Ewell (SR) 1978; chassis rebuilt and given new chassis number ETS1078 10/78; rebodied Plaxton C53F (7911AC018S) and re-registered CPM 520T 6/79;

Workforce (dealer), London E1 4/87; Zarb, Birkirkara (O-M) 4/87; re-registered Y 0883 by 10/88; re-registered JCY 883 c1996.

HOD 40E (40): Western National Omnibus Co Ltd, Exeter (DN) 40 1/71; re-seated to B39F 1971; withdrawn 11/79; T Carpenter (dealer), Exeter 3/80; Gould (dealer), Taunton for scrap 4/80.

HOD 41E (41): Western National Omnibus Co Ltd, Exeter (DN) 41 1/71; re-seated to B39F 1974; withdrawn 11/79; CF Booth Ltd (dealer), Rotherham 7/80.

HOD 42E (42): Western National Omnibus Co Ltd, Exeter (DN) 42 1/71; re-seated to B39F 1971; withdrawn 12/79; CF Booth Ltd (dealer), Rotherham 7/80.

HOD 43E (43): Western National Omnibus Co Ltd, Exeter (DN) 43 1/71; re-seated to B39F 1972; withdrawn 11/79; DJ Green (dealer), Weymouth

HOD 44E (44): Western National Omnibus Co Ltd, Exeter (DN) 44 1/71; re-seated to B39F 1974; withdrawn 10/79; C Meynell (dealer), Carlton 4/80.

Vehicle on loan from Transport Vehicles (Daimler) Ltd, Coventry:

CVC 124C	Daimler Roadliner	36002	Marshall	B3490	B50F	11/65

Notes:

CVC 124C: This vehicle was on site during 1/67, but was not used in service due to a mechanical fault.

Vehicle on loan from Ford Motor Co Ltd, Warley:

SVW 275D	Ford R192	BC04FM40116	Willowbrook	65394	B45F	11/66

Notes:

SVW 275D: This vehicle, which also had Duple Group body number CF1439 was on demonstration and used in service during 10/67.

1968

New Vehicles:

45	LUO 45F	AEC Reliance	6U3ZR6924	Willowbrook	80727		DP49F	3/68	1/71
46	LUO 46F	AEC Reliance	6U3ZR6925	Willowbrook	80726		DP49F	3/68	1/71
47	LUO 47F	AEC Reliance	6U3ZR6926	Willowbrook	80728		DP49F	3/68	1/71
48	LUO 48F	AEC Reliance	6U32R6927	Willowbrook	80730		B51F	4/68	1/71
49	LUO 49F	AEC Reliance	6U32R6928	Willowbrook	80729		B51F	4/68	1/71
50	LUO 50F	AEC Reliance	6U32R6929	Willowbrook	80731		B51F	4/68	1/71
51	LUO 51F	AEC Reliance	6U32R6930	Willowbrook	80732		B51F	4/68	1/71
52	LUO 52F	AEC Reliance	6U32R6931	Willowbrook	80733		B51F	4/68	1/71
53	LUO 53F	AEC Reliance	6U32R6932	Willowbrook	80734		B51F	4/68	1/71
54	LUO 54F	AEC Reliance	6U32R6933	Willowbrook	80735		B51F	4/68	1/71
55	LUO 55F	AEC Reliance	6MU3RV6934	Marshall	B4081		B41F	3/68	1/71
56	LUO 56F	AEC Reliance	6MU3RV6935	Marshall	B4082		B41F	3/68	1/71
57	LUO 57F	AEC Reliance	6MU3RV6936	Marshall	B4083		B41F	3/68	1/71
532	NDV 532G	Leyland PDR1/1	703740	MCW			H43/32F	10/68	1/71
533	NDV 533G	Leyland PDR1/1	703741	MCW			H43/32F	10/68	1/71
534	NDV 534G	Leyland PDR1/1	703791	MCW			H43/32F	11/68	1/71
535	NDV 535G	Leyland PDR1/1	703792	MCW			H43/32F	11/68	1/71
536	NDV 536G	Leyland PDR1/1	703846	MCW			H43/32F	11/68	1/71
537	NDV 537G	Leyland PDR1/1	703872	MCW			H43/32F	11/68	1/71
538	NDV 538G	Leyland PDR1/1	703873	MCW			H43/32F	11/68	1/71
539	NDV 539G	Leyland PDR1/1	703874	MCW			H43/32F	12/68	1/71
540	NDV 540G	Leyland PDR1/1	703951	MCW			H43/32F	12/68	1/71

Notes:

LUO 45-47F (45-47): Were 36ft long x 8ft 2½in and were intended for express service 46 (Exeter-Torquay).

LUO 45F (45): Also had Duple Group body number CF1558; re-seated to DP41F before entering service; reverted to DP49F 7/68.

LUO 46F (46): Also had Duple Group body number CF1557; re-seated to DP41F before entering service; reverted to DP49F 7/68.

LUO 47F (47): Also had Duple Group body number CF1559; re-seated to DP41F before entering service; reverted to DP49F 7/68.

LUO 48-54F (48-54): Were 36ft long x 8ft 2½in.

LUO 48F (48): Also had Duple Group body number CF1592

LUO 49F (49): Also had Duple Group body number CF1591

LUO 50-54F (50-54): Also had Duple Group body numbers CF1593-1597.
LUO 55-57F (55-57): Were 32ft 8in long x 8ft 2½in wide.
NDV 532-540G (532-541): Bodies completed by Laird (Anglesey) Ltd, Beaumaris.

Disposals:

LUO 45F (45): Western National Omnibus Co Ltd, Exeter (DN) 45 1/71; reseated to DP47F 1976; withdrawn 11/80; Ensign Bus Co Ltd (dealer), Purfleet) 4/81; Kingsforth (dealer), Thurscroft 9/81; WG Weaver, Tredegar (GT) 11/81; withdrawn 5/82; still owned 5/83.

LUO 46F (46): Western National Omnibus Co Ltd, Exeter (DN) 46 1/71; reseated to DP47F 1971; withdrawn 5/80; W Norths (PV) Ltd (dealer), Sherburn in Elmet 8/80; D Rollinson (Bus Centre) Ltd (dealer), Carlton by 3/81.

LUO 47F (47): Western National Omnibus Co Ltd, Exeter (DN) 47 1/71; reseated to DP47F 1971; withdrawn 11/80; Ensign Bus Co Ltd (dealer), Purfleet 4/81; Kirkby Kingsforth Ltd (dealer), Thurcroft 5/81; Dawlish Coaches Ltd, Dawlish (DN) 5/81; DM Munslow, Torquay (DN) 7/85; A Younge, Bishops Stortford for preservation 4/86; 47 Group, Newton Abbot for preservation 12/87; Ingram, Truro for preservation by 6/01; dismantled for spares at premises of Falmouth Coaches Ltd, Falmouth (CO) by 8/07.

LUO 48F (48): Western National Omnibus Co Ltd, Exeter (DN) 48 1/71; reseated to B49F 1972; withdrawn 5/80; CF Booth Ltd (dealer), Rotherham for scrap 8/80.

LUO 49F (49): Western National Omnibus Co Ltd, Exeter (DN) 49 1/71; reseated to B49F 1973; withdrawn 6/80; dismantled for spares; remains to Stoneman (dealer), Plymouth for scrap 8/80.

LUO 50F (50): Western National Omnibus Co Ltd, Exeter (DN) 50 1/71; reseated to B49F 1974; withdrawn 6/80; Kinross Plant & Construction Ltd (contractor), Kinross (XTE) 9/80; sold by 2/82.

LUO 51F (51): Western National Omnibus Co Ltd, Exeter (DN) 51 1/71; reseated to B49F 1974; withdrawn 6/80; W Norths (PV) Ltd (dealer), Sherburn in Elmet 8/80; café at junction of A1/A642, Micklefield by 2/81; returned to W Norths (PV) Ltd (dealer), Sherburn in Elmet 7/81; sold 11/81.

LUO 52F (52): Western National Omnibus Co Ltd, Exeter (DN) 52 1/71; reseated to B49F 1974; withdrawn after an accident 12/76; broken up at Laira Bridge by Rundle (dealer), Plymouth 8/77.

LUO 53F (53): Western National Omnibus Co Ltd, Exeter (DN) 53 1/71; reseated to B49F 1974; withdrawn 6/80; W Norths (PV) Ltd (dealer), Sherburn in Elmet 8/80; M Parton & Allen (dealer), Carlton 8/80.

LUO 54F (54): Western National Omnibus Co Ltd, Exeter (DN) 54 1/71; reseated to B49F 1973; withdrawn 5/80; CF Booth Ltd (dealer), Rotherham 7/80.

LUO 55F (55): Western National Omnibus Co Ltd, Exeter (DN) 55 1/71; reseated to B39F 1973; withdrawn 6/80; W Norths (PV) Ltd (dealer), Sherburn in Elmet 7/80; Grovehill Baseball Club, Beverley (XEY) by 2/81; returned to W Norths (PV) Ltd (dealer), Sherburn in Elmet by 9/81.

LUO 56F (56): Western National Omnibus Co Ltd, Exeter (DN) 56 1/71; reseated to B39F 1975; withdrawn 6/80; W Norths (PV) Ltd (dealer), Sherburn in Elmet 8/80; chassis to Central Motors (Ripponden) Ltd, Ripponden (WY) for rebodying 3/81; not proceeded with; sold by 5/82.

LUO 57F (57): Western National Omnibus Co Ltd, Exeter (DN) 57 1/71; reseated to B39F 1971; withdrawn 5/80; A Barraclough (dealer), Carlton 8/80.

NDV 532-533G (532-533): Western National Omnibus Co Ltd, Exeter (DN) 532-533 1/71; Devon General Ltd, Exeter (DN) 532-533 1/83; withdrawn 1983; Hartwood Exports (Machinery) Ltd (dealer), Barnsley 2/84; DC Morris {DC Commercials} (dealer), Carlton 2/84.

NDV 534G (534): Western National Omnibus Co Ltd, Exeter (DN) 534 1/71; Devon General Ltd, Exeter (DN) 534 1/83; withdrawn 1983; Hartwood Exports (Machinery) Ltd (dealer), Barnsley 2/84 and scrapped at an unknown date.

NDV 535G (535): Western National Omnibus Co Ltd, Exeter (DN) 535 1/71; Devon General Ltd, Exeter (DN) 535 1/83; withdrawn 1984; Hartwood Exports (Machinery) Ltd (dealer), Barnsley 2/84; DC Morris {DC Commercials} (dealer), Carlton 2/84.

NDV 536G (536): Western National Omnibus Co Ltd, Exeter (DN) 536 1/71; Devon General Ltd, Exeter (DN) 536 1/83; withdrawn 1982; Hartwood Exports (Machinery) Ltd (dealer), Barnsley 2/84 and scrapped at an unknown date.

NDV 537G (537): Western National Omnibus Co Ltd, Exeter (DN) 537 1/71; withdrawn 10/82; P Platt, Exeter for preservation 11/82; R Follwell & P Morrey, Newcastle under Lyme for preservation 9/83; R Follwell, Stableford for preservation by 5/85; current 8/08; S Cope, Longton for preservation by 12/14.

NDV 538G (538): Western National Omnibus Co Ltd, Exeter (DN) 538 1/71; Devon General Ltd, Exeter (DN) 538 1/83; withdrawn 1984; Hartwood Exports (Machinery) Ltd (dealer), Barnsley 2/84; DC Morris {DC Commercials} (dealer), Carlton 2/84.

NDV 539-540G (539-540): Western National Omnibus Co Ltd, Exeter (DN) 539-540 1/71; Devon General Ltd, Exeter (DN) 539-540 1/83; withdrawn 1983; Hartwood Exports (Machinery) Ltd (dealer), Barnsley 2/84; DC Morris {DC Commercials} (dealer), Carlton 2/84.

Vehicles reacquired from Court Garages, Torquay (DN) 10/68:

893	893 ADV	AEC Reliance	2MU3RV2352	Willowbrook	59369	C41F	5/59	10/68
894	894 ADV	AEC Reliance	2MU3RV2353	Willowbrook	59370	C41F	5/59	10/68

Notes:

These vehicles were new to Devon General and had been transferred to Court Garages in 9/66.

Disposals:

893 ADV (893): Transport (Passenger Equipment) Ltd (dealer), Macclesfield 10/68; JT Mullen, Blackwood (GT) 1/69; withdrawn 1972; sold for scrap 1/73.

894 ADV (894): Transport (Passenger Equipment) Ltd (dealer), Macclesfield 10/68; Edmunds Omnibus Services Ltd, Rassau (GT) 11/68; written off 1/69 following an accident in 4/69; chassis still on premises 1/70.

1969

New Vehicles:

541	NDV 541G	Leyland PDR1/1	703952	MCW		H43/32F	2/69	1/71
58	OTA 58G	AEC Reliance	2MU3RV7052	Marshall	B4253	B41F	3/69	1/71
59	OTA 59G	AEC Reliance	2MU3RV7053	Marshall	B4254	B41F	3/69	1/71
60	OTA 60G	AEC Reliance	2MU3RV7054	Marshall	B4255	B41F	3/69	1/71
61	OTA 61G	AEC Reliance	2MU3RV7055	Marshall	B4256	B41F	3/69	1/71
62	OTA 62G	AEC Reliance	2MU3RV7056	Marshall	B4260	B41F	3/69	1/71
63	OTA 63G	AEC Reliance	2MU3RV7057	Marshall	B4262	B41F	3/69	1/71
64	OTA 64G	AEC Reliance	2MU3RV7058	Marshall	B4263	B41F	3/69	1/71
65	OTA 65G	AEC Reliance	2MU3RV7059	Marshall	B4264	B41F	3/69	1/71
66	OTA 66G	AEC Reliance	2MU3RV7060	Marshall	B4265	B41F	3/69	1/71
67	OTA 67G	AEC Reliance	2MU3RV7061	Marshall	B4261	B41F	3/69	1/71
68	OTA 68G	AEC Reliance	2MU3RV7062	Marshall	B4257	B41F	3/69	1/71
69	OTA 69G	AEC Reliance	2MU3RV7063	Marshall	B4258	B41F	3/69	1/71
70	OTA 70G	AEC Reliance	2MU3RV7064	Marshall	B4259	B41F	3/69	1/71
71	OTA 71G	AEC Reliance	2MU3RV7065	Marshall	B4268	B41F	3/69	1/71
72	OTA 72G	AEC Reliance	2MU3RV7066	Marshall	B4266	B41F	3/69	1/71
73	OTA 73G	AEC Reliance	2MU3RV7067	Marshall	B4267	B41F	3/69	1/71

Notes:

NDV 541G (541): Body completed by Laird (Anglesey) Ltd, Beaumaris.

OTA 58-73G: Were 32ft 8in long x 8ft 2½in wide.

Disposals:

NDV 541G (541): Western National Omnibus Co Ltd, Exeter (DN) 541 1/71; Devon General Ltd, Exeter (DN) 541 1/83; withdrawn 1983; Hartwood Exports (Machinery) Ltd (dealer), Barnsley 2/84; DC Morris {DC Commercials} (dealer), Carlton 2/84.

OTA 58G (58): Western National Omnibus Co Ltd, Exeter (DN) 58 1/71; reseated to B39F 1972; withdrawn 6/80; Kinross Plant & Construction Co Ltd (contractor), Kinross (XTE) 8/80; Kettle Produce, Kingskettle (XFE) by 12/80; Muir (dealer), Kirkcaldy 7/83; T Wigley (dealer), Carlton by 8/85.

OTA 59G (59): Western National Omnibus Co Ltd, Exeter (DN) 59 1/71; reseated to B39F 1972; withdrawn 6/80; CF Booth Ltd (dealer), Rotherham 7/80; Bentley St Peters Church, Doncaster (XSY) by 10/81; last licensed 5/86; Wombwell Diesels Co Ltd (dealer), Wombwell by 8/86.

OTA 60G (60): Western National Omnibus Co Ltd, Exeter (DN) 60 1/71; reseated to B39F 1979; withdrawn 11/80; CF Booth Ltd (dealer), Rotherham 12/80; DE Allmey (dealer), Eastcote 9/81; Booth of Anston Ltd (dealer), Anston by 12/81.

OTA 61G (61): Western National Omnibus Co Ltd, Exeter (DN) 61 1/71; reseated to B39F at an unknown date; withdrawn 6/80; CF Booth Ltd (dealer), Rotherham 7/80.

OTA 62G (62): Western National Omnibus Co Ltd, Exeter (DN) 62 1/71; reseated to B39F 1976-77; withdrawn 5/80; Kinross Plant & Construction Co Ltd (contractor), Kinross (XTE) 8/80; Kettle Produce, Kingskettle (XFE) by 12/80; Thomas Muir (Metals) Ltd (dealer), Kirkcaldy 7/83.

OTA 63G (63): Western National Omnibus Co Ltd, Exeter (DN) 63 1/71; reseated to B39F 1976-77; withdrawn 11/80; CF Booth Ltd (dealer), Rotherham 12/80.

OTA 64G (64): Western National Omnibus Co Ltd, Exeter (DN) 64 1/71; reseated to B39F 1972; withdrawn 6/80; Kinross Plant & Construction Co Ltd (contractor), Kinross (XTE) 8/80; GP Ripley (dealer), Carlton 2/82.

OTA 65G (65): Western National Omnibus Co Ltd, Exeter (DN) 65 1/71; reseated to B39F 1976-77; withdrawn 11/80; CF Booth Ltd (dealer), Rotherham 12/80.

OTA 66G (66): Western National Omnibus Co Ltd, Exeter (DN) 66 1/71; reseated to B39F 1976-77; withdrawn 11/80; CF Booth Ltd (dealer), Rotherham 12/80; Poppleton, Pontefract (XWY) 8/82; Walsall Metropolitan Borough Council (XWM) as a playbus by 12/83; unknown dealer, Barnsley for scrap by8/86.

OTA 67G (67): Western National Omnibus Co Ltd, Exeter (DN) 67 1/71; reseated to B39F 1973; withdrawn 6/80; CF Booth Ltd (dealer), Rotherham 12/80.

OTA 68G (68): Western National Omnibus Co Ltd, Exeter (DN) 68 1/71; reseated to B39F 1973; withdrawn 6/80; A Baraclough (dealer), Carlton 8/80.

OTA 69G (69): Western National Omnibus Co Ltd, Exeter (DN) 69 1/71; reseated to B39F 1972; withdrawn 11/80; CF Booth Ltd (dealer), Rotherham 12/80.

OTA 70G (70): Western National Omnibus Co Ltd, Exeter (DN) 70 1/71; reseated to B39F 1973; withdrawn 6/80; dismantled for spares at Newton Road depot by T Carpenter (dealer), Exeter by 6/80.

OTA 71G (71): Western National Omnibus Co Ltd, Exeter (DN) 71 1/71; reseated to B39F 1972; withdrawn 11/80; T CF Booth Ltd (dealer), Rotherham 12/80.

OTA 72G (72): Western National Omnibus Co Ltd, Exeter (DN) 72 1/71; reseated to B39F 1972; withdrawn 11/80; T CF Booth Ltd (dealer), Rotherham 12/80.

OTA 73G (73): Western National Omnibus Co Ltd, Exeter (DN) 73 1/71; reseated to B39F 1973; withdrawn11/80; T CF Booth Ltd (dealer), Rotherham 12/80.

Vehicle on loan from Western National Omnibus Co Ltd, Exeter (DN):

OTA 291G	Bristol VRT/SL6G	123	ECW	17316	H39/31F	3/69

Notes:

OTA 291G: Was Western National 1057 and on loan from 5/69 until 6/69.

Vehicle on loan from Black & White Motorways Ltd, Cheltenham (GL):

RDG 309G	Daimler SRP8	36303	Plaxton	693360	C47F	6/69

Notes:

RDG 309G: Was Black & White D309 and was on loan from 9/69 until 5/70 for use as the Torquay United FC team coach.

1970

New Vehicles:

499	RFJ 828H	AEC Reliance	6U3ZR7418	Plaxton	708905	C49F	6/70	1/71
211	TDV 211J	Leyland PSUR1B/1R	7001303	Marshall	B4533	B47D	9/70	1/71
212	TDV 212J	Leyland PSUR1B/1R	7001304	Marshall	B4532	B47D	9/70	1/71
213	TDV 213J	Leyland PSUR1B/1R	7001465	Marshall	B4535	B47D	9/70	1/71
214	TDV 214J	Leyland PSUR1B/1R	7001466	Marshall	B4534	B47D	9/70	1/71
215	TDV 215J	Leyland PSUR1B/1R	7001569	Marshall	B4538	B47D	9/70	1/71
216	TDV 216J	Leyland PSUR1B/1R	7001570	Marshall	B4536	B47D	9/70	1/71
217	TDV 217J	Leyland PSUR1B/1R	7001594	Marshall	B4537	B47D	9/70	1/71

Notes:

RFJ 828H (499): Had Panorama Elite style bodywork and was ordered by Greenslades Tours Ltd, Exeter (DN), but delivered to Devon General in white Grey Cars livery.

TDV 211-217J (211-217): These vehicles were an Exeter Corporation order which were to have been numbered 11-17. They were delivered during 8/70 in Western National Omnibus Co shades of green and cream but to the Exeter Corporation layout. All carried 'EXETER' fleet names and Devon General style fleet numbers.

Disposals:

RFJ 828H (499): Western National Omnibus Co Ltd, Exeter (DN) 499 1/71; renumbered 399 1/75; renumbered 199 4/77; National Travel (South West) Ltd 199 6/77; withdrawn 11/77; Martin's Bus & Coach Sales Ltd (dealer), Middlewich 2/78; Smith of Rainhill Ltd, Rainhill (MY) 2/78; withdrawn 8/78.

TDV 211J (211): Western National Omnibus Co Ltd, Exeter (DN) 211 1/71; repainted into NBC poppy red livery 5/73; fitted with 3-track number blinds 7/73; withdrawn 10/80; Wood (dealer), Crediton for scrap 6/81.

TDV 212J (212): Western National Omnibus Co Ltd, Exeter (DN) 212 1/71; repainted into NBC poppy red livery11/72; withdrawn 10/80; Ensign Bus Co Ltd (dealer), Purfleet 4/81; Stanlake Passenger Transport Co Ltd, Ipswich (SK) 10/81; returned to Ensign Bus Co Ltd (dealer), Purfleet 4/83; C Meynell (dealer), Carlton for scrap 10/83.

TDV 213J (213): Western National Omnibus Co Ltd, Exeter (DN) 213 1/71; repainted into NBC poppy red livery1/73; to NBC leaf green livery with Devon General fleetnames 2/80; withdrawn 10/80; Ensign Bus Co Ltd (dealer), Purfleet 4/81; GHN Whybrow {Kelvedon Coaches}, Kelvedon (EX) 9/81; C Meynell (dealer), Carlton 4/83.

TDV 214J (214): Western National Omnibus Co Ltd, Exeter (DN) 214 1/71; repainted into Devon General BET-style red and ivory livery 8/72, later repainted into NBC poppy red livery; withdrawn 10/80; Ensign Bus Co Ltd (dealer), Purfleet 4/81; GHN Whybrow {Kelvedon Coaches}, Kelvedon (EX) 9/81; returned to Ensign Bus Co Ltd (dealer), Purfleet 12/81; A Hodnett {Tame Valley Coaches}, Tamworth (ST) 5/83; Burman, Cradley Heath (HW) 1/84; Wacton Trading/Coach Sales (dealer), Bromyard 6/84; Athelstan Coaches Ltd, Malmesbury (WI) 6/84.

TDV 215J (215): Western National Omnibus Co Ltd, Exeter (DN) 215 1/71; to NBC red livery 10/72; withdrawn 10/80; Ensign Bus Co Ltd (dealer), Purfleet 7/81; GHN Whybrow {Kelvedon Coaches}, Kelvedon (EX) 9/81; A Hodnett & C Bentley {Tame Valley Coaches}, Tamworth (ST) 4/83; becoming A Hodnett {Tame Valley Coaches}, Tamworth (ST) 5/83; Tame Valley Coaches, Coleshill (WK) 8/83.

TDV 216J (216): Western National Omnibus Co Ltd, Exeter (DN) 216 1/71; repainted into Devon General BET-style red and ivory livery 9/72; repainted into NBC poppy red livery 4/76; to NBC leaf green livery with Devon General fleet names by 8/80; withdrawn 10/80; Wood (dealer), Crediton for scrap 6/81.

TDV 217J (217): Western National Omnibus Co Ltd, Exeter (DN) 217 1/71; repainted into NBC poppy red with white window surrounds 12/72; repainted NBC poppy red with white band 12/76; withdrawn 1980; transferred to ancillary stock L8 as an office and/or mobile exhibition bus 5/80; renumbered 9415; Devon General Ltd, Exeter (XDN) 9415 in 1/83; Western National Ltd, Truro (XCO) 9415 as a mobile exhibition bus by 10/86; converted to mobile travel shop; First Western National Buses Ltd, Truro (XCO) 9415 3/99; West Country Historic Omnibus & Transport Trust for preservation 12/00; still owned 1/15.

Vehicles acquired from Exeter City Transport (DN) 4/70:

13	HFJ 140	Leyland PD2/1	480631	Leyland		H30/26R	2/48	7/70
14	HFJ 141	Leyland PD2/1	480634	Leyland		H30/26R	2/48	7/70
15	HFJ 142	Leyland PD2/1	480632	Leyland		H30/26R	2/48	7/70
17	HFJ 144	Leyland PD2/1	480630	Leyland		H30/26R	2/48	7/70
18	HFJ 145	Leyland PD2/1	480635	Leyland		H30/26R	3/48	7/70
250	TFJ 808	Guy Arab IV	FD73287	Massey	2250	H30/26R	11/56	9/70
251	UFJ 291	Guy Arab IV	FD73679	Massey	2251	H30/26R	6/57	1/71
252	UFJ 292	Guy Arab IV	FD73680	Massey	2252	H30/26R	6/57	9/70
253	UFJ 293	Guy Arab IV	FD73686	Massey	2254	H30/26R	6/57	1/71
254	UFJ 294	Guy Arab IV	FD73687	Massey	2253	H30/26R	6/57	9/70
255	UFJ 295	Guy Arab IV	FD73574	Park Royal	B39413	H30/26R	6/57	9/70
256	UFJ 296	Guy Arab IV	FD73580	Park Royal	B39414	H30/26R	6/57	1/71
257	UFJ 297	Guy Arab IV	FD73581	Park Royal	B39415	H30/26R	6/57	9/70
258	UFJ 298	Guy Arab IV	FD73582	Park Royal	B39416	H30/26R	6/57	9/70
259	UFJ 299	Guy Arab IV	FD73586	Park Royal	B39417	H30/26R	6/57	1/71
260	VFJ 995	Leyland PD2/40	581113	Weymann	M8049	H31/26R	6/58	1/71
261	VFJ 996	Leyland PD2/40	581114	Weymann	M8046	H31/26R	6/58	1/71
262	VFJ 997	Leyland PD2/40	581115	Weymann	M8048	H31/26R	6/58	1/71
263	VFJ 998	Leyland PD2/40	581116	Weymann	M8050	H31/26R	6/58	1/71
264	VFJ 999	Leyland PD2/40	581117	Weymann	M8047	H31/26R	6/58	1/71
265	XFJ 750	Guy Arab IV	FD74278	Weymann	M8889	H31/26R	9/59	1/71
266	XFJ 751	Guy Arab IV	FD74279	Weymann	M8887	H31/26R	9/59	1/71
267	XFJ 752	Guy Arab IV	FD74280	Weymann	M8891	H31/26R	9/59	1/71

268	XFJ 753	Guy Arab IV	FD74281	Weymann	M8890	H31/26R	9/59	1/71
269	XFJ 754	Guy Arab IV	FD74282	Weymann	M8888	H31/26R	9/59	1/71
270	970 AFJ	Guy Arab IV	FD74585	Massey	2381	H31/26R	7/60	1/71
271	971 AFJ	Guy Arab IV	FD74587	Massey	2380	H31/26R	7/60	1/71
272	972 AFJ	Guy Arab IV	FD74588	Massey	2379	H31/26R	7/60	1/71
273	973 AFJ	Guy Arab IV	FD74589	Massey	2382	H31/26R	7/60	1/71
274	974 AFJ	Guy Arab IV	FD74590	Massey	2383	H31/26R	7/60	1/71
275	475 CFJ	Leyland PD2A/30	610082	Massey	2418	H31/26R	4/61	1/71
276	476 CFJ	Leyland PD2A/30	610083	Massey	2421	H31/26R	4/61	1/71
277	477 CFJ	Leyland PD2A/30	610084	Massey	2419	H31/26R	4/61	1/71
278	478 CFJ	Leyland PD2A/30	610090	Massey	2420	H31/26R	4/61	1/71
279	479 CFJ	Leyland PD2A/30	610091	Massey	2422	H31/26R	4/61	1/71
280	480 EFJ	Leyland PD2A/30	620405	Massey	2468	H31/26R	4/62	1/71
281	481 EFJ	Leyland PD2A/30	620406	Massey	2469	H31/26R	4/62	1/71
282	482 EFJ	Leyland PD2A/30	620423	Massey	2466	H31/26R	4/62	1/71
283	483 EFJ	Leyland PD2A/30	620424	Massey	2470	H31/26R	4/62	1/71
284	484 EFJ	Leyland PD2A/30	620425	Massey	2467	H31/26R	4/62	1/71
285	85 GFJ	Leyland PD2A/30	L00490	Massey	2525	H31/26R	5/63	1/71
286	86 GFJ	Leyland PD2A/30	L00491	Massey	2527	H31/26R	5/63	1/71
287	87 GFJ	Leyland PD2A/30	L00526	Massey	2528	H31/26R	5/63	1/71
288	88 GFJ	Leyland PD2A/30	L00527	Massey	2524	H31/26R	5/63	1/71
289	89 GFJ	Leyland PD2A/30	L00528	Massey	2526	H31/26R	5/63	1/71
290	AFJ 90B	Leyland PD2A/30	L20493	Massey	2569	H31/26R	6/64	1/71
291	AFJ 91B	Leyland PD2A/30	L20494	Massey	2568	H31/26R	6/64	1/71
292	AFJ 92B	Leyland PD2A/30	L20547	Massey	2566	H31/26R	6/64	1/71
293	AFJ 93B	Leyland PD2A/30	L20548	Massey	2565	H31/26R	6/64	1/71
294	AFJ 94B	Leyland PD2A/30	L20549	Massey	2567	H31/26R	6/64	1/71
295	DFJ 895C	Leyland PD2A/30	L41916	Massey	2630	H37/28R	10/65	1/71
296	DFJ 896C	Leyland PD2A/30	L41917	Massey	2629	H37/28R	10/65	1/71
297	DFJ 897C	Leyland PD2A/30	L41918	Massey	2628	H37/28R	9/65	1/71
298	DFJ 898C	Leyland PD2A/30	L42168	Massey	2631	H37/28R	10/65	1/71
299	DFJ 899C	Leyland PD2A/30	L42169	Massey	2632	H37/28R	10/65	1/71
201	GFJ 601D	Leyland PSU4/2R	L62213	Massey	2675	B41D	10/66	1/71
202	GFJ 602D	Leyland PSU4/2R	L62532	Massey	2676	B41D	10/66	1/71
203	GFJ 603D	Leyland PSU4/2R	L62533	Massey	2679	B41D	10/66	1/71
204	GFJ 604D	Leyland PSU4/2R	L62631	Massey	2678	B41D	10/66	1/71
205	GFJ 605D	Leyland PSU4/2R	L62644	Massey	2677	B41D	10/66	1/71
206	MFJ 386G	Leyland PSUR1A/1R	801544	Marshall	B4146	B47D	1/69	1/71
207	MFJ 387G	Leyland PSUR1A/1R	801545	Marshall	B4147	B47D	1/69	1/71
208	MFJ 388G	Leyland PSUR1A/1R	801649	Marshall	B4145	B47D	1/69	1/71
209	MFJ 389G	Leyland PSUR1A/1R	801650	Marshall	B4149	B47D	1/69	1/71
210	MFJ 390G	Leyland PSUR1A/1R	801746	Marshall	B4148	B47D	1/69	1/71

Previous history:

All these vehicles were new to Exeter Corporation. HFJ 140-145 (13-18) retained their Exeter fleet numbers, although HFJ 132 was subsequently renumbered 245. The double-deckers, which became Devon General 250-299, being originally numbered 50-99. The single-deckers which became Devon General 201-210 were numbered 1-10 with Exeter Corporation.

Notes:

HFJ 142 (15): Renumbered 245 4/70.
TFJ 808 (250): Had a Gardner 6LW engine.
UFJ 291-299 (251-259): Had Gardner 6LW engines.
XFJ 750-754 (265-269): Had Gardner 6LW engines.
970-974 AFJ (270-274): Had Gardner 6LW engines.

Disposals:

HFJ 140 (13): W Norths (PV) Ltd (dealer), Sherburn-in-Elmet 7/70; Armoride Ltd, Earby (XLA) 9/70.
HFJ 141 (14): W Norths (PV) Ltd (dealer), Sherburn-in-Elmet 7/70; unknown contractor, Scunthorpe area 1970.
HFJ 142 (15): J Gobbin, St Austell for preservation 11/70; Roselyn Coaches, Par (CO) for preservation 7/12; still owned 1/15.
HFJ 144 (17): in 4/70; withdrawn 5/70; G Glover, Winkleigh for preservation 7/70; T Robbins, Leatherhead for preservation 3/94; still owned 1/15.

HFJ 145 (18): withdrawn 5/70; W Norths (PV) Ltd (dealer), Sherburn-in-Elmet 8/70; Armoride Ltd, Earby (XLA) 9/70.

TFJ 808 (250): Withdrawn 9/70; CT Shears, Winkleigh for preservation 12/70; B Parnell, Exeter for preservation 9/80; CT Shears, Winkleigh for preservation by 10/89; S Cope, Longton for preservation 10/00; DJ Shears, Northam (DN) 12/07; still current 1/15.

UFJ 291 (251): Western National Omnibus Co Ltd, Exeter (DN) 1/71; withdrawn 7/71; W Norths (PV) Ltd (dealer), Sherburn in Elmet 10/72; unidentified dealer, Barnsley for scrap 1/73.

UFJ 292 (252): Withdrawn 9/70; Western National Omnibus Co Ltd, Exeter (DN) 252 as a withdrawn vehicle 1/71; W Norths (PV) Ltd (dealer), Sherburn in Elmet 1/71; J & W Shaw Bros, Byers Green (DM) 5/71; United Automobile Services Ltd, Darlington (DM) 1/75; not used; C Durham et al, Meopham for preservation 3/75; T Snow, Kentisbeare for preservation 1/84; A Beadnell, Saltburn-by-the-Sea for preservation 3/92; J Shaw, Willington for preservation 10/92; restored in Shaw Bros livery; still owned 1/15.

UFJ 293 (253): Western National Omnibus Co Ltd, Exeter (DN) 253 1/71; repainted Tilling green and cream with NBC style fleet names 7/74; to NBC poppy red livery 4/78; Devon Bus Preservation Group, Exeter for spares 8/80; South Molton Cricket Club, South Molton (XDN) 9/81; still there 9/99; R Greet (preservationist), Broadhempston for spares by 12/04; scrapped c2005.

UFJ 294 (254): Withdrawn 9/70; Western National Omnibus Co Ltd, Exeter (DN) 254 as a withdrawn vehicle 1/71; W Norths (PV) Ltd (dealer), Sherburn in Elmet 1/71; Johnston, Glasgow (LK) 3/71; R Irvine {Tiger Coaches} (dealer), Salsburgh by 7/72.

UFJ 295 (255): Withdrawn 9/70; Western National Omnibus Co Ltd, Exeter (DN) 255 as a withdrawn vehicle 1/71; W Norths (PV) Ltd (dealer), Sherburn in Elmet 1/71; Scarlet Band Motor Services Ltd, West Cornforth (DM) 83 3/71; withdrawn 7/74; Paul Sykes Organisation Ltd (dealer), Blackerhill 8/74; J & J Sykes (dealer), Carlton for scrap 8/74.

UFJ 296 (256): Western National Omnibus Co Ltd, Exeter (DN) 256 1/71; transferred to Torquay depot as driver trainer 12/72; repainted in traditional City of Exeter green and cream livery complete with crest and fleet name 6/74; withdrawn 10/79; Devon Bus Preservation Group, Exeter 3/80; AS Simm, Tiverton for preservation 11/86; R Greet, Broadhempston for preservation 1992; operated as a psv on an irregular basis between 5/01 and 11/03 as R Greet, Broadhempston and between 11/03 and 12/11 as Nostalgic Transport Ltd, Broadhempston (DN); still owned 1/15.

UFJ 297 (257): Withdrawn 9/70; Western National Omnibus Co Ltd, Exeter (DN) 257 as a withdrawn vehicle 1/71; W Norths (PV) Ltd (dealer), Sherburn in Elmet 1/71; sold for scrap 3/72.

UFJ 298 (258): Withdrawn 9/70; Western National Omnibus Co Ltd, Exeter (DN) 258 as a withdrawn vehicle 1/71; W Norths (PV) Ltd (dealer), Sherburn in Elmet 1/71; Scarlet Band Motor Services Ltd, West Cornforth (DM) 82 3/71; withdrawn 7/74; Paul Sykes Organisation Ltd (dealer), Blackerhill 8/74; J & J Sykes (dealer), Carlton for scrap 8/74.

UFJ 299 (259): Western National Omnibus Co Ltd, Exeter (DN) 259 1/71; withdrawn 3/71; W Norths (PV) Ltd (dealer), Sherburn in Elmet 10/72; unidentified dealer, Barnsley for scrap 1/73.

VFJ 995 (260): Western National Omnibus Co Ltd, Exeter (DN) 260 1/71; to NBC poppy red livery 3/74; to driver trainer at Exeter 11/74; withdrawn 2/79; P Rossiter, Winkleigh for preservation 4/79; B Geenty, Herne Bay for preservation by 5/83; Kent Metro, Burham (XKT) as a driver tuition vehicle 10/88; J Wagstaff, Croydon for preservation 3/93; D Shears, Northam for preservation 9/09; still owned 1/15.

VFJ 996 (261): Western National Omnibus Co Ltd, Exeter (DN) 261 1/71; to NBC poppy red livery 1/74; withdrawn 11/76; sold 12/76; Suntrekkers Ltd, Newport (GT) 1977; used as driver trainer; Winged Fellowship Trust, London W1 (XLN) 6/78; returned to Suntrekkers 1979; used as a seat store.

VFJ 997 (262): Western National Omnibus Co Ltd, Exeter (DN) 262 1/71; to NBC poppy red livery 6/74; withdrawn 11/76; sold 12/76; A Finlay (dealer), Birdwell by 3/77.

VFJ 998 (263): Western National Omnibus Co Ltd, Exeter (DN) 263 1/71; to NBC poppy red livery 6/74; withdrawn 11/76; sold 12/76; unidentified dealer, Blackerhill by 7/77 (probably P Sykes).

VFJ 999 (264): Western National Omnibus Co Ltd, Exeter (DN) 264 1/71; to NBC poppy red livery 6/74; withdrawn 10/76; sold 12/76; Suntrekkers Ltd, Newport (GT) by 4/77; Ashford Garden Centre, Barnstaple (XDN) as a canteen storeroom 8/83; DL Hoare (preservationist), Chepstow for spares by 9/90; unidentified dealer, Barnsley for scrap at an unknown date.

XFJ 750-751 (265-266): Western National Omnibus Co Ltd, Exeter (DN) 265 1/71; withdrawn 7/71; W Norths (PV) Ltd (dealer), Sherburn in Elmet 10/71; M Parton & Allen (dealer), Carlton for scrap 3/72.

XFJ 752 (267): Western National Omnibus Co Ltd, Exeter (DN) 267 1/71; to full Devon General BET-style red and ivory livery complete with Devon General BET-style style fleet name and fleet numbers 2/71; withdrawn 7/71; W Norths (PV) Ltd (dealer), Sherburn in Elmet 10/71; M Parton & Allen (dealer), Carlton for scrap 3/72.

XFJ 753-754 (268-269): Western National Omnibus Co Ltd, Exeter (DN) 268-269 1/71; withdrawn 7/71;
W Norths (PV) Ltd (dealer), Sherburn in Elmet 10/71; M Parton & Allen (dealer), Carlton for
scrap 3/72.

970 AFJ (270): Western National Omnibus Co Ltd, Exeter (DN) 270 1/71; withdrawn 6/72; W Norths (PV)
Ltd (dealer), Sherburn in Elmet 10/72; unidentified dealer, Barnsley for scrap 1/73.

971-972 AFJ (271-272): Western National Omnibus Co Ltd, Exeter (DN) 271-272 1/71; withdrawn 4/72;
W Norths (PV) Ltd (dealer), Sherburn in Elmet 5/72; unidentified dealer, Barnsley for scrap
1972.

973 AFJ (273): Western National Omnibus Co Ltd, Exeter (DN) 273 1/71; withdrawn 2/72; W Norths (PV)
Ltd (dealer), Sherburn in Elmet 5/72; unidentified dealer, Barnsley for scrap 1972.

974 AFJ (274): Western National Omnibus Co Ltd, Exeter (DN) 274 1/71; withdrawn 6/72; W Norths (PV)
Ltd (dealer), Sherburn in Elmet 10/72; CT Shears, Winkleigh for preservation 10/72; on loan
to T Jackson and others, Kingsbridge for preservation (but still kept at Winkleigh) by 5/91; off
loan by 6/95; S & C Blood, North Tawton 5/97 for preservation; still owned 1/15.

475 CFJ (275): Repainted dark green with single cream band 6/70; repainted into standard Exeter green
and cream livery 7/70; Western National Omnibus Co Ltd, Exeter (DN) 275 1/71; withdrawn
3/73; used for spares from 3/73; Rundle (dealer), Plymouth for scrap 10/73.

476 CFJ (276): Western National Omnibus Co Ltd, Exeter (DN) 276 1/71; Devon General BET–style
red/ivory livery, NBC-style Devon General fleet names 11/71; to NBC poppy red livery by
9/76; withdrawn 1/78; W Norths (PV) Ltd (dealer), Sherburn in Elmet 4/78.

477 CFJ (277): Western National Omnibus Co Ltd, Exeter (DN) 277 1/71; withdrawn 3/73; used for
spares from 3/73; Rundle (dealer), Plymouth for scrap 10/73.

478 CFJ (278): Western National Omnibus Co Ltd, Exeter (DN) 278 1/71; to Devon General BET–style
red/ivory livery 7/71; to NBC poppy red livery by 9/76; withdrawn 1/78; W Norths (PV) Ltd
(dealer), Sherburn in Elmet 4/78; Doncaster Gliding Club, Doncaster (XSY) 10/78; M Parton
& Allen (dealer), Carlton 5/83.

479 CFJ (279): Repainted green and cream livery with 'EXETER' as fleet name on both sides; Western
National Omnibus Co Ltd, Exeter (DN) 279 1/71; to NBC poppy red livery 1/74; withdrawn
3/79; British Double Decker Corporation (dealer), Wotton-under-Edge 5/79; George Hotel,
Swindon as a mobile bar 8/79; Lorien, Salisbury as a mobile caravan 1980; new owner, near
Salisbury as a mobile caravan 4/82; Hippies (caravan) by 9/86; still owned 6/88; Ribbs and
Lynne, Dulverton for preservation by 10/00; still owned 12/11.

480 EFJ (280): Western National Omnibus Co Ltd, Exeter (DN) 280 1/71; to Devon General BET–style
red/ivory livery, NBC-style Devon General fleet names by 10/71; to NBC poppy red livery
9/74; withdrawn 9/79; W Norths (PV) Ltd (dealer), Sherburn in Elmet 12/79.

481 EFJ (281): Western National Omnibus Co Ltd, Exeter (DN) 281 1/71; to Devon General BET–style
red/ivory livery 3/71; to NBC poppy red livery 8/74; withdrawn 9/79; W Norths (PV) Ltd
(dealer), Sherburn in Elmet 12/79; M Parton & Allen (dealer), Carlton for scrap 3/80.

482 EFJ (282): Western National Omnibus Co Ltd, Exeter (DN) 282 1/71; to Devon General BET–style
red/ivory livery 7/71; to NBC poppy red livery 8/74; withdrawn 9/79; W Norths (PV) Ltd
(dealer), Sherburn in Elmet 11/79; J Whiting (dealer), Carlton for scrap 12/79.

483 EFJ (283): Western National Omnibus Co Ltd, Exeter (DN) 283 1/71; to Devon General BET–style
red/ivory livery 7/71; to NBC poppy red livery 8/74; withdrawn 9/79; W Norths (PV) Ltd
(dealer), Sherburn in Elmet 12/79; M Parton & Allen (dealer), Carlton 7/80 for scrap.

484 EFJ (284): Western National Omnibus Co Ltd, Exeter (DN) 284 1/71; to NBC poppy red livery 11/74;
withdrawn 9/79; W Norths (PV) Ltd (dealer), Sherburn in Elmet 11/79; J Whiting (dealer),
Featherstone 12/79; Home Office Fire Service Training College, Moreton-in-Marsh (XGL)
10/80; Nottingham Heritage Centre for preservation 11/98; P Platt, Exeter for preservation
10/99; J Shorland, Exeter for preservation by 6/00; still owned 1/15.

85 GFJ (285): Western National Omnibus Co Ltd, Exeter (DN) 285 1/71; to Devon General BET–style
red/ivory livery by 12/71; to NBC poppy red livery 11/74; withdrawn 8/80; Paul Sykes
Organisation Ltd (dealer), Barnsley 9/80; J Sykes (dealer), Carlton 10/80.

86 GFJ (286): Western National Omnibus Co Ltd, Exeter (DN) 286 1/71; to Devon General BET–style
red/ivory livery 3/72; to NBC poppy red livery 10/75; withdrawn 1980; D Godley, Crediton for
preservation 10/80; Musterphantom Ltd {Solent Blue Line}, Southampton (HA) 01 as driver
training vehicle 11/87; P Fricker, Worthing for preservation 10/91; Wyatt, Brighton for
preservation 10/92; Exeter City Council 2/96; on loan to West Country Historic Omnibus &
Transport Trust for preservation 4/05; still on loan 1/15

87 GFJ (287): To NBC poppy red livery 1/74; Western National Omnibus Co Ltd, Exeter (DN) 287 1/71;
withdrawn 1980; Paul Sykes Organisation Ltd (dealer), Barnsley 9/80; J Sykes (dealer),
Carlton for scrap 10/80.

88 GFJ (288): Western National Omnibus Co Ltd, Exeter (DN) 288 1/71; to NBC poppy red livery 5/73;
withdrawn 1980; Paul Sykes Organisation Ltd (dealer), Barnsley 9/80; J Sykes (dealer),
Carlton for scrap 10/80.

89 GFJ (289): Western National Omnibus Co Ltd, Exeter (DN) 289 1/71; to NBC poppy red livery 2/74; withdrawn 1980; Paul Sykes Organisation Ltd (dealer), Barnsley 9/80; J Sykes (dealer), Carlton for scrap 10/80.

AFJ 90B (290): Western National Omnibus Co Ltd, Exeter (DN) 290 1/71; to NBC poppy red livery 7/73; withdrawn 8/80; Paul Sykes Organisation Ltd (dealer), Barnsley 9/80; J Sykes (dealer), Carlton for scrap 10/80.

AFJ 91B (291): Western National Omnibus Co Ltd, Exeter (DN) 291 1/71; to NBC poppy red livery 10/73; withdrawn 8/80; Paul Sykes Organisation Ltd (dealer), Barnsley 9/80; J Sykes (dealer), Carlton for scrap 10/80.

AFJ 92B (292): Western National Omnibus Co Ltd, Exeter (DN) 292 1/71; to NBC poppy red livery 11/73; withdrawn 8/80; Paul Sykes Organisation Ltd (dealer), Barnsley 9/80; J Sykes (dealer), Carlton for scrap 10/80.

AFJ 93B (293): Western National Omnibus Co Ltd, Exeter (DN) 293 1/71; to NBC poppy red livery 12/73; withdrawn 8/80; Paul Sykes Organisation Ltd (dealer), Barnsley 9/80; J Sykes (dealer), Carlton for scrap 10/80.

AFJ 94B (294): Western National Omnibus Co Ltd, Exeter (DN) 294 1/71; to NBC poppy red livery 3/73; withdrawn 8/80; Paul Sykes Organisation Ltd (dealer), Barnsley 9/80; J Sykes (dealer), Carlton for scrap 10/80.

DFJ 895C (295): Western National Omnibus Co Ltd, Exeter (DN) 295 1/71; to NBC poppy red livery 9/73; withdrawn 8/78; W Norths (PV) Ltd (dealer), Sherburn in Elmet 10/78; M Parton & Allen (dealer), Carlton 2/81.

DFJ 896C (296): Western National Omnibus Co Ltd, Exeter (DN) 296 1/71; to NBC poppy red livery 2/73; withdrawn 8/78; W Norths (PV) Ltd (dealer), Sherburn in Elmet 10/78; M Parton & Allen (dealer), Carlton for scrap 11/78.

DFJ 897C (297): Western National Omnibus Co Ltd, Exeter (DN) 297 1/71; to NBC poppy red livery 10/73; withdrawn 8/78; W Norths (PV) Ltd (dealer), Sherburn in Elmet 10/78; M Parton & Allen (dealer), Carlton 7/80.

DFJ 898C (298): Western National Omnibus Co Ltd, Exeter (DN) 298 1/71; to NBC poppy red livery 2/74; withdrawn 8/78; W Norths (PV) Ltd (dealer), Sherburn in Elmet 10/78; M Parton & Allen (dealer), Carlton for scrap 11/78.

DFJ 899C (299): Western National Omnibus Co Ltd, Exeter (DN) 299 1/71; to NBC poppy red livery 2/73; withdrawn 8/78; W Norths (PV) Ltd (dealer), Sherburn in Elmet 10/78; M Parton & Allen (dealer), Carlton for scrap 11/78.

GFJ 601D (201): Western National Omnibus Co Ltd, Exeter (DN) 201 1/71; to Devon General BET–style red/ivory livery 4/72; to NBC poppy red with white band 10/73; withdrawn 10/79; DJ Green (dealer), Weymouth 11/79; Hartwood Exports (Machinery) Ltd (dealer), Barnsley 12/79; Livingstone, Staines (XSR) as a mobile dining bus 12/79; withdrawn and sold 7/83.

GFJ 602D (202): Western National Omnibus Co Ltd, Exeter (DN) 202 1/71; to Devon General BET–style red/ivory livery 4/72; to NBC poppy red with white window surrounds 11/73; to NBC poppy red with white band; withdrawn 10/79; DJ Green (dealer), Weymouth 11/79; Hartwood Exports (Machinery) Ltd (dealer), Barnsley 12/79; Leonard Taylor & Sons (Tours) Ltd, East Morton (WY) 5/80; Central, Keighley (WY) by 9/81; Stanley Hughes & Co Ltd (dealer), Gomersal 2/82; J Sykes (dealer), Carlton for scrap 2/82.

GFJ 603D (203): Western National Omnibus Co Ltd, Exeter (DN) 203 1/71; to Devon General BET–style red/ivory livery 4/72, later to NBC poppy red livery 11/73; withdrawn 10/79; DJ Green (dealer), Weymouth 11/79; Hartwood Exports (Machinery) Ltd (dealer), Barnsley 12/79; C Meynell (dealer), Carlton for scrap 2/80.

GFJ 604D (204): Western National Omnibus Co Ltd, Exeter (DN) 204 1/71; to Devon General BET–style red/ivory livery 5/72; to NBC poppy red with white window surrounds 11/73; withdrawn 11/79; DJ Green (dealer), Weymouth 11/79; Hartwood Exports (Machinery) Ltd (dealer), Barnsley 12/79; D Rollinson (Bus Centre) Ltd (dealer), Carlton for scrap 2/80.

GFJ 605D (205): Western National Omnibus Co Ltd, Exeter (DN) 205 1/71; to Devon General BET–style red/ivory livery 7/72; to NBC poppy red with white window surrounds 11/73; withdrawn 10/79; DJ Green (dealer), Weymouth 11/79; Hartwood Exports (Machinery) Ltd (dealer), Barnsley 12/79; Middletons (Rugeley) Ltd, Rugeley (ST) 58 1/80; withdrawn 10/80; sold 1/81.

MFJ 386G (206): Western National Omnibus Co Ltd, Exeter (DN) 206 1/71; to Devon General BET–style red/ivory livery 11/71, later to NBC poppy red livery; withdrawn 6/80; Booth of Aston Ltd (dealer), Aston for scrap 12/80.

MFJ 387G (207): Western National Omnibus Co Ltd, Exeter (DN) 207 1/71; to Devon General BET–style red/ivory livery 1972, later to NBC poppy red livery; withdrawn 6/80; Booth of Aston Ltd (dealer), Aston 12/80 for scrap 12/80.

MFJ 388G (208): Western National Omnibus Co Ltd, Exeter (DN) 208 1/71; to Devon General BET–style red/ivory livery 12/71, later to NBC poppy red livery; withdrawn 6/80; Booth of Aston Ltd (dealer), Aston 12/80 for scrap 12/80.

MFJ 389G (209): Western National Omnibus Co Ltd, Exeter (DN) 209 1/71; to Devon General BET–style red/ivory livery 12/71, later to NBC poppy red livery; withdrawn 6/80; Booth of Aston Ltd (dealer), Aston for scrap 12/80.

MFJ 390G (210): Western National Omnibus Co Ltd, Exeter (DN) 210 1/71; to Devon General BET–style red/ivory livery 1972, later to NBC poppy red livery; withdrawn 6/80; Booth of Aston Ltd (dealer), Aston for scrap 12/80.

Vehicles acquired from Court Garages (Torquay) Ltd (DN) 10/70:

493	JTA 763E	Bedford SB5	7802536	Duple	1212/2	C41F	4/67	1/71
494	JTA 764E	Bedford SB5	7802556	Duple	1213/3	C41F	4/67	1/71
495	JTA 765E	Bedford SB5	7803235	Duple	1213/1	C41F	4/67	1/71
496	CXF 256G	Bedford SB5	9T466343	Duple	1224/24	C41F	4/69	1/71
497	CXF 257G	Bedford SB5	9T466109	Duple	1224/25	C41F	4/69	1/71

Previous history:
These vehicles were all new to Court Garages.

Notes:
These vehicles retained their cream and orange Court Garages livery with Devon General.

Disposals:
JTA 763E (493): Western National Omnibus Co Ltd, Exeter (DN) 493 1/71; repainted into Grey Cars white livery 2/71; Greenslades Tours Ltd, Exeter (DN) 493 5/71; renumbered 483 at an unknown date; Dawlish Coaches Ltd {Tomlinson's}, Dawlish (DN) 11/74; Waverley Coaches Ltd, St Brelade, Jersey (CI) 3 4/76; re-registered J 29255; PJ Powell, St Helier, Jersey (CI) 4/89; Wacton Trading/Coach Sales (dealer), Bromyard c7/94.

JTA 764E (494): Western National Omnibus Co Ltd, Exeter (DN) 494 1/71; repainted into Grey Cars white livery 2/71; Greenslades Tours Ltd, Exeter (DN) 494 5/71; renumbered 484 at an unknown date; A & AR Turner, Chulmleigh (DN) 1/75; Wacton Trading/Coach Sales (dealer), Bromyard for scrap 1/85.

JTA 765E (495): Western National Omnibus Co Ltd, Exeter (DN) 495 1/71; repainted into Grey Cars white livery 2/71; Greenslades Tours Ltd, Exeter (DN) 495 5/71; renumbered 485 at an unknown date; A & AR Turner, Chulmleigh (DN) 1/75; Moseley in the South Ltd (dealer), Taunton by 8/86; JW Pugsley {Blue Embassy Coaches}, Atherington (DN) by10/86; Stark, Harris & Doe {Country Bus}, Atherington (DN) 6/88; Wacton Trading/Coach Sales (dealer), Bromyard for scrap 8/88.

CXF 256G (496): Western National Omnibus Co Ltd, Exeter (DN) 496 1/71; repainted into Grey Cars white livery 2/71; Greenslades Tours Ltd, Exeter (DN) 496 5/71; renumbered 386 1/75; DC Venner {Scarlet Coaches}, Minehead (SO) 8/76; not operated; BJ Redwood {Redwood Services} Hemyock (DN) 11/76; A & R Millman, Buckfastleigh (DN) 1/80; withdrawn 7/80; BJD Whitehead {Flashes Coaches}, Newent (GT) 2/81; Wacton Trading/Coach Sales (dealer), Bromyard 3/82; Exors of AO Sherrin, Carhampton (SO) 4/82; Autojade Ltd, Tiverton (DN) by 6/84.

CXF 257G (497): Western National Omnibus Co Ltd, Exeter (DN) 497 1/71; repainted into Grey Cars white livery 2/71; Greenslades Tours Ltd, Exeter (DN) 497 5/71; renumbered 387 1/75; Mascot Motors Ltd, St Helier, Jersey (CI) 25 7/76; re-registered J 51937; Waverley Coaches Ltd, St Brelade, Jersey (CI) 4 4/84; renumbered 13 by 11/91; renumbered 19 by 5/98; sold by 4/04; Glen Hamel, St Clement, Jersey (XCI) 2007; Carlton leFevre {Amazin Adventure Park}, St Peter, Jeresy (XCI) by 1/10 as static playbus; N Cottilard {Amazin Adventure Park}, St Peter, Jersey (XCI) by 12/12 as static party bus; Talbot, St Helier, Jersey (CI) c1/13; M Wyles, Hinckley 4/13 for preservation.

Vehicles on order by Devon General at time of Western National takeover:

74-87	TUO 74-87J	AEC Reliance - Willowbrook B43F
218-224	VOD 218-224K	Leyland PSUR1B/1R - Marshall B47D

These vehicles were delivered direct to Western National Omnibus Co Ltd. The Leyland Panthers were originally an Exeter Corporation order, that had been transferred to Devon General, prior to being taken over by Western National. They were eventually delivered c12/71 and entered service with Western National, in Devon General livery in 1/72.

An order for a further six AEC Reliance/Willowbrook 36ft long single-deckers was cancelled and replaced by the Bristol LHS order (below), purchased as replacements for Albion Nimbuses.

88-93	VOD 88-93K	Bristol LHS6L - Marshall B33F

Five Bristol RELH6L/Plaxton coaches intended to have been delivered to Devon General in Grey Cars livery as 450-454 passed instead to Greenslades as their UUO 450-454J (305-309).

In addition four Leyland PDR1/1 with Willowbrook H44/33F bodies, which were to have become Devon General OTT 542-545G (542-545) were reallocated to Yorkshire Traction Co Ltd, Barnsley (WR) registered RHE 447-450G and were replaced by Bristol VRT/ECW vehicles, delivered to Western National.

ANCILLARY FLEET

Fleet numbers were not carried until 1956. V13 always carried its previous number M103; those bracketed did not carry their fleet numbers.

Fleet	Reg	Make	Chassis	Body	Date 1	Date 2	Date 3
	T 7518	Wolseley 25 hp	5455	dropside lorry	-/14	11/19	-/21
	T 8874	Humber	4085	Van	-/07	-/20?	-/--
	FJ 1779	Ford Y	4593560	Van	7/21	7/21	3/29
	TA 1870	FIAT F2	?	Van	7/21	-/27	3/29
	TA 6434	Lancia Z1	4097	Van	5/23	-/27	12/34
	UO 1618	Morris Z	2855Z	Van	3/27	3/27	5/36
	DV 113	Morris TX	?	Van	3/29	3/29	6/36
	FJ 1782	Daimler Y	7312	Lorry	7/21	-/29	c-/31
	TA 3098	Leyland G7	12373	Van	3/22	-/29	c-/31
	DV 5836	Morris TX	4853TX	Van	6/30	6/30	-/38
	TA 1803	AEC B	B204	Tower Wagon	-/10	6/33	12/38
V5	AMU 544	Morris 30 cwt	?	Van	1/35	1/35	-/39
V6	AUO 445	Morris (L?) 12 cwt	25444	Van	7/35	7/35	-/51
V7	AOD 211	Morris C.11/30	750C24045	Van	4/36	4/36	-/46
V8	AOD 212	Morris C.11/30	750C24118	Van	4/36	4/36	2/41
V9	Reserved for conversion of SL133 (UO 9779) which did not take place						
V10	EOD 978	Morris 12/4	SY/TWV862	Van	6/40	6/40	1/54
V11	FTA 503	Morris 12 cwt	AV45448	Van	2/41	2/41	-/53
V12	GUO 772	Morris CV.11/30	62976	Van	11/46	11/46	4/58
RV1	(t/p))	AEC Matador	?	Recovery Vehicle	-/--	-/47	1/71
M103	AUO 512	Leyland KP2	3954	Van	6/35	-/48	-/51
V14	MTT 393	Morris JR	?	Van	12/50	12/50	8/59
V15	MUO 296	Morris PV	?	Van	1/51	1/51	8/59
V16	NTA 115	Morris PV	?	Van	7/51	7/51	5/58
XR424	DDV 424	AEC Regal	O6623304	(See notes)	4/39	-/52	-/70
SR469	DOD 469	AEC Regal	O6623447	Tree lopper	1/40	-/52	-/52
V17	OTT 621	Morris JR	?	Van	1/53	1/53	8/60
V18	NUO 692	Morris JR	?	Van	11/53	11/53	3/60
DR215	OD 7502	AEC Regent	O6612450	Tree lopper	3/34	-/53	6/56
DG322	GTT 422	Guy Arab II	FD27923	Tree lopper	11/45	10/57	8/59
DR204	OD 7491	AEC Regent	O6622438	Tree lopper	1/34	-/57	n/a
V20	XOD 377	Morris LD-	?	Van	3/58	3/58	6/66
V19	XOD 376	Morris LC05M	?	Lorry	4/58	4/58	5/67
V21	711 BOD	Morris LD-	?	Van	6/59	6/59	-/66
V22	712 BOD	Morris LD-	?	Van	7/59	7/59	-/66
V23	709 DOD	Morris LD-	?	Van	3/60	3/60	-/67
	DJF 327	AEC Regent II	O6617521	Storage unit	2/46	7/60	1/71
	DJF 328	AEC Regent II	O6617522	Storage unit	3/46	7/60	1/71
	DJF 330	AEC Regent II	O6617526	Storage unit	3/46	7/60	1/71
V24	710 DOD	Morris LD-	?	Van Publicity	7/60	7/60	-/--
DR205	OD 7492	AEC Regent	O6612436	Tree lopper	1/34	4/61	8/61
DR720	DDV 423	AEC Rebuild	O6623303	Tree lopper	-/54	3/63	9/63
DR667	NTT 667	AEC Regent III	9613A7161	Tree lopper	7/52	10/64	3/70
V25	FOD 948D	Morris 1 ton	?	Van	5/66	5/66	1/71
V26	GTA 641D	Morris 1 ton	?	Van	5/66	5/66	1/71
V27	GTA 642D	Morris 1 ton	?	Van	5/66	5/66	1/71
	GFJ 735D	Hillman Hunter	?	Van	-/66	-/66	1/71
V28	JDV 833E	Morris FGK30	?	Lorry	4/67	4/67	1/71
V29	KTA 518E	Morris LDM20	?	Van	6/67	6/67	1/71
V30	MUO 656F	Morris LDM20	?	Van	5/68	5/68	1/71
V31	ODV 294G	Austin Mini	?	Van	2/69	2/69	1/71
	HFJ 133	Leyland PD2/1	472573	Tree-lopper	11/47	4/70	8/70
	ADV 969B	Austin A60	?	Van	-/64	-/70	1/71
RV7	(t/p)	AEC Matador	?	Recovery vehicle	-/--	-/70	1/71

Previous history:
T 7518: Acquired from Torquay Tramways (qv).
T 8874: Acquired from an unknown source.
FJ 1782: Previously bus 17.

OD 7491-7492 (DR204-205): Previously buses DR204-205.
OD 7502: Previously bus DR215.
TA 1803: Acquired from Torquay Tramways (qv).
TA 1870: Acquired from Croscols Ltd, Tiverton (DN) 3/24 as a bus (qv).
TA 3098: Previously bus 98.
TA 6434: Previously Ch14 with Fleet Cars Ltd (qv).
AUO 512: Previously bus M103.
DDV 423 (DR720): Previously bus DR720.
DDV 424 (XR424): Previously bus XR424.
DJF 327-328: Previously buses DR701-702.
DJF 330: Previously bus DR703.
DOD 469 (SR469): Previously bus SR469.
GTT 422 (DG322): Previously bus DG322.
HFJ 133: New as Exeter City Transport (DN) bus 6; converted to open-top for use as tree lopper 7/64.
NTT 667 (DR667): Previously bus DR667.
ADV 969B: Acquired from Western National Omnibus Co Ltd, Exeter (GDN).
GFJ 735D: Acquired from Greenslades Tours Ltd, Exeter (GDN).
RV1 (t/p): Acquired from Air Ministry {Royal Air Force} (GOV).
RV7 (t/p): Acquired from Vass (dealer), Ampthill.

Notes:

DV 113: Devon Motor Tax records this with chassis number ZNZ6 and engine 15263TX, both of which appear to be incorrect.
FJ 1782: Used for rubbish collection.
OD 7491 (DR204): Not used.
OD 7502 (DR215): Converted to open-top.
TA 1803: Latterly used as a carnival float.
AOD 211-212 (V7-8): Allocated to Engineering Department.
AUO 445 (V6): Parcel van at Torquay, later Publicity Department.
AUO 512 (M103): Converted into a stores van by Devon Coachbuilders 1948 and ran as such until 1951; allocated Ancillary Fleet number V13 but never carried.
DDV 423 (DR720): Roof removed for use as tree-lopper.
DDV 424 (RV2): Used initially as a tree lopper during 1952; chassis shortened, fitted with recovery vehicle body by Longwell Green and numbered RV2 1955; subsequently operated on trade plates.
DJF 327-328: Bodies scrapped 7/60; chassis converted to storage racks to carry the roofs of the convertible top Leyland Atlanteans.
DJF 330: Body scrapped 7/60; chassis converted to storage racks to carry the roofs of the convertible top Leyland Atlanteans.
DOD 469 (SR469): Mechanical units used in the construction of 'Light Six' rebuild in 1954 (qv).
EOD 978 (V10): Parcels van at Exeter, later Publicity Department.
FTA 503 (V11): Parcels van at Torquay, later Publicity Department; operated for a period on 'town gas' from 3/43 until 2/44.
GTT 422 (DG322): Roof removed for use as tree-lopper.
GUO 772 (V12): Allocated to Torquay Engineering Department.
MTT 393 (V14): Parcels van at Torquay.
MUO 296 (V15): Allocated to Exeter Engineering Department.
NTA 115 (V16): Allocated to Torquay Engineering Department.
NTT 667 (DR667): Roof removed for use as tree-lopper.
NUO 692 (V18): Parcels van at Exeter.
OTT 621 (V17): Allocated to Publicity Department.
XOD 376 (V19): Torquay stores lorry.
XOD 377 (V20): Allocated to Torquay Engineering Department.
709 BOD (V23): Allocated to Exeter Engineering Department.
710 BOD (V24): Publicity Department van.
711 BOD (V21): Parcels van at Torquay.
712 BOD (V22): Parcels van at Exeter.
FOD 948D (V25): Allocated to Torquay Engineering Department.
GTA 641D (V26): Parcels van at Exeter.
GTA 642D (V27): Parcels van at Torquay.
JDV 833E (V28): Allocated to Torquay Engineering Department.
KTA 518E (V29): Allocated to Exeter Engineering Department.
MUO 656F (V30): Allocated to Publicity Department, Torquay.

RV1 (t/p): Torquay (Newton Road) recovery vehicle.

Disposals:

T 7518: Last known owner Moor & Son, South Molton (GDN) at an unknown date.

T 8874: No disposal known.

DV 113: No further owner.

DV 5836: Last licensed to Southern Railway 12/39.

FJ 1779: Scrapped 3/29.

FJ 1782: WJ Lavinder Ltd (dealer), Worcester Park 9/31.

OD 7491 (DR204): Mitchley (dealer), Birmingham 9/57.

OD 7492 (DR205): Passenger Vehicle Disposals Ltd (dealer) Dunchurch for scrap 8/61.

OD 7502 (DR215): Mitchley (dealer), Birmingham 8/56.

TA 1803: No disposal known.

TA 1870: No futher owner.

TA 3098: Biggs, Leighton Buzzard (GBD) as lorry at an unknown date; last licensed 3/35.

TA 6434: No disposal known.

UO 1618: No disposal known.

AMU 544 (V5): No disposal known.

AOD 211 (V7): Last licensed to AWT Sanders, Bow (GDN) 11/49.

AOD 212 (V8): Scrapped.

AUO 445 (V6): Last licensed to AHA Packer, Torquay 1/62.

AUO 512 (M103): , Mitchley (dealer), Birmingham 1951; JC Lodge (showman), Redditch as a mobile canteen at an unknown date; last licensed 9/55.

DDV 423 (DR720): Transport (Passenger Equipment) Ltd (dealer), Macclesfield 9/63; Berresford Motors Ltd, Cheddleton (ST) for use as tree lopper and tow bus 9/63, later used for spares; GP Ripley (dealer), Barnsley 6/87; scrapped on site.

DDV 424 (RV2): Scrapped at Torquay.

DJF 327-328: Western National Omnibus Co Ltd, Exeter (XDN) N577-578 1/71; Devon General Ltd, Exeter (XDN) 9877-9878 1/83. The rolling chassis of one of these two vehicles, or that of DJF 330 (below) sold to West of England Transport Collection, Winkleigh by 10/94.

DJF 330: Western National Omnibus Co Ltd, Exeter (XDN) N579 1/71; Devon General Ltd, Exeter (XDN) 9879 1/83. See also note above for DJF 327-328.

DOD 469 (SR469): No disposal known.

EOD 978 (V10): No disposal known.

FTA 503 (V11): No disposal known.

GTT 422 (DG322): W Bower, Barlborough, Derbyshire (contractor) (1959?); noted at Rotherham as a messroom 7/60; last licensed 12/61.

GUO 772 (V12): Mitchley (dealer), Birmingham 5/58.

HFJ 133: DJ Hoare, Chepstow for preservation 1970; dismantled at Chepstow 9/71

MTT 393 (V14): No disposal known.

MUO 296 (V15): No disposal known.

NTA 116 (V16): No disposal known.

NTT 667 (DR667): Mitchley (dealer), Birmingham 3/70; not traced further.

NUO 692 (V18): No disposal known.

OTT 621 (V17): No disposal known.

XOD 376-377 (V19-20): No disposals known.

709-710 BOD (V23-24): No disposals known.

711-712 BOD (V21-22): No disposals known.

ADV 969B: Western National Omnibus Co Ltd 1/71; not traced further.

FOD 948D (V25): Western National Omnibus Co Ltd 1/71; not traced further.

GFJ 735D: Western National Omnibus Co Ltd 1/71; not traced further.

GTA 641D (V26): Western National Omnibus Co Ltd 1/71; not traced further.

GTA 642D (V27): Western National Omnibus Co Ltd 1/71; sold 1973.

JDV 833E (V28): Western National Omnibus Co Ltd 1/71; sold 1977.

KTA 518E (V29): Western National Omnibus Co Ltd 1/71; sold 1973.

MUO 656F (V30): Western National Omnibus Co Ltd 1/71; P Platt, exeter for preservation 1978; W Hulme, Yatton for preservation at an unknown date; C Jeavons, Kingswinford for preservation at an unknown date; C Shears, Winkleigh for preservation at an unknown date; unidentified owner, Cornwall for preservation at an unknown date; P Derek, Plymouth for preservation at an unknown date; still owned 1/15.

ODV 294G (V31): Western National Omnibus Co Ltd 1/71; not traced further.

(t/p) (RV1): Western National Omnibus Co Ltd 1/71; withdrawn 1982; believed to be still extant in Midlands 4/15.

(t/p) (RV7): Western National Omnibus Co Ltd 1/71; registered PFJ 849M 1974; withdrawn 1981.

OPERATORS ACQUIRED BY DEVON GENERAL

March 1924	Croscols Ltd, Tiverton
November 1924	Fleet Cars Ltd, Torquay (operated as a subsidiary until November 1933)
January 1927	Torquay-Chelston Car Company Ltd, Torquay
May 1927	EO Babington {Blue Cars}, Ashburton
March 1932	Grey Cars Ltd, Torquay (operated as a subsidiary until November 1933)
August 1935	AC Aggett, Marldon
February 1936	H Fraser & G Rossiter {Teignmouth Motor Car Co}, Teignmouth
March 1952	Mrs WA Hart, Budleigh Salterton
October 1952	Balls Ltd {Balls Bus Service}, Newton Abbot
April 1954	AE Townsend, Torquay
September 1954	Balls Ltd {Balls Tours}, Newton Abbot
June 1957	Falkland Garages Ltd, Torquay
October 1966	Court Garages (Torquay) Ltd

In addition Devon General paid compensation to the following operators for them to abandon their competing Paignton to Brixham services, with effect from on 31st March 1931. No vehicles were acquired.

S Cooper {Dandy Cars}, Paignton
WH Dalton {Waverley Cars), Paignton
J Geddes {Burton Cars}, Brixham
J Low {Dennis Cars}, Paignton
J Mills {Blue Ensign}, Paignton
Prout Bros, Churston
F Slatter {Slavic Cars}, Paignton
Soul & Sanders (Paignton) Ltd {Redcliffe Cars}, Paignton

Goodwill of the following operators was acquired as follows:-

April 1934	Sidmouth Motor Co & Dagworthy Ltd, Sidmouth (stage services)
July 1934	RP Summers, Ottery St Mary (services)
September 1936	HJ Lee {East Devon Motor Co}, Ottery St Mary (excursions and tours)
1936	Milton's Services (Crediton) Ltd, Crediton (stage services)
May 1938	Miller & Sons, Exmouth (stage services)
April 1940	WJ Abbott (Exmouth) Ltd, Exmouth (stage services)
January 1948	Greenslades Tours Ltd, Exeter (Witheridge area stage services)
January 1955	HD Gourd & Sons, Bishopsteignton (stage services)

VEHICLES OF ACQUIRED OPERATORS

AC Aggett — Church House Cottage, Marldon (DN)

DV 2458	Ford AA	1376608	Mumford	B14-	9/29	11/31?	-/34
JY 3912	Ford BB	5310820	Mumford	B20-	6/34	6/34	6/35

Previous history:
DV 2458: New to CB Foxworthy {Dart Bus}, Paignton (DN) from whom it was acquired; date of acquisition uncertain, may be 12/30.

Disposals:
DV 2458: JA Watson, Gunnislake (CO) 1934; last licensed 12/36.
JY 3912: Devon General 104 6/35 (qv).

EO Babington — Ashburton Motor Works, East Street, Ashburton (DN)
Blue Saloon Motor Bus Service/Blue Cars

EB 2186	Ford	364178	hackney/lorry	-14-	4/20	4/20	9/30
EB 2187	FIAT 15/20hp	?	Dowell	Ch14	4/20	4/20	*
EB 2188	FIAT 15/20hp	?	Dowell	Ch14	4/20	4/20	*
EB 2399	FIAT 53A 15/20 hp	N24843	Dowell	Ch19	-/20	-/20	9/26
EB 2589	FIAT 20/30 hp	?	?	-18-	-/21	-/21	6/25
TA 4850	Berliet	CBL5001	?	B20-	11/22	11/22	-/--
TA 7490	Lancia Tetraiota	203	?	B20F	8/23	8/23	*
TA 8913	Berliet 35 hp	50121	?	B20-	2/24	2/24	12/24
TT 1761	Lancia Pentaiota	539	?	B20F	11/24	11/24	*
TA 5449	Maxwell 30 cwt	E21890	?	Ch14-	2/23	5/25	*
TA 7282	Berliet 35 cwt	10583	?	B20F	7/23	5/25	*
?	Maxwell 30 cwt	?	?	Ch14-	-/--	5/25	*
TT 6254	Albion PJ24	4129G	?	B24F	12/25	12/25	*
TT 6255	Albion PJ24	4129K	?	B24F	12/25	12/25	*
TT 8954	Berliet	30754	?	B20F	7/26	7/26	*
UO 97	Berliet CBOH	30762	?	B20F	11/26	11/26	*

Previous history:
TA 5449, TA 7282 and the unidentified Maxwell were new to Turner {Speedwell}, Kingsteignton (DN); from whom they were acquired.

Disposals:
EB 2186: Retained by Babington until 9/30; not traced further.
TA 4850: Wessex Auto Co (dealer?), London W19 at an unknown date; last licensed 3/26; scrapped by JG Auto Spares Co., location unknown.
TA 8913: Last licensed 12/24; no further operator.

The following vehicles marked with an asterisk (*) above, transferred to Devon General 5/27 (qv):
EB 2187-2188, TA 5449, 7282, 7490, TT 1761, 6254-6255, 8954, UO 97 & the unidentified Maxwell.

Balls Ltd (1921-1949) — Newtonian — 65 Queen Street, Newton Abbot (DN)
Balls Bus Service Ltd (1949-1952) — Balls Bus Service
Balls Tours Ltd (1952-1954) — Balls Tours

TA 2521	FIAT 20 hp	24754	?	Ch14	11/21	11/21	9/29
TA 3301	FIAT	25962	?	Ch16	4/22	4/22	12/30
TA 4009	FIAT	21128	?	Ch20	6/22	6/22	9/28
TA 1912	Guy 25 hp	1183	?	Ch20	7/21	c-/24	8/31
TT 1123	Ford	9129968	?	B14-	9/24	9/24	12/27
UO 4577	Morris Z	4652Z	Mumford	B14F	12/27	12/27	c-/31
UO 5963	Guy BA	BA2558	?	C20-	4/28	4/28	c-/40
DV 946	Chevrolet LQ	51757	?	C14R	5/29	5/29	12/47
DV 4851	Chevrolet U	65048	?	-14-	4/30	4/30	9/36
UO 2667	Lancia	1459	?	-20-	6/27	9/30	9/36
OD 638	Bedford WLB	108147	Mumford	B20F	11/31	11/31	c-/45

	DXE 697	Bedford WLB	109455	?			B20F	3/37	3/37	5/53
	OD 2144	Bedford WLB	108520	Mumford			C20F	4/32	c-/38	c-/43
	FTT 800	Bedford OWB	21332	Duple	38863		B32F	8/44	8/44	10/52
	JDV 789	Bedford OB	67110	Mulliner	T170		B31F	12/47	12/47	9/54
	OD 6113	Ford BB	5194796	?			B20-	6/33	1/48	12/49
	CTA 930	Commer PN3	46549	Mumford			C20F	11/36	7/48	9/49
	KTT 44	Commer Commando	17A1113	Whitson			C29F	10/48	10/48	9/54
	LTT 44	Bedford OB	115780	Mulliner			B28F	9/49	9/49	9/54
	LUO 444	Commer Avenger	23A0146	Harrington	643		C32F	12/49	12/49	9/54
	MOD 44	Commer Avenger	23A0564	Heaver			C33C	5/51	5/51	9/54

Previous history:

OD 2144: New to Townsend, Torquay (DN); from whom it was acquired.
OD 6113: New to Stover School, Newton Abbot (XDN); from whom it was acquired.
TA 1912: New to Winsor Bros, Bovey Tracey (DN); from whom it was acquired.
UO 2667: New to Oliver and Parker Torquay (DN) as 19 seat; from whom it was acquired.
CTA 930: New to Osborne Hotel Ltd, Torquay (DN) as C14F; from whom it was acquired.

Notes:

CTA 930: Also recorded as being C17F, date unknown.

Disposals:

DV 946: Mrs LF Walbank, Kingsbridge (DN) 2/48; Mrs LF Lord, South Milton (DN) at an unknown date;
    withdrawn 2/50.
DV 4851: Last licensed 9/36; burnt out (1937?).
OD 638: AE Thomas, Chagford (DN) 1945; Phillips & Co, North Tawton (DN) 1/47; last licensed 3/54.
OD 2144: PA Norman {Kingston Coach Tours}, Combe Martin (DN) (1943?); Phillips & Co, North Tawton
    (DN) 7/47; last licensed 12/51.
OD 6113: Sold for scrap 12/49.
TA 1912: Last licensed 8/31; no further operator.
TA 2521: Last licensed 9/29; no further operator.
TA 3301: Last licensed 12/30; no further operator.
TA 4009: Last licensed 9/29; no further operator.
TT 1123: Last licensed 12/27; no further operator.
UO 2667: Last licensed 12/36; burnt out 1937.
UO 4577: ES Haddy & Son, Kingsand (DN) at an unknown date; last licensed 12/36.
UO 5963: PA Norman {Kingston Coach Tours}, Combe Martin (DN); last licensed 3/43.
CTA 930: Millman & Sons, Buckfastleigh (DN) 9/49; re-seated to C14F at an unknown date; last licensed
    12/56.
DXE 697: Rebuilt as a recovery vehicle.
FTT 800: Devon General 10/52 (qv).
JDV 789: Devon General SB746 9/54 (qv).
KTT 44: Devon General SC745 9/54 (qv).
LTT 44: Devon General SB744 9/54 (qv).
LUO 444: Devon General TC747 9/54 (qv).
MOD 44: Devon General TC748 9/54 (qv).

Croscols
Croscols Ltd (from 7/21)   8A Fore Street, Tiverton (DN)

	FM 1941	Daimler CK	?	Eaton		B26R	c1/21	c1/21	*
	FM 1942	Daimler CK	?	Eaton		B26R	c1/21	c1/21	*
	TA 1258	Daimler Y	6363	?		Ch26	-/16	5/21	12/22
	TA 1870	FIAT F2	?	?		Ch14	7/21	7/21	*
	T 9364	Napier 25/30 hp	3213N	?		Ch19	7/20	12/21	*
8?	TA 2580	Daimler	?	Roberts?		B22R	-/16	12/21	12/22
	Y 5667	Austin 20 hp	?	?		-24-	6/19	7/22	c1924
5?	TA 4851	Daimler CB	1918	Roberts?		B20F	12/22	12/22	*
6?	TA 5391	Daimler CB	2469	Roberts?		B20F	2/23	2/23	*

Previous history:

T 9364: New to Eastmond & Son Ltd, Tiverton (DN); from whom it was acquired.
Y 5667: New to J Alpin, Kilve (SO); from whom it was acquired.

FM 1941-1942: First licensed as B35R, which probably included tip-up seats.

TA 1258: Refurbished ex War Department (GOV) chassis; rebodied and re-registered prior to entering service on date shown.

TA 2580: Refurbished ex War Department (GOV) chassis; rebodied and re-registered prior to entering service on the date shown; body supplied by JM Roberts (dealer), London W12 but likely to have actually been built by a sub-contractor.

TA 4851: Body supplied by JM Roberts (dealer), London W12 but likely to have actually been built by a sub-contractor.

TA 5391: Body supplied by JM Roberts (dealer), London W12 but likely to have actually been built by a sub-contractor.

Notes:

TA 1870: Quoted with engine number 16044, chassis number unknown.

Disposals:

Y 5667: Unknown owner, Middlesex (GMX) c1924.

TA 1258: JM Roberts (dealer), London W12 12/22; scrapped 11/23

TA 2580: No further operator.

The following vehicles marked with an asterisk (*) above, transferred to Devon General 3/24 (qv):

T 9364; FM 1941-1942; TA 1870, 4851, 5391

Minshull, Thornwill & Co (1920-2/21)   Lime Avenue, Torquay (DN)
Clarke, Thornwill & Co (2/21-1928)   **Windsor Cars**
Mrs ED Minshull (1928-1935)
RI Colley (1935-1937)   **Falkland Cars**
Falkland Garages Ltd (1935-1957)

Livery was brown and cream.

T 8412	Garford 22.5 hp	25601	?		Ch15-	4/20	4/20	-/--
TT 4343	Lancia Pentaiota	791	?		-19-	6/25	6/25	9/34
UO 7115	Lancia	348	?		C20-	6/28	6/28	-/--
JY 5949	Bedford WLB	110024	Mumford		C23F	5/35	5/35	3/38
JY 8218	Bedford WLB	110606	Mumford		C23F	7/36	7/36	1/41
ACO 521	Bedford WTB	111236	Mumford		C25F	5/37	5/39	10/49
BJY 562	Bedford WTB	14565	Mumford		C26F	5/39	5/39	5/52
BJY 563	Bedford WTB	16689	Mumford		C26F	6/39	6/39	3/52
FOD 945	Bedford OB	72313	Duple	46944	C29F	3/48	3/48	12/55
JUV 297	Bedford OB	61365	Duple	46369	C29F	1/48	12/49	3/55
LTT 690	Bedford OB	118450	Duple	46945	C29F	3/50	3/50	1/57
MOD 363	Bedford SB	2181	Duple	56906	C33F	7/51	7/51	*
NDV 44	Bedford SB	9600	Duple	1020/7	C33F	5/52	5/52	*
BEN 500	Bedford SB	10157	Yeates	326	C35F	3/53	12/55	*
SUO 826	Bedford SBG	37378	Duple	1055/300	C36F	5/55	5/55	*

Previous history:

JY 5949: Supplied through and registered by the bodybuilder, Mumford.

JY 8218: Supplied through and registered by the bodybuilder, Mumford.

ACO 521: New as a demonstrator for W Mumford Ltd, Plymouth; from whom it was acquired.

BEN 500: New to Auty's Tours Ltd, Bury (LA); from whom it was acquired.

JUV 297: New to Bradshaw's Super Coaches Ltd, London SE18 (LN); from whom it was acquired.

Notes:

The first vehicle operated is believed to have registration serial numbers 3603, but nothing else is known.

T 8412: Re-seated to Ch18 by 2/21; also seated 14 at an unknown date.

Disposals:

T 8412: May, Bodmin (CO) at an unknown date; last licensed 12/28.

JY 5949: NTD Weston, East Looe (CO) 3/38; withdrawn 12/49; LW Skewtesbury, Liskeard (CO) 5/50; MG Rowe, Dobwalls (CO) 8/51; AT Tilley, Crackington Haven (CO) 11/51; withdrawn 11/55; last licensed 12/55.
JY 8218: AJ Rowsell {Otter Coaches}, Ottery St Mary (DN) 1/41; WJ Down {Otter Coaches}, Ottery St Mary (DN) 1952; withdrawn 3/56.
TT 4343: No further operator.
UO 7115: GH Cooper, Dartmouth (DN) as C19- at an unknown date; Couch & Stoneman Ltd, Dartmouth (DN) at an unknown date; Green & Cream Coaches Ltd, Cullompton (DN) at an unknown date; last licensed 11/48.
ACO 521: WJO Jennings, Morwenstow (CO) 4/50; last licensed 9/53.
BJY 562: LFJ Ley {Treley Coaches}, St Buryan (CO) 5/52; withdrawn 5/55; J Hitchens, Newlyn (CO) 8/55; withdrawn and scrapped 8/57.
BJY 563: J Repik {Anglo Continental}, Torquay (DN) 3/52; N Pike, Wareham (DT) 6/53; withdrawn 2/54.
FOD 945: WH Hobbs, Uffculme (DN) 6/56; last licensed 8/71.
JUV 297: WJH Jones, Crantock (CO) 3/55; withdrawn 10/57; West Kirkby County Grammar School, West Kirkby (XLA) (1957?); not traced further.
LTT 690: AO Sherrin, Carhampton (SO) 1/57; withdrawn 2/67; Mrs E Lidgey {Fal Service}, Tregony (CO) 5/67; withdrawn 1/70.

The following vehicles marked with an asterisk (*) above, transferred to Devon General 6/57 (qv):
BEN 500, MOD 363, NDV 44 & SUO 826.

P Hart (until 1927)　　　　Hart's Bus Services　　　3 Clinton Terrace, Budleigh Salterton (DN)
Mrs WA Hart (1927-1952)　　Hart's Bus Services
Mrs WA Hart (1952-1957)　　Harts Services & Tours
Mrs WA Hart & Mrs KAM Bentham (From 1957)
　　　　　　　　　　　　　Harts Services & Tours

Livery was maroon with yellow waistband, except for AYC 106 which ran in its previous operator's blue livery.

UO 2032	Chevrolet LM	15528	Spurling?		-14-	4/27	4/27	-/31
UO 4789	Chevrolet LM	17670	?		-14-	12/27	12/27	-/31
UO 8692	GMC T20C	208896	?		B20-	11/28	11/28	-/--
UO 8963	Chevrolet LP	45683	?		C14-	12/28	12/28	by-/32
DV 959	Chevrolet (LQ?)	51436	?		-14-	5/29	5/29	c-/31
DV 5169	Star VB4	1165	Bence		Ch24-	5/30	5/30	6/39
DV 5364	Bean Model 8	H3263/8	Tiverton		B18F	5/30	5/30	7/32
DV 8395	Chevrolet U	71935	Willmott		-14-	3/31	3/31	9/49
DV 8641	Chevrolet (U?)	72863	Tiverton		-14-	3/31	3/31	-/33
GW 9093	Bedford WLB	108124	Willmott		B20F	12/31	12/31	6/34
OD 420	Bedford WLB	108077	Tiverton?		C20F	10/31	10/31	c-/34
YC 9718	Morris Viceroy	067Y	Dunn		C20-	6/30	7/32	c-/34
OD 5112	Commer B40	46181	Tiverton		B20F	3/33	3/33	10/49
OD 8725	Commer B50	56034	Tiverton		B20F	3/34	3/34	*
OD 8726	Commer B50	56033	Tiverton		B20F	3/34	3/34	*
BTT 186	Commer B3	63010	Tiverton		B20F	3/35	3/35	*
DTA 499	Albion PK115	25012H	Tiverton		B30F	1/37	1/37	*
DUO 558	Bedford WTB	112217	Tiverton		C25F	4/38	4/38	3/59
COD 184	Albion PK115	25025F	Tiverton		C27F	5/39	5/39	12/57
GTT 596	Bedford OWB	27883	Duple	41274	B32F	7/45	7/45	3/59
HDV 75	Bedford OB	57043	Duple	46936	C27F	7/47	7/47	3/59
AYC 106	Albion PK115	25002D	Harrington		C27C	4/35	8/48	*
KOD 477	Albion FT3AB	70740E	Tiverton		C31F	6/49	6/49	3/59
KFJ 173	Albion FT3AB	70755D	Tiverton		C33F	7/49	11/49	3/59
NDV 533	Albion FT39N	73113E	Duple	110/5	C31F	6/52	6/52	3/59
JFJ 179	Bedford OB	55508	Tiverton		C25F	6/48	6/53	3/59

Previous history:
YC 9718: New to EJ Dunn, Taunton (SO); from whom it was acquired.
AYC 106: New to Porlock Weir, Porlock & Minehead Motor Service Co Ltd {Blue Motors}, Minehead (SO); from whom it was acquired.
KFJ 173: New to Greenslades Tours Ltd, Exeter (DN) as C31F; from whom it was acquired.

JFJ 179: New to Greenslades Tours Ltd, Exeter (DN); from whom it was acquired.

Notes:
HDV 75: Re-seated to C29F at an unknown date.

Disposals:
DV 959: BR Shreeve & Sons Ltd, Lowestoft (EK) c1931; last licensed 9/38.
DV 5169: Sold for scrap 10/39.
DV 5364: HF Phillips, Hornchurch (EX) 7/32; London Passenger Transport Board, London SW1 (LN) BN5 12/33; not operated; GJ Dawson (Clapham) Ltd (dealer), London SW9 7/35.
DV 8395: No further operator.
DV 8641: SK Hill, Stibb Cross (DN) 1933; last licensed 9/35.
GW 9093: C Phillips, Over Stowey (SO) 6/34; Quantock Hauliers Ltd, Watchet (SO) 8/42; scrapped 10/42.
OD 420: Mrs EP EP Down, Mary Tavy (DN) c1934; FG Young Aspatria (CU) at an unknown date; last licensed 12/43.
OD 5112: Scrapped 10/49.
UO 2032: Lancing College (XWS) c1931; Jones (showman), Bedminster at an unknown date; last licensed 9/39.
UO 4789: AW Giles, Cricklade (WI) c1931; Ansell, Pitsea (GEX) as lorry (1931?); last licensed 9/32.
UO 8692: AJ & SE Smith, Potterspury (NO) at an unknown date; operated for JE Louch, Woodmansterne (SR) date unknown, possibly prior to operating for Smith; last licensed 3/37.
UO 8963: Kingston, Fritwell (OX) at an unknown date; last licensed 6/32.
COD 184: Clemens (contractor), East Budleigh (XDN) c1958; last licensed 9/60.
DUO 558: GS Carnall, Aylesbeare (DN) 3/59; last licensed 3/60.
GTT 596: Clements (contractor), East Budleigh (XDN) 1959; last licensed 6/60.
HDV 75: SA Kingdom {Tivvy Coaches}, Tiverton (DN) as C27F 6/59; last licensed 6/64.
JFJ 179: SA Kingdom {Tivvy Coaches}, Tiverton (DN) 6/59; withdrawn 4/64; Alf Moseley & Son Ltd (dealer), Loughborough 1/65.
KFJ 173: GS Carnall, Aylesbeare (DN) 1/60; W Bennetto {Majestic}, Fraddon (CO) 9/60, licensed 1/61; W & B Bennetto {W Bennetto & Son / Majestic}, Fraddon (CO) 8/62; withdrawn 10/62.
KOD 477: GS Carnall, Aylesbeare (DN) 10/60; Mitchell, Exeter (DN) 4/63; withdrawn 10/63.
NDV 533: AJ Deeble, Darleyford (CO) 9/59; WH Hobbs, Uffculme (DN) 9/72; withdrawn 5/74.

The following vehicles marked with an asterisk (*) above, transferred to Devon General 3/52 (qv):
OD 8725-8726; AYC 106; BTT 186 & DTA 499

Teignmouth Motor Car Co Ltd (1910-1930)   6 Bank Street, Teignmouth (DN)

H Fraser & G Rossiter		Teignmouth Motor Car Co							
BM 1317	Commer 36 hp	?	?			Ch22	6/10	6/10	-/16
BM 1668	Commer WP2	290	?			Ch22-	7/11	7/11	9/22
T 7836	Karrier 50 hp	WDS2977	?			Ch27	1/20	1/20	9/24
DB 1841	Dennis	?	?			Ch28	3/20	3/20	-/27
TA 1204	Dennis Chara	25009	?			Ch20	5/21	5/21	9/29
TA 5814	Karrier C	20107	?			Ch14	3/23	3/23	5/30
TT 360	Dennis	25085	?			-18-	6/24	6/24	5/30
DV 2755	Commer 5P	27027	Willowbrook	2359	B20-	10/29	10/29	5/30
DV 5335	Commer 6TK	28052	Willowbrook	2382	C20D	6/30	6/30	*
DV 5336	Commer 6TK	28111	Willowbrook	2394	C20D	6/30	6/30	*
UO 2380	Karrier H	1054	?			C20-	5/27	6/33	*

Previous history:
UO 2380: New to Miller & Son, Exmouth (DN); from whom it was acquired.

Notes:
DB 1841: Also operated with an interchangeable lorry body.
TT 360: Also recorded as 19 seat.

Disposals:
T 7836: Later tipper lorry with unknown owner.
DB 1841: Unknown owner as lorry 1927.
DV 2755: T Cousins, Sketty (GG) at unknown date; last licensed 3/33.
TA 1204: MB Down & Co, Kingsteignton (GDN) as lorry at an unknown date; last licensed 12/31.

TT 360: Plympton Trading Co (dealer?) at unknown date; last licensed as lorry 10/37.

The following vehicles marked with an asterisk (*) above, transferred to Devon General 7/2/36 (qv):
DV 5335-5336; UO 2380.

Torquay-Chelston Steam Car Co Ltd				**9 Fleet Street, Torquay (DN)**			
Torquay-Chelston Car Co Ltd							
T 2086	Clarkson Mk IV 30 hp Steam	?	?	B26-	6/11	6/11	3/22
T 2087	Clarkson Steam	?	?	B(26?)-	6/11	6/11	-/23
TA 3098	Leyland G7	12371	Leyland	B31D	3/22	3/22	1/27
TT 8164	Leyland LSC1	45154	Leyland	B31F	5/26	-/26	1/27

Notes:
> T 2087: This vehicle was reputedly built from parts of three earlier Clarkson steam buses, CA 150-151 & 155, which had previously operated for the Vale of Llangollen Engineering Bus & Garage Co, Llangollen (DH) and were acquired from the Torquay Road Car Co (DN); the first two dated from 11/04 and were new to the Sussex Motor Road Co Ltd, Pulborough (WS) registered BP 319 and possibly, BP 317 respectively.

Disposals:
> T 2086-T2087: No disposals known.
> TA 3098: Devon General 98 1/27 (qv).
> TT 8164: Devon General 99 1/27 (qv).

AE Townsend					**147 Reddenhill Road, Torquay (DN)**			
					(Garage) Petitot Road, Torquay			

The business of A Wilson {Ideal Coaches}, Torquay (DN) was purchased early 1931.

DV 9005	Overland C101	19535	Mumford		C14F	5/31	5/31	-/--
OD 2144	Bedford WLB	108520	Mumford		C20F	4/32	4/32	-/--
UO 7044	Graham Bros	GB4880	?		C14F	5/28	-/33	-/34
OD 9735	Bedford WLB	109529	Mumford		C20R	6/34	6/34	-/37
GC 4850	AEC Mercury	640010	Harrington		C23D	6/30	9/35	11/41
JY 6075	Bedford WTL	874736	Mumford		C26R	6/36	6/36	-/--
CTT 608	Bedford WTB	111428	Mumford		C25F	4/37	4/37	4/41
BCO 66	Dodge SBF	SBF757	?		C26-	5/38	5/38	2/49
DUO 505	Bedford WTB	112212	Mumford		C20F	4/38	4/38	-/--
OD 2887	Dennis Lancet	170230	Duple	2943	C26R	7/32	by-/34	2/49
HTA 924	Bedford OWB	11809	Mulliner		B32F	1/43	1/43	8/48
FTT 807	Bedford OWB	21356	Duple	38862	B32F	8/44	8/44	7/48
JTT 964	Bedford OB	35033	Duple	42359	C29F	7/46	7/46	1/52
JTT 965	Bedford OB	24952	Duple	42360	C29F	7/46	7/46	5/50
JOD 638	Dennis Lancet III	393J3	Dutfield		C33F	6/48	6/48	*
JOD 639	Dennis Lancet III	439J3	Dutfield		C33F	7/48	6/48	*
JOD 640	Bedford OB	80407	Duple	43369	C29F	7/48	7/48	1/53
HHA 435	Bedford OB	21307	Duple	42285	C29F	7/46	8/48	5/51
KOD 116	Dennis Lancet III	608J3	Dutfield		C33F	6/49	6/49	*
KOD 117	Dennis Lancet III	620J3	Dutfield		C33F	5/49	5/49	*
MTA 567	TSM K6---	9619	Dutfield		FC33F	9/50	9/50	*
MTT 44	Bedford OB	145707	Duple	43370	C29F	10/50	10/50	2/54
NTT 246	Bedford SB	5851	Duple	1006/497	C33F	11/51	11/51	*
OUO 587	Bedford SB	16254	Duple	1030/17	C35F	3/53	3/53	*

Previous history:
> GC 4850: New to A Timpson & Sons Ltd, London SE6 (LN) 226 as C22D; transferred to Grey Cars as 6 7/31; Devon General 310 11/33 (qv); from whom it was acquired via GJ Dawson (dealer), London SW9.
> JY 6075: Supplied through and registered by the bodybuilder, Mumford.
> OD 2887: New to WE Cawdle, Torquay (DN); from whom it was acquired.
> UO 7044: New to Miller & Son, Exmouth (DN); from whom it was acquired.

HHA 435: New to Gliderways Coaches Ltd, Smethwick (ST); from whom it was acquired.

Notes:

The first two vehicles operated have been identified only by their registration serial numbers, 8091 and 9586; one of which was an Austin 20 hp tourer c1927; no further details known.

Disposals:

DV 9005: L Truscott, Liskeard (CO) at an unknown date; withdrawn 6/38; to PV Trenwith, St Mary's (IS) 1938; becoming PV Trenwith & Perry {Blue & Cream Coaches}, St Mary's (IS) by 1946; withdrawn at an unknown date and abandoned at Old Town.

GC 4850: SH Blake, Delabole (CO) 11/41; SK Hill, Stibb Cross (DN) 1942; Dunn's Motors Ltd, Taunton (SO) at an unknown date; withdrawn 5/50.

JY 6075: E Isaacs, Ugborough (DN) at an unknown date; last licensed 9/55.

OD 2144: Balls Ltd {Newtonian}, Newton Abbot (DN) c1938; PA Norman {Kingston Coach Tours}, Combe Martin (DN) (1943?); Phillips & Co, North Tawton (DN) 7/47; last licensed 12/51.

OD 2887: HD Gourd & Sons, Bishopsteignton (DN) as C29R 2/49; last licensed 12/51.

OD 9735: Cooper, Dalton & Slatter {Waverley Cars}, Paignton (DN) 1937; becoming Waverley Motor Coach Tours Ltd, Paignton (DN) 10/47; JH Clark {Tally Ho! Coaches}, East Allington (DN) 11/47; last licensed 11/54; in use as shed by 7/60.

UO 7044: CA Gayton, Ashburton (DN) 1934; last licensed 3/42.

BCO 66: FVG & EE Bixley, Callington (CO) 4/49; DR Pickett, Fringford (OX) 1/52; last licensed 5/54.

CTT 608: AA Woodbury, Wellington (SO) 4/41; Baker & Bowden, Bradninch (DN) 4/52; last licensed 9/55.

DUO 505: J Griffiths & Sons, Haverfordwest (PE) 5/41; HH, TJ & BH Harries, Haverfordwest (PE) 6/51; withdrawn 4/55.

FTT 807: PF McCafferty {Avonley Coaches}, London SE14 (LN) 9/48; rebodied Duple C29F (55793) 1950; withdrawn 4/58; Byrne Bros (Leek) Ltd, Leek (ST) 6/59; Seddon (contractor), Farnworth (XLA) 6/63; last licensed 7/67.

HHA 435: A Jago & Son {Trehawke Service}, Liskeard (CO) 5/51; withdrawn and scrapped 5/62.

HTA 924: Mrs A Fry, Tintagel (CO)

JOD 640: Beacon Tours Ltd, St Austell (CO) 1/53; last licensed 7/66.

JTT 964: EC, FH & RE Gale, Haslemere (SR) 2/52; EC & CF Budden, West Tytherley (HA) 1/53; last licensed 1/61.

JTT 965: Salcombe Motor & Marine Engineering Co Ltd, Salcombe (DN) 5/50; Tally Ho! Coaches Ltd, East Allington (DN) 5/62; last licensed 9/66.

MTT 44: TW Mundy {Silver Queen}, Camborne (CO) 5/54; Grenville Motors Ltd, Camborne (CO) 6/65; withdrawn 7/67.

Vehicles marked with an asterisk (*) above transferred to Devon General 1/4/54:

JOD 638-639, KOD 116-117, MTA 567, NTT 246 & OUO 587.

FLEET CARS LTD, PAIGNTON

Fleet Cars Ltd was formed in July 1919 by Captain Hutt with a pair of yellow Dennis charabancs on tours from Torquay and Paignton. In November 1924 Devon General bought the business and operated the company as a subsidiary. The following year, the existing fleet was transferred to Devon General and replaced by twenty-one new Lancia coaches. The business of WP Tucker {Comfy Cars} Paignton (DN) was acquired 1st January 1926, together with five Lancia charabancs and a small Buick. This business was originally W Langbridge & WP Tucker {Comfy Cars}, Paignton (DN), becoming WP Tucker alone, probably in 1924. The livery was maroon, with the 'Fleet Cars' name in script style and used a separate series of fleet numbers. The garage was in Orient Road, Paignton.

An earlier business of GG Gullick {White Heather}, Torquay, together with nine vehicles had been taken over by Grey Cars in April 1925. Gullick then recommenced operations using the Heather Tours fleetname during 1927. This operation was then acquired by Fleet Cars with two vehicles in May 1928.

In 1932 Devon General also gained control of the Torquay touring fleet of A Timpson & Sons Ltd ('The Grey Cars'). Both Fleet Cars and the newly acquired Grey Cars business continued to operate independently as subsidiaries until the following year. On 1st November 1933, the three operations were integrated when the vehicles and assets of both Grey Cars and Fleet Cars were transferred to Devon General, with both subsidiaries being wound up on 1st January 1934.

FLEET DETAILS

1919

New vehicles:

DB 1567	Dennis 35 hp	? ?	Ch28	7/19	-/25
DB 1569	Dennis 35 hp	? ?	Ch28	7/19	-/25

Disposals:
DB 1567: Transferred to Devon General 1925 (qv).
DB 1569: Transferred to Devon General 1925 (qv).

1920

New vehicles:

DB 1723	Dennis 35 hp	? ?	Ch28	1/20	-/25
DB 1724	Dennis 35 hp	? ?	Ch28	1/20	-/25

Disposals:
DB 1723-1724: Transferred to Devon General 1925 (qv).

1923

New vehicles:

TA 6347	Lancia Tetraiota	189 ?	Ch18	5/23	1/24

Disposals:
TA 6347: Transferred to Devon General 1925 (qv).

1925

New vehicles:

3	TT 3162	Lancia Pentaiota	711	?	C18F	3/25	11/33
10	TT 3163	Lancia Pentaiota	725	?	C18F	3/25	11/33
15	TT 3164	Lancia Pentaiota	726	?	C18F	3/25	11/33
2	TT 3165	Lancia Pentaiota	727	?	C18F	3/25	11/33
13	TT 3328	Lancia Pentaiota	754	?	C18F	4/25	11/33
9	TT 3620	Lancia Pentaiota	755	?	C18F	5/25	11/33
4	TT 3621	Lancia Pentaiota	756	?	C18F	5/25	11/33
8	TT 3840	Lancia Pentaiota	786	?	C18F	5/25	11/33
6	TT 3841	Lancia Pentaiota	782	?	C18F	5/25	11/33
16	TT 4105	Lancia Pentaiota	784	?	C18F	5/25	11/33
14	TT 4667	Lancia Pentaiota	865	?	C18F	7/25	11/33
11	TT 4668	Lancia Pentaiota	863	?	C18F	7/25	11/33
	TT 4893	Lancia Pentaiota	877	?	C20F	7/25	11/33

| 7 | TT 4894 | Lancia Pentaiota | ? | ? | C20F | 7/25 | 11/33 |
| 12 | TT 4895 | Lancia Pentaiota | 878 | ? | C20F | 7/25 | 11/33 |

Notes:

All were open coaches with detachable canvas roofs and celluloid side-screens.

TT 3162-3163: Re-seated to C20F at an unknown date.

Disposals:

TT 3162-3165: Transferred to Devon General 11/33 (qv).
TT 3328: Transferred to Devon General 11/33 (qv).
TT 3620-3621: Transferred to Devon General 11/33 (qv).
TT 3840-3841: Transferred to Devon General 11/33 (qv).
TT 4105: Transferred to Devon General 11/33 (qv).
TT 4667-4668: Transferred to Devon General 11/33 (qv).
TT 4893-4895: Transferred to Devon General 11/33 (qv).

1926

New vehicle:

| 5 | TT 8647 | Lancia Pentaiota | 1046 | ? | C18F | 6/26 | 11/33 |

Notes:

TT 8647: Re-seated to C20F at an unknown date.

Disposal:

TT 8647: Transferred to Devon General 11/33 (qv).

Vehicles acquired from WP Tucker {Comfy Cars}, Paignton (DN) 1/1/26:

1	TA 3753	Lancia Tetraiota	64	?	Ch--	5/22	11/33
	TA 6433	Lancia Tetriaota	137	?	Ch18	5/23	-/26
	TA 6434	Lancia Z1	4097	?	Ch14	5/23	-/27
	TA 9441	Lancia Tetriaota	163	?	Ch18	4/24	-/27
	TT 3356	Lancia Pentaiota	625	?	Ch20	4/25	-/27
	?	Buick	?	?	Ch8		-/--

Previous history:

These vehicles had all been new to the Comfy Cars business which was originally a partnership between W Langridge & WP Tucker, becoming WP Tucker alone, probably in 1924.

Notes:

TA 3753: Rebodied Weymann C20F (C337) 1932.

Disposal:

TA 3753 (1): Transferred to Devon General 11/33 (qv).
TA 6433: Transferred to Devon General 1926 (qv).
TA 6434: Transferred to Devon General 1927 (qv).
TA 9441: Transferred to Devon General 1927 (qv).
TT 3356: Transferred to Devon General 1927 (qv).
Unidentified Buick: No disposal known.

1927

New vehicles:

19	UO 2720	Lancia Pentaiota	1483	?	C20D	6/27	11/33
20	UO 2721	Lancia Pentaiota	1484	?	C20D	6/27	11/33
18	UO 2722	Lancia Pentaiota	1485	?	C20D	6/27	11/33
21	UO 2723	Lancia Pentaiota	1486	?	C20D	6/27	11/33
17	UO 2724	Lancia Pentaiota	1487	?	C20D	6/27	11/33

Notes:

These vehicles were all-weather coaches with detachable canvas roofs and celluloid side screens.

Disposals:
UO 2720-2721 (19-20): Transferred to Devon General as 336-337 11/33 (qv).
UO 2722 (18): Transferred to Devon General as 335 11/33 (qv).
UO 2723 (21): Transferred to Devon General as 338 11/33 (qv).
UO 2724 (17): Transferred to Devon General as 334 11/33 (qv).

1928

Vehicles acquired from GG Gullick {Heather Tours}, Paignton (DN) 5/28:

ML 4014	Lancia	342	?	Ch18	4/27	4/27	-/28
UO 2811	Lancia 30 hp	3813	?	Ch18	6/27	6/27	-/28

Previous history:
ML 4014: Supplied through and registered by Lancia dealer, Curtis Automobile Co Ltd, London NW10 to Gullick.
UO 2811: New to Gullick.

Disposals:
ML 4014: Transferred to Devon General 109 1928 (qv).
UO 2811: Transferred to Devon General 108 1928 (qv).

GREY CARS

The Grey Cars originated in February 1913 when the two coaches owned by RH Grist of Torquay were taken over by a new company, the South Devon Garages and Motor Touring Company Ltd of Market Street, Torquay, formed by Mr Grist in conjunction with several other partners. New coaches were purchased and operated local tours under the name of 'The Grey Torpedo Cars'. The 'Torpedo' part of the name was dropped at an early stage and after the First World War the size of the fleet expanded rapidly, charabancs purchased being mainly of AEC and Daimler manufacture. A small number of open-tourer type cars were also operated. A stage service between Torquay and Brixham was also operated for short periods in 1915-1916 and 1920-1921.

The coach side of the business was incorporated as 'Grey Cars Ltd' on 17th May 1920 and commenced trading in August 1920, by which time fourteen coaches were being operated, rising to eighteen in 1921. It was in 1921 that the 'Grey Cars' emblem first appeared on the sides of the coaches, with the legal ownership passing to the new company prior to the beginning of the 1921 season. Despite the change of entity, certain coaches continued to show 'South Devon Garages and Motor Touring Co Ltd' as a legal owner at this time. South Devon Garages continued trading, henceforward concentrating on the motor garage, sales and service part of the business. Another notable occurrence in 1921 was the appearance of pneumatic tyres on the first Daimler coach, with the remaining Daimlers and Leylands being so equipped during 1922.

From 1923 powerful Lancia charabancs began to replace the earlier fleet. At Easter 1928 control of Grey Cars Ltd passed to established operator, A Timpson & Sons Ltd of London SE6, who also had an operation at Hastings. They retained the 'Grey Cars' fleetname for the Torquay based fleet and built a new two-level garage at Torwood Street, Torquay which opened in 1931. Between 1930 and 1932 most of the Lancias were replaced by AEC Mercury and Ranger coaches, including some nearly new examples transferred from the London operation. Please note that during the period Grey Cars was owned by Timpson, only those vehicles known to have operated from Torquay are included. Further details of other Timpson vehicles can be found in publication PN7.

Devon General came into the picture when control of Grey Cars Ltd passed to them on 1st March 1932. Both Grey Cars and Fleet Cars, which had been operated as a subsidiary since 1925, continued to operate independently as subsidiaries until the following year. On 1st November 1933, the three operations were integrated when the vehicles and assets of both Grey Cars and Fleet Cars were transferred to Devon General, with both subsidiaries being wound up on 1st January 1934.

Operators acquired prior to 1928:

1913	RH Grist, Torquay (DN)
April 1925	GG Gullick {White Heather}, Torquay (DN) (see next items below). It is believed that A Haigh, Babbacombe may have acquired this business before the sale to Grey Cars took place, but this cannot be confirmed.
	Gullick subsequently recommenced operations from Paignton trading as Heather Tours and was acquired by Fleet Cars 5/28 (qv).
September 1927	WJ Brockman, Torquay (DN).

Operators acquired during Timpson ownership of Grey Cars:

November 1928	E Green {Cosy Cars}, Torquay (DN).
February 1929	FE Hall {Court Cars}, Torquay (DN).
August 1929	AC Bulpin {Pride of the Moor}, Newton Abbot (DN).
September 1929	Hampton Motor Co Ltd, Torquay (DN). This business had gone into liquidation 11/28.

The early fleet carried fleet numbers, but these cannot be attributed to known registrations. In 1920, fleet numbers in use were 1-12, 14, 15. Of these 1, 2, 5, 7, 8, 12, 14, 15 were 22 seaters; 3 & 4 had 27 seats and 6, 9-11 had 18 seats.

Numbers 16-19 and a new number 6 were added for the 1921 season; 6 & 17 were 22 seaters; whilst 16, 18 & 19 had 18 seats. These seating capacities did not include driver and guide. Number 9 received pneumatic tyres in 1921.

FLEET DETAILS

T 2020	Commer 40 hp (CC?)	? ?		Ch22	4/11	5/13	2/15
T 2040	Commer 40 hp (CC?)	? ?		Ch22	6/10	5/13	2/15
T 3382	Commer 40 hp (CC?)	? ?		Ch24	8/13	8/13	-/19

	Reg	Make	Chassis	Body	Type	Date	Date	Date
	T 3994	Commer WP-	?	?	Ch24	4/14	4/14	-/--
	T 4042	Commer 40 hp (CC?)	?	?	Ch24	7/14	7/14	by10/20
	T 4366	Dennis 40 hp	?	?	Ch28	7/14	7/14	4/20
	T 5018	Daimler 58 hp	4570	?	Ch14	6/15	6/15	-/19
	T 5118	Whiting Federal	?	?		-/15	-/15	-/--
	T 6660	AEC YD	13573	?	Ch22	3/19	3/19	4/21
	T 6662	AEC YD	13574	?	Ch22	3/19	3/19	11/20
	T 6804	AEC YC	13575	?	Ch27	5/19	5/19	1/21
	T 6806	AEC YC	13576	?	Ch27	5/19	5/19	-/23
	T 6998	Daimler 30 hp	?	?	Ch--	6/19	6/19	-/20
	T 7012	AEC YD	14123	?	Ch22	6/19	6/19	-/23
	T 7174	Dennis 4 ton subsidy	12621	Torquay Carriage	Ch32	8/19	8/19	6/24
	T 7340	Daimler CK	3167	?	Ch25	10/19	10/19	-/24
	OB 1569	Dennis	?	?	Ch--	-/15	by-/20	-/--
	T 8594	Daimler CK22	3584	?	Ch18	5/20	5/20	-/25
	T 8596	Daimler CK22	3610	?	Ch18	5/20	5/20	-/24
	T 8908	Daimler CK22	3442	?	Ch18	6/20	6/20	-/25
	T 8950	AEC YD	15066	?	Ch22	6/20	6/20	-/25
	T 9268	AEC YD	15065	?	Ch22	7/20	7/20	-/25
	T 9406	AEC YD	15067	?	Ch22	8/20	8/20	-/25
	T 9512	Leyland 36/40 hp	10941	?	Ch22	8/20	8/20	1/24
	T 9715	Daimler CK22	3618	?	Ch18	10/20	10/20	-/25
	T 9717	Daimler CK22	3567	?	Ch18	10/20	10/20	-/25
	TA 731	Leyland 40/48 hp	12240	?	Ch32	3/21	3/21	6/24
	TA 732	Leyland 40/48hp	12241	?	Ch26	3/21	3/21	-/25
	TT 164	Lancia Pentaiota	502	Bartle	Ch20	6/24	6/24	-/30
	TT 165	Lancia Pentaiota	501	Bartle	Ch20	6/24	6/24	-/30
	TT 320	Lancia Pentaiota	503	Bartle	Ch20	6/24	6/24	-/30
	TT 321	Lancia Pentaiota	504	Bartle	Ch20	6/24	6/24	-/30
	PP 816	Lancia	?	?	Ch--	8/23	4/25	11/33
	TA 3247	Lancia Tetraiota	30	?	B20-	3/22	4/25	-/29?
	TA 3835	Lancia Tetraiota	1254	?	-20-	6/22	4/25	-/30
	TA 4081	Lancia Tetraiota	69	?	Ch20	7/22	4/25	-/30
	TA 4139	Lancia Tetraiota	93	?	Ch20	7/22	4/25	-/30
	TA 6571	Lancia Tetraiota	176	?	Ch19	5/23	4/25	-/30
	TA 7245	Lancia Tetraiota	209	?	Ch20	7/23	4/25	-/30
	TA 7246	Lancia Tetraiota	213	?	Ch20	7/23	4/25	-/30
	TA 7429	Lancia Tetraiota	212	?	Ch17	8/23	4/25	-/30
43?	TT 4046	Lancia Pentaiota	836	Bartle?	Ch20	5/25	5/25	9/32
44?	TT 4047	Lancia Pentaiota	837	Bartle?	Ch20	5/25	5/25	9/31
45?	TT 4048	Lancia Pentaiota	838	Bartle?	Ch20	5/25	5/25	9/31
46?	TT 4049	Lancia Pentaiota	840	Bartle?	Ch20	5/25	5/25	9/31
47?	TT 4545	Lancia Pentaiota	887	Bartle?	Ch20	6/25	6/25	6/29
48?	TT 4546	Lancia Pentaiota	897	Bartle?	Ch20	6/25	6/25	9/33
49	TT 8217	Lancia Pentaiota	1223	?	Ch20	5/26	5/26	11/33
50	TT 8218	Lancia Pentaiota	1229	?	Ch20	5/26	5/26	11/33
51	TT 8816	Lancia Pentaiota	1230	?	Ch19	7/26	7/26	9/33
	DL 2344	Lancia Z	5006	?	Ch14	7/21	9/27	by-/30
56	UO 6715	Lancia Pentaiota	2446	?	C25-	5/28	5/28	11/33
57	UO 7253	Lancia Pentaiota	2437	?	C26F	6/28	6/28	11/33
58	UO 7254	Lancia Pentaiota	2447	?	C26F	6/28	6/28	11/33
59	UO 7255	Lancia Pentaiota	2448	?	C26F	6/28	6/28	11/33
60	UO 7256	Lancia Pentaiota	2449	?	C26F	6/28	6/28	11/33
61	UO 7257	Lancia Pentaiota	2450	?	C26F	6/28	6/28	11/33
	T 8604	Garford Overland	EE845	?	Ch18	5/20	11/28	n/a
	TA 6411	Lancia Z	4161	?	Ch18	5/23	11/28	c-/29
	UO 2823	Lancia Tetraiota	345	?	Ch18	6/27	11/28	n/a
94	DY 3969	Albion PF26	5002F	?	C18F-	4/26	2/29	-/--
96	DY 4084	Albion PF26	5005C	?	C18F	5/26	2/29	11/32
152	TA 3841	Lancia Tetraiota	44	?	Ch18	6/22	2/29	9/30
151	TA 5790	Lancia Tetraiota	118	?	Ch18	4/23	2/29	-/30
	TA 6863	Lancia Tetraiota	126	?	Ch20	6/23	2/29	n/a
	XA 876	Lancia Z	?	?	Ch18	-/20	2/29	n/a
53	DY 4573	Lancia Pentaiota	?	?	C26D	5/27	4/29	11/33

54	DY 4575	Lancia Pentaiota	?	?	C26D	5/27	4/29	11/33
55	DY 4574	Lancia Pentaiota	?	?	C26D	5/27	6/29	11/33
	TT 3267	Reo Pullman	W636	Mumford	C20-	4/25	8/29	-/--
	UO 1957	Dennis 30 cwt	51387	?	Ch14	4/27	8/29	-/--
41	DV 1521	Lancia Tetraiota	131	?	Ch20	7/23	9/29	9/33
42	DV 2242	Lancia Tetraiota	214	?	Ch20	7/23	9/29	11/33
	TA 9378	Vandys SPA	8651	?	Ch20	4/24	9/29	-/--
	TT 918	Lancia	352E	?	Ch20	8/24	9/29	-/--
52	UO 2694	Lancia Pentaiota	1472	?	Ch20	5/27	9/29	11/33
24	GN 7305	AEC Ranger	665013	Harrington	C26D	5/31	5/31	11/33
25	GN 7306	AEC Ranger	665016	Harrington	C26D	5/31	5/31	11/33
26	GN 7307	AEC Ranger	665015	Harrington	C26D	5/31	5/31	11/33
27	GN 7308	AEC Ranger	665019	Harrington	C26D	5/31	5/31	11/33
28	GN 7309	AEC Ranger	665020	Harrington	C26D	5/31	5/31	11/33
29	GN 7310	AEC Ranger	665021	Harrington	C26D	5/31	5/31	11/33
30	GN 7311	AEC Ranger	665022	Harrington	C26D	5/31	5/31	11/33
6	GC 4846	AEC Mercury	640011	Harrington	C23D	7/30	7/31	11/33
7	GC 4847	AEC Mercury	640012	Harrington	C23D	6/30	7/31	11/33
8	GC 4848	AEC Mercury	640007	Harrington	C23D	6/30	7/31	11/33
9	GC 4849	AEC Mercury	640005	Harrington	C23D	6/30	7/31	11/33
10	GC 4850	AEC Mercury	640010	Harrington	C23D	6/30	7/31	11/33
13	GN 7318	AEC Mercury	640071	Harrington	C22D	3/31	7/31	11/33
14	GN 7319	AEC Mercury	640070	Harrington	C22D	3/31	7/31	11/33
15	GN 7320	AEC Mercury	640068	Harrington	C22D	3/31	7/31	11/33
16	GN 7321	AEC Mercury	640072	Harrington	C22D	3/31	7/31	11/33
17	GN 7322	AEC Mercury	640073	Harrington	C22D	5/31	7/31	11/33
18	GN 7323	AEC Mercury	640128	Harrington	C22D	3/31	7/31	11/33
1	GC 4841	AEC Mercury	640009	Harrington	C23D	6/30	7/32	11/33
2	GC 4842	AEC Mercury	640004	Harrington	C23D	6/30	7/32	11/33
3	GC 4843	AEC Mercury	640013	Harrington	C23D	6/30	7/32	11/33
4	GC 4844	AEC Mercury	640008	Harrington	C23D	6/30	7/32	11/33
5	GC 4845	AEC Mercury	640006	Harrington	C23D	7/30	7/32	11/33
21	GN 7302	AEC Ranger	665014	Harrington	C26D	5/31	7/32	11/33
22	GN 7303	AEC Ranger	665017	Harrington	C26D	5/31	7/32	11/33
23	GN 7304	AEC Ranger	665018	Harrington	C26D	5/31	7/32	11/33
11	GN 7316	AEC Mercury	640063	Harrington	C22D	3/31	7/32	11/33
12	GN 7317	AEC Mercury	640069	Harrington	C22D	3/31	7/32	11/33

Previous history:

T 2020: New to RH Grist, Torquay (DN), from whom it was acquired.

T 2040 (ex BM 1317): New to Teignmouth Motor Car Co Ltd (DN) registered BM 1317; RH Grist, Torquay (DN) re-registered T 2040 5/11; from whom it was acquired.

T 8604: A third vehicle, together with TA 6411 & UO 2823 (see below) was acquired from E Green {Cosy Cars}, Torquay (DN), but it is not confirmed it was T 8604, which was new to Langridge, Paignton (DN) as Ch20; from whom it was acquired 2/21.

DL 2344: Original operator unknown; WJ Brockman, Torquay (DN) at an unknown date; from whom it was acquired.

DV 1521 (ex TA 6901) (41): New to Hampton Motor Co Ltd, Torquay (DN) registered TA 6901; from whom it was acquired, having been rebodied by an unknown manufacturer as Ch20 and re-registered DV 1521 6/29.

DV 2242 (ex TA 7231) (42): New to Hampton Motor Co Ltd, Torquay (DN) registered TA 7231; from whom it was acquired, having been rebodied by an unknown manufacturer as Ch20 and re-registered DV 2242 8/29.

DY 3969 (94): New to A Timpson & Sons Ltd, London SE6 (LN); operated at Hastings; transferred to Grey Cars 2/29.

DY 4084 (96): New to A Timpson & Sons Ltd, London SE6 (LN); operated at Hastings; transferred to Grey Cars 2/29.

DY 4573 (53): New to A Timpson & Sons Ltd, London SE6 (LN) 98; operated at Hastings; transferred to Grey Cars 4/29.

DY 4574 (55): New to A Timpson & Sons Ltd, London SE6 (LN) 100; operated at Hastings; transferred to Grey Cars 6/29.

DY 4575 (54): New to A Timpson & Sons Ltd, London SE6 (LN) 99; operated at Hastings; transferred to Grey Cars 4/29.

GC 4841-4845 (1-5): New to A Timpson & Sons Ltd, London SE6 (LN) 221-225 as C22D; transferred to Grey Cars 7/32.

GC 4846-4850 (6-10): New to A Timpson & Sons Ltd, London SE6 (LN) 226-230 as C22D; transferred to Grey Cars 7/31.

GN 7302-7304 (19-21): New to A Timpson & Sons Ltd, London SE6 (LN) 302-304; transferred to Grey Cars 7/32.

GN 7316-7317 (11-12): New to A Timpson & Sons Ltd, London SE6 (LN) 316-317; transferred to Grey Cars 7/32.`

GN 7318-7323 (13-18): New to A Timpson & Sons Ltd, London SE6 (LN) 328-323; transferred to Grey Cars 7/31.

PP 816: New to an unidentified operator; GG Gullick {White Heather}, Torquay (DN) at an unknown date; from whom it was acquired.

TA 3247: New to GG Gullick {White Heather}, Torquay (DN); from whom it was acquired.

TA 3835: New to GG Gullick {White Heather}, Torquay (DN); from whom it was acquired.

TA 3841 (152): New to FE Hall {Court Cars}, Torquay (DN), from whom it was acquired.

TA 4081: New to GG Gullick {White Heather}, Torquay (DN); from whom it was acquired.

TA 4139: New to GG Gullick {White Heather}, Torquay (DN); from whom it was acquired.

TA 5790 (151): New to FE Hall {Court Cars}, Torquay (DN), from whom it was acquired.

TA 6411: New to E Green {Cosy Cars}, Torquay (DN), from whom it was acquired.

TA 6571: New to GG Gullick {White Heather}, Torquay (DN); from whom it was acquired.

TA 6863: New to FE Hall {Court Cars}, Torquay (DN), from whom it was acquired.

TA 7245-7246: New to GG Gullick {White Heather}, Torquay (DN); from whom it was acquired.

TA 7429: New to GG Gullick {White Heather}, Torquay (DN); from whom it was acquired.

TA 9378: New to Hampton Motor Co Ltd, Torquay (DN); from whom it was acquired.

TT 918: New to Hampton Motor Co Ltd, Torquay (DN); from whom it was acquired.

TT 3267: New to AC Bulpin {Pride of the Moor}, Newton Abbot (DN), from whom it was acquired.

UO 1957: New to AC Bulpin {Pride of the Moor}, Newton Abbot (DN), from whom it was acquired.

UO 2694: New to Hampton Motor Co Ltd, Torquay (DN), from whom it was acquired.

UO 2823: New to E Green {Cosy Cars}, Torquay (DN), from whom it was acquired; probably not operated.

XA 876: Believed supplied through and registered by Lancia dealer Curtis Automobile Co Ltd, London NW10 to FE Hall {Court Cars}, Torquay (DN), from whom it was acquired; not operated.

Notes:

T 3382: Re-seated to Ch19 at an unknown date.

T 3994: Has been quoted with the incorrect chassis number WP690114 (engine number possibly); had interchangeable lorry body. Either this vehicle, or T 4042, may have originally been registered LC 6739.

T 4042: Also operated with an interchangeable lorry body. Either this vehicle, or T 3994, may have originally been registered LC 6739.

T 5018: Laid up on delivery; not operated.

T 5118: Laid up on delivery; not operated.

T 6660: Also operated with an interchangeable lorry body.

T 6662: Also operated with an interchangeable lorry body.

T 6804: Also operated with an interchangeable lorry body.

T 6806: Also operated with an interchangeable lorry body.

T 6998: Also operated with an interchangeable lorry body.

T 7012: Also operated with an interchangeable lorry body and quoted as 40 seat.

T 7340: Also operated with an interchangeable lorry body.

T 8594: Also operated with an interchangeable lorry body.

T 8908: Also operated with an interchangeable lorry body and quoted as Ch20.

T 9268: Also quoted as Ch26.

T 9406: Also operated with an interchangeable lorry body.

T 9715: Also quoted as Ch18.

PP 816: The registration is not confirmed, it has also been quoted (probably incorrectly) as PP 8816.

TT 8816: Re-seated to Ch20 at an unknown date.

Various vehicles are known to have been fitted with lorry bodies during the winter months, therefore the list of such vehicles above, may be incomplete.

Disposals:

T 2020: War Department (GOV) 2/15; subsequently re-registered for unknown owner.

T 2040 (ex BM 1317): War Department (GOV) 2/15; subsequently re-registered for unknown owner.

T 3382: No disposal known.

T 3994: Condensed Milk Co, Clonmel (GEI) as lorry at an unknown date; last licensed 9/23.

T 4042: Re-registered Y 7271 for (Northcott, Taunton (SO)?) 10/20.

T 4366: Registration void 10/20.

T 5018: Bridport Fire Brigade (GDT) as a fire tender (1919?); last licensed 12/24.

T 5118: No disposal known.

T 6660: SC Clegg, Southampton (HA) 4/21; unidentified owner, Bristol at an unknown date; R Spendlove, Chapelizod (EI) at an unknown date; last licensed 6/26.

T 6662: R Roberts, Cwmcarn (MH) 11/20; G Owen, Flint (GFT) by 12/21; last licensed 6/32.

T 6804: A Trott, Skewen (GGG) as lorry 1/21; last licensed 6/29.

T 6806: W Leysham, Merthyr Tydfil (GGG) as lorry at an unknown date; last licensed 3/33.

T 6998: Unidentified owner Denbighshire (1920?), probably re-registered.

T 7012: PA Sercombe, Hounslow (GMX) as lorry (1923?); last licensed 3/30.

T 7174: Greyhound Motors Ltd, Bristol (GL) 8 6/24; sold 8/31; Goodman Price Ltd, London E8 (GLN) as lorry 9/33; last licensed 8/35.

T 7340: George Henderson & Co Ltd, Duns (BW) 1924; Brook & Amos Ltd, Galashiels (SI) 29 9/24; Scottish Motor Traction Co Ltd, Edinburgh (MN) 1928; A McLeod, Leith (GMN) as lorry at an unknown date; JB Elliott, Edinburgh (GMN) at an unknown date; last licensed 12/32.

T 8594: Sheppey Motor Transport Co Ltd, Sheerness (KT) as Ch20 1925; withdrawn 9/29; Maidstone & District Motor Services Ltd, Maidstone (KT) 1/30; not operated; Leyland Motors Ltd (as dealer), Leyland 10/30; no further operator.

T 8596: George Henderson & Co Ltd, Duns (BW) as Ch26 1924; Brook & Amos Ltd, Galashiels 28 (SI) 9/24; Scottish Motor Traction Co Ltd, Edinburgh (MN) 1928; withdrawn 1929; last licensed 6/29.

T 8604: WA Tremain {One and All}, Zelah (CO) at an unknown date; last licensed 6/30.

T 8908: J & H Doloughan, Cleaton Moor (GCU) as lorry 1925; last licensed 3/34.

T 8950: Bulwark Transport Ltd, London N7 (LN) as Ch27 1925; last licensed 9/29.

T 9268: CJ Nicholls Ltd, Cheriton (GKT) as lorry 1925; last licensed 6/35.

T 9406: J Dennis & Son, Braunton (DN) as Ch32 1925; last licensed 3/31; scrapped 10/31.

T 9512: Unknown operator, High Wycombe (BK) (1/24?); Brookes Bros, Rhyl (GFT) as a van at an unknown date; last licensed 3/36.

T 9715: Belfast Omnibus Co Ltd, Belfast (AM) 1925; last licensed 12/28.

T 9717: F Collins, Ilfracombe (DN) 1925; WH Robins {Osborne Cars), Ilfracombe (DN) at 1927; Glover & Uglow, Callington (GDN) as lorry at an unknown date; last licensed 6/36.

Y 7271 (ex T 4042): No disposal known.

DL 2344: WR Davey, East Ham (GEX) as lorry by 12/33; registration void 11/38.

DY 3969 (94): Transferred to Timpson Ancillary Fleet as lorry (at Hastings?) before 11/33.

DY 4084 (96): AEC Ltd, Southall in part exchange 11/32; Bouts Tillotson, London E3 (GLN) 146 as a van 3/33.

TA 731: Brook & Amos Ltd, Galashiels (SI) 44 9/24; Scottish Motor Traction Co Ltd, Edinburgh (MN) 1928; T Little, Dumfries (GDF) as lorry at an unknown date; last licensed 9/34.

TA 732: T Barnes, Oldham (GLA) 1925; last licensed 9/33.

TA 3247: GF Sissons & Sons {Loftus Motor Services}, Guisborough (NR) (1929?); Eastern Express Motors Ltd, West Hartlepool (DM) 6/29; United Automobile Services Ltd, York (YK) 9/29; chassis to J Westwood (dealer), Middlesbrough for scrap 2/30; body to Blair, use and location unknown 2/30.

TA 3835: T False, London SE3 (GLN) as lorry 1930; last licensed 12/40; destroyed by enemy action 3/41.

TA 3841 (152): AEC Ltd, Southall in part exchange 10/30; Tovee {Lancia Coaches} (dealer), London SW17 1/31; Ajax Builders, Mitcham (GSR) as lorry; last licensed 6/33.

TA 4081: Taylor, Ryde (IW) 1930: last licensed 12/36.

TA 4139: Slater, Weston-super-Mare 1930; last licensed 9/30.

TA 5790 (151): AEC Ltd, Southall in part exchange 10/30; Tovee {Lancia Coaches} (dealer), London SW17 1/31.

TA 6411: GH Buckingham, Plymouth (DN) at an unknown date; last licensed 9/32.

TA 6571: SA Blake & Sons, Delabole (CO) 1930; last licensed 9/33.

TA 6863: Unidentified dealer, London SW17 at an unknown date; Holly, Cheam (GSR) as lorry at an unknown date; last licensed 6/34.

TA 7245: Paterson, Worcester Park (SR) 1930 ; last licensed 9/32.

TA 7246: Taylor, Bristol (GGL) as lorry 1930; last licensed 6/33.

TA 7429: EJ Dunn, Taunton (SO) 1932; E Smith {Rambler}, Taunton (SO) 5/33; last licensed 5/34; scrapped 3/39.

TA 9378: J Shrimpton, London E17 (GLN) as lorry at an unknown date; last licensed 9/33.

TT 164: Calcott, London WC1 (GLN) as lorry 1930; last licensed 3/39.

TT 165: Kimber, London EC3 (GLN) as lorry 1930; last licensed 12/32.

TT 320: Carley, Gillingham (GKT) as lorry 1930; last licensed 9/36.

TT 321: Marks {Devon Touring Co}, Paignton (DN) 1930; last licensed 9/34; scrapped by Kitson (dealer), Honiton 4/61.
TT 918: RW Cure, Torquay (DN) at an unknown date; Noyce, Kingsbridge (GDN) at an unknown date; last licensed 12/34.
TT 3267: Fleming, London E12 (GLN) as lorry at an unknown date; last licensed 9/35.
UO 1957: Reading, location and date unknown as lorry; last licensed 6/36.
UO 2823: Boyd, Liskeard (GCO) as lorry at an unknown date; last licensed 6/36.
UO 6715 (56): Goodman Price Ltd, London E8 (GLN) as a tipper at an unknown date; last licensed 6/37.
XA 876: No disposal known.

The following vehicles marked with an asterisk (*) above, transferred to Devon General as withdrawn vehicles 1/11/33:
PP 816; TT 4046-4049, 4545-4546, 8816.

The following vehicles marked with an asterisk (*) above, transferred to Devon General 1/11/33:
DV 1521, DV 2242, DY 4573-4575, GC 4841-4850, GN 7302-7311, 7316-7323, TT 8217-8218, UO 2694, 6715, 7253-7257.

COURT GARAGES

JR Bond (1928-1932)
JR Bond, RC & SH Vanscolina (1932-8/35)
Court Garages (Torquay) Ltd (from 8/35)

Court Garages, Belgrave Road, Torquay (DN)

Devon General acquired the share capital of this company on 1st October 1966 and ran it as a separate subsidiary company until the coaches were transferred to Devon General in October 1970 and the company was wound up in February 1971.

FLEET DETAILS

Reg	Make/Model	Chassis	Body	Body No	Type			
DR 3686	Buick Master 6	139974	?		Car7	5/28	2/30	7/31
DR 3687	Reo Pullman Junior	FB461	Mumford		-14-	-/28	11/30	-/34
MK 7968	Studebaker Big 6	2064253	?		Car8	7/26	11/30	12/35
UO 6828	Studebaker	3174---	?		-14-	5/28	-/30	-/35
RL 8257	Chevrolet LO	42789	?		C14-	7/28	1/31	by-/39
JY 3258	Bedford WLB	109371	Mumford		C20-	3/34	3/34	4/49
JY 5950	Bedford WLB	110025	Mumford		C20-	5/35	5/35	6/43
RO 5092	Austin 6PT	5929	?		Car7	-/27	by4/36	by4/38
GC 4846	AEC Mercury	640011	Harrington		C23D	7/30	5/36	3/46
GC 4847	AEC Mercury	640011	Harrington		C23D	6/30	5/36	11/46
GJ 5879	Ch (LQ?)	61743	?		C14-	7/30	7/30	5/37
JD 169	AEC Regal	662095	Metcalfe		C32D	2/30	2/38	5/50
HX 340	AEC Regal	662287	Wilton		C32R	6/30	-/43	3/51
GDV 584	Bedford OB	54439	Duple	43371	C27F	-/47	-/47	11/53
KTT 688	Guy Vixen	LLV40776	Wadham		C29F	11/48	11/48	1/55
KTT 689	Guy Vixen	LLV40298	Wadham		C29F	11/48	11/48	1/56
LUO 227	Guy Vixen	LLV41566	DCB		C30F	1/50	1/50	2/56
MTT 214	Bedford OB	146068	Duple	43372	C29F	12/50	12/50	1/57
HBU 107	Bedford SB	5192	Duple	1006/422	C33F	4/52	4/54	11/58
JNT 833	Bedford SB	14712	Burlingham	5548	C35F	-/53	1/55	12/57
BEN 303	Bedford SB	9630	Duple	1014/32	C35F	7/52	4/56	11/59
UUO 314	Bedford SBG	45192	Duple	1060/298	C41F	4/56	4/56	10/60
VOD 710	Bedford SBG	51584	Duple	1074/209	C41F	5/57	5/57	10/61
XOD 403	Bedford SB3	60377	Duple	1090/82	C41F	5/58	5/58	10/62
108 BUO	Bedford SB3	68482	Duple	1105/153	C41F	4/59	4/59	11/63
165 ETA	Bedford SB3	78595	Duple	1120/311	C41F	4/60	4/60	11/65
690 GUO	Bedford SB3	87319	Duple	1123/275	C41F	4/61	4/61	-/67
877 KDV	Bedford SB3	89134	Duple	1145/279	C41F	4/62	4/62	10/64
544 NUO	Bedford SB3	91684	Duple	1159/215	C41F	4/63	4/63	-/67
610 STT	Bedford SB3	94136	Duple	1170/253	C41F	4/64	4/64	-/67
CUO 149C	Bedford SB3	96944	Duple	1183/338	C41F	4/65	4/65	-/67
FTT 432D	Bedford SB3	6817637	Duple	1207/11	C41F	3/66	3/66	-/67
893 ADV	AEC Reliance	2MU3RV2352	Willowbrook	59369	C41F	5/59	9/66	10/68
894 ADV	AEC Reliance	2MU3RV2353	Willowbrook	59370	C41F	5/59	9/66	10/68
JTA 763E	Bedford SB5	7802536	Duple	1212/2	C41F	4/67	4/67	10/70
JTA 764E	Bedford SB5	7802556	Duple	1213/3	C41F	4/67	4/67	10/70
JTA 765E	Bedford SB5	7803235	Duple	1213/1	C41F	4/67	4/67	10/70
CXF 256G	Bedford SB5	9T466343	Duple	1224/24	C41F	4/69	4/69	10/70
CXF 257G	Bedford SB5	9T466109	Duple	1224/25	C41F	4/69	4/69	10/70

Previous history:

Details of early vehicles are sketchy. An unidentified Lancia and a Reo for which no further details are available, are believed to have been the first vehicles operated, followed by an unidentified vehicle of which the registration serial numbers were 8273. Two new Studebakers were acquired in 4/28, followed by a third in 1/29 and an unidentified 18 seat charabanc in 5/29. One of these four may have been the vehicle with registration serial 8273.

DR 3686-3687: No disposals known.

GC 4846-4847: New to A Timpson & Sons Ltd, London SE6 (LN) 226-227 as C22D; transferred to Grey Cars as C23D 7/31; transferred to Devon General 306-307 11/33 (qv).

GJ 5879: Supplied through and registered by H Lane & Co Ltd (dealer), London SW10 to HA Harrison, Torquay (DN); Mrs S Harrison, Torquay (DN) 1933; from whom it was acquired.

HX 340: New to Modern Super Coaches Ltd, Lower Edmonton (MX); Taylor, Plymouth (DN) c3/40; from whom it was acquired.

JD 169: New to HPC Britten, London E8 (LN) 3; from whom it was acquired.

JY 3258: Registered by the bodybuilder Mumford.

JY 5950: Registered by the bodybuilder Mumford.

MK 7968: Not traced, possibly private owner; registration has also been quoted as both MK 8968 and 9968; WTA Traffic Commissioners confirm MK 7968.

RL 8257: New to A Jago & Son {Trehawke Service}, Liskeard (CO); from whom it was acquired.

RO 5092: Original operator unknown; believed acquired from Mrs S Harrison, Torquay (DN).

UO 6828: New to Oliver & Parker {Glorious Devon Cars}, Torquay (DN); RW Cure, Torquay (DN) at an unknown date; from whom it was acquired.

BEN 303: New to Auty's Tours Ltd, Bury (LA); from whom it was acquired.

HBU 107: New to Shaw Motors Ltd, Oldham (LA); from whom it was acquired.

JNT 833: New to Greatrex Motor Coaches Ltd, Stafford (ST) 82; from whom it was acquired.

893-894 ADV: Transferred from Devon General 893-894 (qv).

Notes:

GC 4846: Re-seated to C25D 3/38.

GC 4847: Re-seated to C25D 6/38.

Disposals:

DR 3686: RL Wall & Son, Dartmouth (DN) 7/31; not traced further.

DR 3687: Probably to Hancock Bros, Ilfracombe (DN).

GC 4846: Sunbeam Garages (Torquay) Ltd, Torquay (DN) 3/48; withdrawn 5/49; scrapped 12/49.

GC 4847: WE Pirt, Torquay (DN) 4/47; not operated; scrapped by Cream Cars (Torquay) Ltd, Torquay (DN) 1956.

GJ 5879: Truscott, Rilla Mill (CO) 5/37; withdrawn by 4/38.

HX 340: Blakes (Continental) Tours Ltd, Plymouth (DN) 3/51; withdrawn 1/52.

JD 169: F Stoneman {Currian Road Tours}, Nanpean (CO) 5/50; withdrawn 10/50; John Williams (contrtactor), location unknown (XCO) (1950?).

JY 3258: Mrs LF Lord, South Milton (DN) 11/49; last licensed 9/51; scrapped.

JY 5950: CT Baker, Weston-super-Mare (SO) 6/43; A Perdue {Chiltonian Coaches}, Chilton Foliat (WI) 6/44; withdrawn 8/49; last licensed 12/49.

MK 7968: No disposal known.

RL 8251: Scrapped 12/35.

RO 5092: Hawkey, Wadebridge (CO) 6/39; withdrawn 10/50.

UO 6828: Scrapped (1935?).

BEN 303: TW MacLean {La Bassie Coaches}, London EC2 (LN) 4/60; Arlington Motor Co Ltd (dealer), Enfield c1962; D Balfour, Hounslow (MX) 9/62; withdrawn 4/65.

GDV 584: Craven Park Coaches Ltd {Craven Blue}, London NW10 (LN) 11/53; Barnard & Barnard (dealer), London SE26 4/58.

HBU 107: DA Waterhouse, Burwash (ES) 12/58; withdrawn 3/61; Windsorian Motor Coach Services Ltd, Windsor (BE) 5/62; becoming Windsorian Coaches Ltd, Windsor (BE) 10/62; withdrawn 1/66; D James, Llangeitho (CG) 3/66; derelict at Penuwch by 3/75; still there 7/81; used as shed on B4577 between Bethania and Drefaes from an unknown date.

JNT 833: E Grant & AW Tedd {Kingston Coaches}, Middle Winterslow (WI) 12/57; withdrawn 4/60; Salem Ali Abdul {Khormaksar Bus Service}, Crater (O-ADN) re-registered L 3117 10/60.

KTT 688: Moorhaven Hospital, Ivybridge (XDN) as staff transport 1/55; last licensed (9/64?).

KTT 689: CW & WHM Terraneau, South Molton (DN) 1/56; C Davis {Clifford's Coaches}, Staple Hill (GL) 2/57; withdrawn 8/66; Empire Sports Club, Bristol (XGL) 12/66.

LUO 227: G Woolston {Keysonian}, Keysoe (BD) as C30F 2/56; EJ Sweeney {Lismore Coaches}, London NW3 (LN) 3/56; withdrawn 8/57; Dettridge Bros, London --- (XLN) 10/57; last licensed 12/61.

MTT 214: Cannings Coaches Ltd, Kings Sutton (NO) 3/57; withdrawn 5/64; Wainfleet Motor Services Ltd, Nuneaton (WK) 6/64; noted with unidentified operator, Warwickshire 12/71.

UUO 314: ER Lipscombe {Dorking Coaches}, Dorking (SR) 3/61; not traced further.

VOD 710: GE Wright {Bow Belle}, Bow (DN) 1/62; Phillips & Co, North Tawton (DN) 1/65; withdrawn 10/76.

XOD 403: Arlington Motor Co Ltd (dealer), Enfield 10/62; not traced further.

893-894 ADV: Returned to Devon General (qv).

108 BUO: Combs Coaches Ltd, Ixworth (WF) 5/64; Embankment Motor Co (Plymouth) Ltd, Plymouth (DN) 6/65; EG & NEG Bryant & LM Clarke {Bryant's Coaches}, Williton (SO) 11/65; withdrawn 12/78; DJ Liveley {Western Coaches}, Hereford (HW) 5/79.

165 ETA: GR Pallott, Gorey, Jersey (CI) 1 re-registered J 7717 3/66; Tantivy Motors Ltd, St Helier, Jersey (CI) 27 3/70; De la Salle College, St Saviour, Jersey (XCI) 10/76.

690 GUO: GAJ Morse {Roseland Motors}, Veryan (CO) 5/67; withdrawn by 10/83; scrapped 9/87.

877 KDV: AA Pitcher Ltd {Tantivy Motors}, St Helier, Jersey (CI) 21 re-registered J 24586 3/65; becoming Tantivy Motors Ltd, St Helier, Jersey (CI) 21 12/68; withdrawn 7/79.

544 NUO: AE Sawyer {Blue Coach Tours}, St Helier, Jersey (CI) 2 re-registered J 10632 6/67; CA Evans, Wrexham (CL) reverted to original registration 544 NUO 9/78; JB, G, S & D Jones, Ponciau (CL) 6/85; withdrawn 9/85; sold by 9/88.

610 STT: AA Pitcher Ltd {Tantivy Motors}, St Helier,Jersey (CI) 6 re-registered J 22095 3/67; becoming Tantivy Motors Ltd, St Helier, Jersey (CI) 12/68; Educational Holidays Guernsey Ltd {Island Coachways}, St Peter Port, Guernsey (CI) re-registered 3989 6/83; Traject Ltd {Abbeyways}, Halifax (WY) 11/89; not operated; J Sykes (dealer), Carlton 8/94; WH Fowler & Sons (Coaches) Ltd, Holbeach Drove (LI) as preserved vehicle 8/94; CL Harmer {Renown European}, Bexhill (ES) as preserved vehicle (probably for spares) 3/98; becoming Renown Coaches Ltd 10/98; sold by 4/02.

CUO 149C: JJ Kavanagh, Urlingford (EI) 5/67.

FTT 432D: AE Sawyer {Blue Coach Tours}, St Helier, Jersey (CI) 14 re-registered J 36404 5/67; Fishmore Hall School, Ludlow (XSH) reverted to original registration (FTT 432D) 7/79; Caldicot Labour Club, Caldicot (XGT) 7/83; Pontypool United Rugby Football Club, Pontypool (XGT) 7/87; DJ Brown (dealer), Builth Wells 2/89; Wacton Trading/Coach Sales (dealer), Bromyard 3/89.

JTA 763-764E: Devon General 10/70 (qv).

JTA 765E: Devon General 10/70 (qv).

CXF 256-257G: Devon General 10/70 (qv).

CROSS REFERENCE OF REGISTRATIONS

Reg	No	Reg	No	Reg	No	Reg	No	Reg	No
T 2020	126	T 9715	127	DV 5055	26	DV 9339	26	GN 7302	128
T 2040	126	T 9717	127	DV 5169	119	DV 9572	26	GN 7303	31
T 2086	121	Y 5667	117	DV 5335	40	DV 9655	26	GN 7303	128
T 2087	121	Y 7271	130	DV 5335	120	DV 9721	26	GN 7304	31
T 3382	126			DV 5336	40	DV 9722	27	GN 7304	128
T 3994	127	AY 101	61	DV 5336	120	DY 3969	127	GN 7305	31
T 4042	127	BM 1317	120	DV 5364	119	DY 4084	127	GN 7305	128
T 4366	127	BM 1317	128	DV 5475	24	DY 4573	31	GN 7306	31
T 5018	127	BM 1668	120	DV 5476	24	DY 4573	127	GN 7306	128
T 5118	127	DB 1567	17	DV 5477	24	DY 4574	31	GN 7307	31
T 6660	127	DB 1567	123	DV 5478	24	DY 4574	128	GN 7307	128
T 6662	127	DB 1569	17	DV 5479	24	DY 4575	31	GN 7308	31
T 6804	127	DB 1569	123	DV 5480	24	DY 4575	128	GN 7308	128
T 6806	127	DB 1723	17	DV 5481	24	EB 2186	116	GN 7309	31
T 6942	11	DB 1723	123	DV 5482	24	EB 2187	20	GN 7309	128
T 6944	11	DB 1724	17	DV 5483	24	EB 2187	116	GN 7310	31
T 6946	11	DB 1724	123	DV 5484	24	EB 2188	20	GN 7310	128
T 6998	127	DB 1841	120	DV 5765	24	EB 2188	116	GN 7311	31
T 7012	127	DL 2344	127	DV 5766	24	EB 2399	116	GN 7311	128
T 7174	127	DR 3686	132	DV 5767	24	EB 2589	116	GN 7316	31
T 7340	127	DR 3687	132	DV 5834	24	FJ 1696	12	GN 7316	128
T 7518	10	DV 113	112	DV 5835	24	FJ 1697	12	GN 7317	31
T 7518	112	DV 116	22	DV 5836	112	FJ 1698	12	GN 7317	128
T 7750	11	DV 160	22	DV 6853	24	FJ 1779	112	GN 7318	31
T 7752	11	DV 225	22	DV 7307	24	FJ 1780	12	GN 7318	128
T 7836	120	DV 226	22	DV 7308	24	FJ 1781	12	GN 7319	32
T 8188	9	DV 925	22	DV 7424	24	FJ 1782	12	GN 7319	128
T 8188	13	DV 926	22	DV 7425	24	FJ 1782	112	GN 7320	32
T 8190	9	DV 946	116	DV 7426	24	FJ 1794	12	GN 7320	128
T 8190	13	DV 959	119	DV 7428	24	FJ 1795	12	GN 7321	32
T 8192	9	DV 1044	22	DV 7429	24	FJ 1796	12	GN 7321	128
T 8192	9	DV 1521	31	DV 7430	24	FM 1941	16	GN 7322	32
T 8192	13	DV 1521	128	DV 7709	24	FM 1941	117	GN 7322	128
T 8194	9	DV 1616	22	DV 7710	24	FM 1942	16	GN 7323	32
T 8194	13	DV 2149	22	DV 7712	24	FM 1942	117	GN 7323	128
T 8196	9	DV 2242	31	DV 7713	24	GC 4841	31	GW 9093	119
T 8196	13	DV 2242	128	DV 7714	24	GC 4841	128	HX 340	132
T 8198	9	DV 2304	22	DV 7715	24	GC 4842	31	JD 169	132
T 8198	13	DV 2326	22	DV 7890	26	GC 4842	128	JY 3258	132
T 8200	9	DV 2355	22	DV 8082	26	GC 4843	31	JY 3912	38
T 8200	13	DV 2356	22	DV 8083	26	GC 4843	128	JY 3912	116
T 8202	9	DV 2458	116	DV 8084	26	GC 4844	31	JY 5949	118
T 8202	13	DV 2755	120	DV 8395	119	GC 4844	128	JY 5950	132
T 8204	9	DV 3898	23	DV 8504	26	GC 4845	31	JY 6075	121
T 8204	13	DV 3899	23	DV 8505	26	GC 4845	128	JY 8218	118
T 8232	12	DV 3900	23	DV 8506	26	GC 4846	31	LF 8399	12
T 8234	12	DV 3901	23	DV 8507	26	GC 4846	128	LU 8066	12
T 8328	11	DV 3902	23	DV 8508	26	GC 4846	132	LU 8153	12
T 8330	11	DV 3903	23	DV 8509	26	GC 4847	31	MK 7968	132
T 8412	118	DV 4114	23	DV 8641	119	GC 4847	128	ML 4014	21
T 8594	127	DV 4115	23	DV 9005	121	GC 4847	132	ML 4014	125
T 8596	127	DV 4116	24	DV 9216	26	GC 4848	31	MT 1257	23
T 8604	127	DV 4117	24	DV 9217	26	GC 4848	128	MX 9272	15
T 8874	112	DV 4118	24	DV 9218	26	GC 4849	31	OB 1569	127
T 8908	127	DV 4119	24	DV 9219	26	GC 4849	128	OD 420	119
T 8950	127	DV 4120	24	DV 9220	26	GC 4850	31	OD 638	116
T 9234	11	DV 4121	24	DV 9333	26	GC 4850	121	OD 832	27
T 9268	127	DV 4851	116	DV 9334	26	GC 4850	128	OD 1827	28
T 9364	16	DV 4889	24	DV 9335	26	GJ 5879	132	OD 1828	28
T 9364	117	DV 4890	24	DV 9336	26	GK 1008	50	OD 1829	28
T 9406	127	DV 4891	24	DV 9337	26	GK 1026	50	OD 1830	28
T 9512	127	DV 4925	24	DV 9338	26	GN 7302	31	OD 1831	28

OD 1832	28	OD 7502	112	TA 2580	117	TA 6434	20	TT 4048	32
OD 1833	28	OD 7503	35	TA 3094	9	TA 6434	112	TT 4048	127
OD 1834	28	OD 7504	35	TA 3094	13	TA 6434	124	TT 4049	32
OD 1835	28	OD 7505	35	TA 3094	14	TA 6571	127	TT 4049	127
OD 1836	28	OD 7506	35	TA 3098	19	TA 6863	127	TT 4077	17
OD 2144	117	OD 7507	35	TA 3098	112	TA 6901	32	TT 4078	17
OD 2144	121	OD 7508	35	TA 3098	121	TA 6901	128	TT 4079	17
OD 2259	28	OD 7509	35	TA 3247	127	TA 7157	15	TT 4080	17
OD 2260	28	OD 7510	35	TA 3301	116	TA 7231	32	TT 4105	34
OD 2261	28	OD 8725	68	TA 3753	34	TA 7231	128	TT 4105	123
OD 2290	28	OD 8725	119	TA 3753	124	TA 7245	127	TT 4343	118
OD 2291	28	OD 8726	68	TA 3794	10	TA 7246	127	TT 4545	32
OD 2291	49	OD 8726	119	TA 3794	13	TA 7256	15	TT 4545	127
OD 2292	28	OD 9484	35	TA 3795	10	TA 7282	20	TT 4546	32
OD 2293	28	OD 9485	35	TA 3795	13	TA 7282	116	TT 4546	127
OD 2294	28	OD 9486	35	TA 3796	10	TA 7429	127	TT 4563	17
OD 2540	28	OD 9487	35	TA 3796	13	TA 7490	20	TT 4564	17
OD 2541	28	OD 9488	35	TA 3797	10	TA 7490	116	TT 4565	17
OD 2542	28	OD 9489	35	TA 3797	13	TA 8913	116	TT 4566	17
OD 2543	28	OD 9735	121	TA 3798	10	TA 9378	128	TT 4567	17
OD 2544	28	PP 816	32	TA 3798	13	TA 9408	16	TT 4568	17
OD 2545	28	PP 816	127	TA 3799	10	TA 9409	16	TT 4667	34
OD 2836	28	RL 8257	132	TA 3799	13	TA 9441	20	TT 4667	123
OD 2837	29	RO 5092	132	TA 3800	10	TA 9441	124	TT 4668	34
OD 2838	29	TA 731	127	TA 3800	13	TA 9540	16	TT 4668	123
OD 2887	121	TA 732	127	TA 3801	10	TT 164	127	TT 4893	34
OD 5112	119	TA 820	12	TA 3801	13	TT 165	127	TT 4893	123
OD 5854	30	TA 1004	9	TA 3802	10	TT 193	16	TT 4894	34
OD 5855	30	TA 1004	13	TA 3802	13	TT 194	16	TT 4894	124
OD 5856	30	TA 1005	9	TA 3803	10	TT 320	127	TT 4895	34
OD 5857	30	TA 1005	13	TA 3803	14	TT 321	127	TT 4895	124
OD 5858	30	TA 1006	9	TA 3835	127	TT 360	120	TT 6254	20
OD 5859	30	TA 1006	13	TA 3841	127	TT 485	16	TT 6254	116
OD 5860	30	TA 1008	9	TA 3848	10	TT 486	16	TT 6255	20
OD 5861	30	TA 1008	13	TA 3848	14	TT 918	128	TT 6255	116
OD 5862	30	TA 1009	9	TA 3849	10	TT 1123	116	TT 8164	19
OD 5863	30	TA 1009	13	TA 3849	14	TT 1761	20	TT 8164	121
OD 5864	30	TA 1010	9	TA 4009	116	TT 1761	116	TT 8217	32
OD 5865	30	TA 1010	13	TA 4081	127	TT 2236	17	TT 8217	127
OD 5866	30	TA 1168	9	TA 4139	127	TT 3162	34	TT 8218	32
OD 5867	30	TA 1168	13	TA 4625	15	TT 3162	123	TT 8218	127
OD 5868	30	TA 1169	9	TA 4645	15	TT 3163	34	TT 8647	34
OD 5869	30	TA 1169	13	TA 4701	15	TT 3163	123	TT 8647	124
OD 6113	117	TA 1170	9	TA 4754	15	TT 3164	34	TT 8816	32
OD 6148	30	TA 1170	13	TA 4850	116	TT 3164	123	TT 8816	127
OD 6149	30	TA 1204	120	TA 4851	16	TT 3165	34	TT 8954	20
OD 7487	35	TA 1258	117	TA 4851	117	TT 3165	123	TT 8954	116
OD 7488	35	TA 1676	9	TA 5222	15	TT 3267	128	TT 9268	18
OD 7489	35	TA 1676	13	TA 5223	15	TT 3328	34	TT 9269	18
OD 7490	35	TA 1677	10	TA 5391	16	TT 3328	123	TT 9270	18
OD 7491	35	TA 1677	13	TA 5391	117	TT 3356	20	TT 9271	18
OD 7491	112	TA 1678	10	TA 5440	15	TT 3356	124	TT 9480	18
OD 7492	35	TA 1678	13	TA 5441	15	TT 3620	34	TT 9494	18
OD 7492	112	TA 1679	10	TA 5449	20	TT 3620	123	UO 97	20
OD 7493	35	TA 1679	13	TA 5449	116	TT 3621	34	UO 97	116
OD 7494	35	TA 1803	10	TA 5708	18	TT 3621	123	UO 845	19
OD 7495	35	TA 1803	112	TA 5790	127	TT 3840	34	UO 846	19
OD 7496	35	TA 1870	16	TA 5814	120	TT 3840	123	UO 927	19
OD 7497	35	TA 1870	112	TA 6339	15	TT 3841	34	UO 928	19
OD 7498	35	TA 1870	117	TA 6347	17	TT 3841	123	UO 980	19
OD 7499	35	TA 1912	116	TA 6347	123	TT 4046	32	UO 1618	112
OD 7500	35	TA 1934	10	TA 6411	127	TT 4046	127	UO 1957	128
OD 7501	35	TA 1934	13	TA 6433	18	TT 4047	32	UO 2032	119
OD 7502	35	TA 2521	116	TA 6433	124	TT 4047	127	UO 2380	40

UO 2380	120	UO 9759	22	AYC 106	68	CTA 89	41	DDV 444	46
UO 2667	116	UO 9779	22	AYC 106	119	CTA 90	41	DDV 445	46
UO 2694	32	UO 9780	22	BCO 66	121	CTA 91	41	DDV 446	46
UO 2694	128	UO 9813	22	BDV 1	39	CTA 92	41	DDV 446	70
UO 2720	34	XA 876	127	BDV 1	51	CTA 93	41	DDV 447	46
UO 2720	124	YC 9718	119	BDV 2	39	CTA 94	41	DDV 448	46
UO 2721	34			BDV 2	51	CTA 95	41	DDV 449	46
UO 2721	124	ACO 521	45	BDV 3	39	CTA 96	41	DDV 450	46
UO 2722	34	ACO 521	118	BDV 3	51	CTA 97	41	DDV 451	46
UO 2722	124	AJG 31	49	BDV 4	39	CTA 98	41	DDV 452	46
UO 2723	34	AJG 32	49	BDV 4	51	CTA 99	41	DDV 453	46
UO 2723	124	AJG 33	49	BDV 5	39	CTA 100	41	DJF 324	67
UO 2724	34	AJG 34	49	BDV 5	51	CTA 101	41	DJF 325	67
UO 2724	124	AJG 35	49	BDV 6	39	CTA 102	41	DJF 326	67
UO 2811	21	AMU 544	112	BDV 6	51	CTA 103	41	DJF 327	67
UO 2811	125	AOD 211	112	BDV 7	39	CTA 104	41	DJF 327	112
UO 2823	127	AOD 212	112	BDV 7	51	CTA 105	41	DJF 328	67
UO 4164	19	AOD 599	39	BDV 8	39	CTA 106	41	DJF 328	112
UO 4165	19	AOD 600	39	BDV 8	55	CTA 107	41	DJF 330	67
UO 4189	19	AOD 601	39	BDV 9	39	CTA 108	41	DJF 330	112
UO 4227	19	AOD 602	39	BDV 9	51	CTA 109	41	DOD 454	48
UO 4577	116	AOD 603	39	BDV 10	39	CTA 110	41	DOD 454	70
UO 4675	19	AOD 604	39	BDV 11	39	CTA 110	51	DOD 455	48
UO 4676	19	AOD 605	39	BDV 12	39	CTA 111	41	DOD 455	70
UO 4789	119	AOD 606	39	BDV 13	39	CTA 112	41	DOD 456	48
UO 4960	20	AOD 607	39	BDV 14	39	CTA 113	41	DOD 457	48
UO 4961	20	AOD 608	39	BDV 15	39	CTA 114	41	DOD 458	48
UO 5963	116	AUO 72	37	BDV 16	39	CTA 930	117	DOD 459	48
UO 5995	23	AUO 73	37	BEN 303	132	CTT 608	121	DOD 460	48
UO 6715	32	AUO 73	51	BEN 500	80	CTT 660	41	DOD 461	48
UO 6715	127	AUO 74	37	BEN 500	118	CTT 661	41	DOD 462	48
UO 6828	132	AUO 74	51	BJY 562	118	CVA 430	56	DOD 463	48
UO 6853	20	AUO 75	37	BJY 563	118	DDV 420	46	DOD 464	48
UO 6854	20	AUO 75	51	BTT 186	68	DDV 420	70	DOD 465	48
UO 6855	20	AUO 76	37	BTT 186	119	DDV 421	46	DOD 466	48
UO 7044	121	AUO 77	37	COD 184	119	DDV 421	70	DOD 467	48
UO 7115	118	AUO 77	51	CTA 61	39	DDV 422	46	DOD 468	48
UO 7253	32	AUO 78	37	CTA 62	39	DDV 422	73	DOD 469	48
UO 7253	127	AUO 79	37	CTA 63	39	DDV 423	46	DOD 469	73
UO 7254	32	AUO 79	51	CTA 64	39	DDV 423	73	DOD 469	112
UO 7254	127	AUO 80	37	CTA 65	39	DDV 423	112	DOD 470	48
UO 7255	32	AUO 80	51	CTA 66	39	DDV 424	46	DOD 471	48
UO 7255	127	AUO 81	37	CTA 67	39	DDV 424	73	DOD 472	48
UO 7256	32	AUO 81	51	CTA 68	39	DDV 424	112	DOD 473	48
UO 7256	127	AUO 82	37	CTA 69	41	DDV 425	46	DOD 474	48
UO 7257	32	AUO 83	37	CTA 70	41	DDV 425	73	DOD 475	48
UO 7257	127	AUO 83	51	CTA 71	41	DDV 426	46	DOD 476	48
UO 7303	21	AUO 84	37	CTA 72	41	DDV 427	46	DOD 477	48
UO 7304	21	AUO 84	55	CTA 73	41	DDV 428	46	DOD 478	48
UO 7430	23	AUO 85	37	CTA 74	39	DDV 429	46	DOD 479	48
UO 7469	21	AUO 85	51	CTA 75	41	DDV 430	46	DTA 499	68
UO 7470	21	AUO 86	37	CTA 76	41	DDV 431	46	DTA 499	119
UO 7471	21	AUO 86	51	CTA 77	41	DDV 432	46	DTT 47	41
UO 7851	21	AUO 87	37	CTA 78	41	DDV 433	46	DTT 48	41
UO 7852	21	AUO 88	37	CTA 79	41	DDV 434	46	DUO 317	44
UO 7910	21	AUO 88	51	CTA 80	41	DDV 435	46	DUO 317	70
UO 7911	21	AUO 89	37	CTA 81	41	DDV 436	46	DUO 318	44
UO 7950	21	AUO 90	37	CTA 82	41	DDV 437	46	DUO 319	44
UO 7951	21	AUO 91	37	CTA 83	41	DDV 438	46	DUO 319	70
UO 8692	119	AUO 198	37	CTA 84	41	DDV 439	46	DUO 320	44
UO 8963	119	AUO 199	37	CTA 85	41	DDV 440	46	DUO 320	70
UO 9690	22	AUO 445	112	CTA 86	41	DDV 441	46	DUO 321	44
UO 9691	22	AUO 512	37	CTA 87	41	DDV 442	46	DUO 321	70
UO 9692	22	AUO 512	112	CTA 88	41	DDV 443	46	DUO 322	44

Reg	Val	Reg	Val	Reg	Val	Reg	Val	Reg	Val
DUO 322	70	HFC 953	68	HUO 517	56	JTA 544	50	KOD 586	60
DUO 323	44	HFC 954	68	HUO 518	56	JTA 545	50	KOD 587	62
DUO 324	44	HFC 955	68	HUO 519	56	JTA 546	53	KOD 588	62
DUO 324	56	HFC 956	68	HUO 520	56	JTA 547	53	KOD 589	62
DUO 325	44	HFJ 133	112	HUO 521	56	JTA 548	53	KOD 590	62
DUO 326	44	HFJ 140	105	HUO 522	56	JTA 549	53	KOD 591	62
DUO 327	44	HFJ 141	105	HUO 523	56	JTT 508	54	KOD 592	62
DUO 327	70	HFJ 142	105	HUO 524	57	JTT 964	121	KTT 44	74
DUO 328	44	HFJ 144	105	HUO 525	57	JTT 965	121	KTT 44	117
DUO 328	70	HFJ 145	105	HUO 526	57	JUO 549	57	KTT 688	132
DUO 329	44	HHA 435	121	HUO 527	57	JUO 550	57	KTT 689	132
DUO 329	70	HMX 552	29	HUO 528	57	JUO 551	57	LJW 336	73
DUO 330	44	HMX 553	29	HUO 529	57	JUO 552	57	LRF 697	38
DUO 331	44	HMX 554	29	HUO 530	57	JUO 553	57	LTA 623	62
DUO 332	44	HTA 302	50	HUO 531	57	JUO 554	57	LTA 624	62
DUO 505	121	HTA 740	50	HUO 532	57	JUO 555	57	LTA 625	62
DUO 558	119	HTA 881	50	HUO 533	57	JUO 556	57	LTA 626	62
DXE 697	117	HTA 882	50	HUO 534	57	JUO 557	57	LTA 627	62
EFJ 548	60	HTA 924	121	HUO 535	57	JUO 558	57	LTA 628	62
EOD 978	112	HTT 326	56	HUO 536	57	JUO 559	57	LTA 629	62
ESL 876	87	HTT 327	56	HUO 537	57	JUO 560	57	LTA 630	62
ETG 295	75	HTT 328	54	HUO 538	57	JUO 561	57	LTA 631	62
ETT 985	44	HTT 329	56	HUO 539	57	JUO 562	57	LTA 632	62
ETT 986	44	HTT 330	56	HUO 540	57	JUO 563	57	LTA 633	62
ETT 987	44	HTT 331	56	HUO 541	57	JUO 564	57	LTA 634	62
ETT 988	44	HTT 332	54	HUO 542	57	JUO 565	57	LTT 44	74
ETT 989	44	HTT 333	56	HUO 543	57	JUO 566	57	LTT 44	117
ETT 990	44	HTT 480	54	HUO 544	57	JUO 600	57	LTT 690	118
ETT 991	44	HTT 481	54	HUO 545	57	JUO 601	57	LUO 227	132
ETT 992	44	HTT 482	54	HUO 546	57	JUO 602	57	LUO 444	74
ETT 993	44	HTT 483	54	HUO 547	57	JUO 603	57	LUO 444	117
ETT 994	44	HTT 484	54	HUO 548	57	JUO 604	57	LUO 593	63
ETT 994	70	HTT 485	54	JDV 789	74	JUO 605	57	LUO 594	63
ETT 995	44	HTT 486	54	JDV 789	117	JUO 606	57	LUO 595	63
ETT 995	70	HTT 487	54	JFJ 179	119	JUO 607	57	LUO 596	63
ETT 996	44	HTT 488	54	JNT 833	132	JUO 608	57	LUO 597	63
ETT 997	44	HTT 489	54	JOD 611	60	JUO 609	57	MOD 44	74
ETT 998	44	HTT 490	54	JOD 612	60	JUV 297	118	MOD 44	117
ETT 999	44	HTT 491	54	JOD 613	60	KFJ 173	119	MOD 363	80
ETX 832	53	HTT 492	54	JOD 614	60	KOC 242	62	MOD 363	118
ETX 833	53	HTT 493	54	JOD 615	60	KOD 116	73	MPI 624	70
EUO 192	44	HTT 494	54	JOD 616	60	KOD 116	121	MSJ 499	88
EUO 193	44	HTT 495	54	JOD 617	60	KOD 117	73	MTA 567	73
FOD 945	118	HTT 496	54	JOD 618	60	KOD 117	121	MTA 567	121
FTA 503	112	HTT 497	54	JOD 619	60	KOD 477	119	MTA 747	64
FTT 800	68	HTT 498	54	JOD 620	60	KOD 567	60	MTT 44	121
FTT 800	117	HTT 499	54	JOD 621	60	KOD 568	60	MTT 214	132
FTT 807	121	HTT 500	54	JOD 622	60	KOD 569	60	MTT 393	112
GDV 584	132	HTT 501	54	JOD 638	73	KOD 570	60	MTT 635	64
GKF 20	27	HTT 502	54	JOD 638	121	KOD 571	60	MTT 636	64
GTT 420	53	HTT 503	54	JOD 639	73	KOD 572	60	MTT 637	64
GTT 421	53	HTT 504	54	JOD 639	121	KOD 573	60	MTT 638	64
GTT 422	53	HTT 505	54	JOD 640	121	KOD 574	60	MTT 639	64
GTT 422	112	HTT 506	54	JTA 308	50	KOD 575	60	MTT 640	64
GTT 423	53	HTT 507	54	JTA 309	50	KOD 576	60	MTT 641	65
GTT 424	53	HUC 273	31	JTA 310	50	KOD 577	60	MTT 642	65
GTT 425	53	HUO 509	56	JTA 311	50	KOD 578	62	MTT 643	65
GTT 596	119	HUO 510	56	JTA 312	50	KOD 579	60	MTT 644	65
GUO 772	112	HUO 511	56	JTA 313	50	KOD 580	62	MTT 645	65
GUY 434	31	HUO 512	56	JTA 314	50	KOD 581	62	MTT 646	65
HBU 107	132	HUO 513	56	JTA 315	50	KOD 582	62	MTT 647	65
HDV 75	119	HUO 514	56	JTA 316	50	KOD 583	62	MTT 648	65
HFC 951	68	HUO 515	56	JTA 317	50	KOD 584	62	MTT 649	65
HFC 952	68	HUO 516	56	JTA 543	50	KOD 585	60	MTT 650	65

MTT 651	65	PDV 725	71	UFJ 292	105	XTA 826	81	879 ATA	84
MTT 652	65	PDV 726	71	UFJ 293	105	XTA 827	81	880 ATA	84
MTT 653	65	PDV 727	71	UFJ 294	105	XTA 828	81	881 ATA	84
MTT 654	65	PDV 728	71	UFJ 295	105	XTA 829	81	882 ATA	84
MTT 655	65	PDV 729	71	UFJ 296	105	XTA 830	81	883 ATA	84
MTT 656	65	PDV 730	71	UFJ 297	105	XTA 831	81	884 ATA	84
MTT 657	65	PDV 731	71	UFJ 298	105	XTA 832	81	885 ATA	84
MTT 658	65	PDV 732	71	UFJ 299	105	XTA 833	81	886 ATA	84
MTT 659	65	PDV 733	71	UUO 314	132	XTA 834	81	887 ATA	84
MUO 296	112	PDV 734	71	VDV 793	78	XTA 835	81	888 ATA	84
NDV 44	80	PDV 735	71	VDV 794	78	XTA 836	81	711 BOD	112
NDV 44	118	POD 908	71	VDV 795	78	XTA 837	81	712 BOD	112
NDV 533	119	RKR 120	73	VDV 796	78	XTA 838	81	108 BUO	132
NSG 298	80	ROD 749	75	VDV 797	78	XTA 839	81	475 CFJ	106
NTA 115	112	ROD 750	75	VDV 798	78	XTA 840	81	476 CFJ	106
NTT 246	73	ROD 751	76	VDV 799	78	XTA 841	81	477 CFJ	106
NTT 246	121	ROD 752	76	VDV 800	78	XTA 842	81	478 CFJ	106
NTT 660	66	ROD 753	76	VDV 801	78	XTA 843	81	479 CFJ	106
NTT 661	66	ROD 754	76	VDV 802	78	XTA 844	81	88 CMV	76
NTT 662	66	ROD 755	76	VDV 803	78	XTA 845	81	330 CTD	83
NTT 663	66	ROD 756	76	VDV 804	78	XTA 846	81	709 DOD	112
NTT 664	66	ROD 757	76	VDV 805	78	XTA 847	81	710 DOD	112
NTT 665	66	ROD 758	76	VDV 806	78	XTA 848	81	895 DTT	86
NTT 666	66	ROD 759	76	VDV 807	78	XTA 849	81	896 DTT	86
NTT 667	66	ROD 760	75	VDV 808	78			897 DTT	86
NTT 667	112	ROD 761	76	VDV 809	78	7194 H	73	898 DTT	86
NTT 668	66	ROD 762	76	VDV 810	78	2498 PK	94	899 DTT	86
NTT 669	66	ROD 763	76	VDV 811	79	4559 VC	94	900 DTT	86
NTT 670	66	ROD 764	76	VDV 812	79			901 DTT	86
NTT 671	66	ROD 765	76	VDV 813	79	889 ADV	83	902 DTT	86
NTT 672	66	ROD 766	76	VDV 814	79	890 ADV	83	903 DTT	86
NTT 673	66	ROD 767	76	VDV 815	79	891 ADV	83	904 DTT	86
NTT 674	66	ROD 768	76	VDV 816	79	892 ADV	83	905 DTT	86
NTT 675	66	ROD 769	76	VDV 817	79	893 ADV	83	906 DTT	86
NTT 676	66	ROD 770	75	VDV 818	79	893 ADV	103	907 DTT	86
NTT 677	66	ROD 771	75	VDV 819	79	893 ADV	132	908 DTT	86
NTT 678	66	ROD 772	75	VFJ 995	105	894 ADV	84	909 DTT	86
NTT 679	69	ROD 773	75	VFJ 996	105	894 ADV	103	910 DTT	86
NUO 680	69	ROD 774	75	VFJ 997	105	894 ADV	132	911 DTT	86
NUO 681	69	ROD 775	75	VFJ 998	105	970 AFJ	106	912 DTT	86
NUO 682	69	ROD 776	75	VFJ 999	105	971 AFJ	106	913 DTT	86
NUO 683	69	ROD 777	76	VOD 710	132	972 AFJ	106	914 DTT	86
NUO 684	69	ROD 778	75	VZB 225	65	973 AFJ	106	915 DTT	86
NUO 685	69	ROD 779	75	WJU 407	87	974 AFJ	106	916 DTT	86
NUO 686	69	SGD 669	96	XDV 850	81	50 AMC	73	917 DTT	86
NUO 687	69	STF 90	76	XDV 851	81	860 ATA	84	888 DUK	96
NUO 688	69	SUO 826	80	XDV 852	81	861 ATA	84	480 EFJ	106
NUO 689	69	SUO 826	118	XDV 853	81	862 ATA	84	481 EFJ	106
NUO 690	69	TFJ 808	105	XDV 854	81	863 ATA	84	482 EFJ	106
NUO 691	69	TSV 850	95	XDV 855	81	864 ATA	84	483 EFJ	106
NUO 692	112	TTT 780	76	XDV 856	81	865 ATA	84	484 EFJ	106
OFC 403	64	TTT 781	76	XDV 857	81	866 ATA	84	165 ETA	132
ORE 177	30	TTT 782	76	XDV 858	81	867 ATA	84	85 GFJ	106
OTC 738	71	TTT 783	76	XDV 859	81	868 ATA	84	86 GFJ	106
OTT 621	112	TTT 784	76	XFJ 750	105	869 ATA	84	87 GFJ	106
OUO 587	73	TTT 785	76	XFJ 751	105	870 ATA	84	88 GFJ	106
OUO 587	121	TTT 786	76	XFJ 752	105	871 ATA	84	89 GFJ	106
PDV 692	71	TTT 787	76	XFJ 753	106	872 ATA	84	918 GTA	87
PDV 693	71	TTT 788	76	XFJ 754	106	873 ATA	84	919 GTA	87
PDV 694	71	TTT 789	76	XOD 376	112	874 ATA	84	920 GTA	87
PDV 695	71	TTT 790	76	XOD 377	112	875 ATA	84	921 GTA	87
PDV 696	71	TTT 791	76	XOD 403	132	876 ATA	84	922 GTA	87
PDV 697	71	TTT 792	76	XTA 824	81	877 ATA	84	923 GTA	87
PDV 724	71	UFJ 291	105	XTA 825	81	878 ATA	84	924 GTA	87

925 GTA	87	976 MDV	92	WTS 715A	86	EOD 531D	98	MFJ 388G	106
926 GTA	87	977 MDV	92	ADV 969B	112	FOD 948D	112	MFJ 389G	106
927 GTA	87	978 MDV	92	AFJ 90B	106	FTT 432D	132	MFJ 390G	106
928 GTA	87	979 MDV	92	AFJ 91B	106	GFJ 601D	106	NDV 532G	101
929 GTA	87	980 MDV	92	AFJ 92B	106	GFJ 602D	106	NDV 533G	101
930 GTA	87	981 MDV	92	AFJ 93B	106	GFJ 603D	106	NDV 534G	101
931 GTA	87	982 MDV	92	AFJ 94B	106	GFJ 604D	106	NDV 535G	101
932 GTA	87	983 MDV	92	BDV 175B	95	GFJ 605D	106	NDV 536G	101
933 GTA	87	984 MDV	92	YCV 365B	95	GFJ 735D	112	NDV 537G	101
934 GTA	87	985 MDV	92	CTT 18C	96	GTA 641D	112	NDV 538G	101
935 GTA	87	986 MDV	92	CTT 19C	96	GTA 642D	112	NDV 539G	101
936 GTA	87	987 MDV	92	CTT 20C	96	SVW 275D	101	NDV 540G	101
937 GTA	88	988 MDV	92	CTT 21C	96	HOD 32E	99	NDV 541G	103
938 GTA	88	989 MDV	92	CTT 22C	96	HOD 33E	99	ODV 294G	112
939 GTA	88	990 MDV	93	CTT 23C	96	HOD 34E	99	OTA 58G	103
940 GTA	88	991 MDV	93	CTT 509C	96	HOD 35E	99	OTA 59G	103
941 GTA	88	60 MMD	81	CTT 510C	96	HOD 36E	100	OTA 60G	103
942 GTA	88	544 NUO	132	CTT 511C	96	HOD 37E	100	OTA 61G	103
690 GUO	132	1 RDV	94	CTT 512C	96	HOD 38E	100	OTA 62G	103
943 HTT	90	2 RDV	94	CTT 513C	96	HOD 39E	100	OTA 63G	103
944 HTT	90	3 RDV	94	CTT 514C	96	HOD 40E	100	OTA 64G	103
945 HTT	90	4 RDV	94	CTT 515C	96	HOD 41E	100	OTA 65G	103
946 HTT	90	5 RDV	94	CTT 516C	96	HOD 42E	100	OTA 66G	103
947 HTT	90	6 RDV	94	CTT 517C	96	HOD 43E	100	OTA 67G	103
948 HTT	90	7 RDV	94	CTT 518C	96	HOD 44E	100	OTA 68G	103
949 HTT	90	8 RDV	94	CTT 519C	96	JDV 833E	112	OTA 69G	103
950 HTT	90	9 RDV	94	CTT 520C	96	JTA 763E	110	OTA 70G	103
951 HTT	90	10 RDV	94	CUO 149C	132	JTA 763E	132	OTA 71G	103
952 HTT	90	11 RDV	94	CVC 124C	101	JTA 764E	110	OTA 72G	103
953 HTT	90	12 RDV	94	DFJ 895C	106	JTA 764E	132	OTA 73G	103
954 HTT	90	13 RDV	94	DFJ 896C	106	JTA 765E	110	OTA 291G	104
955 HTT	90	14 RDV	94	DFJ 897C	106	JTA 765E	132	RDG 309G	104
956 HTT	90	15 RDV	94	DFJ 898C	106	KTA 518E	112	RFJ 828H	104
957 HTT	90	16 RDV	94	DFJ 899C	106	LUO 45F	101	TDV 211J	104
958 HTT	90	17 RDV	94	KTD 551C	98	LUO 46F	101	TDV 212J	104
959 HTT	90	501 RUO	94	EOD 24D	98	LUO 47F	101	TDV 213J	104
960 HTT	90	502 RUO	94	EOD 25D	98	LUO 48F	101	TDV 214J	104
961 HTT	90	503 RUO	94	EOD 26D	98	LUO 49F	101	TDV 215J	104
962 HTT	90	504 RUO	94	EOD 27D	98	LUO 50F	101	TDV 216J	104
963 HTT	90	505 RUO	94	EOD 28D	98	LUO 51F	101	TDV 217J	104
964 HTT	90	506 RUO	94	EOD 29D	98	LUO 52F	101	CPM 520T	100
965 HTT	90	507 RUO	94	EOD 30D	98	LUO 53F	101		
966 HTT	90	508 RUO	94	EOD 31D	98	LUO 54F	101	3989	134
967 HTT	90	610 STT	132	EOD 521D	98	LUO 55F	101	6769	95
968 HTT	90	724 XUW	89	EOD 522D	98	LUO 56F	101		
877 KDV	132			EOD 523D	98	LUO 57F	101	J 991	74
969 MDV	92	ABV 669A	89	EOD 524D	98	MUO 656F	112	J 7717	133
970 MDV	92	ADV 299A	88	EOD 525D	98	CXF 256G	110	J 10632	134
971 MDV	92	ADV 435A	88	EOD 526D	98	CXF 256G	132	J 22095	134
972 MDV	92	AFE 387A	89	EOD 527D	98	CXF 257G	110	J 24586	134
973 MDV	92	AFE 388A	89	EOD 528D	98	CXF 257G	132	J 29255	110
974 MDV	92	NAT 747A	89	EOD 529D	98	MFJ 386G	106	J 36404	134
975 MDV	92	NKH 396A	89	EOD 530D	98	MFJ 387G	106	J 51937	110

HISTORICAL COUNTY CODES

GOV   Government Department

Code	County	Code	County
AD	Aberdeenshire	KK	Kirkcudbrightshire
AH	Armagh	KN	Kesteven division of Lincolnshire
AL	Argyllshire	KS	Kinross-shire
AM	Antrim	KT	Kent
AR	Ayrshire	LA	Lancashire
AS	Angus	LC	Lincoln (City)
AY	Isle of Anglesey	LE	Leicestershire
BC	Brecknockshire	LI	Lindsey division of Lincolnshire
BD	Bedfordshire	LK	Lanarkshire
BE	Berkshire	LN	London Postal area
BF	Banffshire	LY	Londonderry
BK	Buckinghamshire	ME	Merionethshire
BU	Buteshire	MH	Monmouthshire
BW	Berwickshire	MN	Midlothian
CG	Cardiganshire	MO	Montgomeryshire
CH	Cheshire	MR	Morayshire
CI	Channel Islands	MX	Middlesex
CK	Clackmannanshire	ND	Northumberland
CM	Cambridgeshire	NG	Nottinghamshire
CN	Caernarvonshire	NK	Norfolk
CO	Cornwall	NN	Nairnshire
CR	Carmarthenshire	NO	Northamptonshire
CS	Caithness	NR	North Riding of Yorkshire
CU	Cumberland	OK	Orkney Islands
DB	Dunbartonshire	OX	Oxfordshire
DE	Derbyshire	PB	Peebles-shire
DF	Dumfries-shire	PE	Pembrokeshire
DH	Denbighshire	PH	Perthshire
DM	County Durham	RD	Rutland
DN	Devon	RH	Roxburghshire
DO	Down	RR	Radnorshire
DT	Dorset	RW	Renfrewshire
EI	Eire	RY	Ross-shire & Cromarty
EK	East Suffolk	SD	Shetland Islands
EL	East Lothian	SH	Shropshire
ER	East Riding of Yorkshire	SI	Selkirkshire
ES	East Sussex	SN	Stirlingshire
EX	Essex	SO	Somerset
EY	Isle of Ely	SP	Soke of Peterborough
FE	Fife	SR	Surrey
FH	Fermanagh	ST	Staffordshire
FT	Flintshire	SU	Sutherland
GG	Glamorgan	TY	Tyrone
GL	Gloucestershire	WF	West Suffolk
HA	Hampshire	WI	Wiltshire
HD	Holland division of Lincolnshire	WK	Warwickshire
HN	Huntingdonshire	WL	West Lothian
HR	Herefordshire	WN	Wigtownshire
HT	Hertfordshire	WO	Worcestershire
IM	Isle of Man	WR	West Riding of Yorkshire
IV	Inverness	WS	West Sussex
IW	Isle of Wight	WT	Westmorland
KE	Kincardineshire	YK	York (City)

Note: A 'G' prefix (eg GLA) indicates the vehicle had been converted to goods (eg lorry or van) and the operator was a goods operator (in this case, in Lancashire).

OVERSEAS COUNTRY CODES

O-ADN	Aden
O-CY	Cyprus
O-D	Germany
O-E	Spain
O-F	France
O-IC	Canary Islands
O-JA	Jamaica
O-M	Malta
O-USA	United States
O-YU	Jugoslavia

ABBREVIATIONS

BTH	British Thomas-Houston Co Ltd.
DCB	Devon Coachbuilders Ltd.
GE	General Electric Co.
LGOC	London General Omnibus Co Ltd.
M & G	Mountain & Gibson Ltd.
MCCW	Metropolitan-Cammell Carriage & Wagon Co Ltd.
MCW	Metropolitan-Cammell Weymann Ltd.
NCME	Northern Counties Motor & Engineering Co Ltd.